# Fodor's 07

W9-AXZ-735

# U.S. & BRITISH VIRGIN ISLANDS

Where to Stay and Eat
for All Budgets

Must-See Sights
and Local Secrets

Ratings You Can Trust

Excerpted from *Fodor's Caribbean*
Fodor's Travel Publications   New York, Toronto, London, Sydney, Auckland
**www.fodors.com**

**FODOR'S U.S. & BRITISH VIRGIN ISLANDS 2007**
**Editor:** Mark Sullivan

**Editorial Production:** Evangelos Vasilakis
**Editorial Contributors:** Carol M. Bareuther, Lynda Lohr
**Maps:** David Lindroth, *cartographer;* Bob Blake and Rebecca Baer, *map editors*
**Design:** Fabrizio La Rocca, *creative director;* Guido Caroti, *art director;* Melanie Marin, *senior photo editor*
**Production/Manufacturing:** Robert B. Shields
**Cover Photo** (St. Croix): Corbis

ISBN-10: 1–4000–1714–9

ISBN-13: 978–1–4000–1714–0

ISSN: 1070–6380

## SPECIAL SALES

This book is available for special discounts for bulk purchases for sales promotions or premiums. Special editions, including personalized covers, excerpts of existing books, and corporate imprints, can be created in large quantities for special needs. For more information, write to Special Markets/ Premium Sales, 1745 Broadway, MD 6-2, New York, New York 10019, or e-mail specialmarkets@ randomhouse.com.

## AN IMPORTANT TIP & AN INVITATION

Although all prices, opening times, and other details in this book are based on information supplied to us at press time, changes occur all the time in the travel world, and Fodor's cannot accept responsibility for facts that become outdated or for inadvertent errors or omissions. So **always confirm information when it matters,** especially if you're making a detour to visit a specific place. Your experiences—positive and negative—matter to us. If we have missed or misstated something, **please write to us.** We follow up on all suggestions. Contact the U.S. & British Virgin Islands editor at editors@fodors.com or c/o Fodor's at 1745 Broadway, New York, New York 10019.

PRINTED IN THE UNITED STATES OF AMERICA

10 9 8 7 6 5 4 3 2 1

# Be a Fodor's Correspondent

Your opinion matters. It matters to us. It matters to your fellow Fodor's travelers, too. And we'd like to hear it. In fact, we *need* to hear it.

When you share your experiences and opinions, you become an active member of the Fodor's community. That means we'll not only use your feedback to make our books better, but we'll publish your names and comments whenever possible. Throughout our guides, look for "Word of Mouth," excerpts of your unvarnished feedback.

Here's how you can help improve Fodor's for all of us.

Tell us when we're right. We rely on local writers to give you an insider's perspective. But our writers and staff editors—who are the best in the business—depend on you. Your positive feedback is a vote to renew our recommendations for the next edition.

Tell us when we're wrong. We're proud that we update most of our guides every year. But we're not perfect. Things change. Hotels cut services. Museums change hours. Charming cafés lose charm. If our writer didn't quite capture the essence of a place, tell us how you'd do it differently. If any of our descriptions are inaccurate or inadequate, we'll incorporate your changes in the next edition and will correct factual errors at fodors.com *immediately.*

Tell us what to include. You probably have had fantastic travel experiences that aren't yet in Fodor's. Why not share them with a community of like-minded travelers? Maybe you chanced upon a beach or bistro or B&B that you don't want to keep to yourself. Tell us why we should include it. And share your discoveries and experiences with everyone directly at fodors.com. Your input may lead us to add a new listing or highlight a place we cover with a "Highly Recommended" star or with our highest rating, "Fodor's Choice."

Give us your opinion instantly at our feedback center at www.fodors.com/feedback. You may also e-mail editors@fodors.com with the subject line "U.S. & British Virgin Islands Editor." Or send your nominations, comments, and complaints by mail to U.S. & British Virgin Islands Editor, Fodor's, 1745 Broadway, New York, NY 10019.

You and travelers like you are the heart of the Fodor's community. Make our community richer by sharing your experiences. Be a Fodor's correspondent.

Happy traveling!

**Tim Jarrell, Publisher**

# CONTENTS

## UNDERSTANDING THE VIRGIN ISLANDS

## MAPS

## CLOSEUPS

# ABOUT THIS BOOK

## Our Ratings

Sometimes you find terrific travel experiences and sometimes they just find you. But usually the burden is on you to select the right combination of experiences. That's where our ratings come in.

As travelers we've all discovered a place so wonderful that its worthiness is obvious. And sometimes that place is so experiential that superlatives don't do it justice: you just have to be there to know. These sights, properties, and experiences get our highest rating, **Fodor's Choice,** indicated by orange stars throughout this book.

Black stars highlight sights and properties we deem **Highly Recommended,** places that our writers, editors, and readers praise again and again for consistency and excellence.

By default, there's another category: any place we include in this book is by definition worth your time, unless we say otherwise. And we will.

Disagree with any of our choices? Care to nominate a place or suggest that we rate one more highly? Visit our feedback center at www. fodors.com/feedback.

## Budget Well

Hotel and restaurant price categories from ¢ to **$$$$** are defined in the opening pages of each chapter. For attractions, we always give standard adult admission fees; reductions are usually available for children, students, and senior citizens. Want to pay with plastic? **AE, D, DC, MC, V** following restaurant and hotel listings indicate if American Express, Discover, Diner's Club, MasterCard, and Visa are accepted.

## Restaurants

Unless we state otherwise, restaurants are open for lunch and dinner daily. We mention dress only when there's a specific requirement and reservations only when they're essential or not accepted—it's always best to book ahead.

## Hotels

Hotels have private bath, phone, TV, and air-conditioning and operate on the European Plan (a.k.a. EP, meaning without meals), unless we specify that they use the Continental Plan (CP, with a Continental breakfast), Breakfast Plan (BP, with a full breakfast), or Modified American Plan (MAP, with breakfast and dinner) or are all-inclusive (including all meals and most activities). We always

list facilities but not whether you'll be charged an extra fee to use them, so when pricing accommodations, find out what's included.

### Many Listings
- ★ Fodor's Choice
- ★ Highly recommended
- ⊠ Physical address
- ✦ Directions
- ⌖ Mailing address
- ☎ Telephone
- 🖶 Fax
- ⊕ On the Web
- ✉ E-mail
- 🎟 Admission fee
- ☉ Open/closed times
- ► Start of walk/itinerary
- ▭ Credit cards

### Hotels & Restaurants
- 🏨 Hotel
- ⇆ Number of rooms
- ♿ Facilities
- ❍ Meal plans
- ✕ Restaurant
- ✑ Reservations
- 🏛 Dress code
- ↘ Smoking
- 🍷 BYOB
- ✕🏨 Hotel with restaurant that warrants a visit

### Outdoors
- 🏌 Golf
- ⛺ Camping

### Other
- ☺ Family-friendly
- ⓘ Contact information
- ⇨ See also
- ⊠ Branch address
- ☞ Take note

# WHAT'S
# WHERE

| | |
|---|---|
| **ST. THOMAS**  | The familiar and foreign mingle on this U.S.-owned island, where you'll recognize everything from major hotel chains to fast food restaurants and at the same time be able to relax in the exotic ambience of a tropical destination. Go for the shopping, sights, and water sports. Stores that sell gold, diamonds, and emeralds line Main Street in Charlotte Amalie. Seventeenth-century-built Fort Christian dates back to the island's colonization, while breathtaking vistas await from Mountain Top and Paradise Point. Opportunities for swimming, snorkeling, scuba diving, sailing, sportfishing, and even submarining abound in the surrounding seas. Don't go for uninhabited tranquility. St. Thomas is the most cosmopolitan of the three U.S. Virgins, and she has a buffet of choices to show visitors a good time. |
| **ST. JOHN**  | Only 3 mi from St. Thomas but still a world apart, St. John is the least developed of the USVI. Although two-thirds of its tropical hills remain protected as a U.S. national park, a bit of hustle and bustle has come to Cruz Bay, the main town. Although many people visit on a day-trip from their cruise ship or from St. Thomas, the island is a great place to unwind for a week or more. If you want to get in touch with nature, go to St. John, where you can enjoy all that Virgin Islands National Park has to offer. This doesn't mean, of course, that you'll have to camp. The island has a couple of posh hotels, some condos, lots of vacation villas, and even some pretty cushy campgrounds. |
| **ST. CROIX**  | The largest of the U.S. Virgin Islands, St. Croix is 40 mi south of St. Thomas. Its northwest is relatively lush, but the drier East End—where you'll find most of the resorts—is spotted with cacti. The main towns are Fredericksted on the West End and Christiansted on the East End. Ironically, the island's best beaches are on the West End, far from the best resorts. Go to St. Croix if you like history. Ruins of old plantations stand crumbling in long-fallow fields and Christiansted National Historic Site beckons with its old fort and other Danish-era remnants. You'll want to linger at interesting restaurants, browse in the island's eclectic collection of stores, or enjoy an afternoon at your hotel's beach when you're finished exploring the island's past. Don't go if you prefer a more back-to-nature experience. |

| | |
|---|---|
| **TORTOLA**<br /> | A day might not be enough to tour this island—all 10-square-mi of it—not because there's so much to see and do but because you're meant to relax while you're here. Time stands still even in Road Town, the biggest community, where the hands of the central square's clock occasionally move, but never tell the right time. The harbor, however, is busy with sailboats—this is the charter-boat capital of the Caribbean. Tortola's roads dip and curve and lead to lovely, secluded accommodations. Go to Tortola if you want to do some shopping and enjoy a larger choice of good restaurants than you'll find on the other British Virgins. |
| **VIRGIN GORDA**<br /> | Progressing from laid-back to more laid-back, mountainous and arid Virgin Gorda fits right in. Its main road sticks to the center of the island, connecting the odd-shaped north and south appendages; sailing is the preferred mode of transportation. Spanish Town, the most noteworthy settlement, is on the southern wing, as are The Baths. Here smooth, giant boulders are scattered about the beach and form delightful sea grottos just offshore. Choose Virgin Gorda if you want better beaches, but the trade-off is fewer restaurants and many fewer shopping opportunities. |
| **JOST VAN DYKE**<br /> | Jost Van Dyke, a sparsely populated island northwest of Tortola, has a disproportionate number of surprisingly lively bars and is a favorite haunt of yachties. There are also a few places to stay here, in case you really want to get away from it all. Go to Jost if you want to get a taste of what the Caribbean used to be like. |
| **ANEGADA**<br /> | Flat Anegada lurks 20 mi northeast of Virgin Gorda. It rises just 28 feet above sea level, but its reef stretches out underwater, practically inviting wrecks. The scores of shipwrecks that encircle the island attract divers and a bounty of fish. Choose Anegada if you're a diver and want easier access to the best BVI dive sights. The beaches are also excellent, but don't expect luxury accommodations or dining. |
| **OTHER VIRGIN ISLANDS**<br /> | There are actually about 50 islands in the British Virgin chain, many of them completely uninhabited, but others have a single hotel or at least a beach that is popular with sailors. Choose one of these resorts if you want to be pampered and pampered some more. A few are exclusive and popular with the jet-set, though more for their potential for relaxation than their lavish amenities. |

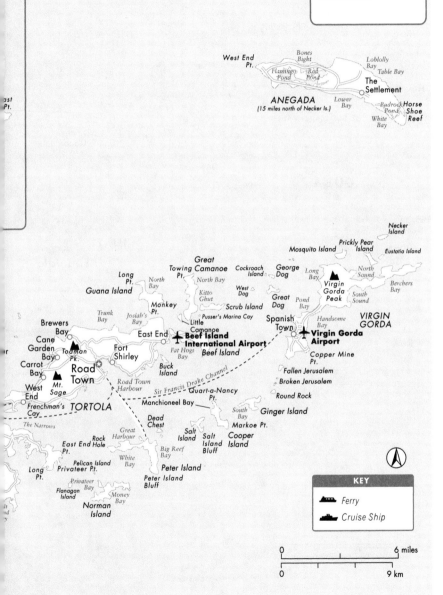

## The Virgin Islands

West End
Pt.

Bones
Bight

Loblolly
Bay    Table Bay

Flamingo
Pond    Rod
Pond

The
Settlement

**ANEGADA**
(15 miles north of Necker Is.)

Lower
Bay

Budrock
Pond    Horse
Shoe
Reef

White
Bay

*ast
Pt.*

Necker
Island

Prickly Pear
Island

Mosquito Island

Eustatia Island

Great
Towing Camanoe    Cockroach    George
Pt.    Island    Dog

Long
Bay

North
Sound

Long
Pt.    North
Bay    North Bay    West
Dog

Berchers
Bay

Guana Island

Kitto
Ghut    Great
Dog

Pond
Bay    Virgin
Gorda
Peak

South
Sound

Monkey
Pt.    Scrub Island

Trunk
Bay    Josiah's
Bay    Little
Camanoe    Pusser's Marina Cay

Spanish
Town

Handsome
Bay    **VIRGIN
GORDA**

Brewers
Bay

East End    **Beef Island
International Airport**

**Virgin Gorda
Airport**

Cane
Garden
Bay    Todman
Pk.    Fort
Shirley    Fat Hogs
Bay    Beef Island

Copper Mine
Pt.

Carrot
Bay    **Road
Town**    Buck
Island

Fallen Jerusalem

West
End    Mt.
Sage    Road Town
Harbour    Sir Francis Drake Channel    Broken Jerusalem

Frenchman's
Cay    **TORTOLA**    Manchioneel Bay    Quart-a-Nancy
Pt.

Round Rock

The Narrows

Dead
Chest    South
Bay    Ginger Island

Great
Harbour    Salt    Markoe Pt.

Rock
East End Hole
Pt.    Salt
Island    Island
Bluff    Cooper
Island

White
Bay    Big Reef
Bay

Pelican Island
Privateer Pt.    Peter Island

Long
Pt.    Privateer
Bay    Money
Bay    Peter Island
Bluff

Flanagan
Island    Norman
Island

*lt
nd
y*

**KEY**

⛴ Ferry

🚢 Cruise Ship

0                                    6 miles

0                                    9 km

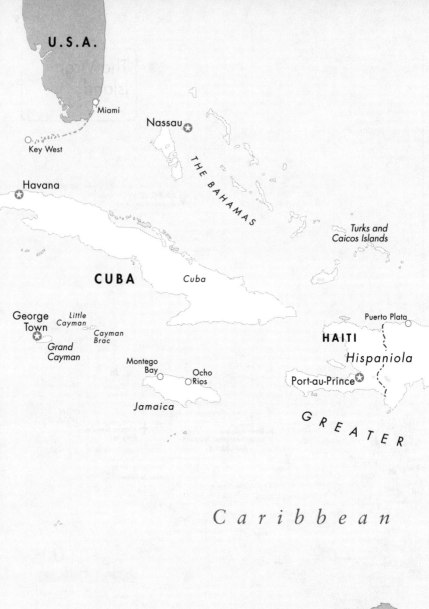

**U.S.A.**

Miami

Key West

Nassau

*THE BAHAMAS*

Havana

*Turks and Caicos Islands*

**CUBA**

*Cuba*

Little
Cayman

George
Town

*Cayman
Brac*

Puerto Plata

**HAITI**

*Grand
Cayman*

Montego
Bay

Ocho
Rios

*Hispaniola*

Port-au-Prince

*Jamaica*

*G R E A T E R*

*C a r i b b e a n*

0                    200 mi

0          200 km

*Panama
Canal*

**PANAMA**

Cartagena

**COLOMBIA**

Maracaibo

# Caribbean

ATLANTIC OCEAN

LEEWARD ISLANDS

**DOMINICAN REPUBLIC**

St. John Tortola
St. Thomas Virgin Gorda
San Juan Anguilla
St. Barthélemy
St. Maarten/
Santo St. Martin Saba Barbuda
Domingo Puerto St. Eustatius Antigua
Rico St. Croix
Croix St. Kitts
Nevis
ANTILLES Montserrat Marie
Guadeloupe Galante

Dominica WINDWARD ISLANDS

Martinique
Fort-de-France

Sea St. Lucia

St. Vincent Barbados
Bequia Bridgetown
The Grenadines
Carriacou
St. George's
Aruba Islas Los Grenada
Curaçao Bonaire Roques
Willemstad Tobago
LESSER ANTILLES
Port of Spain
Trinidad
La Guaira
Caracas

**VENEZUELA**

# WHEN TO GO

°F CHARLOTTE AMALIE, ST. THOMAS °C

°F CHRISTIANSTED, ST. CROIX °C

°F FREDERICKSTED, ST. CROIX °C

The high season in the USBVI is traditionally winter—from December 15 to the week after the St. Thomas Carnival, usually the last week in April—when northern weather is at its worst. During this season, you're guaranteed the most entertainment at resorts and the most people with whom to enjoy it. It's also the most fashionable, the most expensive, and the most popular time to visit—and most hotels are heavily booked. You must make reservations at least two or three months in advance for the very best places (sometimes a year in advance for the most exclusive spots). Hotel prices drop 20% to 50% after April 15; airfares and cruise prices also fall. Saving money isn't the only reason to visit the USBVI during the off-season. Summer is usually one of the prettiest times of the year; the sea is even calmer, and things move at a slower pace (except for the first two weeks of August on Tortola when the BVI celebrates Carnival). The water is clearer for snorkeling and smoother for sailing in the Virgin Islands in May, June, and July.

## Climate

Weather in the USBVI is a year-round wonder. The average daily temperature is about 80°F, and there isn't much variation from the coolest to the warmest months. Rainfall averages 40 to 44 inches per year. But in the tropics, rainstorms tend to be sudden and brief, often erupting early in the morning and at dusk.

In May and June what's known as the Sahara Dust sometimes moves through, making for hazy spring days and spectacular sunsets.

Toward the end of summer, of course, hurricane season begins in earnest, with the first tropical wave passing by in June. Islanders pay close attention to the tropical waves as they form and travel across the Atlantic from Africa. In an odd paradox, tropical storms passing by leave behind the sunniest and clearest days you'll ever see. (And that's saying something in the land of zero air pollution.)

🖪 Forecasts **Weather Channel Connection** (☎ 900/932–8437, 95¢ per minute from a Touch-Tone phone ⊕ www.weather.com).

# IF YOU LIKE . . .

## Beaches

With their warm, clear days, unspoiled sandy strands, and beautiful turquoise water, the Virgin Islands are a beach bum's paradise. Even if you're not a connoisseur, a day or two on the sand is central to a complete vacation here.

Your accommodation may border a beach or provide transportation to one nearby, but you have other options. You could spend one day at a lively, touristy beach that has plenty of water-sports facilities and is backed by a bar and another at an isolated cove that offers nothing but seclusion. Of course, these beaches are just jumping-off points to the underwater world.

In the USVI, public access to beach waters is guaranteed but land access to them isn't, effectively restricting some areas to resort guests. On St. Thomas, **Magens Bay** is among the prettiest (but also the liveliest) public beaches; **Coki Beach** is a fine alternative. St. Croix's **west-end beaches** are deservedly popular, but **Buck Island**'s soft, sandy beach is picture-perfect. Beautiful **Trunk Bay,** St. John, gets a lot of day-trip cruise-ship passengers; **Salt Pond Bay** is remote and mostly undeveloped.

Nowhere in the BVI will you find crowds to match those at the most popular USVI beaches, but **Cane Garden Bay** on Tortola probably comes the closest. **Apple Bay,** also on Tortola, is good for surfing, and **Long Bay West** is quieter. Virgin Gorda's beaches are easiest to get to from the water but are also approachable from land. Swimming among the rock formations at **The Baths** is a priority for many visitors, but this area can be crowded. On the smaller BVI, the lovely beaches are most likely sparsely populated by those who have dropped anchor and made their way in.

## History

Columbus, pirates, European colonizers, and plantation farmers and their slaves are among the people who have left their marks on these islands, all of which are benefiting the tourism industry, a relatively recent development.

In Charlotte Amalie, St. Thomas, **Fort Christian** (1672), **Hotel 1829** (1829), and the **Danish Consulate** (1830) are some noteworthy sights that give glimpses into the town's past; a trip to the **Seven Arches Museum,** a restored 18th-century home, will give you a sense of how St. Thomas residents lived in the colonial heyday. St. Croix's countryside is dotted with ruins of plantation great houses and sugar mills; many of the historic buildings in its main town, **Christiansted,** have been turned into stores and restaurants, but the large, yellow **Fort Christiansvaern** remains. On the island's west end, the **Whim Plantation Museum,** a lovingly restored estate, is the island's best preserved historical treasure. St. John, too, has several plantations in varying degrees of decay; the most popular of these are the ruins of the **Annaberg Plantation,** where the National Park Service sometimes does living-history demonstrations.

Diehard sightseers will find less to keep them busy in the British Virgin Islands. **Fort Burt,** the most intact historical ruin on Tortola, and the **Old Government House Museum**—both in Road Town—are the island's main historical sights; **Mount Healthy National Park** includes the remains of an old 18th-century sugar plantation. **Copper Mine Point,** on Virgin Gorda, is the ruins of a 16th-century mine. The most interesting historic site in the British Virgin Islands is actually underwater; if you're a scuba diver, you may wish to visit the **wreck of the *Rhone,*** which is off Salt Island.

# IF YOU LIKE . . .

## Nightlife

In the Virgin Islands, you're never too far from a Jimmy Buffett tune. Yachties congregate at the waterfront bars, where live guitar music may accompany the rum drinks. On St. Thomas, you may find the liveliest crowd at **Duffy's Love Shack** in Red Hook. In St. John, nightlife is mostly congregated in the main town of **Cruz Bay**, where barhopping is easy on foot; in more isolated Coral Bay, **Skinny Legs** is still the place to go. St. Croix is a bit quieter, but the casino (the USVI's only one) at **Divi Carina Bay** stays open late.

BVI watering holes, especially those on **Jost Van Dyke**, are most likely to be true beach bars, and barhopping here is a genuine island experience. It was on "Jost"—as the island is called locally—that the famous Painkiller drink was first concocted at the Soggy Dollar. These days, you can kill your pain at numerous beach bars, such as Rudy's, Foxy's, and Ali Baba's. Steel-drum, calypso, and reggae music—as well as broken-bottle dancing—are common in shows at larger hotels on Tortola or Virgin Gorda.

## Shopping

**Charlotte Amalie** is *the* place to shop in St. Thomas. As the Virgin Islands' main commercial center, it has the best selection of just about everything. Bargain hunters drool over the duty-free allowances and the lack of sales tax; liquor, china, crystal, and jewelry are especially popular buys. But you should also seek out artwork, crafts, and spices that are sold locally throughout the islands. Upscale stores can be found both in town and in the **Havensight Mall** next to the cruise-ship dock. For crafts and locally made goods, head to **Vendors Plaza** or to **Tillett Gardens**.

## Diving & Snorkeling

Clear water and numerous reefs afford wonderful opportunities for both diving and snorkeling in the Virgin Islands. Serious divers usually head to the BVI, where one of the most famous dive sites in the Caribbean is the **wreck of the *Rhone*,** off the coast of Tortola, but there are many other sites—particularly reef dives that are easily accessible from Tortola. Because the islands are so close together, most of the BVI's dive sites will be accessible to you. **Anegada**, a low-lying coral island, is 14 mi north of the main island group, and while its reefs are a sailor's nightmare, they are a diver's dream. Snorkelers in the BVI need not be disappointed that they can't reach the deeper reefs; **The Baths** in Virgin Gorda, which is dotted with giant round boulders that create numerous tidepools, is a great place to explore underwater from a point closer to the surface.

The reefs surrounding **St. Croix** are also popular with serious divers. The Cane Bay Wall is the most popular dive site on the island, and that's where you'll find the highest concentration of dive operators. Nearby Buck Island is a better destination for snorkelers, who can follow the underwater trail created by the National Park Service.

## Sailing

The area around the Virgin Islands is the most popular sailing destination in the entire Caribbean. The islands' charter yacht business is headquartered in **St. Thomas** and **Tortola,** and if you are looking for a unique and relaxing vacation, you might consider chartering a crewed yacht or, if you are a skipper yourself, a bareboat, and plying the waters for a week or longer.

# ON THE
# CALENDAR

| | |
|---|---|
| | The USBVI's top seasonal events are listed below, and any one of them could provide the stuff of lasting memories. Contact local tourism authorities for exact dates and for further information. |
| **ONGOING** <br><br> Oct.–Apr. | The Candlelight Concert Series at Whim Plantation is an ongoing classical music program—the only such program of its kind on St. Croix—that presents concerts on Friday and Saturday evenings throughout the year on the grounds of the historic plantation. |
| **WINTER** <br><br> Dec. | For the best in local *fungi* bands (bands that make music using household items as instruments), stop by the Scratch–Fungi Band Fiesta during the last two weeks of December. |
| Dec. and Jan. | St. Croix celebrates Carnival with its Crucian Christmas Festival, which starts in late December. After weeks of beauty pageants, food fairs, and concerts, the festival wraps up with a parade in early January. |
| **SPRING** <br><br> Mar. | Locals and yachties gather at Foxy's bar on Jost Van Dyke in the British Virgin Islands for the annual St. Patrick's Day celebration. |
| | The annual St. John Blues Festival brings musicians from all over to play for 5 nights in Coral Bay and Cruz Bay. |
| Mar. and Apr. | During Easter weekend, St. Thomas Yacht Club hosts the Rolex Cup Regatta, which is part of the three-race Caribbean Ocean Racing Triangle (CORT) that pulls in yachties and their pals from all over. |
| | The internationally known BVI Spring Regatta & Sailing Festival, which includes the competition for the Nation's Challenge Cup, begins during the last week in March, continues into the first weekend in April, with parties and sailing competitions on Tortola and Virgin Gorda. |
| May | Every May, hordes of people head to Tortola for the three-day BVI Music Festival to listen to reggae, gospel, blues, and salsa music by musicians from around the Caribbean and the U.S. mainland. |
| | The St. Croix Half Ironman Triathlon attracts international-class athletes as well as amateurs every May for a 1-mi (2-km) swim, a 7-mi (12-km) run, and a 34-mi (55-km) bike ride; it includes a climb up the Beast on Route 69. |
| Apr. | Join the fun at the Virgin Gorda Festival, which culminates with a parade on Easter Sunday. |

# ON THE CALENDAR

| SUMMER | |
|---|---|
| Jun.–July | Events of the St. John Festival celebrating the island's heritage and history continue throughout the month of June—including beauty pageants and a food fair—culminating with the annual parade on Independence Day. |
| July | The St. Thomas Gamefishing Club hosts its July Open Tournament over the Fourth of July weekend. There are categories for serious marlin anglers, just-for-fun fishermen, and even kids who want to try their luck from docks and rocks. |
| | All three islands celebrate Independence Day on July 4 with fireworks, though the biggest celebration is on St. John. |
| Aug. | Try your hand at sportfishing, as anglers compete to land the largest catch at the BVI Sportfishing Tournament. |
| | August sees two weeks of joyful revelry during Tortola's BVI Emancipation Festival celebrations. |

# FODOR'S CHOICE

The sights, restaurants, hotels, and other travel experiences on these pages are our editors' top picks—our Fodor's Choices. They're the best of their type in the area covered by the book—not to be missed and always worth your time. In the destination chapters that follow, you will find all the details.

| | |
|---|---|
| **SPLURGE-WORTHY RESORTS**<br><br>$$$$ | **Caneel Bay Resort,** St. John, U. S. Virgin Islands. With seven beaches spread out over 170 acres, this open-air resort is a sun-worshiper's paradise. Numerous tennis courts, myriad water sports, and good restaurants make it hard to stir from this luxury property. |
| $$$$ | **Peter Island Resort,** Peter Island, British Virgin Islands. A half-hour ferry ride from Tortola puts you at this luxury resort. The rooms are gorgeous, the food is divine, and the staff is at your beck and call. The beaches are close by, and you'll have lots of water sports to fill your hours. |
| $$$$ | **Ritz-Carlton,** St. Thomas, U.S. Virgin Islands. Built like a palatial Italian villa, there's elegance everywhere, from the marbled-floor reception area to a pool that seems to flow right into the sea. |
| **FAMILY-FRIENDLY RESORTS**<br><br>$$$$ | **Bitter End Yacht Club,** Virgin Gorda, British Virgin Islands. In addition to a children's program, the Bitter End includes all non-motorized watersports activities in its rate. You can also sign your kids up for sailing lessons. |
| $$$$ | **Wyndham Sugar Bay Resort & Spa,** St. Thomas, U.S. Virgin Islands. A stellar pool area and great children's programs make this a natural for families; all-inclusive rates make budgeting easier. |
| $ | **Maho Bay Camps,** St. John, U.S. Virgin Islands. Nature reigns at this upscale campground tucked inside Virgin Islands National Park. Yes, you'll have to head down the path for cool showers, but the beach is just a few stairs away, the restaurant serves good cheap meals, and the guests are always an interesting mix. |
| **SMALL INNS**<br><br>$ | **Carringtons Inn,** St. Croix, U.S. Virgin Islands. A stay at this spacious bed-and-breakfast harks back to a gentler time, when people spent the winter, rather than a week, in the Caribbean. |
| $ | **The Green Iguana,** St. Thomas, U.S. Virgin Islands. A perfect mix of views, convenience, and secluded privacy. |
| $ | **Inn at Pelican Heights,** St. Croix, U.S. Virgin Islands. This rambling B&B is another of St. Croix's lovely small inns. |

# FODOR'S CHOICE

| | |
|---|---|
| $ | **Villa Santana,** St. Thomas, U.S. Virgin Islands. Stay here and you get a slice of Virgin Islands history along with all the modern conveniences. |
| **ROMANTIC HIDEAWAYS** $$–$$$ | **Sugar Mill Hotel,** Tortola, British Virgin Islands. With rooms scattered across a hillside above a sandy beach, this cozy resort exudes a romantic, tropical ambience. |
| $–$$ | **Pavilions & Pools Villa Hotel,** St. Thomas, U.S. Virgin Islands. This is the place if you crave privacy, including your own pool. |
| **RESTAURANTS WORTH NOTING** $$$–$$$$ | **Old Stone Farmhouse,** St. Thomas, U.S. Virgin Islands. Throw yourself in chef Brian Katz's capable hands, and he'll fix you a six-course meal that will knock your socks off. |
| $$$–$$$$ | **Zozo's Ristorante,** St. John, U.S. Virgin Islands. Creative takes on old standards coupled with lovely presentation draw the crowds to this restaurant at Gallows Point Resort. |
| $$$ | **The Sugar Mill,** Tortola, British Virgin Islands. In the resort of the same name, The Sugar Mill Restaurant provides a lovely ambience in an old sugar mill. The food is delicious, with a different menu each night. |
| $$$ | **Brandywine Bay,** Tortola, British Virgin Islands. Candles and seaviews set the stage for a romantic dinner. The Tuscan-style food is always interesting, with fresh fish always on the menu. |
| $$$ | **Craig & Sally's,** St. Thomas, U.S. Virgin Islands. While Sally Darash's international menu is constantly changing, husband Craig is a continuous reassuring presence in the dining room. |
| **LOCAL FOOD** $$–$$$ | **Cuzzin's Caribbean Restaurant & Bar,** St. Thomas, U.S. Virgin Islands. Stick to the Virgin Island staples, and you will never go wrong here. |
| ¢–$ | **Skinny Legs Bar & Restaurant,** St. John, U.S. Virgin Islands. Exuding scads of island charm, this may just be the best bar in the Virgin Islands. Owner Moe is a character, as are some of those who frequent the place. |
| $–$$ | **Gladys' Cafe,** St. Thomas, U.S. Virgin Islands. Gladys's smile is almost as good as the local specialties she serves for lunch in her island-style diner. |

| | |
|---|---|
| **BEACHES** | **Cane Garden Bay,** Tortola, British Virgin Islands. This spacious beach can be a bit busy, but if you want to stroll off for a casual lunch, it's the best place on the island. After days at quiet anchorages, this is where sailors head for the action. |
| | **Coki Beach,** St. Thomas, U.S. Virgin Islands. This beach next to Coral World has the best shore diving and snorkeling in St. Thomas. |
| | **Lameshur Bay Beach,** St. John, U.S. Virgin Islands. On the southeast coast, this beach is often quiet, with good snorkeling and easy access to several hiking trails. |
| | **Loblolly Bay,** Anegada, British Virgin Islands. You'll find many miles of beach at this beautiful bay. Best, other than a small beach bar and sun shelters, the expanse is undeveloped and often deserted. |
| | **Magens Bay,** St. Thomas, U.S. Virgin Islands. This picture-postcard perfect heart-shape beach is on many lists of the world's most beautiful. |
| | **Trunk Bay,** St. John, U.S. Virgin Islands. This long, gorgeous beach in Virgin Islands National Park has all the amenities—showers, flush toilets, a snack bar, lifeguards, and even water-sports concessions. The only drawback is that it can be crowded. |
| | **White Bay,** Jost Van Dyke, British Virgin Islands. True to its name, this white stretch of sand is a great swimming beach and easily reached by boat from the bigger British Virgins. |
| **ACTIVITIES** | **Biking,** Water Island, U.S. Virgin Islands. Water Island Adventures has the best guided mountain-biking trip in the USVI on the "newest Virgin Island." |
| | **Diving the Wreck of the *Rhone,*** British Virgin Islands. Off Salt Island you can get a close-up look into BVI history. The ship went down in an 1867 hurricane, leaving the remains ready for underwater exploration. |
| | **Hiking in Virgin Islands National Park,** St. John, U.S. Virgin Islands. Swim, snorkel, and hike at this showpiece of the National Park Service, which occupies a full two-thirds of the island of St. John. |
| | **Kayaking in Salt River Bay National Historical Park & Ecological Preserve,** St. Croix, U.S. Virgin Islands. A guided kayaking trip through one of the island's most pristine areas is a great way to top off a trip to St. Croix and is an activity suitable for all ages. |

# FODOR'S CHOICE

| | |
|---|---|
| | **Playing Golf at Mahogany Run Golf Course,** St. Thomas, U.S. Virgin Islands. This challenging course, designed by George and Tom Fazio, is one of the best in the region. |
| | **Renting a Villa,** St. John, U.S. Virgin Islands. Enjoy all the comforts of home while enjoying all St. John has to offer. Villas—from basic to super-posh—have lovely sea views and the services of a local management team. |
| | **Sailing,** St. Thomas or Tortola, U.S. and British Virgin Islands. With dozens of islands—many with beautiful sandy beaches—the Virgin Islands provide one of the best sailing environments in the world. Set sail for a day, for a week, or for a month with a crew or without. |
| | **Shopping in St. Thomas,** U.S. Virgin Islands. Main Street in Charlotte Amalie is well known for numerous duty-free shops, selling everything from rum to designer fashions and gems. |
| | **Windsurfing,** Tortola, British Virgin Islands. Brisk, steady tradewinds lure windsurfers of all levels. |
| **HISTORICAL SIGHTS** | **Annaberg Plantation,** St. John, U.S. Virgin Islands. The national park's showpiece historic site gives you a glimpse into what life was like when slavery fueled the island's economy. Guides are often on hand to tell the stories. |
| | **Christiansted,** St. Croix, U.S. Virgin Islands. Fort Christiansvaern and other historic sights, which are spread out all over town, let you step back into St. Croix's colonial past. |
| | **Copper Mine Point,** Virgin Gorda, British Virgin Islands. With ruins dating back to the 1600s, this is one of the few places you can view the island's man-made history. |
| | **Fort Christian,** St. Thomas, U.S. Virgin Islands. The center for island life in the 1660s, when the Danes first settled the island, still stands as a centerpiece of downtown Charlotte Amalie. |
| | **Old Government House Museum,** Tortola, British Virgin Islands. A visit here takes you down the island's memory lane. Until recently, this was the governor's office, but now this cozy museum is filled with interesting and eclectic memorabilia from Tortola's past. |
| | **Whim Plantation Museum,** St. Croix, U.S. Virgin Islands. The lovingly restored sugar plantation gives a sense of what life was like for 18th-century Caribbean planters, and it's one of the cultural centers of the island. |

| NATURAL WONDERS | **Anegada**, British Virgin Islands. The island itself is a natural wonder. Gorgeous white-sand beaches stretch forever, and flamingos live in a salt pond. Accommodations are very casual, but you'll always find fresh lobster on restaurant menus. |
| --- | --- |
| | **The Baths**, Virgin Gorda, British Virgin Islands. Giant boulders frame white sandy beaches at this BVI national park. The snorkeling is lovely, and the sunning supreme. |
| | **Coral World Ocean Park**, St. Thomas, U.S. Virgin Islands. If you want to walk on the ocean's floor but aren't a certified diver, try Sea Trekkin' at Coral World, St. Thomas's great marine aquarium. |

# United States Virgin Islands

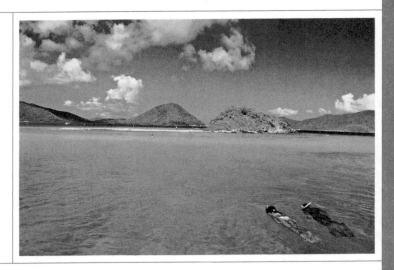

Snorkelers, St. Thomas

**WORD OF MOUTH**

"Magens Bay St. Thomas would be my vote for best and most beautiful beach we've been to."                                                        —Fran

"St. John is where you want to be. We took our whole family last summer and had a wonderful time. Very laid back."

—regansmom

"When on St. Croix, make sure you take a day trip over to Buck Island. . . ."                                                              —Leigh

# WELCOME TO THE UNITED STATES VIRGIN ISLANDS

ATLANTIC

Big Hans Lollick

Picara Pt.

Inner Brass

Santa Maria Bay

Stumpy Bay

Botany Bay

Magens Bay

Lovelund Bay

Thatch Cay

Dorothea

Fortuna

David Pt.

Brewers Bay

Charlotte Amalie

ST. THOMAS

Pillsbury Sound

see detail map pages 32–33

Cyril E. King International Airport

Hassel Island

Nadir

Red Hook

Great St. James Island

Water Island

Frenchman Bay

Bovoni Bay

Long Pt.

Little St. James Island

Charlotte Amalie is the busiest cruise-ship port in the Caribbean. On a busy port day in the high season, as many as 8 ships may anchor in the harbor.

Cane Bay

Davis Bay

Hams Bay

Frederiksted

Henry E. Rohlsen International Airport

Krause Pt.

West End Salt Pond

Long Pt. Bay

Long Pt.

Sandy Pt.

## AMERICA'S CARIBBEAN

About 1,000 mi (1,600 km) from the southern tip of Florida, the U.S. Virgin Islands were acquired from Denmark in 1917. St. Croix, at 84 square mi (216 square km) is the largest of the islands; St. John, at 20 square mi (52 square km) is the smallest. Together, they have a population of around 110,000, half of whom live on St. Thomas.

A perfect combination of the familiar and the exotic, the U.S. Virgin Islands are a little bit of home set in an azure sea. With hundreds of idyllic coves and splendid beaches, chances are that on one of the three islands you'll find your ideal Caribbean vacation spot.

## TOP 4 REASONS TO VISIT THE UNITED STATES VIRGIN ISLANDS

❶ St. Thomas is one of the Caribbean's major sailing centers.

❷ Two-thirds of St. John is a national park, which is criss-crossed by excellent hiking trails.

❸ Though Magens Bay on St. Thomas and Trunk Bay on St. John are two of the most perfect beaches you'll ever find, St. Croix's west-end beaches are fetching in their own way.

❹ Shopping on both St. Thomas and St. Croix is stellar.

## Getting to the U.S. Virgin Islands

Most major airlines fly nonstop to St. Thomas (STT) from the U.S. There are also a few nonstops to St. Croix (STX). Otherwise, you may have to connect in San Juan. It's also possible to take a seaplane between St. Thomas and St. Croix. There are no flights to St. John because it has no airport; the only option is a ferry from either Red Hook or Charlotte Amalie in St. Thomas. Both Caneel Bay and the Westin have private ferries.

St. Thomas's Cyril E. King Airport sits at the western end of the island. St. Croix's Henry Rohlsen Airport sits outside Frederiksted; the east end is 45 minutes away. The ferry dock in St. John is right in the heart of Cruz Bay.

## Activities

St. Thomas is one of the Caribbean's most important centers for **sailing. Beaches** are excellent on both St. Thomas and St. John, good on St. Croix. Of the three, St. Croix is more known for **diving.** Other activities are too varied and numerous to list, particularly on St. Thomas, which is the most developed of the three islands, but you'll find every imaginable kind of water- and land-based activity, **historic sights, golf** (except on St. John), **biking, horseback riding,** and **hiking,** to mention but a few. Since most of St. John is a national park, the island is in pristine condition and well worth exploring on foot. St. Croix's Buck Island and its surrounding reefs are also a protected part of the national park system.

## On the Ground

In St. Thomas, taxi vans are plentiful at the airport. Fees (set by the VI Taxi Commission) are per person. You'll usually be charged a small fee for each piece luggage. East End resorts are typically a half-hour from the airport. In St. Croix, you'll pay $10 to $20 for a taxi to your hotel. In St. John, safari-style taxi vans meet all the ferries and will drop you at your hotel; as on St. Thomas, the rates are per person.

## Renting a Car

If you are renting a villa on any of the three islands, you'll need a car. Otherwise, it's possible to get by with taxis on St. Thomas. You'll probably want a car on St. Croix, if only for a few days, to explore the island; if you are staying near Christiansted and your hotel has a shuttle into Christiansted, you might do without one entirely. In St. John, you will probably need a car to get around and to the beach unless you are staying at Caneel Bay or the Westin.

You need only a valid driver's license and credit card to rent a car; the minimum age for drivers is 18, although many agencies won't rent to anyone under the age of 25. Always make a reservation for a car during the high season.

# Where to Stay

St. Thomas is the most developed of the Virgin Islands; choose it if you want extensive shopping opportunities and a multitude of activities and restaurants. The more luxurious resorts tend to be at the east end of the island. St. John is the least developed of the three and has a distinct following; it's the best choice if you want a small-island feel and easy access to great hiking. However, most villas there aren't directly on the beach. St. Croix is a sleeper. With a wide range of accommodations, from simple inns to luxury resorts, including some dive-oriented resorts on the north coast, it's remarkably diverse, but none of the beaches is as breathtaking as those on St. Thomas and St. John.

**Resorts:** Whether you are looking for a luxury retreat or a moderately-priced vacation spot, there's going to be something for you in the USVI. St. Thomas has the most options. St. John has only two large resorts, both upscale; others are small, but it has some unique eco-oriented camping options. St. Croix's resorts are more mid-sized. The island also has two gay-oriented resorts.

**Small Inns:** Particularly on St. Croix, you'll find a wide range of attractive and accommodating small inns; if you can live without being directly on the beach; these friendly, homey places are a good option. St. Thomas also has a few small inns.

**Villas:** Villas are plentiful on all three islands, but they are especially popular on St. John, where they represent more than half the available lodging. They're always a good bet for families who can do without a busy resort environment.

## Hotel & Restaurant Costs

Assume that hotels operate on the European Plan (**EP**—with no meals) unless we specify that they use either the Continental Plan (**CP**—with a Continental breakfast), Breakfast Plan (**BP**—with full breakfast), or the Modified American Plan (**MAP**—with breakfast and dinner). Other hotels may offer the Full American Plan (**FAP**—including all meals but no drinks) or may be All-Inclusive (**AI**—with all meals, drinks, and most activities).

|  | $$$$ | $$$ | $$ | $ | ¢ |
|---|---|---|---|---|---|
| **Restaurants** | over $30 | $20–$30 | $12–$20 | $8–$12 | under $8 |
| **Hotels\*** | over $350 | $250–$350 | $150–$250 | $80–$150 | under $80 |
| **Hotels\*\*** | over $450 | $350–$450 | $250–$350 | $125–$250 | under $125 |

\*EP, BP, CP    \*\*AI, FAP, MAP

Restaurant prices are for a main course at dinner excluding tip. Hotel prices are for two people in a double room in high season excluding 8% tax, service and energy charges (which can vary significantly), and meal plans (except for all-inclusives).

# When to Go

High season coincides with that on most other Caribbean islands, from December through April or May; before and after that time, rates can drop by as much as 25% to 50%, depending on the resort.

St. Thomas's **International Rolex Regatta** in March is a big draw, as are the big **sport-fishing tournaments**, which usually begin in May and go through the summer. The St. Croix **Half Ironman Triathlon** attracts international-class athletes as well as amateurs every May. In February and March, the **St. Croix Landmarks Society House Tours** give you a chance to peek inside many historic homes that aren't usually open to the public. There aren't too many big events on St. John, but **Carnival** tends to bring many people to all three islands.

By Carol M.
Bareuther &
Lynda Lohr

**WE PILED INTO THE TAXI VAN, BAGS IN THE BACK,** and set off for our hotel on the opposite end of the island. Minutes later, cars slowed as we crept through the heart of town. But this traffic jam came with a view. Ballast-brick-walled 19th-century buildings touted contemporary buys on gold, diamonds, and emeralds, while turquoise seas glittered on the other side. Then our world turned topsy-turvy. Up we drove at a 45-degree angle or steeper, along former donkey trails to the mountain-ridge road that ran down the spine of the island. From this vantage point, the red-roof buildings and harbor below looked like miniatures on a postcard. Back on level ground, we pulled up to a green-painted van parked alongside stands brimming with tropical produce. "Sorry, I didn't have lunch," our driver apologized as he hopped back into his seat while holding a large paper bag. He pulled out a fried-bread oval, took a bite and passed the rest of the bag back to us. "Here, try a johnnycake," he offered. We were still happily munching as we finally pulled into our hotel. In 40 minutes, we had not merely reached where we were going but had a good idea of where we'd come. True, the U.S. flag blows here, but "America's Paradise" is in reality a delightful mix of the foreign and familiar that offers something for everyone to enjoy.

The U.S. Virgin Islands—St. Thomas, St. John, and St. Croix—float in the Greater Antilles between the Atlantic and Caribbean seas and some 1,000 mi (1,600 km) from the southern tip of Florida. History books give credit to Christopher Columbus for "discovering" the New World. In reality, the Virgin Islands, like the rest of the isles in the Caribbean chain, were populated as long ago as 2000 BC by nomadic waves of seagoing settlers as they migrated north from South America and eastward from Central America and the Yucatán Peninsula.

Columbus met the descendants of these original inhabitants during his second voyage to the New World, in 1493. He anchored in Salt River, a natural bay west of what is now Christiansted, St. Croix, and sent his men ashore in search of fresh water. Hostile arrows rather than welcoming embraces made for a quick retreat. In haste, Columbus named the island Santa Cruz (Holy Cross) and sailed north. He eventually claimed St. John, St. Thomas, and what are now the British Virgin Islands for Spain and at the same time named this shapely silhouette of 60-some islands Las Once Mil Virgenes, for the 11,000 legendary virgin followers of St. Ursula. Columbus believed the islands barren of priceless spices, so he sailed off leaving more than a century's gap in time before the next Europeans arrived.

Pioneers, planters, and pirates from throughout Europe ushered in the era of colonization. Great Britain and the Netherlands claimed St. Croix in 1625. This peaceful coexistence ended abruptly when the Dutch governor killed his English counterpart, thus launching years of battles for possession that would see seven flags fly over this southernmost Virgin isle. Meanwhile, St. Thomas's sheltered harbor proved a magnet for pirates like Blackbeard and Bluebeard. The Danes first colonized the island in 1666, naming their main settlement Taphus for its many beer halls. In 1691 the town received the more respectable name of Charlotte Amalie in honor of Danish king Christian V's wife. It wasn't until

1718 that a small group of Dutch planters raised their country's flag on St. John. As on its sibling Virgins, a plantation economy soon developed.

Plantations depended on slave labor, and the Virgin Islands played a key role in the triangular route that connected the Caribbean, Africa, and Europe in the trade of sugar, rum, and human cargo. By the early 1800s a sharp decline in cane prices due to competing beet sugar and an increasing number of slave revolts motivated Governor General Peter von Scholten to abolish slavery in the Danish colonies on July 3, 1848. This holiday is now celebrated as Emancipation Day.

After emancipation, the island's economy slumped. Islanders owed their existence to subsistence farming and fishing. Meanwhile, during the American Civil War, the Union began negotiations with Denmark for the purchase of the Virgin Islands in order to establish a naval base. However, the sale didn't happen until World War I, when President Theodore Roosevelt paid the Danes $25 million for the three largest islands; an elaborate Transfer Day ceremony was held on the grounds of St. Thomas's Legislature Building on March 31, 1917. A decade later, Virgin Islanders were granted U.S. citizenship. Today the U.S. Virgin Islands is an unincorporated territory, meaning that citizens govern themselves, vote for their own senators and governors, but cannot vote for president or congressional representation.

Nowadays, Virgin Islanders hail from more than 60 nations. Descendants of African slaves are the largest segment of the population, so it's not surprising that they also provide the largest percentage of workers and owners of restaurants, resorts, and shops. The Danish influence is still strong in architecture and street names. Americana is everywhere, too, most notably in recognizable fast-food chains, familiar shows on cable TV, and name-brand hotels. Between this diversity and the wealth that tourism brings, Virgin Islanders struggle to preserve their culture. Their rich, spicy West Indian–African heritage comes to full bloom at Carnival time, when celebrating and playing *mas* (with abandon) take precedence over everything else.

About 60,000 people live on 32-square-mi (83-square-km) St. Thomas (about the size of Manhattan); 51,000 on the 84 square mi (216 square km) of pastoral St. Croix; and about 5,000 on 20-square-mi (52-square-km) St. John, two-thirds of which is a national park. The backbone of the islands' economy is tourism, but at their heart is an independent, separate being: a rollicking hodgepodge of West Indian culture with a sense of humor that puts sex and politics in almost every conversation. Lacking a major-league sports team, Virgin Islanders follow the activities and antics of their 15 elected senators with the rabidity of Washingtonians following the Redskins. Loyalty to country and faith in God are the rules in the USVI, not the exceptions. Prayer is a way of life, and ROTC is one of the most popular high-school extracurricular activities.

Although the idyllic images of a tropical isle are definitely here, there's evidence, too, of growing pains. Traffic jams are common, a clandestine drug trade fuels crime, and—particularly on St. Thomas—there are few beaches left that aren't fronted by a high-rise hotel. Virgin Islanders are friendly folks, yet they can be prone to ungracious moments. Saying "Good morning" to the woman behind the jewelry counter, "Good afternoon" to the man who drives your cab, or "Goodnight" as you arrive at a restaurant for dinner will definitely pave the way for more pleasantries. Despite fairly heavy development, wildlife has found refuge here. The brown pelican is on the endangered list worldwide but is a common sight in the USVI. The endangered native boa tree is protected, as is the hawksbill turtle, whose females lumber onto the beaches to lay eggs.

With three islands to choose from, you're likely to find your piece of paradise. Check into a beachfront condo on the east end of St. Thomas; then eat burgers and watch football at a beachfront bar and grill. Or stay at an 18th-century plantation greathouse on St. Croix, dine on everything from local food to Continental cuisine, and go horseback riding at sunrise. Rent a tent or a cottage in the pristine national park on St. John; then take a hike, kayak off the coast, read a book, or just listen to the sounds of the forest. Or dive deep into "island time" and learn the art of limin' (hanging out, Caribbean-style) on all three islands.

# ST. THOMAS

By Carol M.
Bareuther

If you fly to the 32-square-mi (83-square-km) island of St. Thomas, you land at its western end; if you arrive by cruise ship, you come into one of the world's most beautiful harbors. Either way, one of your first sights is the town of Charlotte Amalie. From the harbor you see an idyllic-looking village that spreads into the lower hills. If you were expecting a quiet hamlet with its inhabitants hanging out under palm trees, you've missed that era by about 300 years. Although other islands in the USVI developed plantation economies, St. Thomas cultivated its harbor, and it became a thriving seaport soon after it was settled by the Danish in the 1600s.

The success of the naturally perfect harbor was enhanced by the fact that the Danes—who ruled St. Thomas with only a couple of short interruptions from 1666 to 1917—avoided involvement in some 100 years' worth of European wars. Denmark was the only European country with colonies in the Caribbean to stay neutral during the War of the Spanish Succession in the early 1700s. Thus, products of the Dutch, English, and French islands—sugar, cotton, and indigo—were traded through Charlotte Amalie, along with the regular shipments of slaves. When the Spanish wars ended, trade fell off, but by the end of the 1700s Europe was at war again, Denmark again remained neutral, and St. Thomas continued to prosper. Even into the 1800s, while the economies of St. Croix and St. John foundered with the market for sugarcane, St. Thomas's economy remained strong. This prosperity led to the development of shipyards, a well-organized banking system, and a large merchant class. In 1845 Charlotte Amalie had 101 large importing houses owned by the English, French, Germans, Haitians, Spaniards, Americans, Sephardim, and Danes.

Charlotte Amalie is still one of the most active cruise-ship ports in the world. On almost any day at least one and sometimes as many as eight cruise ships are tied to the dock or anchored outside the harbor. Gently rocking in the shadows of these giant floating hotels are just about every other kind of vessel imaginable: sleek sailing mono- and multi-hulls that will take you on a sunset cruise complete with rum punch and a Jimmy Buffett sound track, private megayachts that spirit busy executives away, and barnacle-bottom sloops—with laundry draped over the lifelines—that are home to world-cruising gypsies. Huge container ships pull up in Sub Base, west of the harbor, bringing in everything from breakfast cereals to tires. Anchored right along the waterfront are down-island barges that ply the waters between the Greater Antilles and the Leeward Islands, transporting goods like refrigerators, VCRs, and disposable diapers.

The waterfront road through Charlotte Amalie was once part of the harbor. Before it was filled to build the highway, the beach came right up to the back door of the warehouses that now line the thoroughfare. Two hundred years ago those warehouses contained indigo, tobacco, and cotton. Today the stone buildings house silk, crystal, linens, and leather. Exotic fragrances are still traded—but by island beauty queens in air-conditioned perfume palaces instead of through open market stalls. The pirates of old used St. Thomas as a base from which to raid merchant ships of every nation, though they were particularly fond of the gold- and silver-laden treasure ships heading to Spain. Pirates are still around, but today's versions use St. Thomas as a drop-off for their contraband: illegal immigrants and drugs.

## Where to Stay

Of the USVI, St. Thomas has the most rooms and the greatest number and variety of resorts. You can let yourself be pampered at a luxurious resort—albeit at a price of $300 to more than $500 per night, not including meals. If your means are more modest, there are fine hotels (often with rooms that have a kitchen and a living area) in lovely settings throughout the island. There are also guesthouses and inns with great views (if not a beach at your door) and great service at about half the cost of what you'll pay at the beachfront pleasure palaces. Many of these are east and north of Charlotte Amalie or overlooking hills—ideal if you plan to get out and mingle with the locals. There are also inexpensive lodgings (most right in town) that are perfect if you just want a clean room to return to after a day of exploring or beach-bumming. You can learn more about the smaller properties on the island from the **St. Thomas–St. John Hotel & Tourism Association** (see ⇨ Visitor Information *in* U.S. Virgin Islands Essentials).

East-end condominium complexes are popular with families. Although condos are pricey (winter rates average $350 per night for a two-bedroom unit, which usually sleeps six), they have full kitchens, and you can definitely save money by cooking for yourself—especially if you bring some of your own nonperishable foodstuffs. (Virtually everything on St. Thomas is imported, and restaurants and shops pass shipping costs on to you.) Though you may spend some time laboring in the kitchen, many condos ease your burden with daily maid service and on-site

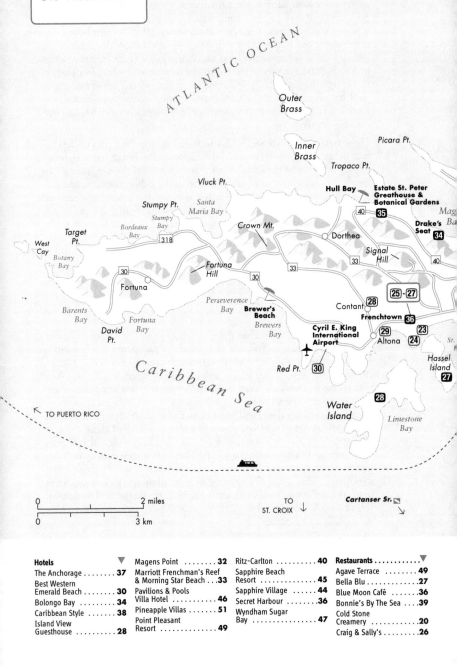

# St. Thomas

ATLANTIC OCEAN

Outer Brass

Inner Brass

Picara Pt.

Tropaco Pt.

Vluck Pt.

Hull Bay

Estate St. Peter Greathouse & Botanical Gardens

Stumpy Pt.

Santa Maria Bay

Stumpy Bay

Bordeaux Bay

Crown Mt.

Dorthea

**40**

**35**

Mag Ba

Drake's Seat **34**

Target Pt.

**318**

West Cay

Botany Bay

Fortuna Hill

Signal Hill

**33**

**40**

**30**

Fortuna

**30**

**33**

**25** - **27**

Barents Bay

Perseverence Bay

Contant

**28**

Fortuna Bay

Brewer's Beach

Frenchtown

**36**

David Pt.

Brewers Bay

Cyril E. King International Airport

**29**

Altona

**23**

**24**

St.

Caribbean Sea

Red Pt. **30**

Hassel Island

**27**

← TO PUERTO RICO

Water Island

**28**

Limestone Bay

0 _____ 2 miles
0 _____ 3 km

TO ST. CROIX ↓

*Cartanser Sr.*

**KEY**

| | |
|---|---|
| ⚓ | Beaches |
| 🚢 | Cruise Ship Terminal |
| ◿ | Dive Sites |
| **1** | Exploring Sights |
| 🚐 | Ferry |
| ① | Hotels & Restaurants |

**UNITED STATES VIRGIN ISLANDS**

*Tortola*

**ST. THOMAS** ---- ST. JOHN

*Distance from St. Thomas to St. Croix approx. 40 miles*

*ST. CROIX*

Hans Lollick

Lovelund Bay

*Aagens Bay*   **Magens Bay**

Mandal Pt.

**The *General Rogers***

**Grass Cay and Congo Cay** ◿→

Thatch Cay

**31**
**33** **Mountain Top**   **32**   42

Mafolie   Mandal

**22**

Tutu Bay

Coki Beach
**32** **Coral World Ocean Park**

**①** - **18**
**1** - **26**
see detail
map
page 63

Frydendal

**51**
**52**   **50**
**49**
**48**
**47**

**44** **45**

Cabes Pt.

40

**Charlotte Amalie**

38

**Sapphire Beach**
Redhook Bay

St. Thomas Harbor   **21**
**20**
**18**   Tutu
**21**

**29** **Paradise Point Tramway**
**Morning Star Beach**
el   **33**

32

**38**
**46**

**41** - **43**
**Vessup Beach**
**Red Hook** **31**

**40**
TO →
ST. JOHN

**Cow and Calf Rocks**

**39**

Paradise Pt.

**35**
**36**
**30**
Nadir

Great Bay

**34**
**Compass Point Marina**
30

**Secret Harbour**
**37**

**38**
St. James Bay

Great St. James Island

Jersey Bay

Coculus Pt.

Long Pt.

Little St. James Island

TO ST. JOHN →

◿ **Frenchcap**

restaurants; a few also have resort amenities, including pools and tennis courts. The east end is convenient to St. John, and it's a hub for the boating crowd, with some good restaurants. The prices below reflect rates in high season, which runs from December 15 to April 15. Rates are 25% to 50% lower the rest of the year.

## Hotels

CHARLOTTE AMALIE  Accommodations in town and near town offer the benefits of being close to the airport, shopping, and a number of casual and fine-dining restaurants. The downside is that this is the most crowded and noisy area of the island. Crime can also be a problem. Don't go for a stroll at night in the heart of town. Use common sense and take the same precautions you would in any U.S. city. Those properties located up along the hillsides are less likely to incur crime problems, plus they command a steady breeze from the cool trade winds. This is especially important if you're visiting in summer and early fall.

**$$$** 🏨 **Best Western Emerald Beach Resort.** You get beachfront ambience at this reasonably priced miniresort tucked beneath the palm trees, but the tradeoff is that it's directly across from a noisy airport runway. You'll definitely want to spend time on the white-sand beach, which can be seen from nearly every room in the four three-story, peach-color buildings. Rooms are acceptable, but the tropical-print bedspreads and rattan furnishings look worn. Stay here if you need the beach on a budget or if you have an early-morning flight. ⊠ *8070 Lindberg Bay, 00802* ☎ *340/777–8800 or 800/233–4936* 🖷 *340/776–3426* ⊕ *www. emeraldbeach.com* ⤳ *90 rooms* ⚐ *Restaurant, refrigerators, cable TV, in-room data ports, tennis courts, pool, gym, beach, boating, volleyball, bar* ☰ *AE, D, MC, V* ⦿❙ *CP.*

**$$** 🏨 **Holiday Inn St. Thomas.** Business travelers, those laying over on the way to the British Virgin Islands, or laid-back vacationers who want the convenience of being able to walk to duty-free shopping, sights, and restaurants stay at this harborfront hotel. But if your ideal Caribbean beach vacation means having the beach at your doorstep, this isn't the place for you, despite the presence of a free beach shuttle. Contemporarily furnished rooms have such amenities as coffeemakers, hair dryers, ironing boards, and irons. An introductory dive lesson with Admiralty Dive Center is complimentary. ⊠ *Waterfront Hwy., Box 640, 00804* ☎ *340/ 774–5200 or 800/524–7389* 🖷 *340/774–1231* ⊕ *www.holidayinn.st-thomas.com* ⤳ *140 rooms, 11 suites* ⚐ *Restaurant, room service, in-room safes, refrigerators, cable TV with movies and video games, in-room data ports, pool, gym, hair salon, dive shop, bar, shops, laundry service, business services, meeting rooms, car rental* ☰ *AE, D, DC, MC, V* ⦿❙ *EP.*

**$–$$**  🏨 **The Green Iguana.** Atop Blackbeard's Hill, this B&B offers the perfect mix of gorgeous harbor views, proximity to town and shopping (five minutes away by foot), and secluded privacy provided by the surrounding flamboyant trees and bushy hibiscus. Accommodations range from a roomy, top-floor junior suite with two queen beds to a balcony room with queen bed and full kitchen. All rooms have air-conditioning, refrigerators, microwave ovens, and coffeemakers. Guests have use of wash-

Fodor'sChoice
★

ers and dryers. There's also a picnic area with a gas barbecue grill. The managing couple live on property and are very helpful in giving restaurant, sightseeing, or beach suggestions. ⌧ *37B Blackbeard's Hill, 00802* ☎ *340/776–7654 or 800/484–8825* ⊟ *340/777–4312* ⊕ *www.thegreeniguana.com* ⤶ *6 rooms* ⚐ *Fans, some kitchens, some kitchenettes, microwaves, refrigerators, cable TV, pool, laundry facilities, no-smoking rooms* ⊟ *AE, D, MC, V* ⦿ *EP.*

**$–$$**  ⛻ **Villa Santana.** Built by exiled general Santa Anna of Mexico, this 1857
**Fodor'sChoice**  landmark provides a panoramic view of the harbor and plenty of West
★  Indian charm, which will make you feel as if you're living in a charming slice of Virgin Islands history with all the modern conveniences. Each of the rooms is unique and lovely. Our two favorites are La Mansion, a former library that is now an elegant villa with a large living area crowned by cathedral ceilings, full kitchen, two baths, and four-poster bed; and El Establo, a three-bedroom house with a full kitchen and laundry facilities that is rented by the week for up to six guests. Modern amenities aren't lacking; you can even sit by the pool with your laptop and indulge in wireless Internet access. ⌧ *2D Denmark Hill, 00802* ☎ *340/776–1311* ⊟ *340/776–1311* ⊕ *www.villasantana.com* ⤶ *6 rooms* ⚐ *Fans, some kitchens, some kitchenettes, Wi-Fi, pool, croquet; no a/c in some rooms, no room phones, no TV in some rooms* ⊟ *AE, MC, V* ⦿ *EP.*

**¢–$$**  ⛻ **Hotel 1829.** Antique charm is readily apparent in this rambling 19th-century merchant's house, from the hand-painted Moroccan tiles to a Tiffany window. Rooms on several levels range from stylish and spacious suites with vaulted ceilings to small and cozy rooms, with prices that range accordingly. The bar is open nightly and attracts locals as well as hotel guests; in the corner, a backgammon table attests to the prowess of the former owner, 1976 world champion Baron Vernon Ball. The second-floor botanical gardens and open-air champagne bar make a romantic spot for sunset viewing. Main Street, with its duty-free shops, is down the hill one block away. ⌧ *Government Hill, Box 1567, 00804* ☎ *340/776–1829 or 800/524–2002* ⊟ *340/776–4313* ⊕ *www.hotel1829.com* ⤶ *15 rooms* ⚐ *Refrigerators, cable TV, pool, bar; no room phones, no kids* ⊟ *AE, D, MC, V* ⦿ *CP.*

**$**  ⛻ **Mafolie Hotel.** The view and the value are the selling points of this 1970s-era family-run hotel perched 700 feet above Charlotte Amalie harbor. The rooms are simply furnished rather than resort elegant, and a few of those at pool level don't have much of a view or a constant flow of trade winds, which makes air-conditioning a must. Rooms above the restaurant are really small and lack privacy in the evening due to the steady stream of diners. The restaurant is known for its well-prepared Continental cuisine, featuring fresh seafood, steaks and chicken. A daily shuttle takes guests to and from Magens Bay Beach. ⌧ *Rte. 35, Box 7091, Estate Mafolie, 00802* ☎ *340/774–2790 or 800/225–7035* ⊟ *340/774–4091* ⊕ *www.mafolie.com* ⤶ *22 rooms* ⚐ *Restaurant, refrigerators, cable TV, pool, bar* ⊟ *AE, MC, V* ⦿ *CP.*

**¢–$**  ⛻ **Island View Guesthouse.** Perched 545 feet up the face of Crown Mountain, this small inn has a homey feel; hands-on owners can book tours or simply offer tips about the best sightseeing spots. Rooms range from a suite with a kitchenette that's perfect for families to two simply furnished veranda rooms that share a bath. Although the two veranda rooms and six poolside rooms have no air-conditioning, at this altitude, there's always a breeze, which makes that less of a burden. All rooms have telephones, six have kitchenettes, and laundry facilities are on-site. There's an honor bar for drinks and snacks and a communal verandah where guests congregate for Continental breakfasts and home-cooked dinners. You'll need a car to explore the island. ☒ *Rte. 332, Box 1903, Estate Contant 00803* ☎ *340/774–4270 or 800/524–2023* 🖷 *340/774–6167* ⊕ *www.islandviewstthomas.com* ➥ *16 rooms, 14 with private bath* ⚐ *Fans, some kitchenettes, cable TV, pool, hot tub, laundry facilities; no a/c in some rooms* ▤ *AE, MC, V* ⦿ *CP.*

EAST END    You can find most of the large, luxurious beachfront resorts on St. Thomas's east end. The downside is that these properties are about a 30-minute drive from town and 45-minute drive from the airport (substantially longer during peak hours). On the upside, these properties tend to be self-contained, plus there are a number of good restaurants, shops, and water-sports operators on the east end. Thus, once you've arrived, you don't need to travel far to have many activities and services at your fingertips.

☉ **$$$$**   🏨 **Ritz-Carlton, St. Thomas.** Everything sparkles at the island's most luxurious resort, from the marble-floor lobby to the infinity pool, which
**Fodor'sChoice**
★   seems to become one with the turquoise sea. Spacious guest rooms, with mahogany furnishings, high-speed Internet access, private balconies, and marble bathrooms with deep soaking tubs, are in six buildings fanning out from the main building. Six tall, somewhat institutional-looking buildings, composing the Ritz-Carlton Club, are two- and three-bedroom condos on their own adjacent beach. The spa, salon, and fitness center serve adults, both body and soul; the Ritz Kids program packs in a full day of activities for kids, including collecting seashells and feeding live iguanas. A 54-foot catamaran is a must-do for a day or sunset sail. ☒ *Rte. 317, Box 6900, Estate Great Bay 00802* ☎ *340/775–3333 or 800/241–3333* 🖷 *340/775–4444* ⊕ *www.ritzcarlton.com* ➥ *200 rooms, 81 condos* ⚐ *4 restaurants, room service, in-room safes, minibars, cable TV with movies and video games, Wi-Fi, 2 tennis courts, 2 pools, health club, hair salon, spa, beach, windsurfing, boating, 5 bars, shops, babysitting, children's programs (ages 4–12), laundry service, concierge, Internet room, business services, meeting rooms, airport shuttle, no-smoking rooms* ▤ *AE, D, DC, MC, V* ⦿ *EP.*

☉ **$$$$**   🏨 **Wyndham Sugar Bay Resort & Spa.** Though this terra-cotta high-rise is
**Fodor'sChoice**
★   surrounded by palm trees and lush greenery, rooms and the walkways between them have a bit of an institutional feel. However, the sixth and seventh levels of building D have spectacular ocean views. Deluxe and superior rooms are spacious and comfortable. The beach is small, although the giant pool is replete with waterfalls that make a day of lounging here idyllic; however, it's a long, 99-step hike down here from guest rooms. Health buffs will enjoy the full-service spa and fitness center, as well as an outdoor fitness trail. If you're feeling lucky, head to the Ocean Club, where more than 50 slot machines were added in early 2005. ☒ *Rte. 38, Box 6500, Estate Smith Bay 00802* ☎ *340/777–7100 or 800/927–7100*

⌂ *340/777–7200* ⊕ *www.wyndham.com* ⇨ *300 rooms, 9 suites* ♿ *2 restaurants, snack bar, room service, fans, in-room safes, refrigerators, cable TV, in-room data ports, Wi-Fi, 4 tennis courts, pool, health club, spa, beach, snorkeling, windsurfing, boating, bar, nightclub, shop, babysitting, children's programs (ages 4–12), laundry service, concierge, business services, meeting rooms, car rental* ▭ *AE, D, DC, MC, V* ⚍ *AI.*

**\$\$\$–\$\$\$\$**    🏨 **Point Pleasant Resort.** Hilltop suites give you an eagle's-eye view of the east end and the BVI beyond, while those in a building adjacent to the reception area offer incredible sea views. Sea-level junior suites are smaller, but the sounds of lapping waves will lull you to sleep. There's a resort shuttle, but some walking is necessary and hills are steep. The beach is very small, though some may call it wonderfully private, but three pools give you more swimming and sunning options. The property also has a labyrinth of well-marked nature trails to explore. If you like seafood, don't miss dinner at the Agave Terrace restaurant; Fungi's on the Beach is a casual alternative. ✉ *6600 Rte. 38, Estate Smith Bay 00802* ☎ *340/775–7200 or 800/524–2300* ⌂ *340/776–5694* ⊕ *www.pointpleasantresort.com* ⇨ *128 suites* ♿ *2 restaurants, in-room safes, kitchenettes, cable TV, in-room data ports, tennis court, 3 pools, gym, beach, bar, shops, laundry facilities, concierge, Internet room* ▭ *AE, D, DC, MC, V* ⚍ *EP.*

🅒 **\$\$\$–\$\$\$\$**    🏨 **Sapphire Beach Resort & Marina.** A beautiful half-mile-long white-sand beach is the real ace here. The buildings have a weathered look, which could be construed as rustic, if not for the needed renovations and refurbishments also lacking in the guest rooms. Some bedspreads, upholstery, and curtains are faded, and bathroom fixtures and kitchen appliances could be replaced. The property is nicely landscaped on the seaside; however, on the land-side is a long-awaited, yet-to-be-built convention center, marina office, and shopping complex that is now a big grassy spot occupied by the odd car and piece of construction equipment. The property came under new management in the fall of 2005, a transition that has eliminated many problems with check in, frequency of maid service, and use of water-sports equipment that occurred when two management companies shared responsibility for separate rooms on the property. The kids club program no longer exists. ✉ *6720 Estate Smith Bay* ☎ *800/524–2090, 340/773–9150, 800/874–7897* ⌂ *340/778–4009* ⊕ *www.antillesresorts.com* ⇨ *171 suites* ♿ *2 restaurants, snack bar, room service, some kitchenettes, cable TV, 4 tennis courts, pool, health club, beach, snorkeling, windsurfing, boating, jet skiing, marina, parasailing, volleyball, bar, shop, babysitting, playground, laundry facilities, concierge, meeting room, car rental* ▭ *AE, MC, V* ⚍ *EP.*

**\$\$\$–\$\$\$\$**    🏨 **Secret Harbour Beach Resort & Villas.** There's no bad view from these low-rise studio, one-, and two-bedroom condos, which are either beachfront or perched on a hill overlooking the inviting cove beyond. All units, which have white-tile floors and tropical-print wood and wicker furnishings, are spacious; even the studios are more than 600 square feet and certainly big enough for a family with two children. The pool is small, but the beach is the real focal point here, where calm seas make for excellent swimming; snorkeling is especially good near the small dock to the east of the cove, where coral outcroppings attract a bevy of marine life. Watch spectacular sunsets from your balcony or at the beachfront bar. Kids under 13 stay free, making this a good value for families. ⊠ *Rte. 317, Box 6280, Estate Nazareth 00802-1104* ☎ *340/775–6550 or 800/ 524–2250* 🖷 *340/775–1501* ⊕ *www.secretharbourvi.com* 🛏 *49 suites, 15 studios* ↺ *Restaurant, fans, kitchens, cable TV, 3 tennis courts, pool, health club, beach, dive shop, snorkeling, windsurfing, boating, bar, shop* ▤ *AE, MC, V* ¶〇¶ *CP.*

**$$–$$$** 🖬 **Magens Point Resort.** This small resort is tucked into the lush, green countryside 10 minutes from town and close to both Magens Bay Beach and the Mahogany Run golf course, to which there are free shuttles. Be forewarned that renovations are needed for the large, multilevel suites, which have full kitchens. Most units are available as time-shares. A plus is the Sunday-morning poolside talk about what to see and do on the island. The restaurant, Indigo, has upscale yet reasonably priced fare served up in a casual, laid-back setting. ⊠ *Rte. 35, Magens Bay Rd., Estate St. Joseph 00802* ☎ *340/777–6000 or 800/524–2031* 🖷 *340/777– 6055* ⊕ *www.magenspoint.com* 🛏 *52 suites* ↺ *Restaurant, cable TV, 2 tennis courts, pool, gym, bar, concierge* ▤ *AE, D, MC, V* ¶〇¶ *EP.*

**$$–$$$**
**Fodor'sChoice**
★
🖬 **Pavilions & Pools Villa Hotel.** Although the rates might lead you to believe you're buying resort ambience, the reality is that you get fairly basic accommodations but also a private swimming pool right outside your bedroom. Perfect for couples who crave privacy, the villas have full kitchens, lots of space, and sunken garden showers. The informal bar and open-air dining area, built around a pond filled with tilapia, is a great place to congregate over a Continental breakfast and chat with other guests. Casual dinners—steak, chicken, and barbecued ribs—are served here every night except Friday, but you can find several restaurants and a small supermarket a mile away in Red Hook. The beach at Sapphire Bay is less than a 10-minute walk away. ⊠ *6400 Rte. 38, Estate Smith Bay 00802* ☎ *340/775–6110 or 800/524–2001* ⊕ *www. pavilionsandpools.com* 🛏 *25 1-bedroom villas* ↺ *Restaurant, in-room safes, kitchens, cable TV, 25 pools* ▤ *AE, D, MC, V* ¶〇¶ *CP.*

SOUTH SHORE   The south shore of St. Thomas connects town to the east end of the island via a beautiful road that rambles along the hillside with frequent peeks between the hills for a view of the ocean and, on a clear day, of St. Croix some 40 mi (60 km) to the south. The resorts here are on their own beaches. They offer several opportunities for water sports, as well as land-based activities, fine dining, and evening entertainment.

↺ **$$$$** 🖬 **Marriott Frenchman's Reef & Morning Star Beach Resorts.** Set majestically on a promontory overlooking the east side of Charlotte Amalie's harbor, Frenchman's Reef is the high-rise full-service superhotel while Morning Star is the even more upscale boutique property nestled surfside along the fine white-sand beach. Meals here include lavish buffets for breakfast and dinner. Live entertainment and dancing, scheduled activities for all ages, and a shuttle boat to town that runs on the hour make having fun easy. ⊠ *Rte. 315, Box 7100, Estate Bakkeroe 00801* ☎ *340/776–8500 or 800/233–6388* 🖷 *340/715–6193* ⊕ *www. marriottfrenchmansreef.com* 🛏 *504 rooms, 27 suites* ↺ *4 restaurants, snack bar, room service, in-room safes, minibars, cable TV with movies, in-room data ports, Wi-Fi, 4 tennis courts, 2 pools, health club, hair salon, spa, beach, boating, volleyball, bar, piano bar, dance club, shops, babysit-*

ting, children's programs (ages 4–12), concierge, business services, convention center ⊟ AE, D, DC, MC, V ⏐◯⏐ EP.

**$$$** ▦ **Bolongo Bay Beach Club.** All the rooms at this small, family-run resort tucked along a 1,000-foot palm-lined beach have balconies with ocean views; down the beach are 12 studio and two-bedroom condos with full kitchens. This place is more homey than resort-fancy, but the friendliness of the longtime staff keeps visitors, including many honeymooners and even some families, coming back. The beach is a bit rocky for swimming, but sails aboard the resort's 53-foot catamaran and excursions arranged by the on-site dive shop are popular. You can opt out of the all-inclusive plan and pay less, but then you'd have to rent a car because the resort is a bit removed from the main parts of the island. The creative Caribbean cuisine at the Beach House, especially the seven-course tasting menu, which is paired with wines, shouldn't be missed. ⊠ *Rte. 30, Box 7150, Estate Bolongo 00802* ☎ *340/775–1800 or 800/ 524–4746* 🖷 *340/775–3208* ⊕ *www.bolongobay.com* ⇆ *65 rooms, 12 studio and 2-bedroom condos* △ *2 restaurants, in-room safes, some kitchenettes, refrigerators, cable TV, 2 tennis courts, pool, beach, dive shop, dock, snorkeling, windsurfing, boating, jet skiing, volleyball, bar, nightclub, shop, babysitting* ⊟ *AE, D, DC, MC, V* ⏐◯⏐ *EP.*

## Villas & Condominiums

All the villa and condominium complexes listed here are on the East End of St. Thomas.

**۞ $$$$** ▦ **The Anchorage.** A beachfront setting and homey conveniences that include full kitchens and washer-dryer units are what you can find in these two- and three-bedroom suites on Cowpet Bay next to the St. Thomas Yacht Club. The complex has two lighted tennis courts, a freshwater pool, and an informal restaurant. ⊠ *Rte. 317, Estate Nazareth* ⏚ *Antilles Resorts, Box 24786, Christiansted, St. Croix 00824-0786* ☎ *800/874–7897* 🖷 *340/778–4009* ⊕ *www.antillesresorts.com* ⇆ *11 suites* △ *Restaurant, kitchens, cable TV, 2 tennis courts, pool, beach, bar, laundry facilities* ⊟ *AE, D, MC, V* ⏐◯⏐ *EP.*

**$$** ▦ **Pineapple Villas.** These light, airy villas are made up of four studios that can be rented separately or combined in various configurations to create a three-bedroom, three-bath unit accommodating 8 to 10 guests. All rooms have private bathrooms, ceiling fans, and kitchenettes; the full villa also offers a complete kitchen. This property is on the grounds of the former Grand Beach Palace Resort, which closed in August 2004. This means the resort's restaurants, water-sports center, and other amenities are no longer available. ⊠ *Rte. 38, at former Grand Beach Palace Resort, Estate Smith Bay 00802* ☎ *340/775–5516 or 800/992– 9232* 🖷 *201/262–7609 reservations only* ⊕ *www.pineapplevillas.com* ⇆ *6 villas* △ *Some kitchens, some kitchenettes, cable TV, pool, beach, dock, volleyball* ⊟ *AE, MC, V* ⏐◯⏐ *EP.*

**$$** ▦ **Sapphire Village.** These high-rise condos have the feel of an apartment house more than a luxury resort, so if you're looking for a home away from home, this might be the place. There are full kitchens, so you can avoid pricey restaurant meals. The view from your balcony is the marina and the Atlantic to the north. The beach, a spectacular half mile of white sand, is a five-minute walk down the hill. There's a restaurant on property and two more down the hill at the Sapphire Beach Resort. Additional restaurants, a shopping complex, and ferries to St. John are a mile away in Red Hook, albeit along a busy road. ⊠ *Rte. 38, Sapphire Bay* ⚓ *Antilles Resorts, Box 24786, Christiansted, St. Croix 00824-0786* ☎ *340/779–1540 or 800/874–7897* 🖷 *340/778–4009* ⊕ *www.antillesresorts.com* 🛏 *15 condos* ⚭ *Restaurant, kitchens, cable TV, 2 tennis courts, 2 pools, beach, dock, snorkeling, windsurfing, boating, jet skiing, marina, parasailing, volleyball, bar, pub, laundry facilities* ▤ *AE, D, MC, V* �𝟙⚭ *EP.*

★ $ 🖥 **Caribbean Style.** Couples will enjoy the romantic feel of these private, individually decorated condos. Each has a king-size bed, a reading and video library, and a kitchen stocked with breakfast foods and special requests, such as your favorite ice cream or preferred brand of rum. You can literally toss an ice cube into the sea from the hammock or lounge chairs on the private porches of the two smaller condos, while the two larger condos are only about 20 feet away from the rocky waterfront. Vessup Beach and water sports are a 10-minute walk away. Couples who would like to tie the knot will find that wedding arrangements, including professional photography, are a specialty of the owner. ⊠ *Rte. 317, at Cabrita Point, Estate Vessup Bay* ⚓ *6501 Red Hook Plaza, Suite 201, 00802* ☎ *340/715–1117 or 800/593–1390* ⊕ *www.cstylevi.com/cstyle_new/html* 🛏 *4 1-bedroom condos* ⚭ *Kitchens, pool, snorkeling, windsurfing, boating; no kids under 15, no smoking* ▤ *AE, MC, V* ⟨⟩ *CP.*

PRIVATE VILLAS  You can arrange private villa rentals through various agents that represent luxury residences and usually have both Web sites and brochures that show photos of the properties they represent. Some are suitable for travelers with disabilities, but be sure to ask specific questions regarding your own needs. **Calypso Realty** (⚓ Box 12178, 00801 ☎ 340/774–1620 or 800/747–4858 ⊕ www.calypsorealty.com) specializes in rental properties in St. Thomas. **McLaughlin-Anderson Villas** (⊠ 100 Blackbeard's Hill, Suite 3, 00802 ☎ 340/776–0635 or 800/537–6246 ⊕www.mclaughlinanderson.com) handles rental villas throughout the U.S. Virgin Islands, British Virgin Islands, and Grenada.

## Where to Eat

The beauty of St. Thomas and its sister islands has attracted a cadre of professionally trained chefs who know their way around fresh fish and local fruits. You can dine on everything from terrific cheap local dishes such as goat water (a spicy stew) and fungi (a cornmeal polenta-like side dish) to imports such as hot pastrami sandwiches and raspberries in crème fraîche.

Restaurants are spread all over the island, although fewer are found on the northwest and far west of the island. Most restaurants out of town are easily accessible by taxi and have ample parking. If you dine in Charlotte Amalie, take a taxi. Parking close to restaurants can be difficult to find, and walking around after dark isn't advisable for safety reasons.

If your accommodations have a kitchen and you plan to cook, there's good variety in St. Thomas's mainland-style supermarkets. Just be prepared for grocery prices that are about 20% higher than those in the United States. As for drinking, outside the hotels a beer in a bar will cost between $2 and $3 and a piña colada $5 or more.

## What to Wear

Dining on St. Thomas is informal. Few restaurants require a jacket and tie. Still, at dinner in the snazzier places shorts and T-shirts are inappropriate; men would do well to wear slacks and a shirt with buttons. Dress codes on St. Thomas rarely require women to wear skirts, but you can never go wrong with something flowing.

## Charlotte Amalie

AMERICAN
☺ $–$$$
✕ **Greenhouse Bar & Restaurant.** The eight-page menu at this bustling waterfront restaurant offers burgers, salads, sandwiches, and pizza served all day long, along with more upscale entrées like peel-and-eat shrimp, Maine lobster, Alaskan king crab, and certified Black Angus prime rib that are reasonably priced. This is generally a family-friendly place, though the Two-for-Tuesdays happy hour and Friday-night live reggae music that starts thumping at 10 PM draw a lively young-adult crowd. ⊠ *Waterfront Hwy. at Storetvaer Gade* ☎ *340/774–7998* ▬ *AE, D, MC, V.*

☺ ¢–$
✕ **Jen's Gourmet Cafe & Deli.** This hole-in-the-wall eatery is the closest thing you'll find to a New York–style Jewish deli. Choose the smoked salmon platter for breakfast or hot pastrami on rye at lunch. Homemade desserts like chocolate layer cake, apple strudel, and peaches-and-cream-cheese strudel are yummy. ⊠ *Grand Galleria, 43-46 Norre Gade* ☎ *340/777–4611* ▬ *AE, MC, V* ☾ *No dinner.*

BARBECUE
☺ ¢–$
✕ **Texas Pit BBQ.** The smell of smoky barbecue ribs, beef brisket, and chicken wafts enticingly from these mobile stands, which set up daily around 4 PM. Austin native and longtime Virgin Islands resident Bill Collins perfected his sauce recipe, which received a thumbs-up from the late culinary great James Beard. Choice of homemade seasoned rice, coleslaw or potato salad, plus a roll, completes the meal. Takeout only. Besides the two Charlotte Amalie branches, you can also find one in Red Hook, next to Marina Market. ⊠ *Waterfront, across from Holiday Inn St. Thomas* ☎ *340/776–9579* ⊠ *Wheatley Center* ☎ *340/714–5775* ▬ *No credit cards* ☾ *No lunch.*

CAFES
☺ ¢
✕ **Cold Stone Creamery.** Ice cream and a dash of showmanship combine in this whimsical shop. Flavors of your choice, as well as candies, nuts, and fruits, are worked into freshly made ice cream on a cold marble stone while you watch. Eat your creation out of a freshly baked waffle cone that doubles as a bowl. There's another outlet in Red Hook. ⊠ *Port of $ale Mall, Rte. 30, next to Havensight Mall* ☎ *340/714–2499* ⊠ *Rte. 32 at American Yacht Harbor, Bldg. B, Red Hook* ☎ *340/777–2777* ▬ *No credit cards.*

CARIBBEAN
$$
Fodor'sChoice
★
✕ **Cuzzin's Caribbean Restaurant & Bar.** The top picks in this restaurant in a 19th-century livery stage are Virgin Islands staples. For lunch, order tender slivers of conch stewed in a rich onion butter sauce, savory braised oxtail, or curried chicken. At dinner, the island-style mutton served in a thick gravy and seasoned with locally grown herbs offers

a tasty treat that's deliciously different. Side dishes include peas and rice, boiled green bananas, fried plantains, and potato stuffing. ⊠ *7 Wimmelskafts Gade, also called Back St.* ☎ *340/777–4711* ⊟ *AE, MC, V.*

**\$–\$\$**
FodorsChoice
★

✕ **Gladys' Cafe.** Even if the local specialties—conch in butter sauce, saltfish and dumplings, hearty red bean soup—didn't make this a recommended café, it would be worth coming for Gladys's smile. While you're here, pick up a \$5 or \$10 bottle of her hot sauce. There are mustard-, oil and vinegar-, and tomato-based versions; the last is the hottest. ⊠ *Waterfront, at Royal Dane Mall* ☎ *340/774–6604* ⊟ *AE* ☉ *No dinner.*

**\$–\$\$**
✕ **Lillian's Caribbean Grill.** This is where the local business community fuels up for its day of selling in Main Street stores. Specialties include dumb bread (baked in a kettle over hot coals) and cheese, cinnamon-spice oatmeal, and bush tea for breakfast, with everything from hamburgers to conch in butter sauce, fish and fungi, souse, curried goat, and tripe soup served for lunch. ⊠ *Grand Galleria* ☎ *340/774–7900* ⊟ *AE, MC, V* ☉ *Closed Sun. No dinner.*

ECLECTIC
**\$\$\$–\$\$\$\$**
FodorsChoice
★

✕ **Banana Tree Grille.** The eagle's-eye view of the Charlotte Amalie harbor from this open-air restaurant is as fantastic as the food. Come before 6 PM and watch the cruise ships depart from the harbor and the sun set over the sea while you have a drink at the bar. Liz Buckalew, who with husband Jerry has been in the island restaurant business since the early 1980s, always greets you with a warm welcome. For starters, try the combination of lobster, shrimp, scallops, and squid marinated in a savory herb vinaigrette. The dark rum, honey, and brown sugar–glazed salmon fillet served with yams is an excellent entrée. ⊠ *Bluebeard's Castle, Bluebeard's Hill* ☎ *340/776–4050* ⌂ *Reservations essential* ⊟ *AE, D, MC, V* ☉ *Closed Mon. No lunch.*

★ **\$\$–\$\$\$**
✕ **Randy's Bar & Bistro.** There's no view here—even though you're at the top of a hill—but the somewhat hidden location has helped to keep this one of the island's best dining secrets. This wine shop and deli caters to a local lunch crowd. At night, you forget you're tucked into a nearly windowless building. The tableside bread for starters is a thick, crusty focaccia flavored with nearly 10 different vegetables. Try the brie-stuffed filet mignon or rack of lamb. After-dinner cigars and wine complete the experience. ⊠ *Al Cohen's Plaza, atop Raphune Hill, ½ mi (¾ km) east of Charlotte Amalie* ☎ *340/777–3199* ⊟ *AE, D, MC, V.*

FRENCH
★ **\$\$\$–\$\$\$\$**
✕ **Hervé Restaurant & Wine Bar.** In the glow of candlelight—at tables impeccably dressed with fine linens, silver settings, and fine crystal—you can start off with French-trained Hervé Chassin's crispy conch fritters served with a spicy-sweet mango chutney, then choose from such entrées as black-sesame-crusted tuna with a ginger raspberry sauce or succulent roast duck with a ginger-and-tamarind sauce. The passion-fruit cheesecake is to die for. For lunch, lighter fare like quiche, salads, and grilled sandwiches is served in the open-air bistro on the first floor. ⊠ *Government Hill* ☎ *340/777–9703* ⌂ *Reservations essential* ⊟ *AE, MC, V.*

ITALIAN
★ **\$\$\$–\$\$\$\$**
✕ **Virgilio's.** For the island's best northern Italian cuisine, don't miss this intimate, elegant hideaway tucked on a quiet side street. Eclectic art covers the two-story brick walls, and the sound of Italian opera sets the stage

for a memorable meal. Come here for more than 40 homemade pastas topped with superb sauces—cappellini with fresh tomatoes and garlic or peasant-style spaghetti in a rich tomato sauce with mushrooms and prosciutto. House specialties include osso buco and tiramisu—expertly crafted by chef Ernesto Garrigos, who has prepared these two dishes on the Discovery Channel's "Great Chefs of the World" series. ✉ *18 Main St.* ☎ *340/776–4920* ⌕ *Reservations essential* ▭ *AE, MC, V* ☺ *Closed Sun.*

**$–$$** ✕ **Café Amici.** Set within the historic stonework and cascading tropical blossoms of A. H. Riise Alley, this charming open-air eatery has an Italian name but boasts a menu with Caribbean flair. Choose anything from brick oven pizzas to fresh salads, open-faced sandwiches, and unique pasta dishes that are cooked to order. House specialties include tamarind barbecued shrimp salad and pizza topped with house-made sausage and apples. ✉ *37 Main St.* ☎ *340/776–0444* ▭ *AE, MC, V* ☺ *Closed Sun. No dinner.*

JAPANESE
**$–$$** ✕ **Beni Iguana's Sushi Bar & Restaurant.** Edible art is an apt description of the sushi and sashimi feast on display at this Japanese restaurant tucked into the historic Grand Galleria Hotel. There are nearly 30 vegetarian and seafood rolls to choose from, including avocado, spicy crab, and red snapper. The real favorite here is steamed mussels in a house-made creamy sesame dressing dubbed "iguana sauce," which is, happily, not made from the spiny reptile that roams the island's hillsides and roadways. ✉ *Grand Galleria, Tolbod Gade at Norre Gade* ☎ *340/777–8744* ▭ *AE, MC, V.*

SPANISH
★ **$$$–$$$$** ✕ **Café Amalia.** Tucked into the alleyway of Palm Passage, this open-air café owned by Antiguan-born Randolph Maynard and his German wife, Helga, serves authentic Spanish cuisine. Try tapas such as mussels in brandy sauce, escargots with mushrooms and herb butter, or Galician-style octopus and baby eels served in a sizzling garlic sauce. Paella is a house specialty, as is the caramel flan. ✉ *Palm Passage, 24 Dronnigens Gade* ☎ *340/714–7373* ▭ *AE, MC, V.*

## East End

AMERICAN
☺ **$$–$$$** ✕ **Blue Moon Café.** Watch the serene scene of sailboats floating at anchor while supping; sunsets are especially spectacular here. Enjoy French toast topped with toasted coconut for breakfast, a grilled mahimahi sandwich with black olive–caper mayonnaise at lunch, or red snapper with pecans, bananas, and a coconut rum sauce for dinner. ✉ *Secret Harbour Beach Resort, Rte. 32, Red Hook* ☎ *340/779–2080* ▭ *AE, D, MC, V.*

CARIBBEAN
☺ **$$–$$$** ✕ **Fungi's on the Beach.** Watch the windsurfers, swimmers, and jet skiers out on the bay as you tuck into native-style foods at this open-air, gaily painted restaurant. Try creole-style fish with a side of fungi. Callaloo, roti bread with a curried chicken or conch filling, and a grilled lobster tail with garlic butter are also good choices. All-American burgers and hot dogs are available, too. ✉ *Point Pleasant Resort, Rte. 38, Estate Smith Bay* ☎ *340/775–4142* ▭ *AE, MC, V.*

ECLECTIC
$$–$$$$
Fodor'sChoice
★

✕ **Old Stone Farmhouse.** Dine in the splendor of a beautifully restored plantation house. You might try the three-day mango Asian duck or something from the excellent sushi menu. For a truly memorable meal, forget the menu entirely. Chef Brian Katz will note your table's likes and dislikes, then surprise you with a customized six-course meal. That kind of personalized attention makes dining here a delight. Finish with one of the tropical fruit sorbets. ⊠ *Rte. 42, 1 mi (1½ km) west of entrance to Mahogany Run Golf Course, Estate Lovenlund* ☎ *340/777–6277* ⚶ *Reservations essential* ▤ *AE, MC, V* ☉ *Closed Mon.*

☾ $$–$$$

✕ **Bonnie's by the Sea.** Wriggle your toes in the sand while you tuck into burgers, sandwiches, and pizza for lunch. For dinner, there's fancier fare like crab cakes, a grilled New York strip steak, or fresh grilled snapper in a butter, banana liqueur, and mango chutney sauce. The island-style pig roast on Sunday afternoons isn't to be missed. ⊠ *Elysian Beach Resort, 6800, Estate Nazareth* ☎ *340/774–8868* ▤ *AE, D, MC, V.*

$

✕ **Duffy's Love Shack.** If the floating bubbles don't attract you to this zany eatery, the lime-green shutters, loud rock music, and fun-loving waitstaff surely will. It's billed as the "ultimate tropical drink shack," and the bartenders shake up such exotic concoctions as the Love Shack Volcano—a 50-ounce flaming extravaganza. The menu has a selection of burgers, tacos, burritos, and salads. Try the grilled mahimahi taco salad or jerk Caesar wrap. Wednesday night is usually a theme party complete with giveaways. ⊠ *Rte. 32, Red Hook* ☎ *340/779–2080* ▤ *No credit cards.*

ENGLISH
$$–$$$

✕ **Toad & Tart English Pub.** You may not notice this unassuming restaurant on first drive-by, but inside, owner Anna Clarke has created a homey, lively pub atmosphere in which to serve favorites like fish-and-chips on Friday and prime rib with Yorkshire pudding on Saturday. There are always three draft beers on tap. Strawberry rhubarb pie is a winner for dessert. ⊠ *Rte. 38, across from Kilnwork's Pottery & Caribbean Art Gallery, Estate Smith Bay* ☎ *340/775–1153* ▤ *AE, MC, V.*

GERMAN
$$–$$$

✕ **Petra's Schnitzel Haus.** If you have a hankering for German food, this is the one and only place on St. Thomas to find it. Owner Petra Dedekind, a native of Hamburg, has crafted a menu that features favorites like Wiener schnitzel and jäger schnitzel, along with pot roast, bratwurst, chicken, and apple streudel to top off the meal. You can also get four brands of imported German beer, or Dedekind makes her own apple schnapps, which is light and delightful. ⊠ *Rte. 32, next to Fish Hawk Marina, Estate Frydenhoj* ☎ *340/776–7198* ⚶ *Reservations essential* ▤ *AE, MC, V* ☉ *Closed Sun.*

IRISH
☾ $$–$$$

✕ **Molly Molone's.** This open-air eatery has a devout following among locals who live and work on boats docked nearby. Traditional Irish dishes include bangers and mash (sausage and mashed potatoes), as well as fresh fish, oversize deli sandwiches, and rich soups and stews. Beware: the iguanas will beg for table scraps—bring your camera. Upstairs, the same owners run A Whale of a Tale, a pricier seafood eatery that also serves freshly made pasta dishes and fine wines. ⊠ *Rte. 32, at American Yacht Harbor, Bldg. D, Red Hook* ☎ *340/775–1270* ▤ *MC, V.*

ITALIAN   ✕ **Romanos.** Inside this huge, old stucco house is a delightful surprise:
★ **$$$–$$$$** a spare yet elegant restaurant serving superb northern Italian cuisine.
Try the pastas, either with a classic sauce or a more unique creation such
as cream sauce with mushrooms, prosciutto, pine nuts, and Parmesan.
✉ *Rte. 388, at Coki Point, Estate Frydendal* ☎ *340/775–0045* ⌖ *Reservations essential* ▭ *MC, V* ☺ *Closed Sun. No lunch.*

SEAFOOD   ✕ **Agave Terrace.** At this open-air restaurant in the Point Pleasant Resort, fresh fish is the specialty, served as steaks or fillets, and the catch
**$$–$$$$** of the day is listed on the blackboard. More than a dozen sauces, including teriyaki-mango and lime-ginger, liven up your entrée. If you get
lucky on a sportfishing day charter, the chef will cook your catch if you
bring the fish in by 3 PM. Come early and have a drink at the Lookout
Lounge, which has breathtaking views of the British Virgins. ✉ *Point
Pleasant Resort, Rte. 38, Estate Smith Bay* ☎ *340/775–4142* ▭ *AE,
MC, V* ☺ *No lunch.*

**$$–$$$** ✕ **Off the Hook.** The fish is so fresh here that you may see it coming in
from one of the boats tied up at the dock just steps away. For starters,
try the crispy conch fritters with sweet-hot banana-chili chutney. Entrées include a rib-sticking fish stew with scallops, shrimp, mahimahi,
mussels, conch, and calamari swimming in a coconut curry broth. Steak,
poultry, and pasta lovers will also find something to please at this open-air eatery. There's also a children's menu. ✉ *Rte. 32, Red Hook* ☎ *340/
775–6350* ▭ *AE, MC, V* ☺ *No lunch.*

## Frenchtown

AMERICAN   ✕ **Tickle's Dockside Pub.** Nautical types as well as the local working
☺ **$–$$** crowd come here for casual fare with homey appeal: chicken-fried steak,
meat loaf and mashed potatoes, and baby back ribs. Hearty breakfasts
feature eggs and pancakes, while lunch is a full array of burgers, salads, sandwiches, and soups. From November through April, the adjacent marina is full of megayachts that make for some great eye candy
while you dine. ✉ *Crown Bay Marina, Rte. 304, Estate Contant* ☎ *340/
776–1595* ▭ *AE, D, MC, V.*

CARIBBEAN   ✕ **Victor's New Hide-Out.** Although it's a little hard to find—it's up the
**$$–$$$** hill between the Nisky shopping center and the airport—this landmark
restaurant is worth the search. Local food, including steamed fish, marinated pork chops, and local lobster, is offered in a casual, friendly West
Indian spot. While you eat, enjoy live local music. ✉ *Sub Base* ☎ *340/
776–9379* ▭ *AE, MC, V.*

ECLECTIC   ✕ **Oceana Restaurant & Wine Bar.** In the old Russian consulate greathouse
**$$$–$$$$** at the tip of the Frenchtown peninsula, this restaurant offers superb views
along with fresh seafood dishes expertly prepared by longtime Virgin
Islands chef Patricia LaCourte and her staff. Specialties include a pan-seared sea bass served on a saffron risotto cake with white truffle butter as well as bouillabaisse chock-full of mussels, manila clams, shrimp,
and Caribbean lobster simmered in a tomato-saffron broth. ✉ *Villa Olga*
☎ *340/774–4262* ▭ *AE, D, MC, V* ☺ *No dinner Sun.*

**$$–$$$**
**Fodor'sChoice**
★

✗**Craig & Sally's.** In the heart of Frenchtown, culinary wizard Sally Darash creates menus with a passionate international flavor using fresh ingredients and a novel approach that makes for a delightful dining experience at this friendly, casual eatery. Sally's constantly changing menu is never the same, which means your favorite dish may not appear again, but then again there's always something new to tantalize your taste buds. Husband Craig maintains a 300-bottle wine list that's received accolades. ⊠ *22 Honduras at Rue Normandie* ☎ *340/777–9949* ▭ *AE, MC, V* ⊙ *Closed Mon. and Tues. No lunch weekends.*

MEDITERRANEAN
☾ **$$–$$$$**

✗**Bella Blu.** Tucked into a quaint building in Frenchtown, the former Alexander's Café has thrown over its Austrian menu—though the menu still has a couple of schnitzels—and lightened up the decor. Alexander Treml's Mediterranean-style menu now includes souvlaki or skewered lamb, snapper Provençal, and chicken breast stuffed with spinach, feta, and pine nuts. ⊠ *Frenchtown Mall, 24-A Honduras* ☎ *340/774–4349* ▭ *AE, MC, V* ⊙ *Closed Sun.*

SEAFOOD
☾ **$$**

✗**Hook, Line & Sinker.** Anchored right on the breezy Frenchtown waterfront, adjacent to the pastel-painted boats of the local fishing fleet, this harbor-view eatery serves quality fish dishes. The almond-crust yellowtail snapper is a house specialty. Spicy jerk-seasoned swordfish and grilled tuna topped with a yummy mango-rum sauce are also good bets. This is one of the few independent restaurants that serves Sunday brunch. ⊠ *2 Honduras, in Frenchtown Mall* ☎ *340/776–9708* ▭ *AE, MC, V.*

AMERICAN
☾ **$$–$$$**

✗**Sib's Mountain Bar & Restaurant.** Here you can find live music, football on the TV, burgers, barbecue ribs and chicken, and beer. It's the perfect place for a casual dinner after a day at the beach. ⊠ *Rte. 35, Estate Mafolie* ☎ *340/774–8967* ▭ *AE, MC, V.*

## Beaches

All 44 St. Thomas beaches are open to the public, although you can reach some of them only by walking through a resort. Hotel guests frequently have access to lounge chairs and floats that are off-limits to nonguests; for this reason you may feel more comfortable at one of the beaches not associated with a resort, such as Magens Bay (which charges an entrance fee to cover beach maintenance) or Coki. Whichever one you choose, remember to remove your valuables from the car and keep them out of sight when you go swimming.

**Brewer's Beach.** Watch jets land at the Cyril E. King Airport as you dip into the usually calm seas. Rocks at either end of the shoreline, patches of grass poking randomly through the sand, and shady tamarind trees 30 feet from the water give this beach a wild, natural feel. Civilization is here (one or two mobile food vans park on the nearby road). Buy a fried-chicken leg and johnnycake or burgers, chips, and beverages to munch on at the picnic tables. ⊠ *Rte. 30, west of University of the Virgin Islands.*

**1**

☾ **Coki Beach.** Funky beach huts selling local foods like meat pates (fried
**Fodor'sChoice** turnovers with a spicy ground-beef filling), picnic tables topped with
★ umbrellas sporting beverage logos, and a brigade of hair braiders and
taxi men give this beach overlooking picturesque Thatch Cay a Coney
Island feel. But this is the best place on the island from which to snorkel
and scuba dive. Fish, including grunts, snappers, and wrasses, teem in
schools like an effervescent cloud you can wave your hand through.
Ashore, find conveniences like restrooms, changing facilities, rentals for
masks, fins, air tanks, and even fish food. ☒ *Rte. 388, next to Coral
World Marine Park.*

**Hull Bay.** Watch surfers ride the waves here from December to March,
when huge swells roll in from north Atlantic storms. The rest of the year,
tranquility prevails. Local fishermen keep their runabouts anchored here.
For a small fee, they will take you on a short tour out to Tropaco Point,
where you can look across to the uninhabited isle of Hans Lollick. Enjoy
hot pizza, barbecue ribs, and a game of darts or pool at the Hull Bay
Hideaway bar and restaurant. ☒ *Rte. 37, at end of road on north side.*

☾ **Magens Bay.** Deeded to the island as a public park, this ½-mi (¾-km)
**Fodor'sChoice** heart-shape stretch of white sand is considered one of the most beauti-
★ ful in the world. The bottom of the bay here is flat and sandy, so this is
a place for sunning and swimming rather than snorkeling. On weekends and holidays the sounds of music from groups partying under the
sheds fill the air. There's a bar, snack bar, water-sports-equipment rental
kiosk, and beachwear boutique; bathhouses with toilets, changing
rooms, and saltwater showers are also here. Sunfish and paddleboats
are the most popular rentals. East of the beach is Udder Delight, a one-
room shop at St. Thomas Dairies that serves a Virgin Islands tradition—
a milk shake with a splash of Cruzan rum. Kids can enjoy virgin versions,
which have a touch of soursop, mango, or banana flavoring. If you arrive between 8 AM and 5 PM, you have to pay an entrance fee of $3 per
person, $1 per vehicle, and 25¢ per child under age 12. ☒ *Rte. 35, at
end of road on north side of island.*

★ **Morningstar Beach.** Nature and nurture combine at this ¼-mi-long (½-
km) beach between Marriott Frenchman's Reef and Morning Star Beach
Resorts where amenities range from water-sports rentals to beachside
bar service. A concession rents floating mats, snorkeling equipment, sailboards, Sunfish, and Jet Skis. Swimming is excellent; there are good-
size rolling waves year-round, but do watch the undertow. If you're feeling
lazy, rent a lounge chair with umbrella and order a libation from one
of two full-service beach bars. At 7 AM and again at 5 PM, watch the
mega cruise ships glide majestically out to sea from the Charlotte Amalie
harbor. ☒ *Rte. 315, 2 mi (3 km) southeast of Charlotte Amalie, past
Havensight Mall and cruise-ship dock.*

★ **Sapphire Beach.** A steady breeze makes this beach a boardsailor's Mecca.
The swimming is great, as is the snorkeling, especially at the reef near
Pettyklip Point. Beach volleyball is big here on the weekends. There's
also a restaurant, bar, and water-sports rentals at Sapphire Beach Resort & Marina. ☒ *Rte. 38, Sapphire Bay.*

**Secret Harbour.** Placid waters make it an easy job to stroke your way out
to a swim platform offshore from the Secret Harbour Beach Resort &

Villas. Nearby reefs give snorkelers a natural show. There's a bar and restaurant, as well as a dive shop. ⊠ *Rte. 32, Red Hook.*

★ **Vessup Beach.** This wild, undeveloped beach is lined with sea-grape trees and century plants, and it's close to Red Hook harbor, so you can watch the ferries depart. Calm waters are excellent for swimming. West Indies Windsurfing is here, so you can rent Windsurfers, kayaks, and other water toys. There are no restroom or changing facilities. It's popular with locals on weekends. ⊠ *Off Rte. 322, Vessup Bay.*

## Sports & the Outdoors

AIR TOURS **Air Center Helicopters** (⊠ Waterfront, Charlotte Amalie, St. Thomas ☎ 340/775–7335 or 800/619–0013 ⊕ www.aircenterhelicopters.com), on the Charlotte Amalie waterfront (next to Tortola Wharf), offers two tours, both pretty pricey: a 17-minute tour of St. Thomas and St. John priced at $256 (for up to four passengers) per trip, and a 25-minute tour that includes St. Thomas, St. John, and Jost Van Dyke priced at $348 (for up to four passengers) per trip. If you can afford the splurge, it's a nice ride, but in truth, you can see most of the aerial sights from Mountain Top or Paradise Point, and there's no place you can't reach easily by car or boat.

BOATING & Calm seas, crystal waters, and nearby islands (perfect for picnicking, snor-
SAILING keling, and exploring) make St. Thomas a favorite jumping-off spot for day- or weeklong sails or powerboat adventures. With more than 100 vessels from which to choose, St. Thomas is the charter-boat center of the U.S. Virgin Islands. You can go through a broker to book a sailing vessel with a crew or contact a charter company directly. Crewed charters start at $1,500 per person per week, while bareboat charters can start at $1,200 per person for a 50- to 55-foot sailboat (not including provisioning), which can comfortably accommodate up to six people. If you want to rent your own boat, hire a captain. Most local captains are excellent tour guides.

Single-day charters are also a possibility. You can hire smaller power boats for the day, including the services of a captain if you wish to have someone take you on a guided snorkel trip around the islands.

**Island Yachts** (⊠ 6100 Red Hook Quarter, 18B, Red Hook ☎ 340/775–6666 or 800/524–2019 ⊕ www.iyc.vi) offers sail- or powerboats with or without crews. Luxury is the word at **Magic Moments** (⊠ American Yacht Harbor, Red Hook ☎ 340/775–5066 ⊕ www.yachtmagicmoments.com), where the crew of a 45-foot Sea Ray offers a pampered island-hopping snorkeling cruise that includes icy-cold eucalyptus-infused washcloths to freshen up and a gourmet wine and lobster lunch. **Stewart Yacht Charters** (⊠ 6501 Red Hook Plaza, Suite 20, Red Hook ☎ 340/775–1358 or 800/432–6118 ⊕ www.stewartyachtcharters.com) is run by longtime sailor Ellen Stewart, who is an expert at matching clients with yachts for weeklong crewed charter holidays. Bareboat sail and powerboats, including a selection of stable trawlers, are available at **VIP Yacht Charters** (⊠ South off Rte. 32, Estate Frydenhoj ☎ 340/774–9224 or 866/847–9224 ⊕ www.vipyachts.com), at Compass Point Marina.

**Awesome Powerboat Rentals** (✉ 6100 Red Hook Quarter, Red Hook ☎ 340/775–0860 ⊕ www.powerboatrentalsvi.com), at "P" dock next to the Off the Hook restaurant, offers 22-foot to 26-foot twin-engine catamarans for day charters. Rates range from $185 to $375 for half- or full-day. A captain can be hired, if desired, for $75 to $100 for half- or full-day. **Mangrove Adventures** (✉ Rte. 32, Estate Nadir ☎ 340/779–2155 ⊕ www.viecotours.com) offers inflatable boat rentals for $60 per day to explore and snorkel the east end of St. Thomas. **Nauti Nymph** (✉ 6501 Red Hook Plaza, Suite 201, Red Hook ☎☎ 340/775–5066 ☎ 800/734–7345 ⊕ www.st-thomas.com/nautinymph) has a large selection of 25-foot to 29-foot powerboats for rent. Rates vary from $345 to $540 a day, including snorkel gear, water skis, and outriggers but not including fuel. You can hire a captain for $115 more.

CYCLING **Water Island Adventures** (✉ Water Island ☎ 340/714–2186 or 340/775–
Fodor's Choice 5770 ⊕ www.waterislandadventures.com) offers a cycling adventure to
★ the USVI's "newest" Virgin. You take a ferry ride from the West Indian Company dock near Havensight Mall to Water Island before jumping on a Cannondale mountain bike for a 90-minute tour over rolling hills on dirt and paved roads. Explore the remains of the Sea Cliff Hotel, the inspiration for Herman Wouk's book *Don't Stop the Carnival*, and take a cooling swim at beautiful Honeymoon Beach. Helmets, water, a guide, juices, and ferry fare are included in the $60 cost.

DIVING & Popular dive sites include such wrecks as the ***Cartanser Sr.,*** a beautifully
SNORKELING encrusted World War II cargo ship sitting in 35 feet of water, and the ***General Rogers,*** a Coast Guard cutter with a gigantic resident barracuda resting at 65 feet. Reef dives offer hidden caves and archways at **Cow and Calf Rocks,** coral-covered pinnacles at **Frenchcap,** and tunnels where you can explore undersea from the Caribbean to the Atlantic at **Thatch Cay, Grass Cay,** and **Congo Cay.** Many resorts and charter yachts offer dive packages. A one-tank dive starts at $60; two-tank dives are $80 or more. Call the USVI Department of Tourism to obtain a free eight-page guide to Virgin Islands dive sites. There are plenty of snorkeling possibilities too.

**Admiralty Dive Center** (✉ Holiday Inn St. Thomas, Waterfront Hwy., Charlotte Amalie ☎ 340/777–9802 or 888/900–3483 ⊕ www.admiraltydive. com) provides boat dives, rental equipment, and a retail store. Four-tank to 12-tank packages are available if you want to dive over several days. **Aqua Adventures** (✉ Crown Bay Marina, Rte. 304, Charlotte Amalie ☎ 340/715–0348 ⊕ www.bobusvi.com) offers an alternative to traditional diving in the form of an underwater motor scooter called BOB, or Breathing Observation Bubble. A half-day tour, including snorkel equipment, rum punch, and towels, is $99 per person. **Blue Island Divers** (✉ Crown Bay Marina, Rte. 304, Estate Contant ☎ 340/774–2001 ⊕ www.blueislanddivers.com) is a full-service dive shop that offers both day and night dives to wrecks and reefs. **Chris Sawyer Diving Center** (☎ 340/775–7320 or 877/929–3483 ⊕ www.sawyerdive.vi) is a PADI five-star outfit that specializes in dives to the 310-foot-long *Rhone,* in the British Virgin Islands. Hotel-dive packages are offered through the Wyndham Sugar Bay Beach Club & Resort. **Coki Beach Dive Club**

(⊠ Rte. 388, at Coki Point, Estate Frydendal ☎ 340/775–4220 ⊕ www. cokidive.com) is a PADI Gold Palm outfit run by avid diver Peter Jackson in the fish-filled reefs off Coki Beach. Snorkel and dive tours are available, as are classes from beginner to underwater photography. **Snuba of St. Thomas** (⊠ Rte. 388, at Coki Point, Estate Smith Bay ☎ 340/ 693–8063 ⊕ www.visnuba.com) offers something for nondivers, a cross between snorkeling and scuba diving: a 20-foot air hose connects you to the surface. The cost is $59. Children must be eight or older to participate. **Underwater Safaris** (⊠ Havensight Mall, Bldg. VI, Rte. 30, Charlotte Amalie ☎ 340/774–1350 ⊕ www.scubadivevi.com) is another PADI five-star center that offers boat dives to the reefs around Buck Island and nearby offshore wrecks.

FISHING

★ Fishing here is synonymous with blue marlin angling—especially from June through October. Four 1,000-pound-plus blues, including three world records, have been caught on the famous North Drop, about 20 mi (32 km) north of St. Thomas. A day charter for marlin with up to six anglers costs $1,300 for the day. If you're not into marlin fishing, try hooking up sailfish in the winter, dolphin (the fish, not the mammal; aka mahimahi) come spring, and wahoo in the fall. Inshore trips for two to four hours range in cost from $200 to $550, respectively. To really find the trip that will best suit you, walk down the docks at either American Yacht Harbor or Sapphire Beach Marina in the late afternoon and chat with the captains and crews.

For marlin, Captain Red Bailey's *Abigail III* (☎ 340/775–6024 ⊕ www. sportfishvi.com) operates out of the Sapphire Beach Resort & Marina. The **Charter Boat Center** (⊠ 6300 Red Hook Plaza, Red Hook ☎ 340/ 775–7990 ⊕ www.charterboat.vi) is a major source for sportfishing charters, both marlin and inshore. For inshore trips, **Peanut Gallery Charters** (⊠ Crown Bay Marina, Rte. 304, Estate Contant ☎ 340/775–5274 ⊕ www.fishingstthomas.com) offers trips on its 18-foot *Dauntless* or 28-foot custom sportfishing catamaran. Capt. Eddie Morrison, aboard the 45-foot Viking *Marlin Prince* (⊠ American Yacht Harbor, Red Hook ☎ 340/693–5929 ⊕ www.marlinprince.com), is one of the most experienced charter operators in St. Thomas and specializes in fly-fishing for blue marlin. Captain Mark Lamborn, who pilots the *Prowler* (⊠ American Yacht Harbor, Red Hook ☎340/779–2515), offers marlin and gamefishing trips year-round.

GOLF

Fodor'sChoice

★ The **Mahogany Run Golf Course** (⊠ Rte. 42, Estate Lovenlund ☎ 340/ 777–6006 or 800/253–7103 ⊕ www.mahoganyrungolf.com) attracts golfers for its spectacular view of the British Virgin Islands and the challenging 3-hole Devil's Triangle on this Tom and George Fazio–designed par-70, 18-hole course. Greens and half-cart fees for 18 holes are $130. There's a fully stocked pro shop, snack bar, and open-air club house. The course is open daily, and there are frequently informal weekend tournaments. It's the only course on St. Thomas.

HORSE RACING

The **Clinton Phipps Racetrack** (⊠ Rte. 30, Estate Nadir ☎ 340/775– 4555) schedules races—especially on local holidays—with sanctioned betting. Be prepared for large crowds.

**1**

**PARASAILING**  The waters are so clear around St. Thomas that the outlines of coral reefs are visible from high in the sky. Parasailers sit in a harness attached to a parachute that lifts them off a boat deck until they're sailing up in the air. Parasailing trips average a 10-minute ride in the sky that costs $65 per person. Friends who want to ride along pay $15 for the boat trip. **Caribbean Watersports & Tours** (⊠ 6501 Red Hook Plaza, Red Hook ☏ 340/775–9360) makes parasailing pickups from 10 locations around the island, including many major beachfront resorts. It also rents Jet Skis, kayaks, and floating battery-power chairs.

**SEA EXCURSIONS**  Landlubbers and seafarers alike will enjoy the wind in their hair and salt spray in the air while exploring the waters surrounding St. Thomas. Several businesses can book you on a snorkel-and-sail to a deserted cay for the day that costs on average $85 to $125 per person; a luxury day-long motor-yacht cruise complete with gourmet lunch for $325 or more per person; or an excursion over to the British Virgin Islands starting at $100 per person plus $20 customs fees.

For a soup-to-nuts choice of sea tours, contact the **Adventure Center** (⊠ Marriott's Frenchman's Reef Hotel, Rte. 315, Estate Bakkeroe ☏ 340/774–2992 or 866/868–7784 ⊕ www.adventurecenters.net). The **Charter Boat Center** (⊠ 6300 Red Hook Plaza, Red Hook ☏ 340/775–7990 ⊕ www.charterboat.vi) specializes in day trips to the British Virgin Islands and day- or weeklong sailing charters. The party boat *Kon Tiki* (⊠ Gregorie Channel East Dock, Frenchtown ☏ 340/775–5055) is a kick. Put your sophistication aside, climb on this big palm-thatched raft, and dip into bottomless barrels of rum punch along with a couple hundred of your soon-to-be closest friends. Dance to the steel-drum band, sun on the roof (watch out: you'll fry), and join the limbo dancing on the way home from an afternoon of swimming and beachcombing at Honeymoon Beach on Water Island. This popular 3½-hour afternoon excursion costs $32 for adults, $18 for children under 13 (although few come on this booze cruise). **Limnos Charters** (⊠ Compass Point Marina, Rte. 32, Estate Frydenhoj ☏ 340/775–3203 ⊕ www.limnoscharters.com) offers one of the most popular British Virgin Islands day trips, complete with lunch, open bar, and snorkel gear. Jimmy Loveland at **Treasure Isle Cruises** (⊠ Rte. 32, Box 6616, Estate Nadir ☏ 340/775–9500 ⊕ www.treasureislecruises.com) can set you up with everything from a half-day sail to a seven-day U.S. and British Virgin Islands trip that combines sailing with accommodations and sightseeing trips onshore.

**SEA KAYAKING**  Fish dart, birds sing, and iguanas lounge on the limbs of dense mangroves deep within a marine sanctuary on St. Thomas's southeast shore. Learn about the natural history here in a guided kayak-snorkel tour to Patricia Cay or via an inflatable boat tour to Cas Cay for snorkeling and hiking. Both are 2½ hours long. The cost is $60 per person. **Mangrove Adventures** (⊠ Rte. 32, Estate Nadir ☏ 340/779–2155 ⊕ www.viecotours.com) rents its two-person sit-atop ocean kayaks and inflatable boats for self-guided exploring. In addition, many resorts on St. Thomas's eastern end also rent kayaks.

SIGHTSEEING TOURS **Accessible Adventures** (☎ 340/775–2346 ⊕ www.accessvi.com) provides a 2- to 2½-hour island tour aboard a special trolley that's especially suitable for those in wheelchairs. Tours include major sights like Magens Bay and Mountain Top and provide a stop for shopping and refreshments. The cost is $32 per person. **Tropic Tours** (☎ 340/774–1855 or 800/524–4334 ⊕ www.tropictours-virginislands.com) offers half-day shopping and sightseeing tours of St. Thomas by bus six days a week. The cost is $30 per person. The company also has a full-day ferry tour to St. John that includes snorkeling and lunch. The cost is $85 per person. **V. I. Taxi Association St. Thomas City-Island Tour** (☎ 340/774–4550) gives a two-hour $30 tour for two people in an open-air safari bus or enclosed van; aimed at cruise-ship passengers, this tour includes stops at Drake's Seat and Mountain Top. For just a bit more ($35 to $40 for two) you can hire a taxi and ask the driver to take the opposite route to avoid the crowds. But do see Mountain Top: the view is wonderful.

STARGAZING Without the light pollution so prevalent in more densely populated areas, the heavens appear supernaturally bright. On a **Star Charters Astronomy Adventure** (☎ 340/774–9211) you can peer into the Caribbean's largest telescope—an 18-inch Newtonian reflector—and learn the science and lore of the stars from a well-informed celestial guide.

SUBMARINING Dive 90 feet under the sea to one of St. Thomas's most beautiful reefs without getting wet. **Atlantis Adventures** (✉ Havensight Mall, Bldg. VI, Charlotte Amalie ☎ 340/776–5650 ⊕ www.atlantisadventures.com) has a 46-passenger submarine that takes you to a watery world teeming with brightly colored fish, vibrant sea fans, and an occasional shark. A guide narrates the one-hour underwater journey, while a diver makes a mid-tour appearance for a fish-feeding show. The cost is $89. No children shorter than 36 inches are allowed.

TENNIS The Caribbean sun is hot, so be sure to hit the courts before 10 AM or after 5 PM (many courts are lighted). You can indulge in a set or two even if you're staying in a guesthouse without courts; most hotels rent time to nonguests. **Marriott Frenchman's Reef and Morning Star Beach Resorts** (✉ Rte. 315, Estate Bakkeroe ☎ 340/776–8500 Ext. 6818) has two courts, with nonguests charged $15 per hour per court. Two courts are available at the **Ritz-Carlton, St. Thomas** (✉ Rte. 317, Box 6900, Estate Great Bay ☎ 340/775–3333), where nonguests can reserve lessons for $80 per hour and $40 per half hour. **Sapphire Beach Resort & Marina** (✉ Sapphire Bay ☎ 340/775–6100 Ext. 8135) has four courts that fill up fast in the cool early-morning hours. The cost for nonguests is $15 per hour. At **Wyndham Sugar Bay Beach Club & Resort** (✉ Rte. 38, Box 6500, Estate Smith Bay ☎ 340/777–7100) nonguests can rent any of the four courts for $15 per hour. Lessons are by appointment, and rates start at $45 for a half hour.

**Lindberg Bay Park** (✉ Rte. 302, Estate Lindberg Bay) has two courts that are open to the public; it's opposite the Cyril E. King Airport. There are two public tennis courts at **Sub Base** (✉ Rte. 306, next to Water and Power Authority, Estate Contant), open on a first-come, first-served basis at no cost. Lights are on until 10 PM.

**WALKING TOURS** The *St. Thomas–St. John Vacation Handbook,* available free at hotels and tourist centers, has an excellent self-guided walking tour of Charlotte Amalie on St. Thomas.

**Blackbeard's Castle** (☎ 340/776–1234 or 340/776–1829 ⊕ www.blackbeardscastle.com) conducts a 45-minute to one-hour historic walking tour that starts at Blackbeard's Castle, then heads downhill to Villa Notman, Haagensen House, and the 99-steps. The cost is $35 per person and includes a tour of Haagensen House and rum punch.

**Cindy Born** (☎ 340/714–1672 ⊕ www.st-thomas.com/walktour) conducts a two-hour historical walking tour of Charlotte Amalie at 9:30 each weekday that starts at Emancipation Garden. The tour covers all the in-town sights and can be narrated in Spanish, Danish, German, and Japanese as well as in English. The cost is $20 per person; wear a hat and comfortable walking shoes. The tour is offered again at 12:30, but you must make a reservation.

The **St. Thomas Historical Trust** (☎ 340/774–5541 ⊕ www.stthomashistoricaltrust.org) has published a self-guided tour of the historic district; it's available in book and souvenir shops for $1.95. Trust members also conduct a two-hour guided historic walking tour by reservation only. Call for more information and to make a reservation.

**WINDSURFING** Expect some spills, anticipate the thrills, and try your luck clipping through the seas. Most beachfront resorts rent Windsurfers and offer one-hour lessons for about $45 to $60. One of the island's best-known independent windsurfing companies is **West Indies Windsurfing** (⊠ Vessup Beach, No. 9, Estate Nazareth ☎ 340/775–6530). Owner John Phillips is the board buff who introduced the sport of kite boarding to the USVI; it entails using a kite to lift a boardsailor off the water for an airborne ride. A two-hour, land-based kite-boarding lesson costs $90, while a two-hour lesson with on-the-water time is $175. Go-fast WindRider 17 trimarans are the new water toy here. They rent for $75 an hour or $250 a day.

## Shopping

**Fodor'sChoice** St. Thomas lives up to its billing as a duty-free shopping destination. ★ Even if shopping isn't your idea of how to spend a vacation, you still may want to slip in on a quiet day (check the cruise-ship listings—Monday and Sunday are usually the least crowded) to browse. Among the best buys are liquor, linens, china, crystal (most stores will ship), and jewelry. The amount of jewelry available makes this one of the few items for which comparison shopping is worth the effort. Local crafts include shell jewelry, carved calabash bowls, straw brooms, woven baskets, fragrances, and dolls. Creations by local doll maker Gwendolyn Harley—like her costumed West Indian market woman—have been little goodwill ambassadors, bought by visitors from as far away as Asia. Spice mixes, hot sauces, and tropical jams and jellies are other native products.

On St. Thomas, stores on Main Street in Charlotte Amalie are open weekdays and Saturday 9 to 5. The hours of the shops in the Havensight Mall (next to the cruise-ships dock) are the same, though occasionally some stay open until 9 on Friday, depending on how many cruise ships are at the dock. You may also find some shops open on Sunday if cruise ships are in port. Hotel shops are usually open evenings, as well.

There's no sales tax in the USVI, and you can take advantage of the $1,200 duty-free allowance per family member (remember to save your receipts). Although you can find the occasional salesclerk who will make a deal, bartering isn't the norm.

## Areas & Malls

The prime shopping area in **Charlotte Amalie** is between Post Office and Market squares; it consists of two parallel streets that run east–west (Waterfront Highway and Main Street) and the alleyways that connect them. Particularly attractive are the historic **A. H. Riise Alley, Royal Dane Mall, Palm Passage,** and pastel-painted **International Plaza.**

**Vendors Plaza,** on the waterfront side of Emancipation Gardens in Charlotte Amalie, is a central location for vendors selling handmade earrings, necklaces, and bracelets; straw baskets and handbags; T-shirts; fabrics; African artifacts; and local fruits. Look for the many brightly colored umbrellas.

West of Charlotte Amalie, the pink-stucco **Nisky Center,** on Harwood Highway about ½ mi (¾ km) east of the airport, is more of a hometown shopping center than a tourist area, but there's a bank, clothing store, record shop, and Radio Shack.

**Havensight Mall,** next to the cruise-ship dock, may not be as charming as downtown Charlotte Amalie, but it does have more than 60 shops. It also has an excellent bookstore, a bank, a pharmacy, a gourmet grocery, and smaller branches of many downtown stores. The shops at **Port of Sale,** which adjoins the Havensight Mall (its buildings are pink instead of the brown of the Havensight shops), sell discount goods.

East of Charlotte Amalie on Route 38, **Tillett Gardens** is an oasis of artistic endeavor across from the Tutu Park Shopping Mall. The late Jim and Rhoda Tillett converted this old Danish farm into an artists' retreat in 1959. Today you can watch artisans produce silk-screen fabrics, candles, watercolors, jewelry, and other handicrafts. Something special is often happening in the gardens as well: the Classics in the Gardens program is a classical music series presented under the stars, Arts Alive is an annual arts and crafts fair held in November, and the Pistarckle Theater holds its performances here. **Tutu Park Shopping Mall,** across from Tillett Gardens, is the island's one and only enclosed mall. More than 50 stores and a food court are anchored by Kmart and Plaza Extra grocery store. Archaeologists have discovered evidence that Arawak Indians once lived near the grounds.

Red Hook has **American Yacht Harbor,** a waterfront shopping area with a dive shop, a tackle store, clothing and jewelry boutiques, a bar, and a few restaurants.

Don't forget **St. John.** A ferry ride (an hour from Charlotte Amalie or 20 minutes from Red Hook) will take you to the charming shops of **Mon-**

CLOSE UP

# Made in St. Thomas

1

DATE PALM BROOMS, frangipani-scented perfume, historically clad dolls, sun-scorched hot sauces, aromatic mango candles: these are just a few of the handicrafts made in St. Thomas.

Justin Todman, aka the Broom Man, keeps the dying art of broom-making alive. It's a skill he learned at the age of six from his father. From the fronds of the date palm, Todman delicately cuts, strips, and dries the leaves, a process that can take up to a week. Then he creatively weaves the leaves into distinctively shaped brooms with birch-berry wood for handles. His styles? There are feather brooms, cane brooms, multicolor yarn brooms, tiny brooms to fit into a child's hand, and tall long-handled brooms to reach cobwebs on the ceiling. Some customers buy Todman's brooms—sold at the Native Arts & Crafts Cooperative—not for cleaning but rather for celebrating their nuptials. It's an old African custom for the bride and groom to jump over a horizontally laid broom to start their new life.

Gail Garrison puts the essence of local flowers, fruits, and leaves into perfumes, powders, and body splashes. Her Island Fragrances line includes frangipani-, white-ginger-, and jasmine-scented perfumes; aromatic mango, lime, and coconut body splashes; and bay rum aftershave for men. Garrison compounds, mixes, and bottles the products herself in second-floor offices on Charlotte Amalie's Main Street. You can buy the products in the Tropicana Perfume Shop.

Gwendolyn Harley preserves Virgin Islands culture in the personalities of her hand-sewn, softly sculptured historic dolls for sale at the Native Arts & Crafts Cooperative. There are quadrille dancers clad in long, colorful skirts; French women with their neat peaked bonnets; and farmers sporting hand-woven straw hats. Each one-of-kind design is named using the last three letters of Harley's first name; the dolls have names like Joycelyn, Vitalyn, and Iselyn. From her adoption log, she knows her dolls have traveled as far as Asia.

Cheryl Miller cooks up ingredients like sun-sweetened papayas, fiery Scotch bonnet peppers, and aromatic basil leaves into the jams, jellies, and hot sauces she sells under her Cheryl's Taste of Paradise line. Five of Miller's products—Caribbean Mustango Sauce, Caribbean Sunburn, Mango Momma Jam, Mango Chutney, and Hot Green Pepper Jelly—have won awards at the National Fiery Foods Show in Albuquerque, New Mexico. Miller makes her products in a professional kitchen in the Compass Point Marina and sells them from a storefront there as well as from Cost-U-Less and the Native Arts & Crafts Cooperative.

Jason Budsan traps the tropically enticing aromas of the islands into sumptuously scented candles he sells at his Tillett Gardens workshop and at stores throughout the island such as the Native Arts & Crafts Cooperative. Among the rich scents are Ripe Mango, Night Jasmine, Lime in de Coconut, Frenchie Connection (with vanilla and lavender), and Ripe Pineapple. Some candles, such as the Ripe Mango, are uniquely set in beautiful tonna shells or wrapped in aromatic sea-grape leaves.

goose Junction and Wharfside Village, which specialize in unusual, often island-made articles.

## Specialty Items

ART **Camille Pissarro Art Gallery.** This second-floor gallery, in the birthplace of St. Thomas's famous artist, offers a fine collection of original paintings and prints by local and regional artists. ⊠ *14 Main St., Charlotte Amalie* ☎ *340/774–4621.*

**The Color of Joy.** Find locally made arts and crafts here, including pottery, batik, hand-painted linen and cotton clothing, glass plates and ornaments, and watercolors by owner Corinne Van Rensselaer. There are also original prints by many local artists. ⊠ *Rte. 317, about 100 yards west of Ritz-Carlton, Red Hook* ☎ *340/775–4020.*

**Gallery St. Thomas.** Fine art and collectibles are found in this charming gallery, including paintings, wood sculpture, glass, and jewelry that are from or inspired by the Virgin Islands. ⊠ *1 Main St., 2nd fl., Charlotte Amalie* ☎ *340/777–6363.*

**Kilnworks Pottery & Caribbean Art Gallery.** A 12-foot statue of a green iguana marks the entrance to this pottery paradise. Owner Peggy Seiwert is best known for her lizard collection of ceramic cups, bowls, and platters. There are also pottery pieces by other local artists, as well as paintings and gift items. ⊠ *Rte. 38, across from the Toad & Tart English Pub, Estate Smith Bay* ☎ *340/775–3979.*

**Mango Tango.** Works by popular local artists—originals, prints, and note cards—are displayed (there's a one-person show at least one weekend a month) and sold here. There's also the island's largest humidor and a brand-name cigar gallery. ⊠ *Al Cohen's Plaza, ½ mi (¾ km) east of Charlotte Amalie* ☎ *340/777–3060.*

BOOKS **Dockside Bookshop.** This place is packed with books for children, travelers, cooks, and historians, as well as a good selection of paperback mysteries, best-sellers, art books, calendars, and prints. It also carries a selection of books written in and about the Caribbean and the Virgin Islands. ⊠ *Havensight Mall, Bldg. VI, Rte. 30, Charlotte Amalie* ☎ *340/774–4937.*

CAMERAS & **Boolchand's.** Brand-name cameras, audio and video equipment, and
ELECTRONICS binoculars are sold here. ⊠ *31 Main St., Charlotte Amalie* ☎ *340/776–0794* ⊠ *Havensight Mall, Bldg. II, Rte. 30, Charlotte Amalie* ☎ *340/776–0302.*

**Royal Caribbean.** Shop here for cameras, camcorders, stereos, watches, and clocks. ⊠ *23 Main St., Charlotte Amalie* ☎ *340/776–5449* ⊠ *33 Main St., Charlotte Amalie* ☎ *340/776–4110* ⊠ *Havensight Mall, Bldg. I, Rte. 30, Charlotte Amalie* ☎ *340/776–8890.*

CHINA & CRYSTAL **The Crystal Shoppe at A. H. Riise.** All that glitters is here, from the Swarovski and Waterford crystal to the figurines by Hummel, Daum, and Royal Copenhagen, and china by Belleek, Kosta Boda, and several Limoges factories. There's also a large selection of Lladro figurines. ⊠ *37 Main St., at Riise's Alley, Charlotte Amalie* ☎ *340/776–2303.*

**Little Switzerland.** All of this establishment's shops carry crystal from Baccarat, Waterford, and Orrefors; and china from Kosta Boda, Rosenthal, and Wedgwood, among others. There's also an assortment of Swarovski cut-crystal animals, gemstone globes, and many other affordable collectibles. It also does a booming mail-order business; ask for a catalog. ⊠ *5 Dronningens Gade, across from Emancipation Garden, Charlotte Amalie* ☎ *340/776–2010* ⊠ *3B Main St., Charlotte Amalie* ☎ *340/776–2010* ⊠ *Havensight Mall, Bldg. II, Rte. 30, Charlotte Amalie* ☎ *340/776–2198.*

**Scandinavian Center.** The best of Scandinavia is here, including Royal Copenhagen, Georg Jensen, Kosta Boda, and Orrefors. Owners Søøren and Grace Blak make regular buying trips to northern Europe and are a great source of information on crystal. Online ordering is available if you want to add to your collection once home. ⊠ *Havensight Mall, Bldg. III, Rte. 30, Charlotte Amalie* ☎ *340/776–5030 or 800/524–2063.*

CLOTHING **Fresh Produce.** You won't find lime-green mangoes, peachy-pink guavas, or sunny-yellow bananas in this store. But you will find these fun, casual colors in the Fresh Produce clothing line. This is one of only 16 stores to stock 100% of this California-created, tropical-feel line of apparel for women. Find dresses, shirts, slacks, and skirts in small to plus sizes as well as accessories such as bags and hats. ⊠ *Riise's Alley, Charlotte Amalie* ☎ *340/774–0807.*

**Keep Left.** This friendly shop features something for everyone in the family, including Patagonia dresses, Quiksilver swim wear, Jams World shirts, Watership Trading hats, and NAOT sandals. ⊠ *American Yacht Harbor, Bldg. C, Rte. 32, Red Hook* ☎ *340/775–9964.*

**Local Color.** Men, women, and children will find something to choose from among brand-name wear like Jams World, Fresh Produce, and Urban Safari. There's also St. John artist Sloop Jones's colorful, hand-painted island designs on cool dresses, T-shirts, and sweaters. Find tropically oriented accessories like big-brim straw hats, bold-color bags, and casual jewelry. ⊠ *Royal Dane Mall, at Waterfront, Charlotte Amalie* ☎ *340/774–2280.*

**Nicole Miller.** The New York designer has created an exclusive motif for the USVI: a map of the islands, a cruise ship, and a tropical sunset. Find this print, and Miller's full line of other designs, on ties, scarves, boxer shorts, sarongs, and dresses. ⊠ *24 Main St., at Palm Passage, Charlotte Amalie* ☎ *340/774–8286.*

**Tommy Hilfiger Boutique.** Stop by this shop for classic American jeans and sportswear, as well as trendy bags, belts, ties, socks, caps, and wallets. ⊠ *Waterfront Hwy. at Trompeter Gade, Charlotte Amalie* ☎ *340/777–1189.*

FOODSTUFFS **Caribbean Chocolate.** Everything at this confectionery tastes as good as it smells. Owner and chocolatier David Dawson makes his own confections daily. Specialties include triple chocolate rum truffles. Gift boxes are available. You can also find Starbucks coffee here and Virgin Islands rum cakes. An ice cream parlor selling Häagen-Dazs is next door. ⊠ *17 Main St., Charlotte Amalie* ☎ *340/774–6675.*

**Cost-U-Less.** The Caribbean equivalent of Costco and Sam's Club sells everything from soup to nuts, but in giant sizes and case lots. The meat-and-seafood department, however, has smaller, family-size portions.

⊠ *Rte. 38, ¼ mi (½ km) west of Rte. 39 intersection, Estate Donoe* ☎ *340/ 777–3588.*

**Food Center.** Fresh produce, meats, and seafood, plus an on-site bakery and deli with hot-and-cold prepared foods, are the draw here, especially for those renting villas, condos, or charter boats in the East End area. ⊠ *Rte. 32, Estate Frydenhoj* ☎ *340/777–8806.*

**Fruit Bowl.** For fresh fruits and vegetables, this is the best place on the island to go. ⊠ *Wheatley Center, Rtes. 38 and 313 intersection, Charlotte Amalie* ☎ *340/774–8565.*

**Gourmet Gallery.** Visiting millionaires buy their caviar here. There's also an excellent and reasonably priced wine selection, as well as specialty ingredients for everything from tacos to curries to chow mein. A full-service deli offers imported meats, cheeses, and in-store prepared foods that are perfect for a gourmet picnic. ⊠ *Crown Bay Marina, Rte. 304, Estate Contant* ☎ *340/776–8555* ⊠ *Havensight Mall, Bldg. VI, Rte. 30, Charlotte Amalie* ☎ *340/774–4948.*

**Marina Market.** You won't find better fresh meat or seafood anywhere on the island. ⊠ *Rte. 32, across from Red Hook ferry, Red Hook* ☎ *340/779–2411.*

**Plaza Extra.** This large U.S.-style supermarket has everything you need from produce to meat, including fresh seafood, an excellent deli, and a bakery. There's a liquor department, too. ⊠ *Tutu Park Shopping Mall, Rte. 38, Estate Tutu* ☎ *340/775–5646.*

**PriceSmart.** Everything from electronics to housewares is found in this warehouse-size store. The meat, poultry, and seafood departments are especially popular. A small café in front sells pizzas, hot dogs, and the cheapest bottled water on the island–just 75¢ a pop. ⊠ *Rte. 38, west of Fort Mylner, Estate Tutu* ☎ *340/777–3430.*

**Pueblo Supermarket.** This Caribbean chain carries stateside brands of most products—but at higher prices because of shipping costs to the islands. ⊠ *Sub Base, ½ mi (¾ km) east of Crown Bay Marina, Estate Contant* ☎ *340/774–4200* ⊠ *Rte. 30, 1 mi (1½ km) north of Havensight Mall, Estate Thomas* ☎ *340/774–2695.*

HANDICRAFTS **Caribbean Marketplace.** This is a great place to buy handicrafts from the ᘖ Caribbean and elsewhere. Also look for Sunny Caribee spices, soaps, coffee, and teas from Tortola, and coffee from Trinidad. ⊠ *Havensight Mall, Rte. 30, Charlotte Amalie* ☎ *340/776–5400.*

ᘖ **Dolphin Dreams.** Look for gaily painted Caribbean-theme Christmas ornaments, art) glass from the Mitchell-Larsen studio, and jewelry made from recycled coral. Signature clothing lines include Bimini Bay and Rum Reggae. This boutique is the exclusive Red Hook source for the famous Caribbean Hook Bracelet, originated by the Caribbean Bracelet Company on St. Croix. ⊠ *American Yacht Harbor, Bldg. C, Rte. 32, Red Hook* ☎ *340/775–0549.*

**Down Island Traders.** These traders deal in hand-painted calabash bowls; finely printed Caribbean note cards; jams, jellies, spices, hot sauces, and herbs; teas made of lemongrass, passion fruit, and mango; coffee from Jamaica; and handicrafts from throughout the Caribbean. ⊠ *Waterfront Hwy. at Post Office Alley, Charlotte Amalie* ☎ *340/776–4641.*

**Into the Sea.** Find a wide variety of arts and crafts made by Virgin Islands artists. There are ceramics, glass art, paintings and prints, tropical perfumed soaps, and Caribbean Christmas ornaments. ⊠ *2-A Royal Dane Mall, Charlotte Amalie* ☎ *340/779–1280.*

**Native Arts & Crafts Cooperative.** More than 40 local artists—including schoolchildren, senior citizens, and people with disabilities—create the handcrafted items for sale here: African-style jewelry, quilts, calabash bowls, dolls, carved-wood figures, woven baskets, straw brooms, note cards, and cookbooks. ⊠ *Tolbod Gade, across from Emancipation Garden, Charlotte Amalie* ☎ *340/777–1153.*

JEWELRY   **Amsterdam Sauer.** Many fine one-of-a-kind designs are displayed at this jeweler's three locations. The Imperial Topaz Collection at the Main Street store is a stunner. ⊠ *1 Main St., Charlotte Amalie* ☎ *340/774–2222* ⊠ *Havensight Mall, Rte. 30, Charlotte Amalie* ☎ *340/776–3828* ⊠ *Ritz-Carlton, Rte. 317, Estate Great Bay* ☎ *340/779–2308.*

**Cardow Jewelry.** A chain bar—with gold in several lengths, widths, sizes, and styles—awaits you here, along with diamonds, emeralds, and other precious gems. You're guaranteed 40% to 60% savings off U.S. retail prices or your money will be refunded within 30 days of purchase. ⊠ *33 Main St., Charlotte Amalie* ☎ *340/776–1140* ⊠ *Havensight Mall, Bldg. I, Rte. 30, Charlotte Amalie* ☎ *340/774–0530 or 340/774–5905* ⊠ *Marriott Frenchman's Reef Resort, Rte. 315, Estate Bakkeroe* ☎ *340/774–0434.*

**Colombian Emeralds.** Well known in the Caribbean, this store offers set and unset emeralds as well as gems of every description. The watch boutique carries upscale brands like Ebel, Tissot, and Jaeger LeCoultre. ⊠ *30 Main St., Charlotte Amalie* ☎ *340/777–5400* ⊠ *Waterfront at A. H. Riise Mall, Charlotte Amalie* ☎ *340/774–1033* ⊠ *Havensight Mall, Bldg. V, Rte. 30, Charlotte Amalie* ☎ *340/774–2442.*

**Diamonds International.** Choose a diamond, emerald, or tanzanite gem and a mounting, and you can have your dream ring set in an hour. Famous for having the largest inventory of diamonds on the island, this shop welcomes trade-ins, has a U.S. service center, and offers free diamond earrings with every purchase. ⊠ *31 Main St., Charlotte Amalie* ☎ *340/774–3707* ⊠ *3 Drakes Passage, Charlotte Amalie* ☎ *340/775–2010* ⊠ *7AB Drakes Passage, Charlotte Amalie* ☎ *340/774–1516* ⊠ *Havensight Mall, Bldg. II, Rte. 30, Charlotte Amalie* ☎ *340/776–0040* ⊠ *Wyndham Sugar Bay Beach Club & Resort, Rte. 38, Estate Smith Bay* ☎ *340/714–3248.*

**H. Stern Jewelers.** The World Collection of jewels set in modern, fashionable designs and an exclusive sapphire watch have earned this Brazilian jeweler a stellar name. ⊠ *8 Main St., Charlotte Amalie* ☎ *340/776–1939* ⊠ *Havensight Mall, Bldg. II, Rte. 30, Charlotte Amalie* ☎ *340/776–1223* ⊠ *Marriott Frenchman's Reef Resort, Rte. 315, Estate Bakkeroe* ☎ *340/776–3550.*

**Jewels.** Name-brand jewelry and watches are in abundance here. Designer jewelry lines include David Yurman, Bulgari, Chopard, and Penny Preville. The selection of watches is extensive, with brand names including Jaeger le Coultre, Tag Heuer, Breitling, Movado, and Gucci. ⊠ *Main*

*St., at Riise's Alley, Charlotte Amalie* ☏ *340/777–4222* ✉ *Waterfront at Hibiscus Alley, Charlotte Amalie* ☏ *340/777–4222* ✉ *Havensight Mall, Bldg. II, Rte. 30, Charlotte Amalie* ☏ *340/776–8590.*

**Rolex Watches at A. H. Riise.** As the Virgin Islands' official Rolex retailer, this shop offers one of the largest selections of these fine timepieces in the Caribbean. An After Sales Service Center assures that your Rolex keeps on ticking for your lifetime. ✉ *37 Main St., at Riise's Alley, Charlotte Amalie* ☏ *340/776–2303* ✉ *Havensight Mall, Bldg. II, Rte. 30, Charlotte Amalie* ☏ *340/776–4002.*

LEATHER GOODS **Coach Boutique at Little Switzerland.** Find a full line of fine leather handbags, belts, gloves, and more for women, plus briefcases and wallets for men. Accessories for both sexes include organizers, travel bags, and cellphone cases. ✉ *5 Main St., Charlotte Amalie* ☏ *340/776–2010.*

**Longchamp Boutique.** Classic Longchamp brings you authentic French hand-crafted leather goods like handbags, briefcases, wallets, key chains, belts, and luggage. The exclusive line of canvas and leather travel bags is as beautiful as the items are practical. ✉ *25 Main St., Charlotte Amalie* ☏ *340/777–5240.*

↺ **Zora's.** Fine leather sandals made-to-order are the specialty here. There's also a selection of locally made backpacks, purses, and briefcases in durable, brightly colored canvas. ✉ *Norre Gade, across from Roosevelt Park, Charlotte Amalie* ☏ *340/774–2559.*

LINENS **Fabric in Motion.** Fine Italian linens share space with Liberty's of London silky cottons, colorful batiks, cotton prints, ribbons, and accessories at this small shop. ✉ *Storetvaer Gade, Charlotte Amalie* ☏ *340/774–2006.*

**Mr. Tablecloth.** The friendly staff here will help you choose from the floor-to-ceiling selection of linens, from Tuscany lace tablecloths to Irish linen pillowcases. The prices will please. ✉ *6–7 Main St., Charlotte Amalie* ☏ *340/774–4343.*

LIQUOR & **A. H. Riise Liquors & Tobacco.** This Riise venture offers a large selection
TOBACCO of tobacco (including imported cigars), as well as cordials, wines, and rare vintage Armagnacs, cognacs, ports, and Madeiras. It also stocks fruits in brandy and barware from England. Enjoy rum samples at the tasting bar. ✉ *37 Main St., at Riise's Alley, Charlotte Amalie* ☏ *340/776–2303* ✉ *Havensight Mall, Bldg. I, Rte. 30, Charlotte Amalie* ☏ *340/776–7713.*

**Al Cohen's Discount Liquor.** The wine selection at this warehouse-style store is extremely large. ✉ *Rte. 30 across from Havensight Mall, Charlotte Amalie* ☏ *340/774–3690.*

**Tobacco Discounters.** Find here a full line of discounted brand-name cigarettes, cigars, and tobacco accessories. ✉ *Port of $ale Mall, Rte. 30, next to Havensight Mall* ☏ *340/774–2256.*

MUSIC **Modern Music.** Shop for the latest stateside and Caribbean CD and cas-
↺ sette releases, plus oldies, classical, and New Age music. ✉ *Rte. 30, across from Havensight Mall, Charlotte Amalie* ☏ *340/774–3100* ✉ *Nisky Center, Rte. 30, Charlotte Amalie* ☏ *340/777–8787.*

↺ **Parrot Fish Music.** A stock of standard stateside tapes and CDs, plus a good selection of Caribbean artists, including local groups, can be found here. You can browse through the collection of calypso, soca, steel band, and reggae music online. ✉ *Back St., Charlotte Amalie* ☎ *340/ 776–4514* ⊕ *www.parrotfishmusic.com.*

PERFUME **Tropicana Perfume Shoppe.** Displayed in an 18th-century Danish build-ing is a large selection of fragrances for men and women, including those locally made by Gail Garrison from the essential oils of tropical fruits and flowers like mango and jasmine. ✉ *2 Main St., Charlotte Amalie* ☎ *340/774–0010.*

SUNGLASSES **Davante.** This designer eyewear store carries brands like Cartier, Dun-hill, Giorgio Armani, and Christian Dior. ✉ *Riise's Alley, Charlotte Amalie* ☎ *340/714–1220.*

**Fashion Eyewear.** Take your pick from name-brand eyewear. A real plus here is prescription sunglasses, copied from your present eyewear, ready in a half hour for $99. ✉ *International Plaza, Charlotte Amalie* ☎ *340/ 776–9075.*

TOYS **Quick Pics.** Birds sing, dogs bark, and fish swim in this animated toy land, ☻ which is part of a larger electronics and souvenir store. Adults have as much fun trying out the wares as do kids. ✉ *Havensight Mall, Bldg. IV, Rte. 30, Charlotte Amalie* ☎ *340/774–3500.*

# Nightlife & the Arts

On any given night, especially in season, you can find steel-pan orches-tras, rock and roll, piano music, jazz, broken-bottle dancing (actual danc-ing atop broken glass), disco, and karaoke. Pick up a copy of the free, bright yellow *St. Thomas–St. John This Week* magazine when you ar-rive (it can be found at the airport, in stores, and in hotel lobbies); the back pages list who's playing where. The Friday edition of the *Daily News* carries complete listings for the upcoming weekend.

## Nightlife

BARS **Agave Terrace.** Island-style steel-pan bands are a treat that should not be missed. Pan music resonates after dinner here on Tuesday and Thurs-day. ✉ *Point Pleasant Resort, Rte. 38, Estate Smith Bay* ☎ *340/775– 4142.*

**Duffy's Love Shack.** A live band and dancing under the stars are the big draws for locals and visitors alike. ✉ *Red Hook Plaza, Red Hook* ☎ *340/779–2080.*

**Epernay Bistro.** This intimate nightspot has small tables for easy chat-ting, wine and champagne by the glass, and a spacious dance floor. Mix and mingle with island celebrities. The action runs from 4 PM until the wee hours Monday through Saturday. ✉ *Frenchtown Mall, 24-A Hon-duras, Frenchtown* ☎ *340/774–5348.*

**Greenhouse Bar & Restaurant.** Once this favorite eatery puts away the salt-and-pepper shakers at 10 PM, it becomes a rock-and-roll club with a DJ or live reggae bands raising the weary to their feet six nights a week. ✉ *Wa-terfront Hwy. at Storetvaer Gade, Charlotte Amalie* ☎ *340/774–7998.*

**Iggies Beach Bar.** Sing along karaoke-style to the sounds of the surf or the latest hits at this beachside lounge. There are live bands on the week-ends, and you can dance inside or kick up your heels under the stars. At the adjacent Beach House restaurant, there's Carnival Night, complete with steel-pan music on Wednesday. ⊠ *Bolongo Bay Beach Club & Villas, Rte. 30, Estate Bolongo* ☎ *340/775–1800.*

**Ritz-Carlton, St. Thomas.** On Monday nights, catch pan music at this resort's bar. ⊠ *Rte. 317, Estate Great Bay* ☎ *340/775–3333.*

## The Arts

THEATER **Pistarkle Theater.** This air-conditioned theater with more than 100 seats, which is in the Tillett Gardens complex, is host to a dozen or more productions annually, plus a children's summer drama camp. ⊠ *Tillett Gardens, Rte. 38, across from Tutu Park Shopping Mall, Estate Tutu* ☎ *340/775–7877.*

**Reichhold Center for the Arts.** This amphitheater has its more expensive seats covered by a roof. Schedules vary, so check the paper to see what's on when you're in town. Throughout the year there's an entertaining mix of local plays, dance exhibitions, and music of all types. ⊠ *Rte. 30, across from Brewers Beach, Estate Lindberg Bay* ☎ *340/693–1559.*

# Exploring St. Thomas

St. Thomas is only 13 mi (21 km) long and less than 4 mi (6½ km) wide, but it's extremely hilly, and even an 8- or 10-mi (13- or 16-km) trip could take well over an hour. Don't let that discourage you, though; the mountain ridge that runs east to west through the middle and separates the island's Caribbean and Atlantic sides has spectacular vistas.

## Charlotte Amalie

Look beyond the pricey shops, T-shirt vendors, and bustling crowds for a glimpse of the island's history. The city served as the capital of Denmark's outpost in the Caribbean until 1917, an aspect of the island often lost in the glitz of the shopping district.

Emancipation Gardens, right next to the fort, is a good place to start a walking tour. Tackle the hilly part of town first: head north up Government Hill to the historic buildings that house government offices and have incredible views. Several regal churches line the route that runs west back to the town proper and the old-time market. Virtually all the alleyways that intersect Main Street lead to eateries that serve frosty drinks, sandwiches, burgers, and West Indian fare. There are public restrooms in this area, too. Allow an hour for a quick view of the sights.

A note about the street names: In deference to the island's heritage, the streets downtown are labeled by their Danish names. Locals will use both the Danish name and the English name (such as Dronningens Gade and Norre Gade for Main Street), but most people refer to things by their location ("a block toward the Waterfront off Main Street" or "next to the Little Switzerland Shop"). You may find it more useful if you ask for directions by shop names or landmarks.

*Numbers in the margin correspond to points of interest on the Charlotte Amalie map.*

㉒ **All Saints Anglican Church.** Built in 1848 from stone quarried on the island, the church has thick, arched window frames lined with the yellow brick that came to the islands as ballast aboard ships. Merchants

Charlotte Amalie

KEY

▮ Exploring

▢ Hotels & Restaurants

left the brick on the waterfront when they filled their boats with molasses, sugar, mahogany, and rum for the return voyage. The church was built in celebration of the end of slavery in the USVI. ⊠ *Domini Gade* ☎ *340/774–0217* ⊙ *Mon.–Sat. 9–3.*

**㉕ Cathedral of St. Peter & St. Paul.** This building was consecrated as a parish church in 1848 and serves as the seat of the territory's Roman Catholic diocese. The ceiling and walls are covered with murals painted in 1899 by two Belgian artists, Father Leo Servais and Brother Ildephonsus. The San Juan–marble altar and side walls were added in the 1960s. ⊠ *Lower Main St.* ☎ *340/774–0201* ⊙ *Mon.–Sat. 8–5.*

**㉓ Danish Consulate Building.** Built in 1830, this structure once housed the Danish Consulate. Although the Danish Consul General, Søøren Blak, has an office in Charlotte Amalie, it's now in the Scandinavian Center in Havensight Mall. This building is not open to the public. ⊠ *Take stairs north at corner of Bjerge Gade and Crystal Gade to Denmark Hill.*

**⓫ Dutch Reformed Church.** This church has an austere loveliness that's amazing considering all it's been through. Founded in 1744, it's been rebuilt twice following fires and hurricanes. The unembellished cream-color hall gives you a sense of peace—albeit monochromatically. The only other color is the forest green of the shutters and the carpet. Call ahead if you need to visit at a particular time; the doors are sometimes locked. ⊠ *Nye Gade and Crystal Gade* ☎ *340/776–8255* ⊙ *Weekdays 9–5.*

**❻ Educators Park.** A peaceful place amid the town's hustle and bustle, the park has memorials to three famous Virgin Islanders: educator Edith Williams, J. Antonio Jarvis (a founder of the *Daily News*), and educator and author Rothschild Francis. The last gave many speeches here. ⊠ *Main St., across from post office.*

**㉖ Edward Wilmoth Blyden Marine Terminal.** Locally called Tortola Wharf, it's where you can catch the *Native Son* and other ferries to the BVI. The restaurant upstairs is a good place to watch the Charlotte Amalie harbor traffic and sip an iced tea. Next door is the ramp for the *Seaborne Airlines* seaplane, which offers commuter service to St. Croix, the BVI, and Puerto Rico. ⊠ *Waterfront Hwy.*

**❷ Emancipation Garden.** Built to honor the freeing of slaves in 1848, the garden was the site of a 150th anniversary celebration of emancipation. A bronze bust of a freed slave blowing a symbolic conch shell commemorates this anniversary. The gazebo here is used for official ceremonies. Two other monuments show the island's Danish-American tie—a bust of Denmark's King Christian and a scaled-down model of the U.S. Liberty Bell. ⊠ *Between Tolbod Gade and Fort Christian.*

**⓯ Enid M. Baa Public Library.** Like so many other structures on the north side of Main Street, this large pink building is a typical 18th-century town house. Merchants built their houses (stores downstairs, living quarters above) across from the brick warehouses on the south side of the street. The library was once the home of merchant and landowner Baron von Bretton. It's the island's first recorded fireproof building, meaning it was built of ballast brick instead of wood. Its interior of high ceilings and cool stone floors is the perfect refuge from the afternoon sun. You can browse through historic papers or just sit in the breeze by an open window reading the paper. ⊠ *Main St.* ☎ *340/774–0630* ☉ *Weekdays 9–5, Sat. 10–3.*

**Fort Christian.** St. Thomas's oldest standing structure, this monument was built between 1672 and 1680 and now has U.S. National Landmark status. The clock tower was added in the 19th century. This remarkable building has, over time, been used as a jail, governor's residence, town hall, courthouse, and church. Fort Christian now houses the **Virgin Islands Museum,** where you can see exhibits on USVI history, natural history, and turn-of-the-20th-century furnishings. Local artists display their works monthly in the gallery. A gift shop sells local crafts, books, and other souvenirs. This is also the site of the Chamber of Commerce's Hospitality Lounge, where there are public restrooms, brochures, and a place where you can stash your luggage for some last-minute shopping on the way to the airport. ⊠ *Waterfront Hwy., east of shopping district* ☎ *340/776–4566.*

FodorsChoice ★

**Frederick Lutheran Church.** This historic church has a massive mahogany altar, and its pews—each with its own door—were once rented to families of the congregation. Lutheranism is the state religion of Denmark, and when the territory was without a minister the governor—who had his own elevated pew—filled in. ⊠ *Norre Gade* ☎ *340/776–1315* ☉ *Mon.–Sat. 9–4.*

**Government House.** Built in 1867, this neoclassical white brick-and-wood structure houses the offices for the governor of the Virgin Islands. Inside, the staircases are of native mahogany, as are the plaques handlettered in gold with the names of the governors appointed and, since 1970, elected. Brochures detailing the history of the building are available, but you may have to ask for them. ⊠ *Government Hill* ☎ *340/774–0294* ☒ *Free* ☉ *Weekdays 8–5.*

**Grand Galleria.** This imposing building stands at the head of Main Street. Once the island's premier hotel, it has been converted into offices and shops. ⊠ *Tolbod Gade at Norre Gade* ☎ *340/774–7282* ☉ *Weekdays 8–5, Sat. 9–noon.*

**Haagensen House.** Behind Hotel 1829, this lovingly restored home was built in the early 1800s by Danish entrepreneur Hans Haagensen and is surrounded by an equally impressive cookhouse, outbuildings, and terraced gardens. A lower-level banquet hall now showcases an antique-print and photo gallery. Guided walking tours are available of Haagensen House. The tour begins at the lookout tower at Blackbeard's Castle and continues to the circa-1860s Villa Notman, Haagensen House, and Hotel 1829. The first tour starts at 9:30 AM. ⊠ *Government Hill* ☎ *340/776–1234 or 340/776–1829* ☒ *Tours $20* ☉ *Oct.–May, daily 9–4; June–Sept., by appointment only.*

**Hassel Island.** East of Water Island in Charlotte Amalie harbor, Hassel Island is part of the Virgin Islands National Park, as it has the ruins of a British military garrison (built during a brief British occupation of the

USVI during the 1800s) and the remains of a marine railway (where ships were hoisted into dry dock for repairs). There's a small ferry that runs from the Crown Bay Marina to the island; departure times are posted at Tickles Dockside Pub, and the fare is $5 or $10 round-trip.

**❼ Hotel 1829.** As its name implies, the hotel was built in 1829, albeit as the private residence of a prominent merchant named Lavalette. The building's bright, coral-color exterior walls are accented with fancy black wrought iron, and the interior is paneled in dark wood, which makes it feel delightfully cool. From the terrace there's an exquisite view of the harbor framed by brilliant orange bougainvillea. You can combine a visit to this hotel with a walking tour of Haagensen House, Villa Notman, and the lookout tower at Blackbeard's Castle just behind the hotel. ✉ *Government Hill* ☎ *340/776–1829 or 340/776–1234* ⊕ *www. hotel1829.com* ✉ *Tour $20* ⊙ *Oct.–May, daily 9–4; June–Sept., by appointment only.*

**❼ Legislature Building.** Its pastoral-looking lime-green exterior conceals the vociferous political wrangling of the Virgin Islands Senate inside. Constructed originally by the Danish as a police barracks, the building was later used to billet U.S. Marines, and much later it housed a public school. You're welcome to sit in on sessions in the upstairs chambers. ✉ *Waterfront Hwy., across from Fort Christian* ☎ *340/774–0880* ⊙ *Daily 8–5.*

**❶❻ Market Square.** Formally called Rothschild Francis Square, this is a good place to find local produce. A cadre of old-timers sells mangoes and papayas, strange-looking root vegetables, and herbs; sidewalk vendors offer African fabrics and artifacts and tie-dyed cotton clothes at good prices. ✉ *North side of Main St., at Strand Gade.*

**❶❽ Memorial Moravian Church.** Built in 1884, it was named to commemorate the 150th anniversary of the Moravian Church in the Virgin Islands. ✉ *17 Norre Gade* ☎ *340/776–0066* ⊙ *Weekdays 8–5.*

**☙ ❾ 99 Steps.** This staircase "street," built by the Danes in the 1700s, leads to the residential area above Charlotte Amalie and Blackbeard's Castle. The castle's tower, built in 1679, was once used by the notorious pirate Edward Teach. If you count the stairs as you go up, you will discover, as have thousands before you, that there are more than 99. ✉ *Look for steps heading north from Government Hill.*

**❶❹ Pissarro Building.** Housing several shops and an art gallery, this was the birthplace and childhood home of Camille Pissarro, who later moved to France and became an acclaimed Impressionist painter. The art gallery contains three original pages from Pissarro's sketchbook and two pastels by Pissarro's grandson, Claude. ✉ *Main St., between Raadets Gade and Trompeter Gade.*

**☙ ❶❾ Roosevelt Park.** You can see members of the local legal community head to the nearby court buildings while you rest on a bench in this park—a good spot to people-watch. The small monument on the park's south side is dedicated to USVI war veterans. Kids enjoy the playground made of wood and tires. ✉ *Norre Gade.*

**㉔ Savan.** A neighborhood of small streets and houses, it was first laid out in the 1700s as the residential area for a growing community of middle-class black artisans, clerks, and shopkeepers. There's a row of Rastafarian shops along the first block and restaurants that sell spicy vegetarian fare. It's best not to walk here at night and to exercise caution even in daylight. ⊠ *Turn north off lower Main St. onto General Gade.*

★ ⓴ **Seven Arches Museum.** This restored 18th-century home is a striking example of classic Danish–West Indian architecture. There seem to be arches everywhere—seven to be exact—all supporting a "welcoming arms" staircase that leads to the second floor and the flower-framed front doorway. The Danish kitchen is a highlight: it's housed in a separate building off the main house, as were all cooking facilities in the early days (for fire prevention). Inside the house you can see mahogany furnishings and gas lamps. ⊠ *Government Hill, 3 bldgs. east of Government House* ☎ *340/774–9295* ☜ *$5 suggested donation* ☉ *Oct.–July, daily 10–4; Aug. and Sept., by appointment only.*

⑫ **Synagogue of Beracha Veshalom Vegmiluth Hasidim.** The synagogue's Hebrew name translates to the Congregation of Blessing, Peace, and Loving Deeds. The small building's white pillars contrast with rough stone walls, as does the rich mahogany of the pews and altar. The sand on the floor symbolizes the exodus from Egypt. Since the synagogue first opened its doors in 1833 it has held a weekly Sabbath service, making it the oldest synagogue building in continuous use under the American flag and the second-oldest (after the one on Curaçao) in the western hemisphere. Guided tours are available. Brochures detailing the key structures and history are also available. Next door, the Weibel Museum showcases Jewish history on St. Thomas. ⊠ *15 Crystal Gade* ☎ *340/ 774–4312* ⊕ *new.onepaper.com/synagogue* ☉ *Weekdays 9–4.*

❺ **U.S. Post Office.** While you buy your postcard stamps, contemplate the murals of waterfront scenes by *Saturday Evening Post* artist Stephen Dohanos. His art was commissioned as part of the Works Project Administration (WPA) in the 1930s. ⊠ *Tolbod Gade and Main St.*

☾ ❸ **Vendors Plaza.** Here merchants sell everything from T-shirts to African attire to leather goods. Look for local art among the ever-changing selections at this busy market. ⊠ *Waterfront, west of Fort Christian* ☉ *Weekdays 8–6, weekends 9–1.*

㉘ **Water Island.** This island, once owned by the U.S. Department of the Interior and about ¼ mi (½ km) out in Charlotte Amalie Harbor, was once a peninsula. A channel was cut through so that U.S. submarines could get to their base in a bay just to the west, known as Sub Base. Today, this is the fourth-largest U.S. Virgin Island. A ferry goes between Crown Bay Marina and the island several times daily, at a cost of $5 or $10 round-trip.

⑬ **Weibel Museum.** In this museum next to the synagogue, 300 years of Jewish history on St. Thomas are showcased. The small gift shop sells a commemorative silver coin celebrating the anniversary of the Hebrew congregation's establishment on the island in 1796. There are also tropically inspired items, like a shell seder plate and menorahs painted to resemble palm trees. ✉ *15 Crystal Gade* ☎ *340/774–4312* 💲 *Free* ⊙ *Weekdays 9–4.*

## Around the Island

To explore outside Charlotte Amalie, rent a car or hire a taxi. Your rental car should come with a good map; if not, pick up the pocket-size "St. Thomas–St. John Road Map" at a tourist information center. Roads are marked with route numbers, but they're confusing and seem to switch numbers suddenly. Roads are also identified by signs bearing the St. Thomas–St. John Hotel and Tourism Association's mascot, Tommy the Starfish. More than 100 of these color-coded signs line the island's main routes. Orange signs trace the route from the airport to Red Hook, green signs identify the road from town to Magens Bay, Tommy's face on a yellow background points from Mafolie to Crown Bay through the north side, red signs lead from Smith Bay to Four Corners via Skyline Drive, and blue signs mark the route from the cruise-ship dock at Havensight to Red Hook. These color-coded routes are not marked on most visitor maps, however. Allow yourself a day to explore, especially if you want to stop to take pictures or to enjoy a light bite or refreshing swim. Most gas stations are on the island's more populated eastern end, so fill up before heading to the north side. And remember to drive on the left!

Although the eastern end has many major resorts and spectacular beaches, don't be surprised if a cow or a herd of goats crosses your path as you drive through the relatively flat, dry terrain. The north side of the island is more lush and hush—fewer houses and less traffic. Here there are roller-coaster routes (made all the more scary because the roads have no shoulders) and incredible vistas. Leave time in the afternoon for a swim. Pick up some sandwiches from delis in the Red Hook area for a picnic lunch, or enjoy a slice of pizza at Magens Bay. A day in the country will reveal the tropical pleasures that have enticed more than one visitor to become a resident.

*Numbers in the margin correspond to points of interest on the St. Thomas map.*

**㉚ Compass Point Marina.** It's fun to park your car and walk around this marina. The boaters—many of whom have sailed here from points around the globe—are easy to engage in conversation. Turn south off Route 32 at the well-marked entrance road just east of Independent Boat Yard. ✉ *Estate Frydenhoj.*

☙ **㉜ Coral World Ocean Park.** Coral World has an offshore underwater ob-
**Fodor's**Choice servatory that houses the Predator Tank, one of the world's largest
★ coral-reef tanks, and an aquarium with more than 20 portholes providing close-ups of Caribbean sea life. Sea Trekkin' lets you tour the reef outside the park at a depth of 15 feet, thanks to specialized high-tech headgear and a continuous air supply that's based on the surface. A guide leads the half-hour tour, and the narration is piped through a specialized microphone inside each trekker's helmet; the minimum age to participate is eight years. Adventure Island, added in early 2006, is St.

Thomas's first and only water park. A large catamaran, equipped with two tunnel-like water slides, a water trampoline, water cannon, and other water toys, takes visitors on a fun-filled snorkeling excursion three days a week. The park also has several outdoor pools where you can shake hands with a starfish, pet a baby shark, feed stingrays, and view endangered sea turtles. In addition there's a mangrove lagoon and a nature trail full of lush tropical flora. Daily feedings and talks take place at most every exhibit. ⊠ *Coki Point, north of Rte. 38, Estate Frydendal* ☎ *340/ 775–1555* ⊕ *www.coralworldvi.com* ✏ *$18, Adventure Island $45, Sea Trekkin $50* ☉ *Daily 9–5.*

☾ **❸❹ Drake's Seat.** Sir Francis Drake was supposed to have kept watch over his fleet and looked for enemy ships from this vantage point. The panorama is especially breathtaking (and romantic) at dusk, and if you arrive late in the day you can miss the hordes of day-trippers on taxi tours who stop here to take a picture and buy a T-shirt from one of the many vendors. ⊠ *Rte. 40, Estate Zufriedenheit.*

**❸❺ Estate St. Peter Greathouse & Botanical Gardens.** This unusual spot is perched on a mountainside 1,000 feet above sea level, with views of more than 20 islands and islets. You can wander through a gallery displaying local art, sip a complimentary rum punch while looking out at the view, or follow a nature trail that leads by nearly 200 varieties of trees and plants, including an orchid jungle. ⊠ *Rte. 40, Estate St. Peter* ☎ *340/774–4999* ⊕ *www.greathouse-mountaintop.com* ✏ *$15* ☉ *Mon.–Sat. 9–4:30.*

**❸❻ Frenchtown.** Popular for its several bars and restaurants, Frenchtown is also the home of descendants of immigrants from St. Barthélemy (St. Barths). You can watch them pull up their brightly painted boats and display their equally colorful catch of the day along the waterfront. If you chat with them, you can hear speech patterns slightly different from those of other St. Thomians. Get a feel for the residential district of Frenchtown by walking west to some of the town's winding streets, where tiny wooden houses have been passed down from generation to generation. Next to Joseph Aubain Ballpark, the **French Heritage Museum** (⊠ Intersection of rue de St. Anne and rue de St. Barthélemy ☎ 340/774–2320) houses century-old artifacts such as fishing nets, accordions, tambourines, mahogany furniture, and historic photographs that illustrate the lives of the French descendants during the 18th through 20th centuries. The museum is open Monday through Saturday from 9 AM to 6 PM; admission is free. ⊠ *Turn south off Waterfront Hwy. at post office.*

★ ☾ **❸❸ Mountain Top.** Stop here for a banana daiquiri and spectacular views from the observation deck more than 1,500 feet above sea level. There are also shops that sell everything from Caribbean art to nautical antiques, ship models, and T-shirts. Kids will like talking to the parrots—and hearing them answer back. ⊠ *Head north off Rte. 33, look for signs* ⊕ *www. greathouse-mountaintop.com.*

★ ☾ **❷❾ Paradise Point Tramway.** Fly skyward in a gondola to Paradise Point, an overlook with breathtaking views of Charlotte Amalie and the harbor. There are several shops, a bar, restaurant, and a wedding gazebo; kids enjoy the tropical bird show held daily at 10:30 AM and 1:30 PM. A ¼-mi (½-km) hiking trail leads to spectacular views of St. Croix to the south. Wear sturdy shoes; the trail is steep and rocky. ⊠ *Rte. 30, across from Havensight Mall, Charlotte Amalie* ☎ *340/774–9809* ⊕ *www. paradisepointtramway.com* ☜ *$16* ⊙ *Thurs.–Tues. 9–5, Wed. 9–9.*

**㉛**   **Red Hook.** In this nautical center there are fishing and sailing charter boats, dive shops, and powerboat-rental agencies at the American Yacht Harbor marina. There are also several bars and restaurants, including Molly Molone's, Duffy's Love Shack, and Off the Hook. One grocery store and two delis offer picnic fixings—from sliced meats and cheeses to rotisserie-roasted chickens, prepared salads, and freshly baked breads.

# ST. JOHN

By Lynda Lohr

The sun slipped up over the horizon like a great orange ball, streaking the sky with wisps of gold. Watching from my porch overlooking Coral Bay, I thanked Mother Nature, as I do almost every day, for providing glorious sunrises, colorful rainbows and green hillsides, and the opportunity to enjoy them all. It was a magnificent start to another gorgeous St. John day, an island where nature is the engine that fuels the island's economy and brings more than 800,000 visitors a year.

St. John's heart is Virgin Islands National Park, a treasure that takes up a full two-thirds of St. John's 20 square mi (53 square km). The park helps keep the island's interior in its pristine and undisturbed state, but if you go at midday, you'll probably have to share your stretch of beach with others, particularly at Trunk Bay.

The island is booming, and it can get a tad crowded at the ever-popular Trunk Bay Beach during the busy winter season; parking woes plague the island's main town of Cruz Bay, but you won't find traffic jams or pollution. It's easy to escape from the fray, however: just head off on a hike or go early or late to the beach. The sun won't be as strong, and you may have that perfect crescent of white sand all to yourself.

St. John doesn't have a grand agrarian past like her sister island, St. Croix, but if you're hiking in the dry season, you can probably stumble upon the stone ruins of old plantations. The less adventuresome can visit the repaired ruins at the park's Annaberg Plantation and Caneel Bay Resort.

In 1675 Jorgen Iverson claimed the unsettled island for Denmark. By 1733 there were more than 1,000 slaves working more than 100 plantations. In that year the island was hit by a drought, hurricanes, and a plague of insects that destroyed the summer crops. With famine a real threat and the planters keeping them under tight reign, the slaves revolted on November 23, 1733. They captured the fort at Coral Bay, took control of the island, and held on to it for six months. During this period, about 20% of the island's total population was killed, the tragedy affecting both black and white residents in equal percentages. The rebellion was eventually put down with the help of French troops from Martinique. Slavery continued until 1848, when slaves in St. Croix marched on Frederiksted to demand their freedom from the Danish gov-

1

# St. John Archaeology

CLOSE UP

**ARCHAEOLOGISTS CONTINUE** to unravel St. John's past through excavations at Trunk Bay and Cinnamon Bay, both prime tourist destinations within Virgin Islands National Park.

Work began back in the early 1990s, when the park wanted to build new bathhouses at the popular Trunk Bay. In preparation for that project, the archaeologists began to dig, turning up artifacts and the remains of structures that date to AD 900. The site was once a village occupied by the Taino, a peaceful group that lived in the area for many centuries. A similar but not quite as ancient village was discovered at Cinnamon Bay.

By the time the Tainos got to Cinnamon Bay—they lived in the area from about AD 1000 to 1500—their society had developed to include chiefs, commoners, workers, and slaves. The location of the national park's busy Cinnamon Bay campground was once a Taino temple that belonged to a king or chief. When archaeologists began digging in 1998, they uncovered several dozen *zemis*, which are small clay gods used in ceremonial activities, as well as beads, pots, and many other artifacts.

Near the end of the Cinnamon Bay dig, archaeologists turned up another less ancient but still surprising discovery. A burned layer indicated that a plantation slave village had also stood near Cinnamon Bay campground; it was torched during the 1733 revolt because its slave inhabitants had been loyal to the planters. Since the 1970s, bones from slaves buried in the area have been uncovered at the water's edge by beach erosion.

---

ernment. This time it was granted. After emancipation, St. John fell into decline, with its inhabitants eking out a living on small farms. Life continued in much the same way until the national park opened in 1956 and tourism became an industry.

Of the three U.S. Virgin Islands, St. John, which has 5,000 residents, has the strongest sense of community, which is primarily rooted in a desire to protect the island's natural beauty. Despite the growth, there are still many pockets of tranquility. Here you can truly escape the pressures of modern life for a day, a week—perhaps, forever.

## Where to Stay

St. John doesn't have many beachfront hotels, but that's a small price to pay for all the pristine sand. However, the island's two excellent resorts—Caneel Bay Resort and the Westin St. John Resort & Villas—*are* on the beach. Sandy, white beaches string out along the north coast, which is popular with sunbathers and snorkelers and is where you can find the Caneel Bay Resort and Cinnamon and Maho Bay campgrounds. Most villas are in the residential south-shore area, a 15-minute drive from the north-shore beaches. If you head east you come to the laid-back com-

# St. John

TO
JOST VAN DYKE

Mary Point

Whistling
Cay

Windward Passage

Francis Bay

Francis
Bay

Maho Bay

6

24

23

20

Trunk Bay    Cinnamon Bay

Peace
Hill    8

North Shore Rd.

22

20

Henley
Cay

Hawksnest
Beach

Catherineberg
Ruins

7

Camelberg
Pk.

Caneel Bay

21

25

TO
ST. THOMAS

Elaine Ione Sprauve
Library and Museum

Reef Bay Trail

3

Stephen's
Cay

Cruz Bay

1    2

VIRGIN ISLANDS
NATIONAL PARK

20

19

1 - 16

17

104

18

Great Cruz
Bay

Reef
Bay

Blasbalg Pt.

Chocolate
Hole

Rendezvous
Bay

Fish
Bay

White Pt.

Dever's Bay

Bovocoap Pt.

Dittlif Pt.

Caribbean Sea

0                    1 miles

0            1 km

## KEY

- Beaches
- Dive Sites
- Ferry
- **1** Exploring Sights
- **1** Hotels & Restaurants
- .......... Trail

←TO TORTOLA

TO TORTOLA→

*The Narrows*

*Leinster Bay*

*Brown Bay*

**Annaberg Plantation**

**VIRGIN ISLANDS NATIONAL PARK**

Centerline Rd.

*Sir Francis Drake Channel*

**28**

**10**

**Coral Bay**

**26** - **27**

**5**

Palestina

King Hill Rd.

*Hurricane Hole*

*Coral Harbor*

*Haulover Bay*

*Newfound Bay*

**29**

*East End Pt.*

**4** **Bordeaux Mountain**

**107**

*Sanders Bay*

*Coral Bay*

*Round Bay*

**East End**

*East End Bay*

*Privateer Pt.*

*Lagoon Pt.*

*Long Pt.*

Calabash

**30**

*Privateer Bay*

*John?s Folly Bay*

*Leduck Island*

**Lameshur Bay**

*Drunk Bay*

**31**

**Salt Pond Bay**

*Salt Pond Peninsula*

*Ram Head*

### UNITED STATES VIRGIN ISLANDS

*Tortola*

**ST. THOMAS**

**ST. JOHN**

*Distance from St. Thomas to St. Croix approx. 40 miles*

**ST. CROIX**

munity of Coral Bay, where there are growing numbers of villas and cottages. A stay outside of Coral Bay will be peaceful and quiet.

If you're looking for West Indian village charm, there are a few inns in Cruz Bay. Just know that when bands play at any of the town's bars (some of which stay open until the wee hours), the noise can be a problem. Your choice of accommodations also includes condominiums and cottages near town; two campgrounds, both at the edges of beautiful beaches (bring bug repellent); eco-resorts; and luxurious villas, often with a pool or a hot tub (sometimes both) and a stunning view.

If your lodging comes with a fully equipped kitchen, you'll be happy to know that St. John's handful of grocery stores sell everything from the basics to sun-dried tomatoes and green chilies—though the prices will take your breath away. If you're on a budget, consider bringing some staples (pasta, canned goods, paper products) from home. Hotel rates throughout the island, though considered expensive by some, do include endless privacy and access to most water sports.

For approximate costs, *see* the dining and lodging price chart on the U.S. Virgin Islands Planner, at the beginning of this chapter.

## Hotels & Inns

**$$$$**
**Fodor's Choice**
**★**
**Caneel Bay Resort.** Well-heeled honeymooners, couples celebrating anniversaries, and extended families all enjoy Caneel Bay Resort's laid-back luxury. If you want to spend your days sunning on any one of its seven gorgeous beaches, taking a kayak out for a paddle, or enjoying lingering dinners at its fine restaurants, you'll find no finer resort on St. John. Your room, which has air-conditioning or can be opened to the breezes, won't come with a TV or even a telephone (though management will loan you a cellular)—all the better to get away from it all. Rooms look as if they're modeled right out of a magazine; if you opt for one of the beachfront rooms, you can get out of bed and stumble a few steps across the sand to the Caribbean. Otherwise, you can look out on the gardens or the tennis courts. Nightlife runs to steel-pan music or an easy-listening combo; if you want lots of action, go elsewhere. ⊠ *Rte. 20, Caneel Bay* ⊕ *Box 720, Cruz Bay 00830* ☎ *340/776–6111 or 888/767–3966* 🖷 *340/693–8280* ⊕ *www.caneelbay.com* ⥂ *166 rooms* ♨ *4 restaurants, fans, minibars, Wi-Fi, 11 tennis courts, pool, spa, beach, dive shop, dock, snorkeling, windsurfing, boating, billiards, children's programs (ages infant–12), meeting rooms; no room phones, no room TVs* ⊟ *AE, DC, MC, V* ⏩ *CP.*

**$$$$**
**Westin St. John Resort & Villas.** Other than Caneel Bay, this is the only big resort on the island. Although it doesn't provide the same casual luxury, it does have a nice beachfront location and enough activities to make you never want to leave. That said, most guests rent a car for at least a couple of days to explore the many lovely beaches and the nearby town of Cruz Bay. The hotel is spread over 47 beachfront acres adjacent to Great Cruz Bay, with lushly planted gardens, a white sandy beach that beckons sunbathers, and nice—but not luxurious—rooms with tropical touches. Those strung out behind the beach put you closest to the water, but even the hillside villas are only a seven-minute stroll to the

sand. You can keep very busy here with tennis and water sports, or you can idle the day away at the pool or beach. ☒ *Rte. 104, Great Cruz Bay* ✉ *Box 8310, Cruz Bay 00831* ☎ *340/693–8000 or 800/808–5020* 🖶 *340/779–4985* ⊕ *www.westinresortstjohn.com* 🛏 *282 rooms, 67 villas* ⚭ *4 restaurants, in-room safes, minibars, refrigerators, cable TV, in-room broadband, Wi-Fi, 6 tennis courts, pool, gym, outdoor hot tub, massage, beach, dive shop, snorkeling, windsurfing, boating, fishing, shops, children's programs (ages 3–12), meeting rooms, no-smoking rooms* ☰ *AE, D, DC, MC, V* ⦿ *EP.*

**$$$** 🏨 **Estate Lindholm Bed & Breakfast.** Built among old stone ruins on a lushly planted hill overlooking Cruz Bay, Estate Lindholm provides a charming setting, with the convenience of being close to Cruz Bay's restaurants, shopping, and nightlife. You'll feel as if you're out of the fray but still near enough to run into town when you want. Rooms are sophisticated, with crisp white spreads accented by teak furniture. Although you can easily walk to Cruz Bay, the return trip is up a big hill. To get out and about, rent a car. The sunset views from Asolare restaurant, on the property, provide a stunning end to your day. ✉ *Box 1360, Cruz Bay 00831* ☎ *340/776–6121* 🖶 *800/322–6335* ⊕ *www.estatelindholm. com* 🛏 *10 rooms* ⚭ *Restaurant, fans, microwaves, refrigerators, cable TV, pool, gym; no smoking* ☰ *AE, D, MC, V* ⦿ *CP.*

**$$** 🏨 **Garden by the Sea Bed & Breakfast.** A stay here will allow you to live like a local in a middle-class residential neighborhood near a bird-filled salt pond. This cozy B&B is also an easy walk from Cruz Bay, which makes it convenient. White spreads and curtains provide pristine counterpoints to the blue-and-green hues that predominate your room. Your hosts serve a delightful breakfast—piña colada French toast is a specialty—on the front deck. It's perfect for folks who enjoy peace and quiet: there are no phones or TVs in the rooms. ☒ *Enighed* ✉ *5004A Enighed 87, Cruz Bay 00830* ☎☎ *340/779–4731* ⊕ *www.gardenbythesea.com* 🛏 *3 rooms* ⚭ *Fans, no-smoking rooms; no a/c, no room phones, no room TVs* ☰ *No credit cards* ⦿ *BP.*

**$$** 🏨 **St. John Inn.** A stay here gives you a bit of style at what passes for budget prices in St. John. You might find a four-poster bed or an old-fashioned armoire in rooms painted in lush hues. Tucked down a side street off a busy major thoroughfare, this cozy inn puts you an easy walk from Cruz Bay's shops, restaurants, and even the ferry dock (if you don't have much luggage). ☒ *Off Rte. 104, Box 37, Cruz Bay 00831* ☎ *340/693–8688 or 800/666–7688* 🖶 *340/693–9900* ⊕ *www.stjohninn.com* 🛏 *11 units* ⚭ *Fans, some kitchenettes, refrigerators, cable TV, pool* ☰ *AE, MC, V* ⦿ *CP.*

**$** 🏨 **Inn at Tamarind Court.** If money is an object—and you don't want to camp at Maho—opt for the Inn at Tamarind Court. The rooms have rather pedestrian decor, but they're clean, and you can't beat the location, a five-minute walk from the heart of Cruz Bay's action. If you're up for a bit of a hike, you can even walk to the beach at Salomon Bay; the trip takes you about a mile up and down hill, but you'll be rewarded with a swim at the end. Ask at the national park visitor center for directions. Single rooms share a bath, but the rest have private baths. The hotel's courtyard restaurant, filled with umbrella-covered tables, is popular with locals. ✉ *Rte. 104, Box 350, Cruz Bay 00831* ☎ *340/776–6378 or 800/221–1637* 🖷 *340/776–6722* ⊕ *www.tamarindcourt.com* 🛏 *20 rooms* ♿ *Restaurant, fans, some kitchenettes, refrigerators, cable TV* ▤ *AE, D, MC, V* ⍟ *EP.*

WHERE TO CAMP   🏕 **Cinnamon Bay Campground.** Cinnamon Bay Campground sits in the ⟳ heart of Virgin Islands National Park, a stellar location right at the beach. Tents and rustic cottages are nestled in the trees that stretch behind the shore, and you have easy access to hiking, water sports, and ranger-led evening programs. The amenities are basic but include propane stoves, cooking equipment, and bed linens; reserve early if you'd like a cottage right behind the beach. Only the screened cottages have electric lights; tenters depend on propane lanterns. If you have your own gear, the tent sites are a steal at $27 per night. Showers and flush toilets, as well as a restaurant and a small store, are a short walk away from the camping area. ♿ *BBQs, flush toilets, drinking water, showers (cold), picnic tables, food service, some electricity, public telephone, general store, ranger station, swimming (ocean)* 🛏 *55 tents, 40 cottages, 31 tent sites* ✉ *Rte. 20, Cinnamon Bay* 🕮 *Box 720, Cruz Bay 00830-0720* ☎ *340/776–6330 or 800/539–9998* 🖷 *340/776–6458* ⊕ *www.cinnamonbay.com* 🕮 *Reservations essential* ▤ *AE, MC, V* ��� *Oct.–Aug.*

⟳ 🏕 **Maho Bay Camps.** Tucked into the greenery along the island's north
Fodor'sChoice  shore, Maho Bay Camps is particularly eco-conscious, and it attracts a
★  sociable crowd that likes to explore the undersea world off the campground's beach or attend on-site educational seminars. The "tents" (wooden platforms protected from the elements by canvas and screening) are linked by wooden stairs, ramps, and walkways—all of them elevated—so that you can trek around camp, down to the beach, and to the unheated, coolish public showers without disturbing the terrain. Although the tents have some amenities like real beds and electricity, there are no refrigerators; ice-filled coolers keep your food from spoiling. ♿ *BBQs, Internet room, flush toilets, drinking water, showers (cold), picnic tables, food service, electricity, public telephone, general store, swimming (beach)* 🛏 *114 tent cottages* ✉ *Maho Bay* 🕮 *Box 310, Cruz Bay 00830* ☎ *340/776–6240 or 800/392–9004* 🖷 *340/776–6504* ⊕ *www.maho.org* 🕮 *Reservations essential* ▤ *AE, MC, V.*

## Condominiums & Cottages

Many of the island's condos are just minutes from the hustle and bustle of Cruz Bay, but you'll find more condos and cottages around the island.

**$$$$**  🏨 **Gallows Point Resort.** Gallows Point Resort has an excellent waterfront location just outside Cruz Bay's center. You're a short walk to restaurants and shops, but once you step into your condo, the hustle and bustle are left behind at the door. The upper-level apartments have loft bedrooms and the best views. The harborside villas get better trade winds, but they're a tad noisier. Tropical rooms have wicker furniture, tile floors, and brightly colored spreads in colors that reflect the sea and sky. Zozo's Ristorante, a popular spot for sunset watching, serves northern Italian cuisine above the lobby. ✉ *Gallows Point, Bay St., Box 58, Cruz*

435-575

Bay 00831 ☎ 340/776–6434 or 800/323–7229 🖷 340/776–6520 ⊕ www.gallowspointresort.com ➴ 60 units ⌂ Restaurant, fans, kitchens, cable TV, pool, beach, snorkeling ▤ AE, MC, V �🍽 EP.

$$$–$$$$  🏠 **Coconut Coast Villas.** This small condominium complex with studio, two-, and three-bedroom apartments is a 10-minute walk from Cruz Bay but still insulated from the town's noise in a sleepy suburban neighborhood. You can swim and snorkel at the small beach or relax poolside for some sun. Rooms have a fresh feel; each is a little bit different in decor, with whites, blues, and greens predominating in the color scheme. Colorful artwork by the owner's mother, St. John artist Elaine Estern, graces the walls. ⊠ Turner Bay 🖃 Box 618, Cruz Bay 00831 ☎ 340/693–9100 or 800/858–7989 🖷 340/779–4157 ⊕ www.coconutcoast.com ➴ 9 units ⌂ Fans, kitchens, cable TV, pool, beach ▤ MC, V �🍽 EP.

$$$–$$$$  🏠 **Estate Zootenvaal.** The modest cottages may look dated, but you can't beat the peace and quiet. They are certainly out of the way, along the island's East End Road; the small but very private beach across the road is a major plus. Though you will feel that you're getting away from it all, a five-minute drive will bring you to Coral Bay's few restaurants, a handful of shops, and tiny grocery store. ⊠ Rte. 10, Hurricane Hole, Zootenvaal 00830 ☎ 340/776–6321 ⊕ www.estatezootenvaal.com ➴ 4 units ⌂ Fans, kitchens, beach; no a/c, no room phones, no room TVs ▤ No credit cards �🍽 EP.

$$  🏠 **Harmony Studios.** The condominium-style units sit hillside at Maho Bay, giving you more of the comforts of home—albeit in an ecologically correct environment—than the Maho Bay Camp tents just below. Entryway mats are made of recycled tires, the pristine white walls of recycled newspapers, and your electricity comes from the wind and the sun. Best of all, you share access to interesting evening programs and a nice beach at Maho. Be prepared to hike up and down long flights of steep, wooden stairs. ⊠ Maho Bay 🖃 Box 310, Cruz Bay 00830 ☎ 340/776–6240 or 800/392–9004 🖷 340/776–6504 ⊕ www.maho. org ➴ 12 units ⌂ Restaurant, fans, kitchens, beach, snorkeling, windsurfing, children's programs (ages 10 and over), Internet room, no-smoking rooms; no a/c, no room phones, no room TVs ▤ AE, MC, V �🍽 EP.

$–$$  🏠 **Concordia Studios and Eco-tents.** This off-the-beaten-path resort—under the same management as Maho Bay Camps—is on the remote Salt Pond peninsula. It shares the back-to-nature bent of its sister resorts but with a decent level of comfort. The spacious condominium units are casually comfortable with tile floors, kitchens, and lovely sea views. Next door are 11 "eco-tents," upscale camping structures made of environmentally friendly materials but also equipped with solar power, composting toilets, and kitchenettes. ⊠ 20–27 Estate Concordia, Concordia 00830 ☎ 340/693–5855 or 800/392–9004 🖷 340/693–5960 ⊕ www. maho.org ➴ 9 studios, 25 tents ⌂ Some kitchens, some kitchenettes, pool, beach, no-smoking rooms; no a/c, no room phones, no room TVs ▤ AE, MC, V �🍽 EP.

$–$$  🏠 **Serendip.** We'd pick Serendip for a budget vacation in a residential locale. This complex offers modern apartments on lush grounds with lovely views. Although this is an older property dating from the 1960s, the units don't feel dated. There are colorful spreads, fully equipped kitchens, and bookshelves filled with good vacation reads. You definitely need a car if you stay here, though; it's about 1 mi (1½ km) up a steep hill out of Cruz Bay. ☒ *Enighed* ☎ *Box 273, Cruz Bay 00831* ☎ *340/ 776–6646 or 888/800–6445* ⊕ *www.serendipstjohn.com* ☜ *10 apartments* ♤ *Fans, kitchens, cable TV* ☰ *MC, V* ⦿ *EP.*

## Private Condos & Villas

**Fodor's**Choice ★ Tucked here and there between Cruz Bay and Coral Bay are about 350 private villas and condos (prices range from $ to $$$$). With pools and/ or hot tubs, full kitchens, and living areas, these lodgings provide a fully functional home away from home. They're perfect for couples and extended groups of families or friends. You need a car, since most lodgings are in the hills (very few are at the beach). Villa managers usually pick you up at the dock, arrange for your rental car, and answer questions you have upon arrival as well as during your stay. Prices drop in the summer season, which is generally after April 15, though some companies begin off-season pricing a week or two later, so be sure to ask.

If you want to be close to Cruz Bay's restaurants and boutiques, a villa in the Chocolate Hole and Great Cruz Bay areas will put you just a few minutes away. The Coral Bay area has a growing number of villas, but you'll be about 20 minutes from Cruz Bay. Beaches string out along the North Shore, so you won't be more than 15 minutes away from the water no matter where you stay.

**Book-It VI** (☎ Box 1552, Cruz Bay 00831 ☎ 340/693–8261 or 800/416– 1205 ☎ 340/693–8480 ⊕ www.bookitvi.com) handles villas all across St. John. **Caribbean Villas & Resorts** (☎ Box 458, Cruz Bay 00831 ☎ 340/776–6152 or 800/338–0987 ☎ 340/779–4044 ⊕ www. caribbeanvilla.com) handles condo rentals for Cruz Views and Gallow's Point Resort, as well as for many private villas. **Carefree Get-Aways** (☎ Box 1626, Cruz Bay 00831 ☎ 340/779–4070 or 888/643– 6002 ☎ 340/774–6000 ⊕ www.carefreegetaways.com) manages vacation villas on the island's southern and western edges. **Catered to Vacation Homes** (☒ Marketplace Suite 206, 5206 Enighed, Cruz Bay 00830 ☎340/776–6641 or 800/424–6641 ☎340/693–8191 ⊕www.cateredto. com) has luxury homes, mainly mid-island and on the western edge. **Destination St. John** (☎ Box 8306, Cruz Bay 00831 ☎ 340/779–4647 or 800/562–1901 ☎ 340/715–0073 ⊕ www.destinationstjohn.com) manages villas across the island. **Great Caribbean Getaways** (☎ Box 8317, Cruz Bay 00831 ☎ 340/693–8692 or 800/341–2532 ☎ 340/693–9112 ⊕ www.greatcaribbeangetaways.com) handles private villas from Cruz Bay to Coral Bay. **Island Getaways** (☎ Box 1504, Cruz Bay 00831 ☎ 340/693–7676 or 888/693–7676 ☎ 340/693–8923 ⊕ www.islandgetaways.net) has villas in the Great Cruz Bay–Chocolate Hole area, with a few others scattered around the island.

**On-Line Vacations** (☎ Box 9901, Emmaus 00830 ☎ 340/776–6036 or 888-842-6632 ☎ 340/693–5357) books vacation villas around St. John. **Private Homes for Private Vacations** (☒ 8D Carolina, Mamey Peak 00830 ☎☎ 340/776–6876 ⊕ www.privatehomesvi.com) has homes across the island. **Seaview Vacation Homes** (☎ Box 644, Cruz Bay 00831 ☎ 340/

776–6805 or 888/625–2963 🖷 340/779–4349 ⊕ www.seaviewhomes. com) handles homes with sea views in the Chocolate Hole, Great Cruz Bay, and Fish Bay areas. **Star Villas** (🖅 Box 599, Cruz Bay 00830 ☎ 340/776–6704 or 888/897–9759 🖷 340/776–6183 ⊕ www.starvillas. com) has cozy villas just outside Cruz Bay. **Vacation Vistas** (🖅 Box 476, Cruz Bay 00831 ☎ 340/776–6462 ⊕ www.vacationvistas.com) manages villas mainly in the Chocolate Hole, Great Cruz Bay, and Rendezvous areas. **Windspree** (✉ 7924 Emmaus, Cruz Bay 00830 ☎ 340/693–5423 or 888/742–0357 🖷 340/693–5623 ⊕ www.windspree.com) handles villas mainly in the Coral Bay area.

## Where to Eat

The cuisine on St. John seems to get better every year, with culinary-school-trained chefs vying to see who can come up with the most imaginative dishes. There are restaurants to suit every taste and budget—from the elegant establishments at Caneel Bay Resort (where men may be required to wear a jacket at dinner) to the casual in-town eateries of Cruz Bay. For quick lunches, try the West Indian food stands in Cruz Bay Park and across from the post office. The cooks prepare fried chicken legs, pates (meat- and fish-filled pastries), and callaloo.

Some restaurants close for vacation in September and even October. If you have your heart set on a special place, call ahead to make sure it's open during these months.

For approximate costs, *see* the dining and lodging price chart on the U.S. Virgin Islands Planner, at the beginning of this chapter.

### Bordeaux

CONTEMPORARY ✕ **Chateau Bordeaux.** This rustic restaurant with a to-die-for view of Coral
★ **$$$$** Bay is a bit out of the way but worth the trip. Its interior is made elegant with lace tablecloths, glowing candles, and stylish dinner presentations. Start with a bowl of creamy asparagus soup; then segue into seared sea scallops with sautéed spinach, wild mushrooms, and a potato galette or herb-encrusted rack of lamb with roasted corn and a raspberry sauce. Save room for dessert—the fresh berry cups with Chambord and caramel are wonderful. ✉ *Rte. 10, Bordeaux* ☎ *340/776–6611* 🖃 *AE, MC, V* ⊗ *No lunch.*

### Coral Bay & Environs

AMERICAN ✕ **Skinny Legs Bar & Restaurant.** Sailors who live aboard boats anchored
**¢–$** just offshore and an eclectic coterie of residents gather for lunch and
**Fodor'sChoice** dinner at this funky spot in the middle of a boatyard-cum-shopping com-
★ plex. If owner Moe Chabuz is around, take a gander at his gams; you'll see where the restaurant got its name. It's a great place for burgers, fish sandwiches, and whatever sports event is on the satellite TV. ✉ *Rte. 10, Coral Bay* ☎ *340/779–4982* 🖃 *AE, D, MC, V.*

CARIBBEAN ✕ **Pavillion Restaurant.** At the end of a long, partially paved road at Maho
ⵙ **$$–$$$** Bay Camps, this casual open-air restaurant is worth the drive. The menu changes daily, but there's always a handful of seafood, chicken, and vegetarian entrées. Give your order at the counter. While you wait

for it to be cooked—the chef calls your name when it's done—help yourself to the salad bar, rolls, and iced tea included with your dinner. Arrive early to enjoy the spectacular sunset views. ⊠ *Maho Bay Camps, off Rte. 20* ☎ *340/776–6226* ▭ *AE, MC, V* ✆ *No lunch.*

★ **$$** ✕ **Miss Lucy's Restaurant.** Sitting seaside at remote Friis Bay, Miss Lucy's dishes up Caribbean food with a contemporary flair. Dishes like tender conch fritters, a spicy West Indian stew called callaloo, and fried fish make up most of the menu, but you also find a generous pot of seafood, sausage, and chicken paella on the menu. Sunday brunches are legendary, and if you're around on the full moon, stop by for the monthly full-moon party. The handful of small tables near the water are the nicest, but if they're taken or the mosquitoes are bad, the indoor tables do nicely. ⊠ *Rte. 107, Friis Bay* ☎ *340/693–5244* ▭ *AE, D, MC, V* ✆ *Closed Mon. No dinner Sun.*

★ **¢–$** ✕ **Vie's Snack Shack.** Stop by Vie's when you're out exploring the island. Although it's just a shack by the side of the road, Vie's serves up some great cooking. The garlic chicken legs are crisp and tasty, and the conch fritters are really something to write home about. Plump and filled with fresh herbs, a plateful will keep you going for the rest of the afternoon. Save room for a wedge of coconut pie, called a tart in this neck of the woods. When you're done eating, a spectacular white-sand beach across the road beckons. ⊠ *Rte. 10, Hansen Bay* ☎ *340/693–5033* ▭ *No credit cards* ✆ *Closed Sun. and Mon. No dinner.*

ECLECTIC   ✕ **Donkey Diner.** In an odd combination that works well for Coral Bay
**$$–$$$**   visitors and residents, this tiny spot along the main road through Coral Bay sells yummy breakfasts and tasty pizza. Breakfasts can be as ordinary or as innovative as you like, with the menu running from fried eggs with bacon to blueberry pancakes to scrambled tofu served with home fries. Pizzas are equally eclectic, with toppings that include everything from the usual pepperoni and mushrooms to more exotic corn, raisins, and kalamata olives. ⊠ *Rte. 10, Coral Bay* ☎ *340/693–5240* ▭ *No credit cards* ✆ *Closed Mon. and Tues.*

## Cruz Bay & Environs

BARBECUE   ✕ **Uncle Joe's Barbecue.** Juicy ribs and tasty chicken legs dripping with
☾ **$–$$**   the house barbecue sauce make for one of St. John's best dining deals. An ear of corn, rice, and a generous scoop of macaroni salad or coleslaw round out the plate. This casual spot crowds the edge of a busy sidewalk in the heart of Cruz Bay. Even though there are a few open-air tables for dining "in," the ambience is more than a tad on the pedestrian side, so take-out is a better bet. ⊠ *North Shore Rd., across from post office* ☎ *340/693–8806* ▭ *No credit cards.*

CONTEMPORARY   ✕ **Stone Terrace Restaurant.** A delightful harbor view, soft lantern light, and
**$$$–$$$$**   white-linen tablecloths provide the backdrop for chef Aaron Willis's imaginative cuisine. To standards like rack of lamb, he adds a crisp Dijon mustard–onion crust, a few savory carrot gnocchi, and a Stilton cheese cream sauce and rosemary glaze. He jazzes up the salad course with seared tuna sashimi perched on a spinach salad drizzled with a hoisin vinaigrette. The desserts change daily but are always as intriguing as the other courses. ⊠ *Bay St.* ☎ *340/693–9370* ▭ *D, MC, V* ✆ *Closed Mon. No lunch.*

**1**

★ **$$$–$$$$**   ✕**Tage.** Tage gets rave reviews from locals and visitors alike for its imaginative cuisine. The menu isn't large but changes seasonally; look for dishes like pan-seared yellowfin tuna served with salad of pear, fennel, and arugula drizzled with a champagne truffle vinaigrette. Save room for a dessert such as almond and lemon pound cake topped with a passion fruit–caramel sauce. Although you may be tempted to eat outside, resist the urge—it's much quieter indoors. ⊠ *Rte. 104, across from Julius E. Sprauve School* ☎ *340/715–4270* ▤ *AE, D, MC, V* ✆ *Closed Mon. No lunch.*

**$$$**   ✕**Chloe & Bernard's.** With a focus on Asian cuisine, Chloe & Bernard's is always delightful. The menu changes regularly, but you might start with a tasty wasabi-potato pancake or a pea sprout salad drizzled with a sweet chili-lemongrass dressing. Dinner might be marinated tuna served with mandarin fried rice and a lobster-mango summer roll. ⊠ *Westin St. John Resort & Villas, Rte. 104* ☎ *340/693–8000* ▤ *AE, MC, V* ✆ *No lunch.*

**$$–$$$**   ✕**Lime Inn.** Vacationers and mainland transplants who call St. John home flock to this alfresco spot for the congenial hospitality and good food, including all-you-can-eat shrimp on Wednesday nights. Fresh lobster is the specialty, and the menu also includes shrimp-and-steak dishes and such specials as coconut-encrusted chicken breasts with plantains and Thai curry–cream sauce. ⊠ *Lemon Tree Mall, King St.* ☎ *340/776–6425* ▤ *AE, MC, V* ✆ *Closed Sun. No lunch Sat.*

**$$–$$$**   ✕**Morgan's Mango.** A visit to this alfresco eatery requires you to climb a long flight of stairs, but the good food is well worth the effort. Although fish is the specialty—try the voodoo snapper topped with a many-fruit salsa—the chef also creates a vegetarian platter with black beans, fried plantains, salad, and even an ear of corn. ⊠ *North Shore Rd., across from V. I. National Park Visitors Center* ☎ *340/693–8141* ▤ *AE, MC, V* ✆ *No lunch.*

ECLECTIC   ✕**Fish Trap.** The rooms here all open to the breezes and buzz with a mix
♻ **$$–$$$**   of locals and visitors. Chef Aaron Willis, who also presides over the kitchen at Stone Terrace, conjures up such tasty appetizers as conch fritters and fish chowder (a creamy combination of snapper, white wine, paprika, and secret spices). You can always find steak and chicken dishes, as well as an interesting pasta of the day. ⊠ *Bay and Strand Sts., next to Our Lady of Mount Carmel Church* ☎*340/693–9994* ▤*D, MC, V* ✆ *Closed Mon. No lunch.*

♻ **$$–$$$**   ✕**High Tide.** This casual spot right at Cruz Bay Beach serves everything from hamburgers and flying-fish sandwiches to a fish of the day with sauces like mango chutney or island salsa. The kids' menu includes favorites like chicken tenders and grilled cheese sandwiches. ⊠ *Wharfside Village, Strand St.* ☎ *340/714–6169* ▤ *AE, MC, V.*

**$–$$$**   ✕**Inn at Tamarind Court Restaurant.** There's a different chef—each with a unique style—every night, which makes for an eclectic menu. On Monday, schoolteacher Val serves up gyros and spanokapita from her native Greece; Wednesday is sushi night. Other nights feature a varying rotation of chefs, so you might find Thai, West Indian, or down-home American cooking depending on the night you visit. ⊠ *Rte. 104* ☎ *340/776–6378* ▤ *AE, D, MC, V* ✆ *No lunch.*

**$** ✕ **Sun Dog Cafe.** There's an unusual assortment of dishes at this charming alfresco restaurant, which is tucked into a courtyard in the upper reaches of the Mongoose Junction shopping center. Kudos to the white pizza with artichoke hearts, roasted garlic, mozzarella cheese, and capers. The Jamaican jerk chicken sub and the black-bean quesadilla are also good choices. ⊠ *Mongoose Junction, North Shore Rd.* ☎ *340/693–8340* ▱ *AE, MC, V* ☻ *No dinner.*

**¢–$** ✕ **Chilly Billy's.** Although you might stop by this restaurant at lunchtime for a heartburn-inducing St. John Reuben (with turkey, cheese, sauerkraut, and mustard on rye), this restaurant's claim to fame is breakfast. The stuffed French toast is one step this side of heaven: before it's fried, the bread is soaked in a mixture of eggs and Bailey's. If you're not one for morning sweets, try a savory breakfast burrito stuffed with eggs and jalepeño jack cheese. ⊠ *Lumberyard Shopping Center, Boulon Center Rd.* ☎ *340/693–8708* ▱ *MC, V* ☻ *No dinner.*

ITALIAN ✕ **Zozo's Ristorante.** Creative takes on old standards coupled with lovely
**$$$–$$$$** presentation draw the crowds to this restaurant at Gallows Point Re-
Fodor'sChoice sort. Start with crispy fried calamari served with a pesto mayonnaise.
★ The chef dresses up roasted grouper with a pistachio crust and serves it with a warm goat cheese and arugula salad. The grilled veal chop comes with a pancetta and spinach gratin and crisp fried potatoes. The sunset views will take your breath away. ⊠ *Gallows Point Resort, Bay St.* ☎ *340/693–9200* ▱ *AE, MC, V* ☻ *No lunch.*

�映 **$$–$$$** ✕ **Café Roma.** This casual second-floor restaurant in the heart of Cruz Bay is *the* place for traditional Italian cuisine: lasagna, spaghetti and meatballs, and chicken piccata. There are also excellent pizzas, but they are for takeout only. Rum-caramel bread pudding is a dessert specialty. The place can get crowded in the winter season, so show up early. ⊠ *Vesta Gade* ☎ *340/776–6524* ▱ *MC, V* ☻ *No lunch.*

**$$–$$$** ✕ **Panini Beach Trattoria.** Taking its name from the pressed and grilled sandwiches that are a staple here at lunchtime, this cozy seaside bistro serves delightful northern Italian fare. Lunch includes basics like pizza, soup, and salads; the dinner menu includes everything from freshly made pasta to chicken to seafood dishes cooked with herbs and spices. Save room for dessert, because the chocolate panini is heavenly. The dining room is air-conditioned, but the alfresco beachfront tables are the best spots. ⊠ *Wharfside Village, Strand St.* ☎ *340/693–9119* ▱ *AE, MC, V* ☻ *No lunch weekends.*

PAN-ASIAN ✕ **Asolare.** Contemporary Asian cuisine dominates the menu at this el-
★ **$$$$** egant open-air eatery in an old St. John house. Come early and relax over drinks while you enjoy the sunset lighting up the harbor. Start with an appetizer such as pork dumplings served with a glass noodle salad; then move on to entrées such as beef fillet served with roasted haystack potatoes and napa cabbage, or seared tuna served with an orange-and-greens salad. If you still have room for dessert, try the chocolate pyramid, a luscious cake with homemade ice cream melting in the middle. ⊠ *Estate Lindholm, Rte. 20 on Caneel Hill* ☎ *340/779–4747* ▱ *AE, MC, V* ☻ *No lunch.*

# Beaches

St. John is blessed with many beaches, and all of them fall into the good, great, and don't-tell-anyone-else-about-this-place categories. Those along the north shore are all within the national park. Some are more developed than others—and many are crowded on weekends, holidays, and in high season—but by and large they're still pristine. Beaches along the south and eastern shores are quiet and isolated.

**Cinnamon Bay Beach.** This long, sandy beach faces beautiful cays and abuts the national park campground. The facilities are open to the public and include cool showers, toilets, a commissary, and a restaurant. You can rent water-sports equipment here—a good thing, because there's excellent snorkeling off the point to the right; look for the big angelfish and large schools of purple triggerfish. Afternoons on Cinnamon Bay can be windy—a boon for windsurfers but an annoyance for sunbathers—so arrive early to beat the gusts. The Cinnamon Bay hiking trail begins across the road from the beach parking lot; ruins mark the trailhead. There are actually two paths here: a level nature trail (signs along it identify the flora) that loops through the woods and passes an old Danish cemetery, and a steep trail that starts where the road bends past the ruins and heads straight up to Route 10. Restrooms are located on the main path from the commissary to the beach and scattered around the campground. ⊠ *North Shore Rd., Rte. 20, about 4 mi (6 km) east of Cruz Bay.*

**Francis Bay Beach.** Because there's little shade, this beach gets toasty warm in the afternoon when the sun comes around to the west, but the rest of the day, it's a delightful stretch of white sand. The only facilities are a few picnic tables tucked among the trees and a portable bathroom, but folks come here to watch the birds that live in the swampy area behind the beach. The park offers bird-watching hikes here on Sunday morning; sign up at the Visitor's Center in Cruz Bay. To get here, turn left at the Annaberg intersection. ⊠ *North Shore Rd., Rte. 20, ¼ mi from Annaberg intersection.*

**Hawksnest Beach.** Sea-grape and waving palm trees line this narrow beach, and there are restrooms, cooking grills, and a covered shed for picnicking. A patchy reef just offshore near the middle of the beach offers snorkeling an easy swim away, but the best underwater views are reserved for ambitious snorkelers who head farther to the east along the bay's fringes. Watch out for boat traffic—a channel guides dinghies to the beach, but the occasional boater strays into the swim area. It's the closest drivable beach to Cruz Bay, so it's often crowded with locals and visitors. ⊠ *North Shore Rd., Rte. 20, about 2 mi (3 km) east of Cruz Bay.*

**Lameshur Bay Beach.** This sea-grape-fringed beach is toward the end of a very long, partially paved road on the southeast coast. The reward for your long drive is solitude, good snorkeling, and a chance to spy on some pelicans. The beach has a couple of picnic tables, rusting barbecue grills, and a portable restroom. The ruins of the old plantation are a five-minute walk down the road past the beach. The area has good hiking trails, including the trek (more than a mile) up Bordeaux Mountain before an easy walk to Yawzi Point. ⊠ *Off Rte. 107, about 1½ mi from Salt Pond.*

**Maho Bay Beach.** This popular beach is below Maho Bay Camps—a wonderful hillside enclave of tent cabins. The campground offers breakfast and dinner at its Pavillion Restaurant, water-sports equipment rentals at the beach, and restrooms. After a five-minute hike down a long flight of stairs to the beach, snorkelers head off along rocky outcroppings for a look at all manner of colorful fish. Watch for a sea turtle or two to cross your path. Another lovely strip of sand with the same name sits right along the North Shore Road. Turn left at the Annaberg intersection and follow the signs about 1 mi (1½ km) for Maho Bay Camps. ⊠ *Off North Shore Rd., Rte. 20, Maho Bay.*

**Salt Pond Bay Beach.** If you're adventurous, this rocky beach on the scenic southeastern coast—next to Coral Bay and rugged Drunk Bay—is worth exploring. It's a short hike down a hill from the parking lot, and the only facilities are an outhouse and a few picnic tables scattered about. Tide pools are filled with all sorts of marine creatures, and the snorkeling is good, particularly along the bay's edges. A short walk takes you to a salt pond, where salt crystals collect around the edges. Hike farther uphill past cactus gardens to Ram Head for see-forever views. Leave nothing valuable in your car; reports of thefts are common. ⊠ *Rte. 107, about 3 mi south of Coral Bay.*

Fodor'sChoice   **Trunk Bay Beach.** St. John's most-photographed beach is also the preferred
★   spot for beginning snorkelers because of its underwater trail. (Cruise-ship passengers interested in snorkeling for a day flock here, so if you're looking for seclusion, arrive early or later in the day.) Crowded or not, this stunning beach is one of the island's most beautiful. There are changing rooms with showers, bathrooms, a snack bar, picnic tables, a gift shop, phones, lockers, and snorkeling-equipment rentals. The parking lot often overflows, but you can park along the road. ⊠ *North Shore Rd., Rte. 20, about 2½ mi east of Cruz Bay.*

## Sports & the Outdoors

BOATING &   If you're staying at a hotel or campground, your activities desk will usu-
SAILING   ally be able to help you arrange a sailing excursion aboard a nearby boat.
★   Most day sails leaving Cruz Bay head out along St. John's north coast. Those that depart Coral Bay might drop anchor at some remote cay off the island's east end or even in the nearby British Virgin Islands. Your trip usually includes lunch, beverages, and at least one snorkeling stop. Keep in mind that inclement weather could interfere with your plans, though most boats will still go out if rain isn't too heavy. If you're staying in a villa, or if your hotel or campground doesn't have an affiliated charter sailboat, contact **Connections** (⊠ 1 block up from ferry dock, diagonal to First Bank, Cruz Bay ☎ 340/776–6922 ⊠ Skinny Legs Bar & Restaurant, Coral Bay ☎ 340/779–4994 ⊕ www.connectionsstjohn.com). The very capable staff can find a boat that fits your style and pocketbook. The company also books fishing and scuba trips from both its offices.

For a speedier trip to the cays and remote beaches off St. John, you can rent a power boat from **Ocean Runner** (⊠ On the waterfront, Cruz Bay

☎ 340/693–8809 ⊕ www.oceanrunner.vi). The company rents one- and two-engine boats for around $300 to $400 per day. Gas and oil will run you $75 to $250 a day extra, depending on how far you're going. It's a good idea to have some skill with power boats for this self-drive adventure, but if you don't, you can hire a captain to go along to instruct you.

**DIVING & SNORKELING**  Although just about every beach has nice snorkeling—Trunk Bay, Cinnamon Bay, and Waterlemon Cay at Leinster Bay get the most praise— you need a boat to head out to the more remote snorkeling locations and the best scuba spots. Sign on with any of the island's water-sports operators to get to spots farther from St. John. If you use the one at your hotel, just stroll down to the dock to hop aboard. Their boats will take you to hot spots between St. John and St. Thomas, including the tunnels at **Thatch Cay,** the ledges at **Congo Cay,** and the wreck of the *General Rogers.* Dive off St. John at **Stephens Cay,** a short boat ride out of Cruz Bay, where fish swim around the reefs as you float downward. At **Devers Bay,** on St. John's south shore, fish dart about in colorful schools. **Carval Rock,** shaped somewhat like an old-time ship, has gorgeous rock formations, coral gardens, and lots of fish. It can be too rough here in the winter, though. Count on paying $70 for a one-tank dive and $90 for a two-tank dive. Rates include equipment and a tour. If you've never dived before, try an introductory course, called a resort course. Or if certification is in your vacation plans, the island's dive shops can help you get your card.

**Cruz Bay Watersports** (☎ 340/776–6234 ⊕ www.divestjohn.com) has two locations: in Cruz Bay at the Lumberyard Shopping Complex and at the Westin St. John Resort. Owners Marcus and Patty Johnston offer regular reef, wreck, and night dives and USVI and BVI snorkel tours. The company holds both PADI five-star facility and NAUI Dream Resort status. **Low Key Watersports** (☎ 340/693–8999 or 800/835–7718 ⊕ www.divelowkey.com), at Wharfside Village, offers one- and two-tank dives and specialty courses. It's certified as a PADI five-star training facility.

**FISHING**  Well-kept charter boats—approved by the U.S. Coast Guard—head out to the north and south drops or troll along the inshore reefs, depending on the season and what's biting. The captains usually provide bait, drinks, and lunch, but you need to bring your own hat and sunscreen. Fishing charters run between $550 and $700 per half day for the boat. **Capt. Bryon Oliver** (☎ 340/693–8339) takes you out to the north and south drops or closer in to St. John. **Gone Ketchin'** (☎ 340/714–1175 ⊕ www.goneketchin.com), in St. John, arranges trips with old salt Captain Griz.

**HIKING**  Although it's fun to go hiking with a Virgin Islands National Park guide, don't be afraid to head out on your own. To find a hike that suits your ability, stop by the park's visitor center in Cruz Bay and pick up the free trail guide; it details points of interest, dangers, trail lengths, and estimated hiking times. Although the park staff recommends long pants to protect against thorns and insects, most people hike in shorts because it can get very hot. Wear sturdy shoes or hiking boots even if you're hiking to the beach. Don't forget to bring water and insect repellent.

**Fodor'sChoice** The **Virgin Islands National Park** (☎ 340/776–6201 ⊕ www.nps.gov/
★ viis) maintains more than 20 trails on the north and south shores and offers guided hikes along popular routes. A full-day trip to Reef Bay is a must; it's an easy hike through lush and dry forest, past the ruins of an old plantation, and to a sugar factory adjacent to the beach. It can be a bit arduous for young kids, however. Take the public Vitran bus or a taxi to the trailhead, where you can meet a ranger who'll serve as your guide. The park provides a boat ride back to Cruz Bay for $15 to save you the walk back up the mountain. The schedule changes from season to season; call for times and reservations, which are essential.

HORSEBACK    Clip-clop along the island's byways for a slower-pace tour of St. John.
RIDING    **Carolina Corral** (☎ 340/693–5778) offers horseback trips down scenic roads with owner Dana Barlett. She has a way with horses and calms even the most novice riders. Rates start at $65 for a 1½-hour ride.

SAILING    Even novice sailors can take off in a small sailboat from Cruz Bay Beach with **Sail Safaris** (☎ 340/998–1265 or 866/820-6906 ⊕ www.sailsafaris.net) to one of the small islands off St. John. Guided half-day tours, rentals, and lessons each run $70 per person.

SEA KAYAKING    Poke around crystal bays and explore undersea life from a sea kayak. Rates run about $60 for a full day in a double kayak. Tours start at $50 for a half day. On the Cruz Bay side of the island, **Arawak Expeditions** (☎ 340/693–8312 or 800/238–8687 ⊕ www.arawakexp.com), which operates out of Low Key Watersports in Cruz Bay's Wharfside Village, has professional guides who use traditional and sit-on-top kayaks to ply coastal waters. The company also rents single and double kayaks so you can head independently to nearby islands like Stephen's Cay. Explore Coral Bay Harbor and Hurricane Hole on the eastern end of the island in a sea kayak from **Crabby's Watersports** (✉ Rte. 107, outside Coral Bay ☎ 340/714–2415 ⊕ www.crabbyswatersports.com). If you don't want to paddle into the wind to get out of Coral Bay Harbor, the staff will drop you off in Hurricane Hole so you can paddle downwind back to Coral Bay. Crabby's also rents Sunfish sailboats, dinghies, and fishing tackle.

SIGHTSEEING    In St. John, taxi drivers provide tours of the island, making stops at var-
TOURS    ious sites, including Trunk Bay and Annaberg Plantation. Prices run around $15 a person. The taxi drivers congregate near the ferry in Cruz Bay. The dispatcher will find you a driver for your tour.

WALKING TOURS    Along with providing trail maps and brochures about Virgin Islands National Park, the park service also gives several guided tours on- and off-shore. Some are only offered during particular times of the year, and some require reservations. For more information, contact the **V. I. National Park Visitors Center** (✉ Cruz Bay ☎ 340/776–6201 ⊕ www.nps.gov/viis).

WINDSURFING    Steady breezes and expert instruction make learning to windsurf a snap. Try **Cinnamon Bay Campground** (✉ Rte. 20, Cinnamon Bay ☎ 340/693–5902 or 340/626–4769), where rentals are $30 to $70 per hour. Lessons are available right at the waterfront; just look for the Windsurfers stacked up on the beach. The cost for a one-hour lesson starts at $70. You can also rent kayaks.

# Shopping

## Areas & Malls

Luxury goods and handicrafts can be found on St. John. Most shops carry a little of this and a bit of that, so it pays to poke around. The Cruz Bay shopping district runs from **Wharfside Village,** just around the corner from the ferry dock, through the streets of town to North Shore Road and **Mongoose Junction,** an inviting shopping center with stonework walls (its name is a holdover from a time when those furry island creatures gathered at a nearby garbage bin); steps connect the two sections of the center, which has unusual, upscale shops. Out on Route 104, stop in at the **Marketplace** to explore its handful of gift and crafts shops. At the island's other end, there are a few stores—selling clothes, jewelry, and artwork—here and there from the village of **Coral Bay** to the small complex at **Shipwreck Landing.**

On St. John, store hours run from 9 or 10 to 5 or 6. Wharfside Village and Mongoose Junction shops in Cruz Bay are often open into the evening.

## Specialty Items

ART **Bajo el Sol.** Bajo el Sol sells works by owner Livy Hitchcock plus those from a roster of the island's best artists. Shop for oil and acrylics, jewelry, sculptures, and ceramics. ⊠ *Mongoose Junction, North Shore Rd., Cruz Bay* ☎ *340/693–7070.*

**Coconut Coast Studios.** This waterside shop, a five-minute walk from Cruz Bay, showcases the work of Elaine Estern. She specializes in undersea scenes. ⊠ *Frank Bay, Cruz Bay* ☎ *340/776–6944.*

BOOKS **National Park Headquarters.** The headquarters sells several good histories of St. John, including *St. John Back Time,* by Ruth Hull Low and Rafael Lito Valls, and, for linguists, Valls's *What a Pistarckle!*—an explanation of the colloquialisms that make up the local version of English (*pistarckle* is a Dutch Creole word that means "noise" or "din," which pretty much sums up the language here). ⊠ *Cruz Bay* ☎ *340/776–6201.*

CLOTHING **Big Planet Adventure Outfitters.** You knew when you arrived that some place on St. John would cater to the outdoor enthusiasts who hike up and down the island's trails. Well, this outdoor-clothing store is where you can find the popular Naot sandals and Reef footware, along with colorful and durable cotton clothing and accessories by Billabong. The store also sells children's clothes. ⊠ *Mongoose Junction, North Shore Rd., Cruz Bay* ☎ *340/776–6638.*

**Bougainvillea Boutique.** If you want to look as if you stepped out of the pages of the resort-wear spread in an upscale travel magazine, try this store. Owner Susan Stair carries *very* chic men's and women's resort wear, straw hats, leather handbags, and fine gifts. ⊠ *Mongoose Junction, North Shore Rd., Cruz Bay* ☎ *340/693–7190.*

**The Clothing Studio.** Several talented artists put their original designs on clothing for all members of the family. This shop carries T-shirts, beach cover-ups, pants, shorts, and even bathing suits with beautiful hand-painted creations. ✉ *Mongoose Junction, North Shore Rd., Cruz Bay* ☎ *340/776–6585.*

**Jolly Dog.** Stock up on the stuff you forgot to pack at this store. Sarongs in cotton and rayon, beach towels with tropical motifs, and hats and T-shirts sporting the Jolly Dog logo fill the shelves. ✉ *Shipwreck Landing, Rte. 107, Sanders Bay* ☎ *340/693–5333* ✉ *Skinny Legs Shopping Complex, Rte. 10, Coral Bay* ☎ *340/693–5900.*

**Sloop Jones.** It's worth the trip all the way out to the island's east end to shop for made-on-the-premises clothing, pillows, and fabrics by the yard splashed with tropical bright colors. Fabrics are in cotton, linen, and rayon and are supremely comfortable. ✉ *Off Rte. 10, East End* ☎ *340/779–4001.*

**St. John Editions.** Shop here for nifty cotton dresses that go from beach to dinner with a change of shoes and accessories. Owner Molly Soper also carries attractive straw hats and inexpensive jewelry. ✉ *North Shore Rd., Cruz Bay* ☎ *340/693–8444.*

FOODSTUFFS  If you're renting a villa, condo, or cottage and doing your own cooking, there are several good places to shop for food; just be aware that prices are much higher than those at home.

**Love City Mini Mart.** This market doesn't look like much, but it's just about the only place to shop in Coral Bay and has a surprising selection of items. ✉ *Off Rte. 107, Coral Bay* ☎ *340/693–5790.*

**Simple Feast.** You can get great take-out meals here in addition to its rather limited selection of groceries. ✉ *Palm Plaza, Rte. 104, Cruz Bay* ☎ *340/ 714–7989.*

**Starfish Market.** The island's largest store usually has the best selection of meat, fish, and produce. ✉ *The Marketplace, Rte. 104, Cruz Bay* ☎ *340/779–4949.*

GIFTS  **Bamboula.** Owner Jo Sterling travels the Caribbean and the world to find unusual housewares, art, rugs, bedspreads, accessories, shoes, and men's and women's clothes for this multicultural boutique. ✉ *Mongoose Junction, North Shore Rd., Cruz Bay* ☎ *340/693–8699.*

**Best of Both Worlds.** Pricy metal sculptures and attractive artworks hang from this shop's walls; the nicest are small glass decorations shaped like shells and dragonflies. ✉ *Mongoose Junction, North Shore Rd., Cruz Bay* ☎ *340/693–7005.*

**The Canvas Factory.** If you're a true shopper who needs an extra bag to carry home all your treasures, this store offers every kind of tote and carrier imaginable, from simple bags to suitcases with numerous zippered compartments. All are made of canvas, naturally. It also sells great canvas hats. ✉ *Mongoose Junction, North Shore Rd., Cruz Bay* ☎ *340/ 776–6196.*

**Donald Schnell Studio.** In addition to pottery, this place sells unusual hand-blown glass, wind chimes, kaleidoscopes, fanciful fountains, and more. Your purchases can be shipped worldwide. ✉ *Mongoose Junction, North Shore Rd., Cruz Bay* ☎ *340/776–6420.*

**Every Ting.** As its name implies, this store has some of this and a bit of that. Shop for Caribbean music CDs, books, picture frames decorated with shells, and T-shirts with tropical motifs. Residents and visitors also drop by to have a cup of espresso or to use the Internet terminals. ⊠ *Bay St., Cruz Bay* ☎ *340/693–5820.*

**Fabric Mill.** Shop here for women's clothing in tropical brights, as well as place mats, napkins, and batik wraps. Or take home a brilliant-hued bolt from the upholstery-fabric selection. ⊠ *Mongoose Junction, North Shore Rd., Cruz Bay* ☎ *340/776–6194.*

**Mumbo Jumbo.** With what may be the best prices in St. John, this cozy shop carries everything from tropical clothing to stuffed sea creatures to gift items. ⊠ *Skinny Legs Shopping Complex, Rte. 10, Coral Bay* ☎ *340/779–4277.*

**Pink Papaya.** This store is where you can find the well-known work of longtime Virgin Islands resident M. L. Etre, plus a huge collection of one-of-a-kind gifts, including bright tablecloths, unusual trays, dinnerware, and unique tropical jewelry. ⊠ *Lemon Tree Mall, King St., Cruz Bay* ☎ *340/693–8535.*

**Wicker, Wood and Shells.** Shop the second floor of this store for lovely sculptures and other objets d'art, all with a tropical theme. The first floor houses the island's best selection of greeting cards, notepaper, and other interesting gifts to tuck in your suitcase for friends back home. ⊠ *Mongoose Junction, North Shore Rd., Cruz Bay* ☎ *340/776–6909.*

JEWELRY  **Caravan Gallery.** Owner Radha Speer travels the world to find much of the unusual jewelry she sells here. And the more you look, the more you see—folk art, tribal art, and masks for sale cover the walls and tables, making this a great place to browse. ⊠ *Mongoose Junction, North Shore Rd., Cruz Bay* ☎ *340/779–4566.*

**Free Bird Creations.** Head here for special handcrafted jewelry—earrings, bracelets, pendants, chains—as well as the good selection of water-resistant watches for your excursions to the beach. ⊠ *Wharfside Village, Strand St., Cruz Bay* ☎ *340/693–8625.*

**Jewels.** This branch of a St. Thomas store carries emeralds, rubies, diamonds, and other jewels in attractive yellow- and white-gold settings as well as strings of creamy pearls, watches, and other designer jewelry. ⊠ *Mongoose Junction, North Shore Rd., Cruz Bay* ☎ *340/776–6007.*

**R&I Patton Goldsmiths.** Rudy and Irene Patton design most of the lovely silver and gold jewelry displayed in this shop. The rest comes from various designer friends. Sea fans (those large, lacy plants that sway with the ocean's currents) in filigreed silver, lapis lazuli set in gold, starfish and hibiscus pendants in silver or gold, and gold sand-dollar-shape charms and earrings are choice selections. ⊠ *Mongoose Junction, North Shore Rd., Cruz Bay* ☎ *340/776–6548.*

**Verace.** Jewelry from such well-known designers as John Bagley and Patrick Murphy fill the shelves. Murphy's stunning silver sailboats with gems for hulls will catch your attention. ⊠ *Wharfside Village, Strand St., Cruz Bay* ☎ *340/693–7599.*

PHOTO  **Cruz Bay Photo.** Pick up disposable-film cameras, film, and other photo
DEVELOPING  needs, or when your memory card fills up, download your digital pho-

tos to a disk or print them out. Shop here also for good-quality sunglasses, a must for your tropical vacation. ⊠ *Wharfside Village, Strand St., Cruz Bay* ☎ 340/779–4313.

## Nightlife

St. John isn't the place to go for glitter and all-night partying. Still, after-hours Cruz Bay can be a lively little town in which to dine, drink, dance, chat, or flirt. Notices posted on the bulletin board outside the Connections telephone center—up the street from the ferry dock in Cruz Bay—or listings in the island's two small newspapers (the *St. John Sun Times* and *Tradewinds*) will keep you apprised of special events, comedy nights, movies, and the like.

After a sunset drink at **Zozo's Ristorante** (⊠ Gallows Point Resort, Bay St., Cruz Bay ☎ 340/693–9200), up the hill from Cruz Bay, you can stroll around town (much is clustered around the small waterfront park). Many of the young people from the U.S. mainland who live and work on St. John will be out sipping and socializing, too.

**Lizard's Landing** (⊠ Veste Gade, Cruz Bay ☎ 340/776–6065) is the wild and crazy place. Loud music and drinks like the Sunburned Lizard make this Cruz Bay's hottest late-night spot. There's calypso and reggae on Friday night at **Fred's** (⊠ King St., Cruz Bay ☎ 340/776–6363). Young folks like to gather at **Woody's** (⊠ Road up from ferry, across from Subway restaurant, Cruz Bay ☎ 340/779–4625), where sidewalk tables provide a close-up view of Cruz Bay's action.

On the far side of the island, landlubbers and old salts listen to music and swap stories at **Skinny Legs Bar & Restaurant** (⊠ Rte. 10, Coral Bay ☎ 340/779–4982).

As its name implies, **Island Blues** (⊠ Rte. 107, Coral Bay ☎ 340/776–6800) is the hot place to go for music at the eastern end of the island.

## Exploring St. John

St. John is an easy place to explore. One road runs along the north shore, another across the center of the mountains. There are a few roads that branch off here and there, but it's hard to get lost. Pick up a map at the visitor center before you start out, and you'll have no problems. Few residents remember the route numbers, so have your map in hand if you stop to ask for directions. Bring along a swimsuit for stops at some of the most beautiful beaches in the world. You can spend all day or just a couple of hours exploring, but be advised that the roads are narrow and wind up and down steep hills, so don't expect to get anywhere in a hurry. There are lunch spots at Cinnamon Bay and in Coral Bay, or you can do what the locals do—find a secluded spot for a picnic. The grocery stores in Cruz Bay sell Styrofoam coolers just for this purpose.

If you plan to do a lot of touring, renting a car will be cheaper and will give you much more freedom than relying on taxis; on St. John, taxis are shared safari vans, and they are reluctant to go anywhere until they have a full load of passengers. Although you may be tempted by an open-air Suzuki or Jeep, a conventional car can get you just about everywhere on the paved roads, and you'll be able to lock up your valuables. You may be able to share a van or open-air vehicle (called a safari bus) with other passengers on a tour of scenic mountain trails, secret coves, and eerie bush-covered ruins.

*Numbers in the margin correspond to points of interest on the St. John map.*

★ ❻ **Annaberg Plantation.** In the 18th century, sugar plantations dotted the steep hills of this island. Slaves and free Danes and Dutchmen toiled to harvest the cane that was used to create sugar, molasses, and rum for export. Built in the 1780s, the partially restored plantation at Leinster Bay was once an important sugar mill. Though there are no official visiting hours, the National Park Service has regular tours, and some well-informed taxi drivers will show you around. Occasionally you may see a living-history demonstration—someone making johnnycake or weaving baskets. For information on tours and cultural events, contact the St. John National Park Service Visitors Center. ✉ *Leinster Bay Rd., Annaberg* ☎ *340/776–6201* ⊕ *www.nps.gov/viis* ☉ *Daily sunrise–sunset.*

★ ❹ **Bordeaux Mountain.** St. John's highest peak rises to 1,277 feet. Route 10 passes near enough to the top to offer breathtaking views. Don't stray into the road here—cars whiz by at a good clip along this section. Instead, drive nearly to the end of the dirt road that heads off next to the restaurant and gift shop for spectacular views at Picture Point and the trailhead of the hike downhill to Lameshur. Get a trail map from the park service before you start. ✉ *Rte. 10.*

❼ **Catherineberg Ruins.** At this fine example of an 18th-century sugar and rum factory, there's a storage vault beneath the windmill. Across the road, look for the round mill, which was later used to hold water. In the 1733 slave revolt, Catherineberg served as headquarters for the Amina warriors, a tribe of Africans captured into slavery. ✉ *Rte. 10, Catherineberg.*

❺ **Coral Bay.** This laid-back community at the island's dry, eastern end is named for its shape rather than for its underwater life—the word *coral* comes from *krawl*, Dutch for "corral." It's a small, quiet, neighborhoody settlement—a place to get away from it all. You'll need a four-wheel-drive vehicle if you plan to stay at this end of the island, as some of the rental houses are up unpaved roads that wind around the mountain. If you come just for lunch, a regular car will be fine.

❶ **Cruz Bay.** St. John's main town may be compact (it consists of only several blocks), but it's definitely a hub: the ferries from St. Thomas and the BVI pull in here, and it's where you can get a taxi or rent a car to travel around the island. There are plenty of shops in which to browse, a number of watering holes where you can stop for a breather, many restaurants, and a grassy square with benches where you can sit back and take everything in. Look for the current edition of the handy, amusing "St. John Map" featuring Max the Mongoose. To pick up a useful guide to St. John's hiking trails, see various large maps of the island,

and find out about current park service programs, including guided walks and cultural demonstrations, stop by the **V. I. National Park Visitors Center** (⊠ Near the baseball field, Cruz Bay ☎ 340/776–6201 ⊕ www.nps. gov/viis). It's open daily from 8 to 4:30.

**❷ Elaine Ione Sprauve Library and Museum.** On the hill just above Cruz Bay is the Enighed Estate greathouse, built in 1757. *Enighed* is the Danish word for "concord" (unity or peace). The greathouse and its outbuildings (a sugar factory and horse-driven mill) were destroyed by fire and hurricanes, and the house sat in ruins until 1982. Today it houses a library and museum that contains a dusty collection of Indian pottery and colonial artifacts. ⊠ *Rte. 104, make a right past Texaco station, Cruz Bay* ☎ *340/776–6359* ✉ *Free* ⊙ *Weekdays 9–5.*

**❷ Peace Hill.** It's worth stopping at this spot just past the Hawksnest Bay overlook for great views of St. John, St. Thomas, and the BVI. On the flat promontory is an old sugar mill. ⊠ *Off Rte. 20, Denis Bay.*

**★ ❸ Reef Bay Trail.** Although this is one of the most interesting hikes on St. John, unless you're a rugged individualist who wants a physical challenge (and that describes a lot of people who stay on St. John), you can probably get the most out of the trip if you join a hike led by a park service ranger, who can identify the trees and plants on the hike down, fill you in on the history of the Reef Bay Plantation, and tell you about the petroglyphs on the rocks at the bottom of the trail. A side trail takes you to the plantation's greathouse, a gutted but mostly intact structure that maintains vestiges of its former beauty. Take the safari bus from the park's visitor center. A boat takes you from the beach at Reef Bay back to the visitor center, saving you the uphill climb. ⊠ *Rte. 10, Reef Bay* ☎ *340/776–6201 Ext. 238 reservations* ⊕ *www.nps.gov/viis* ✉ *Free, safari bus $5, return boat trip to Cruz Bay $15* ⊙ *Tours at 10 AM, days change seasonally.*

# ST. CROIX

By Lynda Lohr

As my seaplane skimmed St. Croix's north coast on the flight from St. Thomas, the island's agrarian past played out below. Stone windmills left over from the days when sugar ruled stood like sentinels in the fields. As we closed in on Christiansted, the big yellow Fort Christianvaern loomed on the waterfront, and the city's red roofs created a colorful counterpoint to the turquoise harbor. A visit to St. Croix, once a Danish colony, always puts me in touch with my Danish roots (my grandmother was a Poulsen). Indeed, history is so popular in St. Croix that planes are filled with Danish visitors who, like other vacationers, come to sun at the island's powdery beaches, enjoy pampering at the hotels, and dine at interesting restaurants but mainly wish to explore the island's colonial history.

Until 1917 Denmark owned St. Croix and her sister Virgin Islands, an aspect of the island's past that is reflected in street names in the main towns of Christiansted and Frederiksted as well as surnames of many island residents. Those early Danish settlers, as well as those from other

**CLOSE UP**

# Turtles on St. Croix

LIKE CREATURES from the earth's prehistoric past, green, leatherback, and hawksbill turtles crawl ashore during the annual April-to-November turtle nesting season to lay their eggs. They return from their life at sea every two to seven years to the beach where they were born. Since turtles can live for up to 100 years, they may return many times to nest in St. Croix.

The leatherbacks like Sandy Point National Wildlife Refuge and other spots on St. Croix's western end, the hawksbills prefer Buck Island and the East End. Green turtles are also found primarily on the East End.

All are endangered species that face numerous natural and man-made predators. Particularly in the Frederiksted area, dogs and cats prey on the nests and eat the hatchlings.

Occasionally a dog will attack a turtle about to lay its eggs, and cats train their kittens to hunt at turtle nests, creating successive generations of turtle-egg hunters. In addition, turtles have often been hit by fast-moving boats that leave large slices in their shells if they don't kill them outright.

The leatherbacks are the subject of a project by the international group Earthwatch. Each summer, teams arrive at Sandy Point National Wildlife Refuge to ensure that poachers, both natural and human, don't attack the turtles as they crawl up the beach. The teams also relocate nests that are laid in areas prone to erosion. When the eggs hatch, teams stand by to make sure the turtles make it safely to the sea, and scientists tag them so they can monitor their return to St. Croix.

---

European nations, left behind slews of 18th- and 19th-century ruins, all of them worked by slaves brought over on ships from Africa, their descendants, and white indentured servants lured to St. Croix to pay off their debt to society. Some—such as the Christiansted National Historic site, Whim Plantation, the ruins at St. George Village Botanical Garden, the Nature Conservancy's property at Estate Princess, and the ruins at Estate Mount Washington and Judith's Fancy—are open for easy exploration. Others are on private land, but a drive around the island reveals the ruins of 100 plantations here and there on St. Croix's 84 square mi. Their windmills, greathouses, and factories are all that's left of the 224 plantations that once grew sugarcane, tobacco, and other agriculture products at the height of the island's plantation glory.

The downturn began in 1801 when the British occupied the island. Another British occupation in 1807 through 1815, droughts, the demise of the slave trade in 1803, the development of the sugar beet industry in Europe, political upheaval, and a depression sent the island on a downward spiral.

St. Croix never recovered from these blows. The end of slavery in 1848, followed by labor riots, fires, hurricanes, and an earthquake during the last half of the 19th century, brought what was left of the island's economy to its knees. The start of prohibition in 1922 called a halt to the island's rum industry, further crippling the economy. The situation remained dire—so bad that President Herbert Hoover called the territory an "effective poorhouse" during a 1931 visit—until the rise of tourism in the late 1950s and 1960s. With tourism came economic improvements coupled with an influx of residents from other Caribbean islands and the mainland, but St. Croix depends partly on industries like the huge oil refinery outside Frederiksted to provide employment.

Today, suburban subdivisions fill the fields where sugarcane once waved in the tropical breeze. Condominium complexes line the beaches along the north coast outside Christiansted. Homes that are more elaborate dot the rolling hillsides. Modern strip malls and shopping centers sit along major roads, and it's as easy to find a McDonald's as it is Caribbean fare.

Although St. Croix sits definitely in the 21st century, with only a little effort you can easily step back into the island's past.

## Where to Stay

You can find everything from plush resorts to simple beachfront digs in St. Croix. If you sleep in either the Christiansted or Frederiksted area, you'll be closest to shopping, restaurants, and nightlife. Most of the island's other hotels will put you just steps from the beach. St. Croix has several small but special properties that offer personalized service. If you like all the comforts of home, you may prefer to stay in a condominium or villa. Room rates on St. Croix are competitive with those on other islands, and if you travel off-season, you'll find substantially reduced prices. Many properties offer money-saving honeymoon and dive packages. Whether you stay in a hotel, a condominium, or a villa, you'll enjoy up-to-date amenities. Most properties have room TVs, but at some bed-and-breakfasts there might be only one in the common room.

Although a stay right in historic Christiansted may mean putting up with a little urban noise, you probably won't have trouble sleeping. Christiansted rolls up the sidewalks fairly early, and air-conditioners drown out any noise. Solitude is guaranteed at hotels and inns outside Christiansted and those on the outskirts of sleepy Frederiksted.

For approximate costs, *see* the dining and lodging price chart on the U.S. Virgin Islands Planner, at the beginning of this chapter.

### Hotels

CHRISTIANSTED  **Hotel Caravelle.** Near the harbor, at the waterfront end of a pleasant
$–$$  shopping arcade, the Caravelle's in-town location puts you just steps away from shops and restaurants. Rooms are tasteful and tropical, with white walls and floral-print bedspreads and curtains; most have ocean views. A small pool provides a swimming and sunning option. The ever-popular Rum Runners restaurant sits just off the lobby. Although its location provides city conveniences, use your normal prudence when walking back to the hotel at night. ⊠ *44A Queen Cross St., 00820* ☎ *340/773–0687 or 800/524–0410* 🖷 *340/778–7004* ⊕ *www.hotelcaravelle. com* ➪ *43 rooms, 1 suite* ⟁ *Restaurant, refrigerators, cable TV, in-room*

broadband, Wi-Fi, pool, bar, Internet room, meeting room ▭ AE, D,
DC, MC, V ⦿ EP.

**$–$$** ⬚ **Hotel on the Cay.** Hop on the free ferry to reach this casual spot on
an island in the middle of Christiansted Harbor. Although the location sounds a bit inconvenient, the ferry ride takes no time. The captain zips over to the waterfront whenever he sees someone waiting.
Rooms are pleasantly furnished and have harbor views, balconies or
patios, and kitchenettes for times when you don't want to eat at the
hotel's restaurant. In addition to sunning at the small beach and
strolling the lushly planted grounds, you can try windsurfing and
other water sports. Keep an eye out for one of the endangered St. Croix
ground lizards that call the island home. ⊠ *Protestant Cay, Christiansted
00820-4441* ☎ *340/773–2035 or 800/524–2035* ⊟ *340/773–7046*
⊕ *www.hotelonthecay.com* ⤳ *53 rooms* ⟁ *Restaurant, kitchenettes,
cable TV, Wi-Fi, pool, beach, snorkeling, Internet room* ▭ *AE, D, MC,
V* ⦿ *CP.*

**$–$$** ⬚ **Pink Fancy Hotel.** Offering a connection to the island's elegant past,
the venerable hotel is listed on the National Register of Historic Places.
While the building dates from 1780, it did not become a hotel until 1948.
Rooms are furnished with antiques, mahogany furnishings, and Orien-
tal carpets, and lush gardens meander around the fenced-in compound,
creating a comfortable base for folks who like to get out and about. Guests
gather poolside for breakfast and conversation. Although the hotel
shines brightly, its neighborhood is run-down, so take a taxi back after
nighttime excursions. Continental breakfast isn't offered for the least
expensive rooms. ⊠ *27 Prince St., 00820* ☎ *340/773–8460 or 800/524–
2045* ⊟ *340/773–6448* ⊕ *www.pinkfancy.com* ⤳ *12 rooms* ⟁ *Fans,
kitchenettes, cable TV with movies, in-room data ports, no-smoking rooms*
▭ *AE, MC, V* ⦿ *CP.*

**$** ⬚ **King Christian Hotel.** A stay at the King Christian puts you right in
the heart of Christiansted's historic district. Parts of the building date
back to the mid-1700s, but numerous additions and refurbishments have
brought it up to modern standards. Rooms are a bit on the pedestrian
side, but floral spreads and pastel walls brighten things up considerably.
We recommend this hotel for its location. You can hop a ferry to nearby
Protestant Cay for an afternoon at the beach when you tire of the pool.
Out the front door and you're a quick walk to restaurants, shops, and
water-sports excursions. ⊠ *57 King St., Box 24467, 00824-0467* ☎ *340/
773–6330 or 800/524–2012* ⊟ *340/773–9411* ⊕ *www.kingchristian.
com* ⤳ *39 rooms* ⟁ *Fans, some in-room safes, refrigerators, cable TV,
pool, dive shop, boating, fishing, meeting room, car rental* ▭ *AE, D,
MC, V* ⦿ *EP.*

OUTSIDE ⬚ **Carringtons Inn.** Hands-on owners Claudia and Roger Carrington are
CHRISTIANSTED the real reason to stay here, and they conjure up delicious breakfasts—
**$** rum-soaked French toast is a house specialty—dole out advice, and make
Fodor'sChoice you feel right at home. Formerly a private home, the comfy bed-and-
★ breakfast is a 10-minute drive from Christiansted. Each room is different, with a decorating theme that reflects a namesake flower. Wicker
furniture, hand-woven carpets, and balconies in some rooms, colorful

# St. Croix

↑
TO
ST. THOMAS

Cane Bay

Salt River Bay

**28**  **27**

80

**31**  **30**  **32**

Salt River Bay
National Historical Park  **5**

**26**
**4**  **25**
**23**  **2**

Judith's Fancy

75

Hams Bluff

Hams Bay

North Star

Davis Bay

**33**

Blue Mt.

**29**

North... Rd.

Estate Mount
Washington
Plantation  **8**

Annaly

**6** Mt. Eagle

Little Prince

**34**

Rain
Forest

St. Croix Leap

**69**

Midland Rd.

Sunny Isle

**35**

West End
Beaches

**11**

Mahogany Rd.

**72**

Kingshill

**63**

**9**

St. George
Hill

**76**

Frederiksted

**10**

St. George
Village Botanical
Gardens

**70**  **69**

HOVENSA Oil
Refinery ◆

Frederiksted Pier

Carl & Marie
Lawaetz
Museum

**14**

**7** Cruzan Rum Distillery

**36**-**39**

Centerline Rd.

**40**

**12**

**13** Whim Plantation
Museum

Henry E. Rohlsen
Airport

West End
Salt Pond

Melvin H. Evans Hwy.

Cane

**66**

Krause Pt.

Long Pt.
Bay

Long Pt.

```
                    KEY

⛱     Beaches

◥     Dive Sites
🚢    Cruise Ship Terminal

1     Exploring Sights

1     Hotels & Restaurants

🌴    Rain Forest
```

Buck
Island

Buck Island Reef
National Monument

Green
Cay

14 · 15

Tamarind
Reef
Beach

Pull
Pt.

Coakley
Bay

Cramer's
Park

Cottongarden Pt.

Long
Reef

Christiansted
Harbor

16

82

Teague
Bay

Sugarloaf Hill

6

25

23

22

21 · 1 · 8

18

2

Point Udall

Northside
Rd.

9

17 East End Rd.

24

10 · 11

3

Isaacs Bay

19

Princess Estate
Christiansted

1

12

Gallow's
Bay

Prospect
Hill

20

South Side Rd.

60

Grapetree
Bay

Grassy Pt.

Recovery
Hill

Robin
Bay

62

South Side Rd.

Great Pond
Bay

Milord
Pt.

Canegarden
Bay

Manchenil
Bay

**UNITED STATES VIRGIN ISLANDS**

Tortola

ST. THOMAS

ST. JOHN

Distance from St. Thomas to
St. Croix approx. 40 miles

**ST. CROIX**

*Caribbean   Sea*

0                                    2 miles

0                                    3 km

spreads, and sea or pool views create an inviting atmosphere. The hillside suburban location means you need a rental car if you stay. ⊠ *4001 Estate Hermon Hill, Christiansted 00820* ☎ *340/713–0508 or 877/658–0508* 🖷 *340/719–0841* ⊕ *www.carringtonsinn.com* ⟿ *5 rooms* ⚭ *Fans, some kitchenettes, refrigerators, pool, Internet room; no room TVs, no smoking* ☰ *AE, MC, V* ⍓ *BP.*

EAST END
☼ $$$–$$$$

🏨 **The Buccaneer.** Offering a total resort experience just outside of Christiansted, this property has sandy beaches, swimming pools, and extensive sports facilities. A palm-tree-lined main drive leads to the large, pink main building atop a hill; the rest of the resort sprawls over the grounds of a 300-acre former sugar plantation, where shops, restaurants, and guest quarters are scattered about the manicured lawns. Spacious rooms are Mediterranean in style, with tile floors, four-poster beds, massive wardrobes of pale wood, marble baths, and local works of art. Beachside doubloon rooms are the largest and are steps from the beach, but you can be perfectly comfortable no matter where you stay. All rooms are stocked with hair dryers, irons, and a nice selection of toiletries. ⊠ *Rte. 82, Box 25200, Shoys 00824* ☎ *340/712–2100 or 800/255–3881* 🖷 *340/712–2104* ⊕ *www.thebuccaneer.com* ⟿ *138 rooms* ⚭ *4 restaurants, in-room safes, refrigerators, cable TV, Wi-Fi, 18-hole golf course, 8 tennis courts, 2 pools, gym, spa, beach, snorkeling, hiking, bar, shops, children's programs (ages 4–12), Internet room, meeting rooms, no-smoking rooms* ☰ *AE, D, DC, MC, V* ⍓ *BP.*

$$$–$$$$

🏨 **Divi Carina Bay Resort.** An oceanfront location puts most rooms at the Divi Carina Bay Resort close to the beach, though villas are across the road, behind the main building. Because it has the island's only casino and regular evening entertainment, it's your best choice if you enjoy nonstop nightlife. The rooms have rattan and wicker furniture, white-tile floors, sapphire-and-teal linens, and accessories that complement the creamy white walls. Although its location way out on the island's East End puts you a long way from anywhere, the hotel provides a fair amount of activities to keep you busy. If you still have some energy left after dancing the night away, you'll need a car for treks outside the hotel. ⊠ *25 Rte. 60, Estate Turner Hole 00820* ☎ *340/773–9700 or 877/773–9700* 🖷 *340/773–6802* ⊕ *www.divicarina.com* ⟿ *146 rooms, 2 suites, 20 villas* ⚭ *2 restaurants, snack bar, fans, in-room safes, microwaves, refrigerators, cable TV, in-room data ports, Wi-Fi, 2 tennis courts, pool, gym, outdoor hot tub, beach, dock, snorkeling, billiards, 2 bars, casino, video game room, Internet room* ☰ *AE, D, DC, MC, V* ⍓ *EP.*

☼ $$$

🏨 **Chenay Bay Beach Resort.** The beachfront location and complimentary tennis and water-sports equipment (including kayaks) make this resort a real find, particularly for families with active kids. Recent refurbishment projects have upgraded nearly all the rooms, which have ceramic-tile floors, bright peach or yellow walls, rattan furnishings, and front porches. Gravel paths meander among terraced wood or stucco cottages. Other facilities include a large L-shape pool, a protected beach, a picnic area, and a casual restaurant. There's also a shuttle to grocery stores and shopping areas for a reasonable fee. ⊠ *Rte. 82, Green Cay* ✆ *Box 24600, Christiansted 00824* ☎ *340/773–2918 or*

*800/548–4457* ☎ *340/773–6665* ⊕ *www.chenaybay.com* ⤴ *50 rooms* ♨ *Restaurant, picnic area, kitchenettes, cable TV, in-room data ports, Wi-Fi, 2 tennis courts, pool, outdoor hot tub, beach, snorkeling, boating, volleyball, bar, babysitting, children's programs (ages 4–12)* ⊟ *AE, MC, V* ⦿ *EP.*

**$$**  ⊡ **Tamarind Reef Hotel.** Spread out along a small, sandy beach, these motel-like buildings offer casual comfort. Independent travelers who want the option to eat in or out will enjoy the rooms with basic kitchenettes. The spacious modern rooms have rattan furniture, tropical-print fabrics, and either a terrace or a deck with views of St. Croix's sister islands to the north. Snorkelers can explore a nearby reef, but shallow water makes serious swimming difficult. There's a snack bar just off the beach, and the Galleon Restaurant is next door at Green Cay Marina. ⊠ *5001 Tamarind Reef, off Rte. 82, Annas Hope 00820* ☎ *340/773–4455 or 800/619–0014* ☎ *340/773–3989* ⊕ *www.usvi.net/hotel/tamarind* ⤴ *46 rooms* ♨ *Restaurant, refrigerators, cable TV, in-room data ports, pool, snorkeling, meeting rooms, no-smoking rooms* ⊟ *AE, DC, MC, V* ⦿ *CP.*

FREDERIKSTED   ⊡ **Sandcastle on the Beach.** Right on a gorgeous stretch of white beach, **$–$$$** this hotel caters primarily to gay men and lesbians, but anyone is welcome. The hotel has a tropical charm that harks back to a simpler time in the Caribbean; proximity to Frederiksted's interesting dining scene is also a plus. Rooms, which have contemporary decor, tile floors, and bright fabrics, come in several sizes and locations. All have kitchens or kitchenettes, and most have sea views. Packages that include a car and bar privileges are a good value. ⊠ *127 Smithfield, Rte. 71, Frederiksted 00840* ☎ *340/772–1205 or 800/524–2018* ☎ *340/772–1757* ⊕ *www.sandcastleonthebeach.com* ⤴ *8 rooms, 8 suites, 5 villas* ♨ *Restaurant, fans, in-room safes, some kitchens, some kitchenettes, cable TV, in-room VCRs, 2 pools, gym, massage, beach, snorkeling, laundry facilities; meeting room, no room phones, no kids* ⊟ *AE, D, MC, V* ⦿ *CP.*

**$**  ⊡ **Frederiksted Hotel.** The Frederiksted Hotel offers basic but comfortable waterfront rooms in this sleepy town. If you want a laid-back atmosphere steps from a handful of interesting restaurants and a shop or two, it's a decent choice. Rooms along Strand Street have lovely water views; others overlook the pool. Although the area is perfect for strolling during the day, a few streets inland the neighborhood turns seedy, so use caution at night. Lovely beaches are a short drive away. ⊠ *442 Strand St., Frederiksted 00840* ☎☎ *340/772–0500* ☎ *800/595–9519* ⊕ *www. frederikstedhotel.com* ⤴ *40 rooms* ♨ *Restaurant, fans, microwaves, refrigerators, cable TV, pool* ⊟ *AE, D, DC, MC, V.*

NORTH SHORE   ⊡ **Villa Greenleaf.** This spacious B&B is all about the details—four-**$$$** poster beds with elegant duvets, towels folded just so, hand-stenciled **Fodor's Choice** trim on the walls, and gardens tastefully planted. Staying here is like ★ visiting a well-heeled relative who happens to have home in the Caribbean. The house was built in the 1950s but was totally renovated in 2004. Unless you want to spend your days gazing at the lovely view of St. Croix's north shore or relaxing beside the sparkling pool, you'll need a car for trips around the island. ⊠ *Island Center Rd., Montpelier* ⚓ *Box 675, Christiansted, 00821* ☎ *340/719–1958 or 888/282–1001* 🖷 *340/772–5425* ⊕ *www.villagreenleaf.com* 🖙 *6 rooms* ⚱ *Fans, Wi-Fi, pool; some refrigerators, no room phones, no room TVs* ⊟ *AE, D, MC, V* ⦿ *BP.*

**$$–$$$**  🛏 **Palms at Pelican Cove.** A 10-minute drive from Christiansted's interesting shopping and eclectic restaurants, the resort has a gorgeous strand of white sand at its doorstep. A complete lack of amenities for children makes it a bad choice for families, however. The rooms are fresh with floral accents that reflect the tropics. You need a car if you plan to venture beyond the hotel's gates, but the Hibiscus Beach Hotel, next door, gives you a nearby dinner option other than the very good Elizabeth's restaurant. ⊠ *Off Rte. 752, La Grande Princesse 00820* ☎ *340/778–8920 or 800/548–4460* 🖷 *340/778–9218* ⊕ *www.palmsatpelicancove.com* 🖙 *40 rooms* ⚱ *Restaurant, fans, in-room safes, refrigerators, cable TV, in-room data ports, 2 tennis courts, pool, beach, snorkeling, library, Internet room, meeting room* ⊟ *AE, MC, V* ⦿ *EP.*

**$$**  🛏 **Cane Bay Reef Club.** These modestly sized lodgings sit seaside in the peaceful community of Cane Bay. They're perfect for folks who don't need every amenity but want to be right at the water's edge. All the rooms in the two-story buildings have no-frills kitchenettes, the usual rattan furniture with tropical accents, and balconies or porches that put you almost on the beach. You can rent dive gear nearby to explore St. Croix's famous Cane Bay Wall. ⊠ *Rte. 80, Cane Bay* ⚓ *Box 1407, Kingshill 00851* 🖷🖷 *340/778-2966* ☎ *800/253-8534* ⊕ *www.canebay.com* 🖙 *9 units* ⚱ *Restaurant, fans, cable TV, kitchenettes, pool, Internet room* ⊟ *AE, D, DC, MC, V* ⦿ *EP.*

**$$**  🛏 **Carambola Beach Resort.** We like this resort's stellar beachfront setting and peaceful ambience, even though it means overlooking some chipped paint, a cracked tile here and there, and other problems caused by several changes in ownership. Although a total overhaul is promised within the next year or so, it had not yet begun at this writing. Rooms in the 25 two-story red-roof villas are identical except for the view—ocean or garden—and have terra-cotta floors, ceramic lamps, mahogany ceilings and furnishings, and rocking chairs. Each has a patio and a huge bath (shower only). Lushly planted walkways connect the rooms and the hotel's restaurants and pool. ⊠ *Rte. 80, Davis Bay* ⚓ *Box 3031, Kingshill 00851* ☎ *340/778-3800 or 888/503-8760* 🖷 *340/778-1682* 🖙 *151 rooms* ⚱ *3 restaurants, fans, in-room safes, cable TV, in-room data ports, 2 tennis courts, pool, gym, beach, dive shop, snorkeling, Internet room, meeting rooms* ⊟ *AE, D, DC, MC, V* ⦿ *EP.*

**$$**  🛏 **Hibiscus Beach Hotel.** This hotel is right at a lovely beach, which is the best reason to stay here. Rooms, each named for a tropical flower, show obvious wear and tear, but all have roomy balconies and are decorated with brightly colored fabrics. Bathrooms are clean but nondescript—both the shower stalls and the vanity mirrors are on the small side. You'll need a car to get around, as the surrounding neighborhood doesn't encourage walks through its streets. ⊠ *4131 Estate La Grande Princesse, off Rte. 752, La Grande Princesse 00820-4441* ☎ *340/773-4042 or 800/442-0121* 🖷 *340/773-7668* ⊕ *www.hibiscusbeachresort.*

com ↩ *37 rooms* ⚒ *Restaurant, in-room safes, minibars, microwaves, refrigerators, cable TV, in-room data ports, pool, beach, snorkeling, Internet room* ▭ *AE, D, MC, V* ⑭ *CP.*

**$–$$** 🏨 **Inn at Pelican Heights.** If you don't mind renting a car to explore the island, a stay at this comfortable B&B will make you feel as if you are leaving the rest of the world far behind. The buildings ramble over the hillside, providing sea views and a comfortable ambience. Each room is a bit different, though all have typical tropical decor—brightly colored spreads and wicker or rattan furniture. Innkeeper Fred Laue conjures up elaborate breakfasts that might include anything from breakfast lasagna to pancakes with fruit and sausage. You can walk to the spacious beach at Pelican Cove in 10 minutes. If you need a dose of civilization, Christiansted is a 15-minute drive away. ⊠ *Off Rte. 751, 4201 Estate St. John, Christiansted 00820-4491* ☎ *340/713–8022 or 888/ 445–9458* 🖶 *340/713–8526* ⊕ *www.innatpelicanheights.com* ↩ *6 rooms* ⚒ *Fans, kitchenettes, cable TV, pool, Internet room* ▭ *MC, V* ⑭ *BP.*

**FodorsChoice** ★

**$–$$** 🏨 **Villa Margarita.** This quiet retreat is along a tranquil north-shore beach, about 20 minutes from Christiansted's shops and restaurants. It provides a particularly good base if you want to admire the dramatic views of the windswept coast. You'll want to rent a car to explore the island, as the resort's amenities are limited. Units vary in size but come complete with kitchenettes, tropical furnishings, private balconies, and those spectacular views. Swimming in front of the hotel is a bit difficult because of shallow water, but sandy beaches are steps away. The snorkeling nearby is is excellent. ⊠ *Off Rte. 80, Salt River* 🕭 *9024 Salt River, Christiansted 00820* ☎ *340/713–1930 or 866/274–8811* 🖶 *340/719– 3389* ⊕ *www.villamargarita.com* ↩ *3 units* ⚒ *Fans, kitchenettes, refrigerators, cable TV, pool; no room phones, no kids under 17* ▭ *MC, V* ⑭ *EP.*

**$–$$** 🏨 **Waves at Cane Bay.** St. Croix's famed Cane Bay Wall is just offshore from this resort, giving it an enviable location. It's still a good bet for divers, as the hotel will loan you weights and tanks. Although the hotel's stretch of beach is rocky, you can sunbathe at a small patch of sand beside the pool, which has been carved from the coral along the shore. Two peach-and-mint-green buildings house large, balconied rooms decorated with soft pastel prints. Sadly, maintenance has slipped a bit in recent years. The other drawback is the isolation; you definitely need a car if you stay here. ⊠ *Rte. 80, Cane Bay* 🕭 *Box 1749, Kingshill 00851* ☎ *340/778–1805 or 800/545–0603* 🖶 *340/778–4945* ⊕ *www. canebaystcroix.com* ↩ *12 rooms* ⚒ *Restaurant, fans, in-room safes, kitchenettes, cable TV, in-room data ports, pool, dive shop, snorkeling, bar, Internet room; no room phones* ▭ *AE, MC, V* ⑭ *EP.*

## Condominiums & Villas

In addition to several condo and villa complexes, you can also rent a private home—usually for a week or more. Renting a house gives you the convenience of home as well as top-notch amenities. Many have pools, hot tubs, and deluxe furnishings. Most companies meet you at the airport, arrange for a rental car, and provide helpful information.

If you want to be close to the island's restaurants and shopping, look for a villa or condominium in the hills above Christian or on either side of the town. An East End location gets you out of Christiansted's hustle and bustle, but you're still only 15 minutes from town. North Shore locations are lovely, with gorgeous sea views and lots of peace and quiet.

**Caribbean Property Management** (☎ 340/778–8782 or 800/496–7379 ⊕ www.enjoystcroix.com) has villas on the east end. **Rent A Villa** (☎ 800/533–6863 ⊕ www.rentavillavacations.com) specializes in villas on the island's east end. **Vacation St. Croix** (☎ 340/778–0361 or 877/788–0361 ⊕ www.vacationstcroix.com) has villas all around the island.

★ **$$$–$$$$** ⊞ **Villa Madeleine.** If you like privacy and lovely accommodations, we think you'll like Villa Madeline. The two-story units flow downhill from this condominium resort's centerpiece, a West Indian plantation greathouse. Each villa has a full kitchen and a private pool. The decor evokes the property's natural surroundings: rattan furniture with plush cushions, rocking chairs, and, in some, bamboo four-poster beds. Special touches include pink-marble showers and hand-painted floral wall borders. You definitely need a car for sightseeing and dining out. ⊠ *Off Rte. 82, Teague Bay* ⬩ *52 King St., Christiansted 00820* ☎ *340/773–4850 or 800/237–1959* 🖷 *340/773–8989* ⊕ *www.teaguebayproperties. com* 🛏 *43 villas* ⅛ *Fans, kitchens, cable TV, tennis court, 43 pools* ⊟ *AE, MC, V* ⫶⊙⫶ *EP.*

♺ **$$–$$$$** ⊞ **Sugar Beach.** With all the conveniences of home, Sugar Beach has apartments that are immaculate and breezy. Each has a full kitchen and a large patio or balcony with an ocean view; larger units have washers and dryers. Though the exteriors of these condos are drab beige stucco, the interiors are white with tropical furnishings. The pool occupies the ruins of a 250-year-old sugar mill. A lovely beach is just steps away, and Christiansted's conveniences are an easy 10-minute drive. It's one of a string of condominium complexes near a public housing project, so don't walk in the neighborhood at night. ⊠ *Rte. 752, Estate Golden Rock 00820* ☎ *340/773–5345 or 800/524–2049* 🖷 *340/773–1359* ⊕ *www. sugarbeachstcroix.com* 🛏 *46 apartments* ⅛ *Fans, kitchens, cable TV, 2 tennis courts, pool, beach, Internet room, meeting rooms* ⊟ *AE, D, MC, V* ⫶⊙⫶ *EP.*

♺ **$$** ⊞ **Club St. Croix.** Sitting beachfront just outside Christiansted, this modern condominium complex faces a lovely sandy beach. You have easy access to shopping and restaurants in nearby Christiansted, but you need a car to get there. Breezes restaurant provides full meal service if you tire of cooking in your fully equipped kitchen. Spacious condos come in different sizes: studios, one-, and two-bedrooms; all have balconies or patios. Rooms are modern, with rattan furniture and bright accents. The location near public housing doesn't encourage walks through the neighborhood. ⊠ *Rte. 752, Estate Golden Rock 00824* ☎ *340/773–9150 or 800/524–2025* 🖷 *340/778–4009* ⊕ *www.antillesresorts.com* 🛏 *53 apartments* ⅛ *Restaurant, fans, kitchens, cable TV, in-room data ports, Wi-Fi, 3 tennis courts, pool, beach, Internet room* ⊟ *AE, MC, V* ⫶⊙⫶ *EP.*

**🕐 $$ 🏢 Colony Cove.** In a string of condominium complexes, Colony Cove lets you experience comfortable beachfront living. Units all have two bedrooms, two bathrooms, and washer/dryer combos, making it a good choice for families. They have typical tropical furnishings with most furniture made of rattan and wicker. Floors are tile. The neighborhood isn't the best, so don't plan on strolling too far at night. ⊠ *Rte. 752, Estate Golden Rock 00824* ☎ *340/773–1965 or 800/828–0746* ⊕ *www.antillesresorts.com* 🛏 *62 apartments* ⚲ *Fans, kitchens, cable TV, in-room data ports, Wi-Fi, pool, beach* ▭ *AE, MC, V* ❂ *EP.*

WHERE TO CAMP  **⚠ Mount Victory Camp.** A remarkable quietude distinguishes this out-🕐 of-the-way spread on 8 acres in the island's rain forest. If you really want to commune with nature, you'll be hard-pressed to find a better way to do it on St. Croix. Hosts Bruce and Mathilde Wilson are on hand to explain the environment. You sleep in screened-in tent-cottages perched on a raised platform and covered by a roof. Each has a rudimentary outdoor kitchen. The shared, spotlessly clean bathhouse is an easy stroll away. The location feels remote, but a lovely sand beach and the Sunset Grill restaurant are a 2-mi (3-km) drive down the hill. In another 10 minutes you're in Frederiksted. ⚲ *BBQs, flush toilets, drinking water, showers, picnic tables, public telephone* 🛏 *5 tents* ⊠ *Creque Dam Rd., Frederiksted 00841* ☎ *340/772–1651 or 866/772–1651* ⊕ *www.mtvictorycamp.com* ⚲ *Reservations essential* ▭ *No credit cards.*

## Where to Eat

Seven flags have flown over St. Croix, and each has left its legacy in the island's cuisine. You can feast on Italian, French, and American dishes; there are even Chinese and Mexican restaurants in Christiansted. Fresh local seafood is plentiful and always good; wahoo, mahimahi, and conch are most popular. Island chefs often add Caribbean twists to familiar dishes. For a true island experience, stop at a local restaurant for goat stew, curried chicken, or fried pork chops. Regardless of where you eat, your meal will be an informal affair. As is the case everywhere in the Caribbean, prices are higher than you'd pay on the mainland. Some restaurants may close for a week or two in September or October, so if you are traveling during these months it's best to call ahead.

For approximate costs, *see* the dining and lodging price chart on the U.S. Virgin Islands Planner, at the beginning of this chapter.

### Christiansted

CARIBBEAN  **✗ Harvey's.** The dining room is plain, even dowdy, and plastic lace $–$$ tablecloths constitute the sole attempt at decor—but who cares? The food is delicious. Daily specials, such as mouthwatering goat stew and tender whelks in butter, served with big helpings of rice, fungi, and vegetables, are listed on the blackboard. Genial owner Sarah Harvey takes great pride in her kitchen, bustling out from behind the stove to chat and urge you to eat up. ⊠ *11B Company St.* ☎ *340/773–3433* ▭ *No credit cards* ❂ *Closed Sun. No dinner.*

CONTEMPORARY ✕ **Kendricks.** The chef at this open-air restaurant—a longtime favorite
★ **$$$–$$$$** among locals—conjures up creative contemporary cuisine. To start, try
the Alaskan king crab cakes with lemon black-pepper aioli or the warm
chipotle pepper with garlic and onion soup. Move on to the house spe-
cialty: pecan-crusted roast pork loin with ginger mayonnaise. ⊠ 21–32
Company St. ☎ 340/773–9199 ▭ AE, MC, V ⊙ Closed Sun. No
lunch.

★ **$$–$$$$** ✕ **Restaurant Bacchus.** On the chic side, this restaurant is as notable for
its extensive wine list as it is for its food. The menu changes regularly
but often includes favorites like mussels topped with pieces of slab
bacon and served in a fennel broth. Entrées include a crispy duck con-
fit with a mango rum sauce, steak swimming in a mushroom sauce, and
pasta with Parmesan cheese and truffle oil. For dessert, try the rum-
drenched sourdough-bread pudding. ⊠ Queen Cross St., off King St.
☎ 340/692–9922 ▭ AE, D, DC, MC, V ⊙ Closed Mon. No lunch.

★ **$$–$$$$** ✕ **Savant.** Savant is one of those small but special spots that locals love.
The cuisine is a fusion of Mexican, Thai, and Caribbean—an unusual
combination that works surprisingly well. You can find anything from
vegetables in a red curry sauce to enchiladas stuffed with chicken to maple-
teriyaki pork tenderloin coming out of the kitchen. With 20 tables
crammed into the indoor area and small courtyard, this little place can
get crowded. Call early for reservations. ⊠ 4C Hospital St. ☎ 340/713–
8666 ▭ AE, DC, MC, V ⊙ No lunch.

★ ✕ **Rum Runners.** The view is as stellar as the food at this highly popular
☾ **$$–$$$$** local standby. Sitting right on Christiansted Boardwalk, Rum Runners
serves everything, including a to-die-for salad of crispy romaine lettuce
and tender grilled lobster drizzled with a lemongrass vinaigrette. More
hearty fare includes baby back ribs cooked with the restaurant's special spice blend and Guinness stout. ⊠ Hotel Caravelle, 44A Queen Cross
St. ☎ 340/773–6585 ▭ AE, MC, V.

ECLECTIC ✕ **Avocado Pitt.** Locals gather at this Christiansted waterfront spot for
**$** the breakfast and lunch specials as well as for a bit of gossip. Breakfast
runs to stick-to-the ribs dishes like oatmeal and pancakes. Lunches include such dressed-up basics as the Yard Bird on a Bun, a chicken breast
sandwich tarted up with a liberal dose of hot sauce. The yellowfin tuna
sandwich is made from fresh fish and gives a new taste to a standard
lunchtime favorite. ⊠ King Christian Hotel, 59 Kings Wharf ☎ 340/
773–9843 ▭ No credit cards ⊙ No dinner.

¢–$ ✕ **Morning Glory Coffee & Tea.** Stop by this cozy spot in a popular shop-
ping center for light fare. Lunch runs to wraps and sandwiches filled
with veggies, cheeses, and sliced meats. If you can't decide, try the restaurant's famous chicken salad made with walnuts and grapes. For breakfast, the chef cooks up waffles, beignets, croissants, and eggs cooked
any way you like. Smoothies are a house specialty. ⊠ Gallows Bay
Market Pl. ☎ 340/773–6620 ▭ No credit cards ⊙ Closed Sun. No
dinner.

FRENCH ✕ **Café Christine.** A favorite with the professionals who work in down-
★ **$–$$** town Christiansted, Café Christine's presentation is as lovely as the food.
The small menu changes daily, but look for dishes like a shrimp salad

drizzled with a lovely vinaigrette dressing or a vegetarian plate with quiche, salad, and lentils. Desserts are perfection. If the pear pie topped with chocolate is on the menu, don't hesitate. This tiny restaurant has both air-conditioned indoor tables and an outside porch that overlooks historic buildings. ⊠ *Apothecary Hall Courtyard, 4 Company St.* ☎ *340/713–1500* ⊟ *No credit cards* ⊗ *Closed weekends. No dinner.*

ITALIAN
$$–$$$$

✕ **Tutto Bene.** Its muraled walls, brightly striped cushions, and painted trompe-l'oeil tables make Tutto Bene look more like a sophisticated Mexican cantina than an Italian cucina. One bite of the food, however, will clear up any confusion. Written on hanging mirrors is the daily menu, which includes such specialties as veal saltimbocca, a scallopine of veal with prosciutto and sage, all topped with mozzarella and parmesan cheeses. Desserts, including a decadent tiramisu, are on the menu as well. ⊠ *Hospital St. in Boardwalk shopping center* ☎ *340/773–5229* ⊗ *No lunch* ⊟ *AE, MC, V.*

## Outside Christiansted

ECLECTIC
⟲ $$–$$$

✕ **Breezez.** This aptly named restaurant is poolside at Club St. Croix condominiums. Visitors and locals are drawn by its reasonable prices and good food. This is *the* place on the island to be for Sunday brunch, where the menu includes Caesar salad, burgers, and blackened prime rib with Cajun seasonings and horseradish sauce. For dessert, try the flourless chocolate torte—a wedge of rich chocolate served with a river of chocolate sauce. ⊠ *Club St. Croix, 3220 Golden Rock, off Rte. 752, Golden Rock* ☎ *340/773–7077* ⊟ *AE, D, MC, V.*

$$–$$$

✕ **Elizabeth's.** In the Palms at Pelican Cove resort, this small restaurant has surprisingly imaginative food. Dinner entrées include a tasty ravioli served with mussels, scallops, and shrimp in a sherry cream sauce and tilapia stuffed with crab. Lunch brings out lots of locals for the generous helping of curried chicken salad and a crab cake wrapped in a flavorful tortilla. The piquant horseradish sauce adds a tasty touch. ⊠ *Palms at Pelican Cove, Off Rte. 752, La Grande Princesse* ☎ *340/719–0735* ⊗ *No lunch weekends* ⊟ *AE, D, MC, V.*

## East End

AMERICAN–
CASUAL
⟲ $–$$

✕ **Cheeseburgers in Paradise.** A perennial favorite with local and visiting families, this open-air restaurant in the middle of a field serves up terrific ribs smothered in a spicy house sauce, burgers with toppings that run from mushrooms to fried onions, and, of course, cheeseburgers. There's room for kids to run around before dinner. ⊠ *Rte. 82, Southgate* ☎ *340/773–1119* ⊟ *MC, V.*

ECLECTIC
$$$–$$$$

✕ **The Galleon.** This popular dockside restaurant is always busy. Start with the Caesar salad or perhaps a flaky layered duck napolean. The chef's signature dish is a tender filet mignon topped with fresh local lobster. Pasta lovers should sample the penne with smoked chicken, roasted red peppers, portobello mushrooms, and a smoked garlic cream sauce. Take Route 82 out of Christiansted; then turn left at the sign for Green Cay Marina. ⊠ *Annas Hope* ☎ *340/773–9949* ⊟ *MC, V.*

$$–$$$

✕ **South Shore Cafe.** This casual bistro, popular with locals for its good food, sits near the Great Salt Pond on the island's south shore. The restaurant's menu includes dishes drawn from several different cuisines. Meat lovers and vegetarians can find common ground with a menu that ranges from handmade pasta to prime rib. The selection isn't extensive, but the chef puts together a blackboard full of specials every day. ✉ *Southside Rd. near Great Pond* ☎ *340/773–9311* ▭ *V* ☉ *Closed Mon.–Wed. No lunch.*

## Frederiksted

ECLECTIC
$$–$$$

✕ **Blue Moon.** This terrific little bistro, which has a loyal local following, offers a changing menu that draws on Cajun and Caribbean flavors. Try the spicy gumbo with andouille sausage or crab cakes with a spicy aioli as an appetizer; shrimp scampi loaded with garlic and served over pasta as an entrée; and the Almond Joy sundae for dessert. There's live jazz on Fridays. ✉ *7 Strand St.* ☎ *340/772–2222* ▭ *AE, D, MC, V* ☉ *Closed Mon.*

♺ ¢–$

✕ **Turtles Deli.** Eat outside at this tiny spot just as you enter downtown Frederiksted. Lunches are as basic as a corned beef on rye or as imaginative as "The Raven" (turkey breast with bacon, tomato, and melted cheddar cheese on French bread). Also good is "The Beast," named after the grueling hill that challenges bikers in the annual triathlon. It is piled high with hot roast beef, raw onion, and melted Swiss cheese with horseradish and mayonnaise. Early risers stop by for cinnamon buns and espresso. ✉ *37 Strand St., at Prince Passage* ☎ *340/772–3676* ▭ *No credit cards* ☉ *Closed Sun. No dinner.*

FRENCH
$$–$$$$

✕ **Le St. Tropez.** A ceramic-tile bar and soft lighting set the mood at this Mediterranean-style bistro tucked into a courtyard one street from the waterfront. Seated either inside or on the adjoining patio, you can enjoy grilled meats in delicate sauces. The menu changes daily, often taking advantage of local seafood. The fresh basil, tomato, and mozzarella salad is heavenly. ✉ *227 King St.* ☎ *340/772–3000* ▭ *AE, MC, V* ☉ *Closed Sun. No lunch Sat.*

## Outside Frederiksted

♺ $$–$$$

✕ **Sunset Grill.** As you would expect, this alfresco restaurant is a hot spot for sunset watchers, as well as a social hub for locals. The ever-changing menu features fish, fish, and more fish. Try the almond-crusted grouper in a soy-butter sauce or whatever else the chef whipped up that day. Those who aren't fond of fish can pick from dishes like a rib-eye steak for dinner; on the lunch menu is a buffalo burger. Desserts might include fresh blueberries and strawberries in a rum sauce. ✉ *Rte. 63* ☎ *340/772–5855* ▭ *MC, V* ☉ *Closed Mon.*

## North Shore

ECLECTIC
$–$$
Fodor'sChoice
★

✕ **Off the Wall.** Divers fresh from a plunge at the north shore's popular Cane Bay Wall gather at this breezy spot on the beach. If you want to sit a spell before you order, a hammock beckons. Burgers, quesadillas, and steak sandwiches make up most of the menu. The potato salad that comes with your sandwich is as good as you'd get at home. You might find blues and jazz Tuesday through Sunday nights. ✉ *Rte. 80, Cane Bay* ☎ *340/778–4771* ▭ *AE, MC, V.*

## Beaches

★ **Buck Island.** A visit to this island beach, part of Buck Island Reef National Monument, is a must. The beach is beautiful, but its finest treasures are those you can see when you plop off the boat and adjust your mask, snorkel, and fins to swim over colorful coral and darting fish. To get here you have to charter a boat or go on an organized trip. Don't know how to snorkel? No problem—the boat crew will have you outfitted and in the water in no time. Take care not to step on those black-pointed spiny sea urchins or touch the mustard-color fire coral, which can cause a nasty burn. Most charter boat trips start with a snorkel over the lovely reef before a stop at the island's beach. An easy 20-minute hike leads uphill to an overlook for a bird's-eye view of the reef below. Find restrooms at the beach. Buck Island is 5 mi (8 km) north of St. Croix.

**Cane Bay.** The waters aren't always gentle at this breezy north-shore beach, but there are seldom many people around, and the scuba diving and snorkeling are wondrous. You can see elkhorn and brain corals, and less than 200 yards out is the drop-off called Cane Bay Wall. Cane Bay can be an all-day destination. You can rent kayaks and snorkeling and scuba gear at water-sports shops across the road, and a couple of very casual restaurants beckon when the sun gets too high. The Waves at Cane Bay sits seaside nearby, as do other restaurants, but the beach has no public restrooms. ⊠ *Rte. 80, about 4 mi (6 km) west of Salt River.*

**West End Beaches.** There are several unnamed beaches along the coast road north of Frederiksted, but it's best if you don't stray too far from civilization. For safety's sake, most vacationers plop down their towel near one of the very casual restaurants spread out along Route 63. The beachfront Sunset Grill makes a nice spot for lunch. The beach at the Rainbow Beach Club, a five-minute drive outside Frederiksted, has a bar, a casual restaurant, water sports, and volleyball. If you want to be close to the cruise-ship pier, just stroll on over to the adjacent sandy beach in front of Fort Frederik. On the way south out of Frederiksted, the stretch near Sandcastle on the Beach hotel is also lovely. ⊠ *Rte. 63, north and south of Frederiksted.*

## Sports & the Outdoors

BOAT TOURS  Almost everyone takes a day trip to Buck Island aboard a charter boat. Most leave from the Christiansted waterfront or from Green Cay Marina and stop for a snorkel at the island's eastern end before dropping anchor off a gorgeous sandy beach for a swim, a hike, and lunch. Sailboats can often stop right at the beach; a larger boat might have to anchor offshore a bit farther. A full-day sail runs about $75 with lunch included on most trips. A half-day sail costs about $50. **Big Beard's Adventure Tours** (☎ 340/773–4482 ⊕ www.bigbeards.com) takes you on a catamaran, the *Renegade* or the *Flyer,* from the Christiansted waterfront to Buck Island for snorkeling before dropping anchor at a private beach for a barbecue lunch. **Caribbean Sea Adventures** (☎ 340/773–2628 ⊕ www.caribbeanseadventures.com) departs from the Christiansted waterfront for half- and full-day trips on various boats. The

**Teroro Charters** (☎ 340/773–3161 ⊕ www.visitstcroix.com/captainheinz. html) trimaran *Teroro II* leaves Green Cay Marina for full- or half-day sails. Bring your own lunch.

DIVING &
SNORKELING

At **Buck Island,** a short boat ride from Christiansted or Green Cay Marina, the reef is so nice that it's been named a national monument. You can dive right off the beach at **Cane Bay,** which has a spectacular drop-off called the Cane Bay Wall. Dive operators also do boat trips along the Wall, usually leaving from Salt River or Christiansted. **Frederiksted Pier** is home to a colony of sea horses, creatures seldom seen in the waters off the Virgin Islands. At **Green Cay,** just outside Green Cay Marina in the east end, you can see colorful fish swimming around the reefs and rocks. Two exceptional north-shore sites are **North Star** and **Salt River,** which you can reach only by boat. At Salt River you can float downward through a canyon filled with colorful fish and coral.

The island's dive shops take you out for one- or two-tank dives. Plan to pay about $65 for a one-tank dive and $85 for a two-tank dive, including equipment and an underwater tour. All companies offer certification and introductory courses called resort dives for novices.

Which dive outfit you pick usually depends on where you're staying. Your hotel may have one on-site. If not, others are located close by. If you use the hotel's dive operation, you're just a short stroll away from the dock. Where the dive boat goes on a particular day depends on the weather, but in any case, all St. Croix's dive sites are special. All shops are affiliated with PADI, the Professional Association of Diving Instructors.

If you're staying in Christiansted, **Dive Experience** (⊠ 1111 Strand St., Christiansted ☎ 340/773–3307 or 800/235–9047 ⊕ www.divexp.com) has PADI five-star status and runs trips to the north-shore walls and reefs in addition to offering the usual certification and introductory classes. **St. Croix Ultimate Bluewater Adventures** (⊠ Queen Cross St., Christiansted ☎ 340/773–5994 or 877/567–1367 ⊕ www.stcroixscuba.com) can take you to your choice of more than 75 sites; it also offers a variety of packages that include hotel stays.

Folks staying in the Judith's Fancy area are closest to **Anchor Dive Center** (⊠ Salt River Marina, Rte. 801, Salt River ☎ 340/778–1522 or 800/532–3482 ⊕ www.anchordivestcroix.com). The company also has facilities at the Buccaneer and Carambola Beach Resort. Anchor takes divers to more than 35 sites, including the wall at Salt River Canyon.

**Cane Bay Dive Shop** (⊠ Rte. 80, Cane Bay ☎ 340/773–9913 or 800/338–3843 ⊕ www.canebayscuba.com) is the place to go if you want to do a beach dive or boat dive along the north shore. The famed Cane Bay Wall is 150 yards from the five-star PADI facility. This company also has shops at Pan Am Pavilion in Christiansted, on Strand Street in Frederiksted, and at the Divi Carina Bay hotel.

In Frederiksted, **Scuba Shack** (⊠ Frederiksted Beach, Rte. 631, Frederiksted ☎ 340/772–3483 or 888/789–3483 ⊕ www.stcroixscubashack.com) takes divers right off the beach near the Changes in Latitude restaurant, on night dives off the Frederiksted Pier, or on boat trips to wrecks and

1

reefs. **Scuba West** (⊠ 330 Strand St., Frederiksted ☎ 340/772–3701 or 800/352–0107 ⊕ www.divescubawest.com) runs trips to reefs and wrecks from its base in Frederiksted but specializes in showing divers the sea horses that live around the Frederiksted Pier.

FISHING  Since the early 1980s, some 20 world records—many for blue marlin—have been set in these waters. Sailfish, skipjack, bonito, tuna (allison, blackfin, and yellowfin), and wahoo are abundant. A charter runs about $100 an hour per person, with most boats going out for four-, six- or eight-hour trips. **Caribbean Sea Adventures** (⊠ 59 Kings Wharf, Christiansted ☎ 340/773–2628 ⊕ www.caribbeanseaadventures.com) will take you out on a 38-foot powerboat called the *Fantasy*.

GOLF  St. Croix's courses welcome you with spectacular vistas and well-kept greens. Check with your hotel or the tourist board to determine when major celebrity tournaments will be held. There's often an opportunity to play with the pros. The **Buccaneer** (⊠ Rte. 82, Shoys ☎ 340/712–2144 ⊕ www.thebuccaneer.com) has an 18-hole course that is close to Christiansted and is the centerpiece of the Buccaneer Hotel. Greens fees are $92, not including $18 for a cart rental. The spectacular 18-hole course
★  at **Carambola Golf Club** (⊠ Rte. 80, Davis Bay ☎ 340/778–5638 ⊕ www.golfcarambola.com), in the northwest valley, was designed by Robert Trent Jones, Sr. It sits near Carambola Beach Resort. Greens fees are $79 for 18 holes, which includes the use of a golf cart. The **Reef Golf Course** (⊠ Teague Bay ☎ 340/773–8844), a public course on the island's east end, has 9 holes. Greens fees are $18, and cart rental is $10.

HIKING  Although you can set off by yourself on a hike through a rain forest or along a shore, a guide will point out what's important and tell you why. **Ay-Ay Eco Hike & Tours Association** (⊕ Box 2435, Kingshill 00851 ☎ 340/772–4079), run by Ras Lumumba Corriette, takes hikers up hill and down dale in some of St. Croix's most remote places, including the rain forest and Mount Victory. Some hikes include stops at places like the Carl and Marie Lawaetz Museum and old ruins. The cost is $40 to $50 per person for a three- or four-hour hike. There's a three-person minimum. A jeep tour through the rain forest runs $100 per person.

HORSEBACK RIDING  Well-kept roads and expert guides make horseback riding on St. Croix pleasurable. At Sprat Hall, just north of Frederiksted, Jill Hurd runs **Paul & Jill's Equestrian Stables** (⊠ Rte. 58, Frederiksted ☎ 340/772–2880 or 340/772–2627 ⊕ pws.prserv.net/paul-and-jills). She will take you clip-clopping through the rain forest, across the pastures, along the beaches, and over the hilltops—explaining the flora, fauna, and ruins on the way. A 1½-hour ride costs $60.

KAYAKING  **Caribbean Adventure Tours** (⊠ Columbus Cove Marina, Rte. 80, Salt River
Fodor'sChoice  ☎ 340/778–1522 ⊕ www.stcroixkayak.com) takes you on trips through
★  Salt River Bay National Historical Park and Ecological Preserve, one of the island's most pristine areas. All tours run $45. **Virgin Kayak Tours** (⊠ Rte. 80, Cane Bay ☎ 340/778–0071 ⊕ www.kayakstcroix.com) runs guided kayak trips through the Salt River and also rents kayaks so you can tour around the Cane Bay area by yourself. All tours run $45. Kayak rentals are $15 an hour or $40 for the entire day.

SIGHTSEEING TOURS **St. Croix Safari Tours** (☎ 340/773–6700 ⊕ www.gotostcroix.com/safaritours) offers van tours of St. Croix. Tours depart from Christiansted and last about five hours. Costs run from $25 per person plus admission fees to attractions. **St. Croix Transit** (☎ 340/772–3333) offers van tours of St. Croix. Tours depart from Carambola Beach Resort, last about three hours, and cost from $35 per person plus admission fees to attractions.

TENNIS The public courts in Frederiksted and out east at Cramer Park are in questionable shape. It's better to pay a fee and play at one of the hotel courts. Costs vary by resort, but count on paying up to $8 an hour per person. The **Buccaneer** (✉ Rte. 82, Shoys ☎ 340/773–2100) has eight courts (two lighted), plus a pro and a full tennis shop. **Carambola Beach Resort** (✉ Rte. 80, Davis Bay ☎ 340/778–3800) has four lighted courts. **Chenay Bay Beach Resort** (✉ Rte. 82, Green Cay ☎ 340/773–2918) has two lighted courts. **Club St. Croix** (✉ Rte. 752, Estate Golden Rock ☎ 340/773–4800) has two lighted courts.

WINDSURFING St. Croix's trade winds make windsurfing a breeze. Most hotels rent Windsurfers and other water-sports equipment to nonguests. **St. Croix Watersports** (✉ Hotel on the Cay, Protestant Cay, Christiansted ☎ 340/773–7060 ⊕ www.stcroixwatersports.com) offers Windsurfer rentals, sales, and rides; parasailing; and water-sports equipment such as kayaks. Renting a Windsurfer runs about $25 an hour.

## Shopping

### Areas & Malls

Although the shopping on St. Croix isn't as varied or extensive as that on St. Thomas, the island does have several small stores with unusual merchandise. In Christiansted the best shopping areas are the **Pan Am Pavilion** and **Caravelle Arcade**, off Strand Street, and along **King** and **Company streets.** These streets give way to arcades filled with boutiques. **Gallows Bay** has a blossoming shopping area in a quiet neighborhood. St. Croix shop hours are usually Monday through Saturday 9 to 5, but there are some shops in Christiansted open in the evening. Stores are often closed on Sunday.

The best shopping in Frederiksted is along **Strand Street** and in the side streets and alleyways that connect it with **King Street.** Most stores close Sunday except when a cruise ship is in port. One caveat: Frederiksted has a reputation for muggings, so for safety's sake stick to populated areas of Strand and King streets, where there are few—if any—problems.

### Specialty Items

ART **Maria Henle Studio.** Stunning paintings by Maria Henle hang on the walls, but you can also find prints by her father, the late Fritz Henle. He was an acclaimed St. Croix photographer, whose works chronicle St. Croix's recent history. ✉ *55 Company St., Christiansted* ☎ *340/773–7376.*

BOOKS **Undercover Books.** For Caribbean books or the latest good read, try this bookstore across from the post office in the Gallows Bay shopping area. ✉ *5030 Anchor Way, Gallows Bay* ☎ *340/719–1567.*

**1**

CLOTHING

FodorsChoice
★

**Coconut Vine.** Pop into this store at the start of your vacation, and you'll leave with enough comfy cotton or rayon batik men's and women's clothes to make you look like a local. Although the tropical designs and colors originated in Indonesia, they're perfect for the Caribbean. ✉ *1111 Strand St., Christiansted* ☎ *340/773–1991.*

**From the Gecko.** Come here for the hippest clothes on St. Croix, including superb hand-painted sarongs and other items. ✉ *1233 Queen Cross St., Christiansted* ☎ *340/778–9433.*

**Hot Heads.** Hats, hats, and more hats perch on top of cotton shifts, comfortable shirts, and other tropical wear at this small store. If you forgot your bathing suit, this store has a good selection. ✉ *Kings Alley Walk, Christiansted* ☎ *340/773–7888.*

**Pacificotton.** Round out your tropical wardrobe with something from this store. Shifts, tops, and pants in sherbet colors as well as bags and hats fill the racks. ✉ *1110 Strand St., Christiansted* ☎ *340/773–2125.*

FOODSTUFFS

If you've rented a condominium or a villa, you'll appreciate St. Croix's excellent stateside-style supermarkets. Fresh vegetables, fruits, and meats arrive frequently. Try the open-air stands strung out along Route 70 for island produce.

**Cost-U-Less.** This warehouse-type store across from Sunshine Mall doesn't charge a membership fee. It's east of Sunny Isle Shopping Center. ✉ *Rte. 70, Sunny Isle* ☎ *340/719–4442.*

**Plaza Extra.** Shop here for Middle Eastern foods in addition to the usual grocery-store items. ✉ *United Shopping Plaza, Rte. 70, Sion Farm* ☎ *340/778–6240* ✉ *Rte. 70, Mount Pleasant* ☎ *340/719–1870.*

**Pueblo.** This stateside-style market has branches all over the island. ✉ *Orange Grove Shopping Center, Rte. 75, Christiansted* ☎ *340/773–0118* ✉ *Villa La Reine Shopping Center, Rte. 75, La Reine* ☎ *340/778–1272.*

**Schooner Bay Market.** Although it's on the smallish side, Schooner Bay has good-quality deli items. ✉ *Rte. 82, Mount Welcome* ☎ *340/773–3232.*

GIFTS

**Gone Tropical.** Whether you're looking for inexpensive souvenirs of your trip or a special, singular gift, you can probably find it here. On her travels about the world, Margo Meacham keeps her eye out for special delights for her shop—from tablecloths and napkins in bright Caribbean colors to carefully crafted wooden birds. ✉ *5 Company St., Christiansted* ☎ *340/773–4696.*

**Island Webe.** The coffees, jams, and spices—produced on St. Croix and elsewhere in the Caribbean—will tempt your taste buds. Small *mocko jumbie* dolls depict an African tradition transported to the islands during slave days (they represent the souls of the ancestors of African slaves). The fabric dolls wearing Caribbean costumes will delight kids of all ages. Turn the double dolls upside down to see a white face on one side and a black one on the other. ✉ *210 Strand St., Frederiksted* ☎ *340/772–2555.*

**Many Hands.** Pottery in cool and bright colors, paintings of St. Croix and the Caribbean, prints, and maps—all made by local artists—make perfect take-home gifts. The owners ship all over the world if your purchase is too cumbersome to carry. ✉ *21 Pan Am Pavilion, Strand St., Christiansted* ☎ *340/773–1990.*

**Mitchell-Larsen Studio.** Carefully crafted glass plates, sun-catchers, and more grace the shelves of this interesting store. All made on-site by two St. Croix glassmakers, the pieces are often whimsically adorned with tropical fish, flora, and fauna. ✉ *58 Company St., Christiansted* ☎ *340/719–1000.*

**Fodor's Choice**
★ **Royal Poinciana.** This attractive shop is filled with island seasonings and hot sauces, West Indian crafts, bath gels, and herbal teas. Shop here for tablecloths and paper goods in tropical brights. ✉ *1111 Strand St., Christiansted* ☎ *340/773–9892.*

**Tesoro.** The colors are bold and the merchandise eclectic at this crowded store. Shop for metal sculpture made from retired steel pans, mahogany bowls, and hand-painted place mats in bright tropical colors. ✉ *36C Strand St., Christiansted* ☎ *340/773–1212.*

**Tradewinds Shop.** Whatever the wind blew in seems to land here. Glass sailboats glide across the shelves while metal fish sculptures swim nearby. Candles with tropical motifs, note cards, and costume jewelry jostle for space with Naot sandals. ✉ *53 King St., Christiansted* ☎ *340/719–3918.*

HOUSEWARES **St. Croix Landmarks Museum Store.** If a mahogany armoire or cane-back rocker catches your fancy, the staff will arrange to have it shipped to your mainland home at no charge from its mainland warehouse. Furniture aside, this store has one of the largest selections of local art along with Caribbean-inspired bric-a-brac in all price ranges. ✉ *6 Company St., Christiansted* ☎ *340/713–8102.*

**Up Island Home.** While home decor is the focus—look for Asian-inspired rugs, plush pillows, and other items that give your home a tropical look—the store also carries cute accessories and gift items, like shell-encrusted candles and soaps in exotic scents. ✉ *Hospital St., Christiansted* ☎ *340/692–9867.*

JEWELRY **Crucian Gold.** This store carries the unique gold creations of St. Croix native Brian Bishop. His trademark piece is the Turk's Head ring (a knot of interwoven gold strands), but the chess sets with Caribbean motifs as the playing pieces are just lovely. ✉ *59 Kings Wharf, Christiansted* ☎ *340/773–5241.*

**Nelthropp and Low.** Specializing—of course—in gold jewelry, this store also carries diamonds, emeralds, rubies, and sapphires. Jewelers will create one-of-a-kind pieces to your design. ✉ *1102 Strand St., Christiansted* ☎ *340/773–0365 or 800/416–9078.*

**Gold Worker.** In silver and gold, the hand-crafted jewelry at this tiny store will remind you of the Caribbean. Hummingbirds dangle from silver chains, and sand dollars adorn gold necklaces. The sugar mills in silver and gold speak of St. Croix's past. ✉ *3 Company St., Christiansted* ☎ *340/773–5167.*

**Karavan West Indies.** An assortment of tchotchkes, including handmade Christmas ornaments, and silver and gold jewelry fill the shelves at this eclectic shop. ✉ *5030 Anchor Way, Gallows Bay* ☎ *340/773–9999.*

**Sonya's.** Sonya Hough invented the hook bracelet, popular among locals as well as visitors. With hurricanes hitting the island so frequently, she has added an interesting decoration to these bracelets: the swirling symbol used in weather forecasts to indicate these storms. ⊠ *1 Company St., Christiansted* ☎ *340/778–8605.*

LIQUOR & TOBACCO **Baci Duty Free Liquor and Tobacco.** A walk-in humidor with a good selection of Arturo Fuente, Partagas, and Macanudo cigars is the centerpiece of this store, which also carries sleek Danish-made watches and Lladro figurines. ⊠ *1235 Queen Cross St., Christiansted* ☎ *340/773–5040.*

**Kmart.** The two branches of this discount department store—a large one in the Sunshine Mall and a smaller one mid-island at Sunny Isle Shopping Center—carry a huge line of discounted, duty-free liquor. ⊠ *Sunshine Mall, Rte. 70, Frederiksted* ☎ *340/692–5848* ⊠ *Sunny Isle Shopping Center, Rte. 70, Sunny Isle* ☎ *340/719–9190.*

PERFUMES **Violette Boutique.** Perfumes, cosmetics, and skin-care products are the draws here. ⊠ *Caravelle Arcade, 38 Strand St., Christiansted* ☎ *340/773–2148.*

# Nightlife & the Arts

The island's nightlife is ever-changing, and its arts scene is eclectic—ranging from Christmastime performances of *The Nutcracker* to any locally organized shows. Folk-art traditions, such as quadrille dancers, are making a comeback. To find out what's happening, pick up the local newspapers—*V. I. Daily News* and *St. Croix Avis*—available at newsstands. Christiansted has a lively and eminently casual club scene near the waterfront. Frederiksted has a couple of restaurants and clubs offering weekend entertainment.

## Nightlife

**Hotel on the Cay** (⊠ Protestant Cay, Christiansted ☎ 340/773–2035) has a West Indian buffet on Tuesday nights in the winter season, when you can watch a broken-bottle dancer (a dancer who braves a carpet of shattered glass) and mocko jumbie characters. Although you can gamble at the island's only casino, it's the nightly music that draws big crowds to **Divi Carina Bay Casino** (⊠ Rte. 60, Estate Turner Hole ☎ 340/773–9700). The **Moonraker** (⊠ 43A Queen Cross St., Christiansted ☎ 340/713–8025) attracts a youthful crowd for DJ music on Wednesday through Saturday nights.

**Blue Moon** (⊠ 17 Strand St., Frederiksted ☎ 340/772–2222) a waterfront restaurant, is the place to be for live jazz on Friday from 9 PM to 1 AM. Outside Frederiksted, **Off the Wall** (⊠ Rte. 80, Cane Bay ☎ 340/778–4471) has blues or jazz Tuesday through Sunday from 6 PM to 9 PM.

## The Arts

**Sunset Jazz** (⊠ Waterfront, Frederiksted ☎ 340/277–0692), has become the hot event in Frederiksted, drawing crowds of both visitors and locals at 6 PM on the third Friday of every month to watch the sun go down and hear good music.

The **Whim Plantation Museum** (⊠ Rte. 70, Estate Whim ☎ 340/772–0598), outside of Frederiksted, hosts classical music concerts in winter.

## Exploring St. Croix

Though there are things to see and do in St. Croix's two towns, Christiansted and Frederiksted (both named after Danish kings), there are lots of interesting spots in between them and to the east of Christiansted. Just be sure you have a map in hand (pick one up at rental-car agencies, or stop by the tourist office for an excellent one that's free). Many secondary roads remain unmarked; if you get confused, ask for help.

*Numbers in the margin correspond to points of interest on the St. Croix map.*

### Christiansted & the East

Christiansted is a historic Danish-style town that always served as St. Croix's commercial center. Your best bet is to see the historic sights in the morning, when it's still cool. This two-hour endeavor won't tax your walking shoes and will leave you with energy to poke around the town's eclectic shops. Break for lunch at an open-air restaurant before spending as much time as you like shopping.

An easy drive (roads are flat and well marked) to St. Croix's eastern end takes you through some choice real estate. Ruins of old sugar estates dot the landscape. You can make the entire loop on the road that circles the island in about an hour, a good way to end the day. If you want to spend a full day exploring, you can find some nice beaches and easy walks with places to stop for lunch.

**①**
**Fodor'sChoice**
**★**

**Christiansted.** In the 1700s and 1800s this town was a trading center for sugar, rum, and molasses. Today there are law offices, tourist shops, and restaurants, but many of the buildings, which start at the harbor and go up into the gentle hillsides, still date from the 18th century. You can't get lost. All streets lead gently downhill to the water. If you want some friendly advice, stop by the **Visitor Center** (⊠ 53A Company St. ☎ 340/773–0495) weekdays between 8 and 5 for maps and brochures.

Large, yellow **Fort Christiansvaern** (⊠ Hospital St. ☎ 340/773–1460 ⊕ www.nps.gov/chri) dominates the waterfront. Because it's so easy to spot, it makes a good place to begin a walking tour. In 1749 the Danish built the fort to protect the harbor, but the structure was repeatedly damaged by hurricane-force winds and had to be partially rebuilt in 1771. It's now a national historic site, the best preserved of the few remaining Danish-built forts in the Virgin Islands, and houses the park's visitor center. The $3 admission includes the Steeple Building. Rangers are on hand to answer questions. Hours are weekdays 8 to 4:45 and weekends 9 to 4:45.

When you're tired of sightseeing, stop at **D. Hamilton Jackson Park** (⊠ Between Fort Christiansvaern and Danish Customs House)—on the street side of Fort Christiansvaern—for a rest. It's named for a famed labor leader, judge, and journalist who started the first newspaper not under the thumb of the Danish crown (his birthday, November 1, is a territorial holiday celebrated with much fanfare in St. Croix).

Built in 1830 on foundations that date from 1734, the **Danish Customs House** (✉ King St. ☎ 340/773–1460 ⊕ www.nps.gov/chri), near Fort Christiansvaern, originally served as both a customs house and a post office. In 1926 it became the Christiansted Library, and it's been a national park office since 1972. It's open weekdays from 8 to 5. There's not much to see, other than park staff at work, but the architecture makes it worth a peek inside.

Constructed in 1856, the **Scale House** (✉ King St. ☎ 340/773–1460 ⊕ www.nps.gov/chri) was once the spot where goods passing through the port were weighed and inspected. Park staffers now sell a good selection of books about St. Croix history and its flora and fauna. The Scale House is open weekdays 8 to 4:30 and weekends 9 to 4:30.

Built by the Danes in 1753, the **Steeple Building** (✉ Church St. ☎ 340/773–1460) was the first Danish Lutheran church on St. Croix. It's now a national park museum and contains exhibits that document the island's Indian inhabitants. It's worth the short walk to see the building's collection of archaeological artifacts, displays on plantation life, and exhibits on the architectural development of Christiansted, the early history of the church, and Alexander Hamilton, the first secretary of the U.S. Treasury, who grew up in St. Croix. It's open weekdays from 9 to 4:30; the $3 admission includes Fort Christiansvaern.

The **Post Office Building** (✉ Church St.), built in 1749, was once the Danish West India & Guinea Company warehouse. At this writing, it was closed for a major renovation, but it's worth a look from the outside. One of the town's most elegant structures, **Government House** (✉ King St. ☎ 340/773–1404) was built as a home for a Danish merchant in 1747. Today it houses government offices. If you're here weekdays from 8 to 4:30, slip into the peaceful inner courtyard to admire the still pools and gardens. A sweeping staircase leads you to a second-story ballroom, still used for official government functions.

★ **Buck Island Reef National Monument** (✉ Off north shore of St. Croix ☎ 340/773–1460 ⊕ www.nps.gov/buis) has pristine beaches that are just right for sunbathing, but there's also some shade for those who don't want to fry. The snorkeling trail set in the reef allows close-up study of coral formations and tropical fish. After recovering from the spate of hurricanes that started in 1989, the coral now suffers from a disease called bleaching that that leaves the coral white. The reefs are expected to recover, but how long it will take is anyone's guess. There's an easy hiking trail to the island's highest point, where you'll be rewarded for your efforts by spectacular views of the reef and St. John. Charter-boat trips leave daily from the Christiansted waterfront or from Green Cay Marina, about 2 mi (3 km) east of Christiansted. Check with your hotel for recommendations.

**②** **Point Udall.** This rocky promontory, the easternmost point in the United States, is about a half-hour drive from Christiansted. A paved road takes you to an overlook with glorious views. More adventurous folks can hike down to the pristine beach below. On the way back, look for the castle, an enormous mansion that can only be described as a cross between a Moorish mosque and the Taj Mahal. It was built by an extravagant recluse known only as the Contessa. It's sometimes a popular spot for vandals. Residents advise taking your valuables with you and leaving your car unlocked so they won't break into your car to look inside. ⊠ *Rte. 82, Et Stykkeland.*

## Between Christiansted & Frederiksted

A drive through the countryside between these two towns will take you past ruins of old plantations, many bearing whimsical names (Morningstar, Solitude, Upper Love) bestowed by early owners. The traffic moves quickly—by island standards—on the main roads, but you can pause and poke around if you head down some side lanes. It's easy to find your way west, but driving from north to south requires good navigation. Don't leave your hotel without a map. Allow an entire day for this trip, so you'll have enough time for a swim at a north-shore beach. Although you can find lots of casual eateries on the main roads, pick up a picnic lunch if you plan to head off the beaten path.

**❼ Cruzan Rum Distillery.** A tour of the company's factory, established in 1760, culminates in a tasting of its products, all sold here at bargain prices. It's worth a stop to look at the distillery's charming old buildings even if you're not a rum connoisseur. ⊠ *West Airport Rd., Estate Diamond* ☎ *340/692–2280* ⊕ *www.cruzanrum.com* ☞ *$4* ☺ *Weekdays 9–11:30 and 1–4:15.*

**❹ Judith's Fancy.** In this upscale neighborhood are the ruins of an old greathouse and tower of the same name, both remnants of a circa-1750 Danish sugar plantation. The "Judith" comes from the first name of a woman buried on the property. From the guard house at the neighborhood entrance, follow Hamilton Drive past some of St. Croix's loveliest homes. At the end of Hamilton Drive the road overlooks Salt River Bay, where Christopher Columbus anchored in 1493. On the way back, make a detour left off Hamilton Drive onto Caribe Road for a close look at the ruins. The million-dollar villas are something to behold, too. ⊠ *Turn north onto Rte. 751, off Rte. 75.*

**❸ Little Princess Estate.** If the old plantation ruins decaying here and there around St. Croix intrigue you, a visit to this Nature Conservancy project will give you even more of a glimpse into the past. The staff has carved walking paths out of the bush that surrounds what's left of a 19th-century plantation. It's easy to stroll among well-labeled fruit trees and see the ruins of the windmill, the sugar and rum factory, and the laborers' village. This is the perfect place to reflect on St. Croix's agrarian past fueled with labor from African slaves. ⊠ *Off Rte. 75; turn north at Five Corners traffic light* ☎ *340/773–5575* ☞ *Donations accepted* ☺ *Tues. and Thurs. 3–5.*

**❻ Mt. Eagle.** At 1,165 feet, this is St. Croix's highest peak. Leaving Cane Bay and passing North Star Beach, follow the coastal road that dips briefly into a forest; then turn left on Route 69. Just after you make the turn, the pavement is marked with the words THE BEAST and a set of giant paw prints. The hill you're about to climb is the famous Beast of the St. Croix

1

Half Ironman Triathlon, an annual event during which participants must bike this intimidating slope. ⊠ *Rte. 69.*

**5** **Salt River Bay National Historical Park & Ecological Preserve.** This joint national and local park commemorates the area where Christopher Columbus's men skirmished with the Carib Indians in 1493 on his second visit to the New World. The peninsula on the bay's east side is named for the event: Cabo de las Flechas (Cape of the Arrows). Although the park is just in the developing stages, it has several sights with cultural significance. A ball court, used by the Caribs in religious ceremonies, was discovered at the spot where the taxis park. Take a short hike up the dirt road to the ruins of an old earthen fort for great views of Salt River Bay and the surrounding countryside. The area also encompasses a biodiverse coastal estuary with the largest remaining mangrove forest in the region, a submarine canyon, and several endangered species, including the hawksbill turtle and the roseate tern. A visitor center sits just uphill to the west. The water at the beach can be on the rough side, but it's a nice place for sunning. ⊠ *Rte. 75 to Rte. 80, Salt River* ☎ *340/773–1460* ⊕ *www.nps.gov/sari.*

## Frederiksted & Environs

St. Croix's second-largest town, Frederiksted, was founded in 1751. A stroll around its historic sights will take you no more than an hour. Allow a little more time if you want to browse in the few small shops. The area just outside town has old plantations, some of which have been preserved as homes or historic structures that are open to the public.

**10** **Carl & Marie Lawaetz Museum.** For a trip back in time, tour this circa-1750 farm. Owned by the prominent Lawaetz family since 1896, just after Carl Lawaetz arrived from Denmark, the lovely two-story house is in a valley at La Grange. A Lawaetz family member shows you the four-poster mahogany bed Carl and Marie shared, the china Marie painted, the family portraits, and the fruit trees that fed the family for several generations. Initially a sugar plantation, it was subsequently used to raise cattle and grow produce. ⊠ *Rte. 76, Mahogany Rd., Estate Little La Grange* ☎ *340/772–1539* ⊕ *www.stcroixlandmarks.com* ✉ *$8* ⊙ *Tues., Thurs., and Sat. 10–4.*

**8** **Estate Mount Washington Plantation.** Several years ago, while surveying the property, the owners discovered the ruins of a sugar plantation beneath the rain-forest brush. The grounds have since been cleared and opened to the public. You can take a self-guided walking tour of the mill, the rum factory, and other ruins. There's an antiques shop in what were once the stables. ⊠ *Rte. 63, Mount Washington* ☎ *340/772–1026* ⊙ *Ruins open daily dawn–dusk.*

**9** **Frederiksted.** The town is noted less for its Danish than for its Victorian architecture, which dates from after the slave uprising and the great fire of 1878. One long cruise-ship pier juts into the sparkling sea. It's the perfect place to start a tour of this quaint city. The **Visitor Center** (⊠ 200 Strand St. ☎ 340/772–0357), across from the pier, has brochures from numerous St. Croix businesses. You can stop in weekdays from 8 to 5 to view exhibits on St. Croix. On July 3, 1848, 8,000 slaves marched on the red-brick **Fort Frederik** (⊠ Waterfront ☎ 340/772–2021) to demand their freedom. Danish governor Peter von Scholten, fearing they would burn the town to the ground, stood up in his carriage parked in front of the fort and granted their wish. The fort, completed in 1760, houses a number of interesting historical exhibits as well as an art gallery and a display of police memorabilia. It's within earshot of the visitor center. Admission is $3; it's open weekdays from 8 to 5. **St. Patrick's Roman Catholic Church** (⊠ Prince St.), complete with three turrets, was built in 1843 of coral. Wander inside, and you can see woodwork handcrafted by Frederiksted artisans. The churchyard is filled with 18th-century gravestones. **St. Paul's Anglican Church** (⊠ Prince St.), built circa 1812, is a mix of Georgian and Gothic Revival architecture. The bell tower of exposed sandstone was added later. The simple interior has gleaming woodwork and a tray ceiling (resembling an upside-down platter) popular in Caribbean architecture. Built in 1839, **Apothecary Hall** (⊠ King Cross St.) is a good example of 19th-century architecture; its facade has both Gothic and Greek Revival elements.

**⑪ St. Croix Leap.** This workshop sits in the heart of the rain forest, about a 15-minute drive from Frederiksted. It sells mirrors, tables, bread boards, and mahogany jewelry boxes crafted by local artisans. ⊠ *Rte. 76, Brooks Hill* ☎ *340/772–0421* ⊙ *Weekdays 9–5, Sat. 10–5.*

**⑭ St. George Village Botanical Gardens.** At this 17-acre estate, lush, fragrant flora grows amid the ruins of a 19th-century sugarcane plantation village. There are miniature versions of each ecosystem on St. Croix, from a semi-arid cactus grove to a verdant rain forest. ⊠ *Rte. 70, turn north at sign, St. George* ☎ *340/692–2874* ⊕ *www.sgvbg.org* ⊒ *$6* ⊙ *Daily 9–5.*

**⑫ West End Salt Pond.** A bird-watcher's delight, this salt pond attracts a large number of winged creatures, including flamingos. ⊠ *Veteran's Shore Dr., Hesselberg.*

★ ☾ ⑬ **Whim Plantation Museum.** The lovingly restored estate, with a windmill, cook house, and other buildings, will give you a sense of what life was like on St. Croix's sugar plantations in the 1800s. The oval-shape greathouse has high ceilings and antique furniture and utensils. Notice its fresh, airy atmosphere—the waterless stone moat around the greathouse was used not for defense but for gathering cooling air. If you have kids, the grounds are the perfect place for them to stretch their legs, perhaps while you browse in the museum gift shop. It's just outside of Frederiksted. ⊠ *Rte. 70, Estate Whim* ☎ *340/772–0598* ⊕ *www. stcroixlandmarks.com* ⊒ *$8* ⊙ *Mon., Wed., Fri., and Sat. 10–4.*

# U.S. VIRGIN ISLANDS ESSENTIALS

*To research prices, get advice from other travelers, and book travel arrangements, visit www.fodors.com.*

## Transportation

### BY AIR

One advantage to visiting the USVI is the abundance of nonstop and connecting flights to St. Thomas and St. Croix that can have you at the

1

beach in three to four hours from East Coast airports. Small island-hopper planes and a seaplane connect St. Thomas and St. Croix, and a ferry takes you from St. Thomas to St. John.

American, Continental, Delta, Spirit, United, and US Airways fly to the islands; some flights connect through Puerto Rico. Cape Air and Caribbean Sun fly from San Juan; Cape Air has code-share arrangements with all major airlines, so your luggage can transfer seamlessly. Seaborne Airlines flies between St. Thomas, St. Croix, and San Juan, Puerto Rico.

🛪 Airlines **American/American Eagle** ☎ 340/776-2560 in St. Thomas, 340/778-2000 in St. Croix. **Cape Air** ☎ 340/774-2204 or 800/352-0714 ⊕ www.flycapeair.com. **Caribbean Sun** ☎ 866/864-6272 ⊕ www.flycsa.com. **Continental** ☎ 800/231-0856. **Delta** ☎ 340/777-4177. **Seaborne** ☎ 340/773-6442 ⊕ www.flyseaborne.com. **Spirit** ☎ 800/772-7117 ⊕ www.spiritairlines.com. **United** ☎ 340/774-9190. **US Airways** ☎ 800/622-1015.

🛪 Airports **Cyril E. King Airport** ✉ St. Thomas ☎ 340/774-5100 ⊕ www.viport.com. **Henry Rohlsen Airport** ✉ St. Croix ☎ 340/778-1012 ⊕ www.viport.com.

### BY BOAT & FERRY

Ferries are a great way to travel around the islands. There's frequent service between St. Thomas and St. John and their neighbors, the BVI. There's something special about spending a day on St. John and then joining your fellow passengers—a mix of tourists, local families, and construction workers on their way home—for a peaceful sundown ride back to St. Thomas. Sometimes one of the St. John ferry services offers a special weekend trip to Fajardo, Puerto Rico. Such junkets depart from the waterfront in St. Thomas on a Friday evening and return to the same locale on Sunday afternoon.

Ferries to Cruz Bay, St. John, leave St. Thomas from either the Charlotte Amalie waterfront west of the U.S. Coast Guard dock or from Red Hook. From Charlotte Amalie ferries depart at 9, 11, 1, 3, 4, and 5:30. Ferries from Cruz Bay to Charlotte Amalie leave at 7:15, 9:15, 11:15, 1:15, 2:15, and 3:45. The one-way fare for the 45-minute ride is $8. From Red Hook, ferries to Cruz Bay leave at 6:30 AM and 7:30 AM. Starting at 8 AM, they leave hourly until midnight. Returning from Cruz Bay, ferries leave hourly starting at 6 AM until 11 PM. The 15- to 20-minute ferry ride is $4.

Car ferries, called barges, run about every half hour between Red Hook, St. Thomas, and Cruz Bay, St. John. The ride costs $35 (round-trip). Plan to arrive at least 15 minutes before departure.

*Reefer* is the name of both of the brightly colored 26-passenger skiffs that run between the Charlotte Amalie waterfront and Marriott Frenchman's Reef hotel daily on the half hour from 8 to 5. It's a good way to beat the traffic (and is about the same price as a taxi) to Morning Star Beach, which adjoins the hotel. And you get a great view of the harbor as you bob along in the shadow of the giant cruise ships anchored in the harbor. The captain may be persuaded to drop you at Yacht Haven, but check first. The one-way fare is $5 per person, and the trip takes about 15 minutes.

There's daily service between either Charlotte Amalie or Red Hook, on St. Thomas, and West End or Road Town, Tortola, BVI, by either Smith's Ferry or Native Son, and to Virgin Gorda, BVI, by Smith's Ferry. The times and days the ferries run change, so it's best to call for schedules once you're in the islands. The fare is $22 one-way or $40 round-trip, and the trip from Charlotte Amalie takes 45 minutes to an hour to West End, up to 1½ hours to Road Town; from Red Hook the trip is only a half hour. The twice-weekly 2¼-hour trip from Charlotte Amalie to Virgin Gorda costs $28 one-way and $50 round-trip. From Red Hook and Cruz Bay, the boat goes Thursday and Sunday. Prices vary by barge company, but the most you'll pay is $52 round-trip. Three days a week (Friday, Saturday, and Sunday) a ferry operates between Red Hook, Cruz Bay, and Jost Van Dyke in the BVI; the trip takes 45 minutes and costs $50 per person round-trip.

There's also daily service between Cruz Bay, St. John, and West End, Tortola, aboard an Inter-Island Boat Service ferry. The half-hour trip costs $40 round-trip. You need to present proof of citizenship upon entering the BVI; a passport is best, but a birth certificate with a raised seal in addition to a government-issue photo ID will suffice.

🚢 **Inter-Island Boat Service** ☎ 340/776-6597. **Native Son** ☎ 340/774-8685 ⊕ www.nativesonbvi.com. *Reefer* ☎ 340/776-8500 Ext. 6814 ⊕ www.marriottfrenchmansreef.com. **Smith's Ferry** ☎ 340/775-7292 ⊕ www.smithsferry.com.

### BY BUS

On St. Thomas, the island's large buses make public transportation a very comfortable—though slow—way to get from east and west to Charlotte Amalie and back (service to the north is limited). Buses run about every 30 minutes from stops that are clearly marked with VITRAN signs. Fares are $1 between outlying areas and town and 75¢ in town.

Privately owned taxi vans crisscross St. Croix regularly, providing reliable service between Frederiksted and Christiansted along Route 70. This inexpensive ($1.50 one-way) mode of transportation is favored by locals, and though the many stops on the 20-mi (32-km) drive between the two main towns make the ride slow, it's never dull. Vitran public buses aren't the quickest way to get around the island, but they're comfortable and affordable. The fare is $1 between Christiansted and Frederiksted or to places in between.

Modern Vitran buses on St. John run from the Cruz Bay ferry dock through Coral Bay to the far eastern end of the island at Salt Pond, making numerous stops in between. The fare is $1 to any point.

### BY CAR

Even at a sedate speed of 20 mph, driving can be an adventure—for example, you may find yourself slogging behind a slow tourist-packed safari bus at a steep hairpin turn. It's a good idea to give a little beep at blind turns. Note that the general speed limit on these islands is only 25 to 35 mph, which will seem fast enough for you on most roads. If you don't think you'll need to lock up your valuables, a Jeep or open-air Suzuki with four-wheel drive will make it easier to navigate potholed dirt side roads and to get up slick hills when it rains. All the major roads are paved.

Driving is on the left side of the road, British-style (although your steering wheel will be on the left side of the car, American-style). The law requires *everyone* in a car to wear a seat belt: many of the roads are narrow, and the islands are dotted with hills, so there's ample reason to put safety first.

In St. Thomas traffic can get pretty bad, especially in Charlotte Amalie at rush hour (7 to 9 and 4:30 to 6). Cars often line up bumper to bumper along the waterfront. If you need to get from an East End resort to the airport during these times, find the alternate route (starting from the East End, Route 38 to 42 to 40 to 33) that goes up the mountain and then drops you back onto Veterans Highway. If you plan to explore by car, be sure to pick up the latest edition of "Road Map St. Thomas–St. John," which includes the route numbers *and* the names of the roads that are used by locals. It's available anywhere you find maps and guidebooks.

St. Croix, unlike St. Thomas and St. John, where narrow roads wind through hillsides, is relatively flat, and it even has a four-lane highway. The speed limit on the Melvin H. Evans Highway is 55 mph and ranges 35 to 40 mph elsewhere. Roads are often unmarked, so be patient—sometimes getting lost is half the fun.

In St. John, use caution. The terrain is very hilly, the roads winding, and the blind curves numerous. You may suddenly come upon a huge safari bus careening around a corner or a couple of hikers strolling along the side of the road. Major roads are well paved, but once you get off a specific route, dirt roads filled with potholes are common. For such driving, a four-wheel-drive vehicle is your best bet.

Gas is expensive on St. Thomas and St. John; expect to pay considerably more than in the United States. But on St. Croix, where the big HOVENSA refinery is located, the prices are much closer to what you might expect to pay stateside.

ST. THOMAS  Avis, Budget, and Hertz all have counters at Cyril E. King Airport. Dependable Car Rental offers pickups and drop-offs at the airport and to and from major hotels. Cowpet Rent-a-Car is on the east end of the island. Discount has a location at Bluebeard's Castle hotel. Avis is at the Marriott Frenchman's Reef, Havensight Mall (adjacent to the cruise ship dock), and Seaborn Airlines terminal on the Charlotte Amalie waterfront; Budget has branches at the Sapphire Beach Resort & Marina and at the Havensight Mall, adjacent to the main cruise-ship dock.
🚗 **Avis** ☎ 340/774-1468. **Budget** ☎ 340/776-5774. **Cowpet Rent-a-Car** ☎ 340/775-7376. **Dependable Car Rental** ☎ 340/774-2253 or 800/522-3076. **Discount** ☎ 340/776-4858. **Hertz** ☎ 340/774-1879.

ST. CROIX  Atlas is outside Christiansted but provides pickups at hotels. Avis is at Henry Rohlsen Airport and at the seaplane ramp in Christiansted. Budget has branches at the airport and in the King Christian Hotel in Christiansted. Judi of Croix delivers vehicles to your hotel. Midwest is outside Frederiksted but picks up at hotels. Olympic and Thrifty are outside Christiansted but will pick up at hotels.

🎫 **Atlas** ☎ 340/773-2886 or 800/426-6009. **Avis** ☎ 340/778-9355. **Budget** ☎ 340/778-9636 ⊕ www.budgetstcroix.com. **Judi of Croix** ☎ 340/773-2123 or 877/903-2123 ⊕ www.judiofcroix.com. **Midwest** ☎ 340/772-0438 or 877/772-0438 ⊕ www.midwestautorental.com. **Olympic** ☎ 340/773-8000 or 888/878-4227 ⊕ www.stcroixcarrentals.com. **Thrifty** ☎ 340/773-7200.

ST. JOHN  Best is just outside Cruz Bay near the public library, off Route 10. Cool Breeze is in Cruz Bay across from the Creek. Delbert Hill Taxi & Jeep Rental Service is in Cruz Bay around the corner from the ferry dock, across from Wharfside Village. Denzil Clyne is across from the Creek. O'Connor Jeep is in Cruz Bay at the Texaco Station. St. John Car Rental is across from Wharfside Village shopping center on Bay Street in Cruz Bay. Spencer's Jeep is across from the Creek in Cruz Bay. Sun & Sand is in Cruz Bay across from the Creek.

🎫 **Best** ☎ 340/693-8177. **Cool Breeze** ☎ 340/776-6588 ⊕ www.coolbreezecarrental.com. **Delbert Hill Taxi & Jeep Rental Service** ☎ 340/776-6637. **Denzil Clyne** ☎ 340/776-6715. **O'Connor Jeep** ☎ 340/776-6343 ⊕ www.oconnorcarrental.com. **St. John Car Rental** ☎ 340/776-6103 ⊕ www.stjohncarrental.com. **Spencer's Jeep** ☎ 340/693-8784 or 888/776-6628. **Sun & Sand Car Rental** ☎ 340/776-6374.

### BY TAXI

USVI taxis don't have meters, but you needn't worry about fare gouging if you check a list of standard rates to popular destinations (required by law to be carried by each driver and often posted in hotel and airport lobbies and printed in free tourist periodicals, such as *St. Thomas-St. John This Week* and *St. Croix This Week*) and settle on the fare before you start out. Fares are per person, not per destination, but drivers taking multiple fares (which often happens, especially from the airport) will charge you a lower rate than if you're in the cab alone.

ST. THOMAS  On St. Thomas, taxi vans line up along Havensight and Crown Bay docks when a cruise ship pulls in. If you booked a shore tour, the operator will lead you to a designated vehicle. Otherwise, there are plenty of air-conditioned vans and open-air safari buses to take you to Charlotte Amalie or the beach. The cab fare from Havensight to Charlotte Amalie is $5 per person if you ride alone or $4 per person if you share a cab; you can, however, make the 1½-mi (2½-km) walk into town in about 30 minutes along the beautiful waterfront. From Crown Bay to town the taxi fare is $4 or $3.50 per person if you share; it's a 1-mi (1½-km) walk, but the route passes along a busy highway, so it's not advisable. Transportation from Havensight to Magens Bay for swimming is $8.50 per person ($6 if you share).

Additionally, taxis of all shapes and sizes are available at various ferry, shopping, resort, and airport areas, and they also respond to phone calls. There are taxi stands in Charlotte Amalie across from Emancipation Garden (in front of Little Switzerland, behind the post office) and along the waterfront. But you probably won't have to look for a stand, as taxis are plentiful and routinely cruise the streets. Walking down Main Street,

1

you'll be asked "Back to ship?" often enough to make you never want to carry another shopping bag.

🚩 **East End Taxi** ☎ 340/775-6974. **Islander Taxi** ☎ 340/774-4077. **VI Taxi Association** ☎ 340/774-4550.

ST. CROIX  Taxis, generally station wagons or minivans, are a phone call away from most hotels and are available in downtown Christiansted, at the Henry E. Rohlsen Airport, and at the Frederiksted pier during cruise-ship arrivals.

In Frederiksted all the shops are a short walk away, and you can swim off the beach. Most ship passengers visit Christiansted on a tour; a taxi will cost $24 for one or two people.

🚩 **Antilles Taxi Service** ☎ 340/773-5020. **St. Croix Taxi Association** ☎ 340/778-1088.

ST. JOHN  Taxis meet ferries arriving in Cruz Bay. Most drivers use vans or open-air safari buses. You can find them congregated at the dock and at hotel parking lots. You can also hail them anywhere on the road. You're likely to travel with other tourists en route to their destinations. Paradise Taxi will pick you up if you call, but most of the drivers don't provide that service. If you need one to pick you up at your rental villa, ask the villa manager for suggestions on whom to call or arrange a ride in advance.

Some cruise ships stop at St. John to let passengers disembark for a day. The main town of Cruz Bay is near the area where the ships drop off passengers. If you want to swim, the famous Trunk Bay is a $6 taxi ride per person from town.

🚩 **Paradise Taxi** ☎ 340/714-7913.

## Contacts & Resources

### BANKS & EXCHANGE SERVICES

The American dollar is used throughout the territory, just as in the neighboring BVI. If you need to exchange foreign currency, you need to go to the main branch of major banks. All major credit cards and traveler's checks are generally accepted. Some places will take Discover, though it's not as widely accepted as Visa, MasterCard, and American Express.

Each of the islands has several banks. On St. Thomas, First Bank has locations in Market Square, Waterfront, Estate Thomas, Port of $ale, Red Hook, and Tutu. There are waterfront locations for Banco Popular, as well as branches in Hibiscus Alley, Sugar Estate, Fort Mylner, Red Hook, and Altona, a mile east of the airport. The Scotia Bank has branches at Havensight Mall, Nisky Center, Tutu Park Mall, and the Waterfront.

St. Croix has branches of Banco Popular in Orange Grove and Sunny Isle shopping centers. V. I. Community Bank is in Orange Grove Shopping Center and in downtown Christiansted. Scotia Bank has branches in Sunny Isle, Frederiksted, Christiansted, and Sunshine Mall.

St. John has two banks. First Bank is one block up from the ferry dock, and Scotia Bank is at the Marketplace on Route 107.

## BUSINESS HOURS

Bank hours are generally Monday through Thursday 9 to 3 and Friday 9 to 5; a handful open Saturday (9 to noon). Walk-up windows open at 8:30 on weekdays. Hours may vary slightly from branch to branch and island to island, but they are generally weekdays 7:30 or 8 to 4 or 5:30 and Saturday 7:30 or 8 to noon or 2:30.

On St. Thomas, stores on Main Street in Charlotte Amalie are open weekdays and Saturday 9 to 5. The hours of the shops in the Havensight Mall (next to the cruise-ships dock) are the same, though occasionally some stay open until 9 on Friday, depending on how many cruise ships are at the dock. You may also find some shops open on Sunday if cruise ships are in port. Hotel shops are usually open evenings, as well.

St. Croix shop hours are usually Monday through Saturday 9 to 5, but there are some shops in Christiansted open in the evening.

On St. John, store hours run from 9 or 10 to 5 or 6. Wharfside Village and Mongoose Junction shops in Cruz Bay are often open into the evening.

## ELECTRICITY

The USVI use the same current as the U.S. mainland—110 volts. European appliances will require adaptors. Since power fluctuations occasionally occur, bring a heavy-duty surge protector (available at hardware stores) if you plan to use your computer.

## EMERGENCIES

🔂 Emergency Services **Air Ambulance Network** ☎ 800/327-1966. **Ambulance and fire emergencies** ☎ 911. **Medical Air Services** ☎ 340/777-8580 or 800/643-9023. **Police emergencies** ☎ 911.

🔂 Coast Guard **Marine Safety Detachment** ☎ 340/776-3497 in St. Thomas and St. John, 340/772-5557 in St. Croix. **Rescue Coordination Center** ☎ 787/289-2040 in San Juan, PR.

🔂 Hospital on St. Thomas **Roy L. Schneider Hospital & Community Health Center** ✉ Sugar Estate, 1 mi [1½ km] east of Charlotte Amalie ☎ 340/776-8311.

🔂 Hospitals on St. Croix **Gov. Juan F. Luis Hospital and Health Center** ✉ 6 Diamond Ruby, north of Sunny Isle Shopping Center on Rte. 79, Christiansted ☎ 340/778-6311. **Ingeborg Nesbitt Clinic** ✉ 516 Strand St., Frederiksted ☎ 340/772-0260.

🔂 Hospital on St. John **Myrah Keating Smith Community Health Center** ✉ Rte. 10, about 7 mins east of Cruz Bay, Susannaberg ☎ 340/693-8900.

🔂 Pharmacies on St. Thomas **Havensight Pharmacy** ✉ Havensight Mall, Charlotte Amalie ☎ 340/776-1235. **Kmart Pharmacy** ✉ Tutu Park Mall, Tutu ☎ 340/777-3854. **Doctor's Choice Pharmacy** ✉ Wheatley Shopping Center, across from Roy L. Schneider Hospital, Sugar Estate ☎ 340/777-1400 ✉ Medical Arts Complex, off Rte. 30, 1½ mi east of Cyril E. King Airport ☎ 340/774-8988.

🔂 Pharmacies on St. Croix **Kmart Pharmacy** ✉ Sunshine Mall, Cane Estate ☎ 340/692-2622. **People's Drug Store** ✉ Sunny Isle Shopping Center, Rte. 70, Christiansted ☎ 340/778-5537.

🔂 Pharmacy on St. John **Chelsea Drug Store** ✉ The Marketplace, Rte. 104, Cruz Bay ☎ 340/776-4888.

🔂 Scuba-Diving Emergencies **Roy L. Schneider Hospital & Community Health Center** ✉ Sugar Estate, 1 mi [1½ km] east of Charlotte Amalie ☎ 340/776-2686.

## HOLIDAYS

Public holidays, in addition to the U.S. federal holidays are: Three Kings Day (Jan. 6); Transfer Day (commemorates Denmark's 1917 sale of the territory to the United States, Mar. 31); Holy Thursday and Good Friday; Emancipation Day (when slavery was abolished in the Danish West Indies in 1848, July 3); Columbus Day and USVI–Puerto Rico Friendship Day (always on Columbus Day weekend); and Liberty Day (honoring David Hamilton Jackson, who secured freedom of the press and assembly from King Christian X of Denmark, Nov. 1).

Although the government closes down for 23 days a year, most of these holidays have no effect on shopping hours. Unless there's a cruise-ship arrival, expect most stores to close for Christmas and a few other holidays in the slower summer months.

## INTERNET, MAIL & SHIPPING

The main U.S. Post Office on St. Thomas is near the hospital, with branches in Charlotte Amalie, Frenchtown, Havensight, and Tutu Mall; there are post offices at Christiansted, Frederiksted, Gallows Bay, and Sunny Isle on St. Croix and at Cruz Bay on St. John. Postal rates are the same as if you were in the mainland United States, but Express Mail and Priority Mail aren't as quick.

On St. Thomas, FedEx offers overnight service if you get your package to the office before 5 PM. The FedEx office on St. Croix is in Peter's Rest Commercial Center; try to drop off your packages before 5:30 PM. Shipping services on St. Thomas are also available at Fast Shipping & Communications Nisky Mail Center and at Red Hook Mail Services. On St. John, call for Federal Express pickup.

Beans, Bytes & Websites is an Internet café in Charlotte Amalie. East End Secretarial Services offers long-distance dialing, copying, and fax services. At Little Switzerland, there's free Internet access along with an ATM, big-screen TV, telephones, and a bar with cold drinks. Near Havensight Mall, go to Soapy's Station or the Cyber Zone at Port of $ale, where there are 16 computers. Rates for Internet access range from $4 to $6 for 30 minutes to $8 to $12 per hour. On St. Croix, check your e-mail, make phone calls, and buy postage stamps at Strand Street Station Internet Café in Christiansted. Rates run $5 for a half hour of Internet time. On St. John the place to go to check your e-mail, make phone calls, or receive messages is Connections. You'll pay $5 a half hour for Internet service.

🖪 Internet Cafes **Beans, Bytes & Websites** ✉ Royal Dane Mall, behind Tavern on the Waterfront, Charlotte Amalie, St. Thomas ☎ 340/775-5262 ⊕ www.usvi.net/cybercafe. **Connections** ✉ Cruz Bay, St. John ☎ 340/776-6922 ✉ Coral Bay, St. John ☎ 340/779-4994 ⊕ www.connectionsstjohn.com. **Cyber Zone** ✉ Port of $ale, Charlotte Amalie, St. Thomas ☎ 340/714-7743. **East End Secretarial Services** ✉ Upstairs at Red Hook Plaza, Red Hook, St. Thomas ☎ 340/775-5262. **Little Switzerland** ✉ 5 Dronnigens Gade, across from Emancipation Garden, Charlotte Amalie, St. Thomas ☎340/776-2010. **Soapy's Station** ✉ Havensight Mall, above Budget, Charlotte Amalie, St. Thomas ☎ 340/776-7170. **Strand Street Station** ✉ Pan Am Pavilion, 1102 Strand St., Christiansted, St. Croix ☎ 340/719-6245.

⏻ Shipping **Fast Shipping & Communications** ⊠ Rte. 30, across from Havensight Mall, Charlotte Amalie, St. Thomas ☎ 340/714-7634. **FedEx** ⊠ Cyril E. King Airport, St. Thomas ☎ 340/777-4140 ⊕ www.fedex.com ⊠ Peter's Rest Commercial Center, Rte. 708, Peter's Rest, St. Croix ☎ 800/463-3339 ⊠ St. John ☎ 800/463-3339. **Nisky Mail Center** ⊠ Nisky Center, Rte. 30, Charlotte Amalie, St. Thomas ☎ 340/775-7055. **Red Hook Mail Services** ⊠ Red Hook Plaza, Rte. 32, 2nd fl., Red Hook, St. Thomas ☎ 340/779-1890.

## PASSPORT REQUIREMENTS

Since the U.S. Virgin Islands are a U.S. territory, you won't pass through immigration on arrival if you are coming on a flight from the U.S. However, you must still prove citizenship when you head back home regardless of where you are going. So long as you are a U.S. citizen, you will not have to carry a valid passport to visit the U.S. Virgin Islands starting on January 1, 2007, unless you are flying from another country, including all other Caribbean islands except for St. Croix and Puerto Rico; everyone else—including Canadians—will have to carry a valid passport. For Americans, an original, government-issued birth certificate and photo ID should suffice, though we still strongly recommend that everyone traveling to the USVI carry a valid passport to forestall any difficulties.

## SAFETY

Vacationers tend to assume that normal precautions aren't necessary in paradise. They are. Though there isn't quite as much crime here as in large U.S. mainland cities, it does exist. To be safe, keep your hotel or vacation villa door locked at all times, stick to well-lighted streets at night, and use the same kind of street sense that you would in any unfamiliar territory. Don't wander the streets of Charlotte Amalie, Christiansted, or Frederiksted alone at night. If you plan to carry things around, rent a car—not a Jeep—and lock possessions in the trunk. Keep your rental car locked wherever you park. Don't leave cameras, purses, and other valuables lying on the beach while you snorkel for an hour (or even for a minute), whether you're on the deserted beaches of St. John or the more crowded Magens and Coki beaches on St. Thomas. St. Croix has several good but remote beaches outside Frederiksted and on the East End; it's best to visit them with a group rather than on your own.

## TAXES

There's no sales tax in the USVI, but there's an 8% hotel-room tax (which may be raised to 10% by 2006); most hotels also add a 10% service charge to the bill. The St. John Accommodations Council members ask that hotel and villa guests voluntarily pay a $1 a day surcharge to help fund school and community projects and other good works. Many hotels add additional energy surcharges and the like, so please ask about any additional charges, but these are not government-imposed taxes.

## TELEPHONES

Phone service to and from the Virgin Islands is up-to-date and efficient. Phone cards are used throughout the islands; you can buy them (in several denominations) at many retail shops and convenience stores. They must be used in special card phones, which are also widely available. Dialing a call to or from the USVI is exactly like dialing one in the rest of the U.S. All U.S. calling cards work in the USVI, and most charge domestic long-distance rates. The area code for the USVI is 340.

Cell phones from the U.S. companies Cingular and Sprint work in most locations in the USVI if you have a roaming feature; if you are on St. John's north coast, you may have some difficulties with service, where you may find yourself connected to BoatPhone, a Tortola service. Phones from other companies may work, but only Cingular and Sprint have offices in the USVI. Many cell phone companies treat calls in the USVI just like any other calls in the U.S., but be sure to ask; this is not always the case.

### TIPPING

Many hotels in the USVI add a 10% to 15% service charge to cover the room maid and other staff. However, some hotels may use part of that money to fund their operations, passing on only a portion of it to the staff. Check with your maid or bellhop to determine the hotel's policy. If you discover you need to tip, give bellhops and porters 50¢ to $1 per bag and maids $1 or $2 per day. Special errands or requests of hotel staff always require an additional tip. At restaurants bartenders and waiters expect a 10%–15% tip, but always check your tab to see whether service is included. Taxi drivers in the USVI get a 15% tip.

In the BVI, tip porters and bellhops $1 per bag. Sometimes a service charge of 10% is included on restaurant bills; it's customary to leave another 5% if you liked the service. If no charge is added, 15% is the norm. Cabbies normally aren't tipped because most own their cabs; add 10% to 15% if they exceed their duties.

### VISITOR INFORMATION

🚩 **St. Thomas–St. John Hotel & Tourism Association** ☎ 340/774–6835 ⊕ www.sttstjhta.com. **USVI Division of Tourism** ✉ 78–123 Estate Contant, Charlotte Amalie, St. Thomas 00804 ☎ 340/774–8784 or 800/372–8784 ✉ 53A Company St., Christiansted, St. Croix 00822 ☎ 340/773–0495 ✉ Strand St., Frederiksted, St. Croix 00840 ☎ 340/772–0357 ✉ Henry Samuel St. (next to post office), Cruz Bay, St. John ☎ 340/776–6450 ⊕ www.usvitourism.vi. **Virgin Islands National Park** ✉ At the Creek, Cruz Bay, St. John 00831 ☎ 340/776–6201 ⊕ www.nps.gov/viis.

### WEDDINGS

The Virgin Islands provide a lovely backdrop for a wedding. Many couples opt to exchange vows on a white sandy beach or in a tropical garden. The process is easy but does require advance planning. The U.S. Virgin Islands Department of Tourism publishes a brochure with all the details and relevant contact information; you can also download marriage license applications from the Web site.

You must first apply for a marriage license at the Superior Court; there are offices in St. Thomas (which is also where you apply if you're getting married in St. John) and St. Croix. The fee is $50 for the application and $50 for the license. You have to wait eight days after the clerk receives the application to get married, and licenses must be picked up in person weekdays, though you can apply by mail. To make the process easier, most couples hire a wedding planner. If you plan to get married at a large hotel, most have planners on staff, but if you're staying in a villa, at a small hotel or inn, or are arriving on a cruise ship, you'll have to hire your own. Anne Marie Weddings, a wedding planner on St. John, provides a lovely service.

The wedding planner will help you organize your marriage license application as well as arrange for a location, flowers, music, refreshments, and whatever else you want to make your day special. The wedding planner will also hire a clergyman if you'd like a religious service or a nondenominational officiant if you prefer. Indeed, many wedding planners are licensed by the territory as nondenominational officiants and will preside at your wedding.

🚩 Superior Court Offices In St. Croix ⌂ Box 929, Christiansted 00821 ☎ 340/778-9750. In St. Thomas ⌂ Box 70, St. Thomas 00804 ☎ 340/774-6680.

🚩 Wedding Planners Anne Marie Weddings ✉ 5000-4A Enighed, St. John 00830 ☎ 340/693-5153 or 888/676-5701 ⊕ www.stjohnweddings.com. Weddings the Island Way ⌂ Box 11694, St. Thomas 00801 ☎ 340/777-6505 or 800/582-4784 ⊕ www.weddingstheislandway.com.

# British Virgin Islands

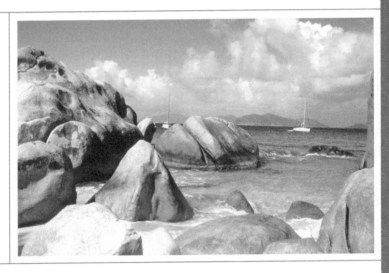

The Baths

**WORD OF MOUTH**

"You'll love Tortola. My best advice is to rent a really good Jeep so you can get around the island. The roads are really steep and if you're not used to it, it can be a bit scary at first."

—Coconut

"The Baths at Virgin Gorda are truly a magical spot, but only if you're not sharing them. . . . If you can, choose to go very early in the morning, or in the late afternoon—before and after the crowds."

—Callaloo

# WELCOME TO THE BRITISH VIRGIN ISLANDS

## NATURE'S LITTLE SECRETS

Most of the 50-some islands, islets, and cays that make up the British Virgin Islands (BVI) are remarkably hilly and volcanic in origin, having exploded from the depths of the sea some 25 million years ago. The exception is Anegada, which is a flat, coral-limestone atoll. Tortola (about 10-square-mi/26-square-km) is the largest member of the chain.

| KEY | |
|---|---|
| 🚤 | Ferry |
| 🚢 | Cruise Ship Terminal |

You can still find traces of a primeval rain forest at the top of Sage Mountain, the highest peak in the BVI.

Long Pt.

Man O'War Bay

JOST VAN DYKE

Little Jost Van Dyke

Great Tobago

Great Harbour

West End Pt.

Brewers Bay

Trunk Bay

Josiah's Bay

White Bay

Pull & Be Damn Pt.

Little Harbour

Todman Pk.

Black Pt.

Cane Garden Bay

Road Town ⭐

Fort Shirley

Little Tobago

Carrot Bay

Apple Bay

Mt. Sage

Great Thatch Island

Long Bay

West End

TORTOLA

Road Harbour

West Pt.

Frenchman's Cay

see map pages 138-139

Great Harbour

ST. JOHN
UNITED STATES VIRGIN ISLANDS

Rock Hole

White Bay

Pelican Island

Privateer Bay

Money Bay

Norman Island

The British Virgin Islands are mostly quiet and casual, so don't expect to party 'til dawn, and definitely leave the tux at home. Luxury here means getting away from it all rather than getting the trendiest state-of-the-art amenities. And the jackpot is the chance to explore the many islets and cays by sailboat.

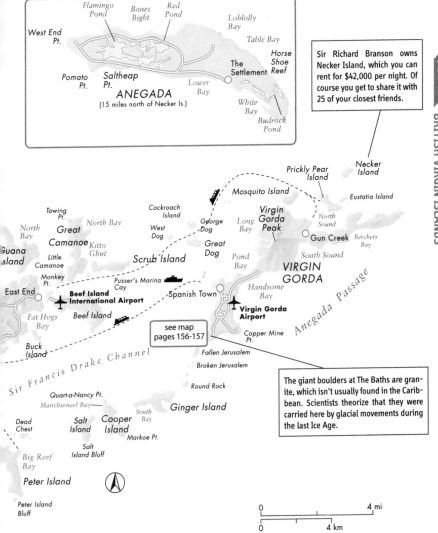

Sir Richard Branson owns Necker Island, which you can rent for $42,000 per night. Of course you get to share it with 25 of your closest friends.

The giant boulders at The Baths are granite, which isn't usually found in the Caribbean. Scientists theorize that they were carried here by glacial movements during the last Ice Age.

see map pages 156-157

# TOP 4 REASONS TO VISIT THE BRITISH VIRGIN ISLANDS

1. With over 50 islands in the chain, sailors can drop anchor at a different, perfect beach every day.

2. Laid-back luxury resorts offer a full-scale retreat from your everyday life.

3. Diving and snorkeling doesn't get any easier than around Anegada, where vibrant reefs are often just feet from the shore.

4. Your trip isn't complete until you've chilled at the casual beach bars on Jost Van Dyke.

# BRITISH VIRGIN ISLANDS PLANNER

## Getting to the British Virgin Islands

There are no direct flights to the British Virgin Islands. To fly into Tortola, you must connect in San Juan or St. Thomas on a propeller-driven plane, regardless of where you are flying from. But it's sometimes just as easy and cheap to use one of the regularly scheduled ferries from either Charlotte Amalie or Red Hook on St. Thomas; these ferries also go to Virgin Gorda, but the only option for Anegada is a flight. The trip to Tortola takes less than an hour. If you're already in St. John, you can get to Tortola from there by ferry as well. Separate ferries go from Tortola to Jost Van Dyke and the other island retreats. You can take a tiny island-hopper flight to either Virgin Gorda or Anegada from Tortola, but you'll have to book it directly with one of the small island-based airlines.

**Hassle Factor:** Medium to High

## Activities

The BVI **sailing** scene is one of the best in the world, with Tortola as one of the major charter yacht centers of the Caribbean. It's no wonder that sailing is so popular; most of the best BVI **beaches** are on deserted islands and are accessible only by boat. The most famous beach in the chain is The Baths on Virgin Gorda, which is lined with giant, round boulders that provide for great off-the-beach snorkeling. The **nightlife** center of the region is actually a series of simple beach bars on Jost Van Dyke, but yachties in the know are happy to bop over for a drink and to hear Foxy Callwood sing at his eponymous bar and restaurant. **Diving** and **game-fishing** in these waters are also good.

## On the Ground

At Tortola's Beef Island airport, taxis hover at the exit from customs. Fares are officially set but are lower per person for more than three passengers. Figure about $15 for up to three people and $5 for each additional passenger for the 20-minute ride to Road Town, and about $20 to $30 for the 45-minute ride to West End. Expect to share your taxi, and be patient if your driver searches for people to fill his cab—only a few flights land each day, and this could be your driver's only run.

On Virgin Gorda, if you're staying on North Sound, a taxi will take you from the airport to the dock, where your hotel launch will meet you, but be sure to make launch arrangements with your hotel before your arrival. If your destination is Leverick Bay, your land taxi will take you there directly. You can also take the North Sound Express directly from the Beef Island airport to Spanish Town or North Sound. On Anegada, your hotel will organize your transportation from the small airstrip.

## Renting a Car

Both Tortola and Virgin Gorda have a number of car-rental agencies. Although taxi service is good, you may wish to rent a car to explore farther afield or try many different beaches. On Anegada it's possible to rent a car, but most people rely on taxis for transportation. Jost Van Dyke has a single road, and visitors travel on foot or by local taxi.

## Where to Stay

## When to Go

Pick your island carefully because each is different, as are the logistics of getting there. Tortola gives you a wider choice of restaurants, shopping, and resorts. Virgin Gorda has fewer off-resort places to eat and shop, but the resorts themselves are often better, and the beaches are exquisite. Anegada is remote and better suited for divers. Jost Van Dyke has some classic Caribbean beach bars, along with fairly basic accommodations. When you want to be pampered and pampered some more, select a remote resort reached only by ferry, or even one of the appealing outer-island resorts that are still somewhat affordable for mere mortals. If you want to enjoy everything the BVI have to offer, charter a sailboat so you can drop anchor where and when you want.

The largest resort in the British Virgin Islands has 120-some rooms, and most have considerably fewer. Luxury here is more about personal service than over-the-top amenities. The best places are certainly comfortable, but they aren't showy. You'll find villas and condos in abundance, and they are a good option for families.

High season doesn't really get into full swing until Christmas and ends sooner (usually by April 1) than on most Caribbean islands. In the off-season, rates can be a third less.

In April, glimpse the colorful spinnakers as sailing enthusiasts gather for the internationally known **BVI Spring Regatta**. In August, try your hand at sport fishing, as anglers compete to land the largest catch at the **BVI Sportfishing Tournament**.

## Hotel & Restaurant Costs

Assume that hotels operate on the European Plan (**EP**—with no meals) unless we specify that they use either the Continental Plan (**CP**—with a Continental breakfast), Breakfast Plan (**BP**—with full breakfast), or the Modified American Plan (**MAP**—with breakfast and dinner). Other hotels may offer the Full American Plan (**FAP**—including all meals but no drinks) or may be All-Inclusive (**AI**—with all meals, drinks, and most activities).

| WHAT IT COSTS in Dollars | | | | | |
|---|---|---|---|---|---|
| | **$$$$** | **$$$** | **$$** | **$** | **¢** |
| **Restaurants** | over $30 | $15–$30 | $10–$15 | $8–$12 | under $8 |
| **Hotels*** | over $350 | $250–$350 | $150–$250 | $80–$150 | under $80 |
| **Hotels**** | over $450 | $350–$450 | $250–$350 | $125–$250 | under $125 |

*EP, BP, CP   **AI, FAP, MAP
Restaurant prices are for a main course excluding 10% service charge. Hotel prices are for two people in a double room in high season and exclude 7% BVI hotel tax, 10% service charge, and meal plans (except at all-inclusives).

Updated by
Carol M.
Bareuther and
Lynda Lohr

**WITH THE SAILS DOWN AFTER A SMOOTH TRIP** across Sir Francis Drake Channel, our boat glided into White Bay at Jost Van Dyke for an afternoon of snorkeling and sun. A fresh-from-the-sea lobster dinner followed at a shoreside restaurant. The next day we anchored at Cane Garden Bay on Tortola's north shore for a dinghy ride ashore to listen to some hot music, and the day after that at a remote bay where we were the only boat. Traveling by sea is the way to hop around this archipelago of small islands and tiny cays. If a sailing trip isn't on your horizon, take one of the ferries that connect all the islands except Anegada.

Once a collection of about 50 sleepy islands and cays, the British Virgin Islands (BVI) are in the midst of transition. The main island of Tortola now sees huge cruise ships crowding its dock outside Road Town. Shoppers clog the downtown area on busy cruise-ship days, and traffic occasionally comes to a standstill. Even the second-largest island, Virgin Gorda, gets its share of smaller ships anchored off the main village of Spanish Town. Despite this explosive growth in the territory's tourism industry, it's still easy to escape the hubbub. Hotels outside Road Town usually provide a quiet oasis, and those on the other islands can be downright serene.

Each island has a different flavor. Want access to lots of restaurants and shopping? Make Tortola your choice. The largest of the BVIs, it covers 10 square mi and sits only a mile from St. John in the United States Virgin Islands (USVI). If you want to kick back at a small hotel or posh resort, try Virgin Gorda. Sitting nearly at the end of the chain, the 8-square-mi (21-square-km) island offers stellar beaches and a laid-back atmosphere. If you really want to get away from it all, the outermost islands, including Anegada and Jost Van Dyke, will fill the bill. Some of the smallest—Norman, Peter, Cooper, and Necker—are home to just one resort or restaurant. Others remain uninhabited specks on the horizon.

No matter what your choice, the scenery is stunning, with lush mountains meeting sandy beaches on all but nearly flat and reef-fringed Anegada. The warm Caribbean Sea beckons no matter which island you choose. Visitors mainly come to relax, though the number of organized activities is growing. The territory stakes its reputation on sailing, and you will find a number of companies renting bare or crewed charter boats.

Visitors have long visited the BVI, starting with Christopher Columbus in 1493. He called the islands *Las Once Mil Virgines*—the 11,000 Virgins—in honor of the 11,000 virgin companions of St. Ursula, martyred in the 4th century AD. Pirates and buccaneers followed, and then came the British, who farmed the islands until slavery was abolished in 1834. The BVI are still politically tied to Britain, so the queen appoints a royal governor, but residents elect a local Legislative Council. Offshore banking and tourism share top billing in the territory's economy, but the majority of the islands' jobs are tourism-related. Despite the growth, you can usually find a welcoming smile.

# TORTOLA

Updated by
Lynda Lohr

Once a sleepy backwater, Tortola is definitely on the busy side these days, particularly when several cruise ships drop anchor off Road Town. Passengers crowd the town's streets and shops, and open-air jitneys filled with cruise-ship passengers create bottlenecks on Tortola's byways. That said, most folks visit Tortola to relax on its deserted sands or linger over lunch at one of its many delightful restaurants. Beaches are never more than a few miles away, and the steep green hills that form Tortola's spine are fanned by gentle trade winds. The neighboring islands glimmer like emeralds in a sea of sapphire. It can be a world far removed from the hustle of modern life, but it simply doesn't compare to Virgin Gorda in terms of beautiful beaches—or even really nice resorts, for that matter.

## Where to Stay

Luxury on Tortola is more about a certain state of mind—serenity, seclusion, gentility, and a bit of Britain in the Caribbean—than about state-of-the-art amenities and facilities. Indeed, don't let a bit of rust on the screen or a chip in the paint mar your appreciation of the ambience. Instead, enjoy getting to know your fellow guests and staff at the island's cozy hotels. Hotels in Road Town don't have beaches, but they do have pools and are within walking distance of restaurants, nightspots, and shops. Accommodations outside Road Town are relatively isolated, but most are on beaches. The Tortola resorts are intimate—only a handful have more than 50 rooms. You will likely spend most of your time outside, so the location, size, or price of a hotel should be more of a factor to you than the decor of the rooms. Guests are treated as more than just room numbers, and many return year after year. This can make booking a room at popular resorts difficult, even off-season, despite the fact that more than half the island's visitors stay aboard their own or chartered boats.

A few hotels lack air-conditioning, relying instead on ceiling fans to capture the almost constant trade winds. Nights are cool and breezy, even in midsummer, and never reach the temperatures or humidity levels that are common in much of the United States in summer. You may assume that all accommodations listed here have air-conditioning unless we mention otherwise. Remember that some places may be closed during the peak of hurricane season—August through October—to give their owners a much-needed break.

### Villas

Renting a villa is growing in popularity. Vacationers like the privacy, the room to get comfortable, and the opportunity to cook their own meals. As everywhere, location counts, so if you want to be close to the beach, opt for a villa on the North Shore. If you want to dine out in Road Town every night, a villa closer to town may be a better bet.

## CLOSE UP

# American or British?

**YES, THE UNION JACK FLUTTERS** overhead in the tropical breeze, schools operate on the British system, place names have British spellings, Queen Elizabeth II appoints the governor—and the Queen's picture hangs on many walls. Indeed, residents celebrate the Queen's birthday every June with a public ceremony. You can overhear that charming English accent from a good handful of expats when you're lunching at Road Town restaurants, and you can buy British biscuits—which Americans call cookies—in the supermarkets.

But you can pay for your lunch and the biscuits with American money, because the U.S. dollar is legal tender here. The unusual circumstance is a matter of geography. The practice started in the mid-20th century, when BVI residents went to work in the nearby USVI. On trips home, they brought their U.S. dollars with them. Soon, they abandoned the barter system, and in 1959, the U.S. dollar became the official form of money. Interestingly, the government sells stamps for use only in the BVI that often carry pictures of Queen Elizabeth II and other royalty with the monetary value in U.S. dollars and cents.

The American influence continued to grow when Americans began to open businesses in the BVI because they preferred its quieter ambience to the hustle and bustle of St. Thomas. Inevitably, cable and satellite TV's U.S.-based programming, along with Hollywood-made movies, further influenced life in the BVI. And most goods are shipped from St. Thomas in the USVI, meaning you'll find more American-made Oreos than British-produced Peak Freens on the supermarket shelves.

---

Prices per week during the winter season run from around $2,000 for a one- or two-bedroom villa up to $10,000 for a five-room beachfront villa. Rates in summer are substantially less. Most, but not all, villa managers accept credit cards.

**Areana Villas** (🖃 Box 263, Road Town ☎ 284/494–5864 🖷 284/494–7626 ⊕ www.areanavillas.com) represents top-of-the-line properties. Homes offer accommodations for 2 to 10 people in one- to five-bedroom villas decorated in soothing pastels. Many have pools, whirlpool tubs, and tiled courtyards.

The St. Thomas–based **McLaughlin-Anderson Luxury Villas** (🖃 1000 Blackbeard's Hill, Suite 3, St. Thomas, VI 00802-6739 ☎ 240/776-0635 or 800/537–6246 ⊕ www.mclaughlinanderson.com) manages nearly three dozen properties spread over Tortola. Villas range in size from one to six bedrooms and come with full kitchens and stellar views. Most have pools. The company can hire a chef and stock your kitchen with groceries.

**Purple Pineapple Villa Rentals** (🖃 Box 305498-314, St. Thomas, VI 00803 ☎ 284/495–3100 🖷 305/723–0855 ⊕ www.purplepineapple.

com) manages eight luxury homes in locations all over the island from its base in Tortola. Most have pools, hot tubs, and other amenities. Villas range in size from one to six bedrooms.

## Hotels & Inns

ROAD TOWN

**$$**  🏨 **Maria's Hotel by the Sea.** Sitting near the water in busy Road Town, Maria's Hotel by the Sea is perfect for budget travelers who want to be near shops and restaurants but who don't need many frills. The least expensive rooms don't have ocean views, but all have bright tropical fabrics and rattan furniture to remind you that you're on an island. ⊠ *Waterfront Dr., Box 2364* ☎ *284/494–2595* 🖷 *284/494–2420* ⊕ *www.mariasbythesea.com* 🛏 *41 rooms* ♨ *Restaurant, refrigerators, cable TV, in-room data ports, pool, bar* ▭ *AE, MC, V* ⏹ *EP.*

**$$**  🏨 **Moorings-Mariner Inn.** If you enjoy the camaraderie of a busy marina, this inn on the fringes of Road Town may appeal to you. It's a hot spot for charter boaters—usually a lively group—heading out for a week-or-more sail around the islands. Rooms are spacious and have balconies or porches that are perfect for an afternoon's relaxing. All have pastel accents that complement the peach exteriors. ⊠ *Waterfront Dr., Box 139* ☎ *284/494–2333 or 800/535–7289* 🖷 *284/494–2226* 🛏 *36 rooms, 4 suites* ♨ *Restaurant, some kitchenettes, refrigerators, cable TV, in-room data ports, pool, dive shop, dock, marina, volleyball, bar, shops, Internet room* ▭ *MC, V* ⏹ *EP.*

**$$**  🏨 **Village Cay Resort & Marina.** If you want to be able to walk to restaurants and shops, you simply can't beat the prime location in the heart of Road Town. It's perfect for charter-yachters who want a night or two in town before heading out to sea, but land-based vacationers like it equally well. Rooms and suites are done in tropical style with tile floors, rattan furniture, and town or marina views. If you're planning on seeing more than Road Town, you'll need a car to explore and sun at the beach. Otherwise, a tiny pool will have to suffice for your morning swim. ⊠ *Wickham's Cay I, Box 145* ☎ *284/494–2771* 🖷 *284/494–2773* ⊕ *www.villagecay.com* 🛏 *21 rooms* ♨ *Restaurant, refrigerators, cable TV, in-room broadband, pool, spa, marina, bar, shops, Internet room* ▭ *AE, MC, V* ⏹ *EP.*

**$–$$**  🏨 **Fort Burt Hotel.** The Fort Burt Hotel surrounds the ruins of an old Dutch fort, giving you a sense of history along with a night's sleep. The hotel attracts many business travelers, who like its location on the fringes of Road Town and the two-line phones and fax machines in the suites and spacious deluxe rooms. Vacationers will enjoy it as well, especially those who think of it as a jumping-off place rather than a place to put down roots. A car will help a great deal in that regard. It's a bit of a hike to Road Town's shopping and restaurants, but there are a couple of stores and eating places right in the neighborhood. ⊠ *Waterfront Dr., Box 3380* ☎ *284/494–2587* 🖷 *284/494–2002* 🛏 *11 rooms, 8 suites* ♨ *Restaurant, some kitchenettes, some microwaves, refrigerators, cable TV, some in-room data ports, pool, bar* ▭ *AE, MC, V* ⏹ *EP.*

OUTSIDE ROAD
TOWN

**$$$$**  🏨 **Long Bay Beach Resort.** Although the service draws complaints, the management has been addressing the frosty attitude of some staff members. Long Bay Beach Resort is still Tortola's only choice if you want

**Tortola**

## Inset: Road Town

**1** J. R. O'Neal Botanic Gardens
Treasure Isle Rd.
Wickhams Cay Rd
Port Purcell
Waterfront Dr.
Free Bottom
**1**
**2** Wickhams Cay 2
Long Bush Rd.
Blyden Yard
**3**
**4**
**6**
**5** Wickhams Cay 1
**7**
Peter Island Ferry
**8**-**11**
Road Town
Romasco Place
Sir Olva Georga's Plaza
Ferry Dock
Customs House
Road Bay
**12**
Waterfront Dr.
Fort Charlotte Rd.
**2** Cedar Rd.
**3** **14**
Old Government House Museum
Fort Burt
Careening Cove
Burnt Point
Road Reef
**13**
MacNamara Rd.
0    1/4 mi
0    1/4 km

The Chikuzen

ATLANTIC OCEAN

Brewers Bay Pinnacle
Shark Bay
Rough Pt.
Hell Hole
Brewers Bay
**27**
Brewers Bay
Dubois Pt.
Mt. Healthy National Park
**10**
Todman Pk.
**26**
Skyworld
**25**
**9** **28**
Cane Garden Bay Rd.
**24**
Cane Garden Bay
**8**
Windy Hill
Joe's Hill Rd
Leonard's
Road Town
Road Town
**1**–**14**
**1**–**3**
see inset
Carrot Bay
Apple Bay
**7**
Sage Mountain National Park
Ridge Rd
**4**
Dolphin Discovery
Long Bay West
**22**
**23**
Sea Cows Bay
Smuggler's Cove
Lower Belmont Bay
**20**
**21**
Mt. Sage
Sea Cows Bay
Great Thatch Island
Steele Pt.
**19**
Zion Hill Rd.
Freshwater Pond
**15**
Soper's Hole
West End
Little Thatch Island
**18** **17**
**6**
Frenchman's Cay
**5** **16**
Fort Recovery
TO ST. THOMAS
0    2 mi
0    2 km
The Indians
ST. JOHN

**Hotels** ▼
Brewers Bay Campground ........ **27**
Fort Burt Hotel ........ **14**
Frenchman's Cay Hotel ............. **17**
Hodge's Creek Marina Hotel ........ **32**
Lambert Beach Resort ............. **30**
Long Bay Beach Resort ............. **20**
Maria's Hotel by the Sea ............. **7**
Moorings-Mariner Inn ... **2**
Myett's ............. **24**
Nanny Cay Hotel ...... **15**
Ole Works Inn ........ **25**
Sebastian's on the Beach ............. **21**
Sugar Mill Hotel ....... **22**
Village Cay Resort ..... **4**
The Villas of Fort Recovery Estates ...... **16**

**Restaurants** ▼
Brandywine Bay ....... **29**
C & F Restaurant ....... **1**
CafeSito .............. **8**
CalaMaya ............. **32**
Capriccio di Mare ..... **10**
The Captain's Table .... **5**

# Tortola

TO ANEGADA ↗

Wash Ballock Pt.

Longman's Pt.

Muskmellon Bay

North Bay

Great Camanoe

Guana Island

White Bay

Kitto Ghut

Lee Bay

Scrub Island

Monkey Pt.

**Elizabeth Beach**

Little Camanoe

Marina Cay

Rogue's Pt.

30

Trellis Bay

**Long Bay, Beef Island**

Ridge Rd.

Buta Mt.

Long Look

East End

**Beef Island International Airport**

Mt. Belle-Vue

Parham Town

Long Swamp

31

Bluff Bay

Baughers Bay

Ft. Shirley

Wickhams Cay

Fat Hogs Bay

Beef Island

Road Harbour

32

Buck Island

Paraquita Bay

29

TO VIRGIN GORDA →

*Sir Francis Drake Channel*

**KEY**

| | |
|---|---|
| 🏖 | Beaches |
| ◣ | Dive Sites |
| ⛴ | Ferry |
| 🚢 | Cruise Ship Terminal |
| **1** | Exploring Sights |
| 1 | Hotels & Restaurants |
| ⋯⋯ | Trail |

**Alice in Wonderland** ◣

◣ **Blonde Rock**
◣ **Painted Walls**
◣ **RMS Rhone**

TO PETER ISLAND ↓

all the resort amenities, including a beach, scads of water sports, tennis, and even a pitch-and-putt golf course. Accommodations range from traditional hotel rooms to three-bedroom villas, with lots of choices in between. All have a modern tropical feel with rattan furniture and brightly colored fabrics. Given its relative isolation on the northwest shore, you may not be inclined to make many excursions. Luckily, the Garden Restaurant serves romantic dinners. ⊠ *Long Bay* ⌂ *Box 433, Road Town* ☎ *284/495–4252 or 800/345–0271* 🖷 *284/495–4677* ⊕ *www. longbay.com* 🛏 *53 rooms, 37 suites* ⌂ *2 restaurants, some in-room safes, some kitchens, some kitchenettes, cable TV, in-room data ports, 2 tennis courts, pool, gym, spa, beach, dive shop, snorkeling, 2 bars, shops, Internet room, meeting rooms* 🖃 *AE, D, MC, V* ⵔ *EP.*

**$$$–$$$$**
**Fodor's**Choice
★

🏨 **Sugar Mill Hotel.** Though it's not a sprawling resort, this is our favorite resort on Tortola. The rooms are attractively decorated with more than the usual floral spreads and have balconies with good views, kitchens or kitchenettes, and even some sofa beds. The grounds get accolades for their attractive gardens, but many say the real reason to stay here is the easy access to the excellent Sugar Mill restaurant, which has both superb food and a stunning setting in the property's old sugar mill. Owners and food-and-travel writers Jeff and Jinx Morgan have brought all their expertise to this well-run small resort. The north-shore location puts you across the road from a nice beach, but you need a car to do anything more than enjoy the sun and sand. ⊠ *Apple Bay* ⌂ *Box 425, Road Town* ☎ *284/495–4355 or 800/462–8834* 🖷 *284/495–4696* ⊕ *www.sugarmillhotel.com* 🛏 *19 rooms, 2 suites, 1 villa, 1 cottage* ⌂ *2 restaurants, some kitchens, some kitchenettes, cable TV, in-room data ports, pool, beach, snorkeling, 2 bars, Internet room; no TV in some rooms* 🖃 *AE, MC, V* ⵔ *EP.*

**$$$–$$$$**

🏨 **The Villas of Fort Recovery Estates.** This is one of those small but special properties, distinguished by friendly service and the chance to get to know your fellow guests rather than the poshness of the rooms and upscale amenities. Villas come in several sizes, and all are quaint—though not fancy—and have good views across the water of St. John. A sandy beach stretches seaside, providing ample opportunity for relaxing. The emphasis on wellness is a welcome touch, and beachside yoga classes are a specialty. The staff is helpful and will arrange day sails and scuba-diving trips. ⊠ *Waterfront Dr., Box 239, Pockwood Pond* 🖷 *284/ 495–4354 or 800/367–8455* 🖷 *284/495–4036* ⊕ *www.fortrecovery.com* 🛏 *29 suites, 1 villa* ⌂ *Kitchens, cable TV, in-room data ports, Wi-Fi, pool, fitness classes, gym, massage, beach, snorkeling, babysitting, laundry service, Internet room* 🖃 *AE, MC, V* ⵔ *CP.*

**$$–$$$$**

🏨 **Lambert Beach Resort.** Although this isolated location on the northeast coast puts you far from Road Town, Lambert Bay is one of the island's loveliest stretches of sand and the main reason to recommend this resort. Rooms are tucked back in the foliage, but you're just a few steps away from an afternoon of sunning and swimming. A handful of restaurants in and around nearby Fat Hogs Bay are within easy reach if you just have to get off that gorgeous beach. At this writing, condo construction was set to begin; ask about their progress if you fear construction noise will be a problem. ⊠ *Lambert Bay, Box 534, East End*

☎ *284/495–2877* ☒ *284/495–2876* ⊕ *www.lambertbeachresort.com*
⊲ *38 rooms, 2 villas, 27 condos* ♿ *Restaurant, some kitchens, refrigerators, some cable TV, some in-room data ports, tennis court, pool, spa, beach, snorkeling, boating, bar, shop, Internet room* ▭ *AE, D, MC, V* ⏏ *EP.*

$$$  ▦ **Frenchman's Cay Hotel.** Tucked away down a narrow road near busy Soper's Hole, Frenchman's Cay provides a quiet oasis for folks who want the option of eating in or out and a bit more space than you'd find in a typical hotel room. All accommodations are villa style, with separate bedrooms and kitchens but no air-conditioning. We like this place for its get-away-from-it-all feel. That said, you can easily walk to Soper's Hole to expand your dining horizons and to do some shopping. ✉ *Frenchman's Cay, Box 1054, West End* ☎ *284/495–4844 or 800/235–4077* ☒ *284/495–4056* ⊕ *www.frenchmans.com* ⊲ *9 villas* ♿ *Restaurant, fans, kitchenettes, tennis court, pool, beach, snorkeling, bar; no a/c, no room TVs* ▭ *AE, D, MC, V* ⏏ *EP.*

$$–$$$  ▦ **Sebastian's on the Beach.** Sitting on the island's north coast, Sebastian's definitely has a beachy feel, and that's its primary charm. Rooms vary in amenities and price, with the remodeled beachfront rooms a bit more up-to-date than those that the hotel calls "beach rear." The beachfront rooms have the best views and put you right on the sand. The less expensive rooms are basic, across the street from the ocean, and lack views. Those nearest the intersection of North Coast Road and Zion Hill Road can also suffer from traffic noise. Although you can eat all your meals at the resort's enjoyable restaurant, the wonderful Sugar Mill Restaurant is just a short drive east. ✉ *Apple Bay* ⏎ *Box 441, Road Town* ☎ *284/495–4212 or 800/336–4870* ☒ *284/495–4466* ⊕ *www.sebastiansbvi.com* ⊲ *26 rooms, 9 villas* ♿ *Restaurant, fans, refrigerators, some in-room data ports, beach, bar, Internet room; no TV in some rooms* ▭ *AE, D, MC* ⏏ *EP.*

$$  ▦ **Hodge's Creek Marina Hotel.** Sitting marina-side out on the island's East End, this hotel puts you in the middle of the nautical action. If you're heading out on a chartered sailboat or if you especially enjoy the marine scene, this is definitely the place for you. Rooms are carpeted and have tiny balconies, but brightly colored spreads and curtains give the rooms a tropical feel. There's a small pool and the CalaMaya Restaurant in the complex, but you need a car to get out and about. ✉ *Hodge's Creek* ⏎ *Box 663, Road Town* ☎ *284/494–5000* ☒ *284/494–7676* ⊕ *www.hodgescreek.com* ⊲ *24 rooms* ♿ *Restaurant, cable TV, pool, dock, boating, marina, shops, Internet room* ▭ *AE, MC, V* ⏏ *EP.*

$$  ▦ **Myett's.** Tucked away in a beachfront garden, this tiny hotel puts you right in the middle of Cane Garden Bay's busy nightlife. The restaurant is one of the area's hottest spots. Rooms have a typical tropical feel, thanks to the tile floors and rattan furniture. If it's available, opt for the one room with a water view. Although you might be content to lounge at the beach and stroll around Cane Garden Bay, you'll need a car to get out and about. ✉ *Cane Garden Bay* ⏎ *Box 556, Cane Garden Bay* ☎ *284/495–9649* ☒ *284/495–9579* ⊕ *www.myettent.com* ⊲ *3 rooms* ♿ *Restaurant, fans, refrigerators, no room TV, beach, shops, Internet room, car rental* ▭ *AE, MC, V* ⏏ *EP.*

**$$** ⌷ **Nanny Cay Hotel.** This quiet oasis is far enough from Road Town to give it a secluded feel but close enough to make shops and restaurants convenient. You're just steps from the hotel's restaurant, boat charters, and the chance to stroll the busy boatyard to gawk at the yachts under repair, but you still have to drive a good 20 minutes to get to the closest beach at Cane Garden Bay. The rooms, which have tile floors, are cheerful, with lots of bright Caribbean colors. ⊠ *Nanny Cay* ⌖ *Box 281, Road Town* ☎ *284/494–2512 or 866/284–4683* ⊟ *284/494–0555* ⊕ *www.nannycay.com* ⇨ *38 rooms* ⚬ *2 restaurants, some kitchenettes, cable TV, tennis court, pool, dive shop, dock, boating, marina, shops, Internet room, meeting rooms* ⊟ *MC, V* ⓘ *EP.*

**$–$$** ⌷ **Ole Works Inn.** The small hotel's location on busy Cane Garden Bay and its ownership by Quito Rhymer, one of the island's most popular musicians, guarantee that it's not a quiet retreat. If you don't mind strolling a short distance to the beach, want to eat in the nearby casual restaurants, and enjoy mixing and mingling with the locals at the village's numerous bars, this is a good choice. Rooms are modest, and most have carpeting rather than tile. Opt for a beach-facing room for the best views. ⊠ *Cane Garden Bay* ⌖ *Box 560, Road Town* ☎ *284/495–4837* ⊟ *284/495–9618* ⇨ *14 rooms, 3 suites* ⚬ *Fans, some kitchenettes, refrigerators, cable TV, in-room data ports, pool* ⊟ *AE, MC, V* ⓘ *EP.*

WHERE TO CAMP ⚠ **Brewers Bay Campground.** If you want to escape to nature and don't mind a rather ramshackle look to where you camp, this is a very sociable place to pitch your tent. It's not a manicured national-park-type place, but you're right on the water and can meet the other campers at the small bar and restaurant. Tarps draped here and there provide privacy and keep the rain off your cooking area. It's a great deal, especially if you bring your own tent. You really need a car unless you want to take expensive taxi rides to see other parts of the island. ⚬ *Restaurant, BBQs, flush toilets, drinking water, showers, public telephone, swimming (ocean)* ⇨ *20 sites* ⊠ *Brewers Bay* ⌖ *Box 185, Road Town* ☎ *284/494–3463* ⊟ *No credit cards.*

## Where to Eat

On Tortola local seafood is plentiful, and although other fresh ingredients are scarce, the island's chefs are a creative lot who apply genius to whatever the supply boat delivers. Contemporary American dishes prepared with a Caribbean influence are very popular. The fancier, more expensive restaurants have dress codes: long pants and collared shirts for men and elegant, casual resort wear for women.

### Road Town

AMERICAN/ ✕ **The Pub.** At this lively waterfront spot, tables are arranged along a
CASUAL terrace facing a small marina and the harbor in Road Town. Hamburg-
**$–$$$** ers, salads, and sandwiches are typical lunch offerings. In the evening you can also choose grilled fish, sautéed conch, sizzling steaks, or barbecued ribs. There's live entertainment on weekends, and locals gather here nightly for spirited games at the pool table. ⊠ *Waterfront Dr.* ☎ *284/494–2608* ⚬ *Reservations not accepted* ⊟ *AE, D, MC, V* ⊙ *No lunch Sun.*

**2**

🕙 **$–$$** ✕ **Pusser's Road Town Pub.** Almost everyone who visits Tortola stops here at least once to have a bite to eat and to sample the famous Pusser's Rum Painkiller (fruit juices and rum). The nonthreatening menu includes cheesy pizza, shepherd's pie, fish-and-chips, and hamburgers. Dine inside in air-conditioned comfort or outside on the veranda, which looks out on the harbor. ⊠ *Waterfront Dr.* ☎ *284/494–3897* ▤ *AE, D, MC, V.*

CARIBBEAN ✕ **C&F Restaurant.** Crowds head to this casual spot for the best barbe-
**$$–$$$** cue in town (chicken, fish, and ribs), fresh local fish and lobster, and excellent curries. Sometimes there's a wait for a table, but it's worth it. The restaurant is just outside Road Town, on a side street past the Moorings and Riteway. ⊠ *Off Canaan Rd., Purcell Estate* ☎ *284/ 494–4941* ◬ *Reservations not accepted* ▤ *AE, D, MC, V* ☺ *No lunch.*

ECLECTIC ✕ **CafeSito.** Don't be put off by the pedestrian decor. The chef at this
**$$$** shopping-center spot conjures up delicious dishes that run the gamut from burgers to lobster to chicken alfredo. It's the place to go for pizza smothered with everything from the standard cheese and tomato to the more unusual chicken and bacon. In winter, the staff will deliver anything from its menu straight to your hotel. ⊠ *Wickham's Cay I, Waterfront Dr.* ☎ *284/494–7412* ▤ *D, MC, V.*

**$–$$$** ✕ **Virgin Queen.** The sailing and rugby crowds head here to play darts, drink beer, and eat Queen's Pizza—a crusty, cheesy pie topped with sausage, onions, green peppers, and mushrooms. Also on the menu is excellent West Indian and English fare: barbecued ribs with beans and rice, bangers and mash, shepherd's pie, and grilled sirloin steak. ⊠ *Fleming St.* ☎ *284/494–2310* ▤ *MC, V* ☺ *Closed Sun.*

FRENCH ✕ **Le Cabanon.** Birds and bougainvillea brighten the patio of this breezy
**$$–$$$$** French restaurant and bar, a popular gathering spot for locals and visitors alike. French onion soup and herring salad are good appetizer choices. From there, move on to roasted pigeon, monkfish in rosemary sauce, or beef tenderloin with green peppercorn sauce. Save room for such tasty desserts as chocolate cake, crème brûlée, or a platter of French cheeses. ⊠ *Waterfront Dr.* ☎ *284/494–8660* ▤ *D, MC, V* ☺ *Closed Sun.*

ITALIAN ✕ **Spaghetti Junction at Beach Club Terrace.** Popular with the boating
★ **$–$$$** crowd, this longtime favorite serves up delightful West Indian food like stewed lobster and fresh local fish along with Italian favorites like penne smothered in a spicy tomato sauce, spinach-mushroom lasagna, and angel-hair pasta with shellfish. For something that combines a bit of both, try the spicy jambalaya pasta. ⊠ *Blackburn Hwy., Baughers Bay* ☎ *284/ 494–4880* ▤ *AE, MC, V* ☺ *Closed Sun.*

★ **$–$$** ✕ **Capriccio di Mare.** The owners of the well-known Brandywine Bay restaurant also run this authentic, little Italian outdoor café. Stop by for an espresso, fresh pastry, a bowl of perfectly cooked linguine, or a crispy tomato and mozzarella pizza. Drink specialties include a mango Bellini, an adaptation of the famous cocktail served at Harry's Bar in Venice. ⊠ *Waterfront Dr.* ☎ *284/494–5369* ◬ *Reservations not accepted* ▤ *D, MC, V* ☺ *Closed Sun.*

SEAFOOD ✕ **The Captain's Table.** Select the lobster you want from the pool, but
$–$$$ be careful not to fall in—it's in the floor right in the middle of the dining room. The menu also includes traditional escargots, filet mignon with blue cheese sauce, duckling with berry sauce, and creative daily specials that usually include freshly caught fish. Ceiling fans keep the dining room cool, but there are also tables on a breezy terrace overlooking the harbor. ⊠ *Wickham's Cay I* ☎ *284/494–3885* ▭ *AE, MC, V* ☉ *No lunch Sat.*

## Outside Road Town

AMERICAN- ✕ **Pusser's Landing.** Yachters flock to this waterfront restaurant. Down-
CASUAL stairs, from late morning to well into the evening, belly up to the out-
♨ $$–$$$ door mahogany bar or sit downstairs for sandwiches, fish-and-chips, and pizzas. At dinnertime head upstairs for a harbor view and a quiet alfresco meal of grilled steak or local fish. ⊠ *Soper's Hole* ☎ *284/495–4554* ▭ *AE, MC, V.*

CARIBBEAN ✕ **Quito's Gazebo.** This rustic beachside bar and restaurant is owned and
$$–$$$$ operated by Quito Rhymer, a multitalented BVI recording star who plays and sings solo on Tuesday and Thursday and performs with his reggae band on Friday and Saturday. The menu is Caribbean, with an emphasis on fresh fish. Try the conch fritters or the chicken roti. ⊠ *Cane Garden Bay* ☎ *284/495–4837* ▭ *AE, MC, V* ☉ *Closed Mon.*

$$–$$$ ✕ **Myett's Garden & Grille.** Right on the beach, this bi-level restaurant and bar is hopping day and night. Chowder made with fresh Anegada lobsters is the specialty, though the menu includes everything from vegetarian dishes to grilled shrimp, steak, and tuna. There's live entertainment every night during the winter. ⊠ *Cane Garden Bay* ☎ *284/495–9649* ▭ *AE, MC, V.*

$–$$$ ✕ **Roti Palace.** You might be tempted to pass this tiny spot on Road Town's
Fodor'sChoice Main Street when you see the plastic tablecloths and fake flowers, but
★ owner Jean Leonard's reputation for dishing up fantastic roti is known far and wide. A flatbread is filled with curried potatoes, onions and lobster, chicken, beef, conch, goat, or vegetables. Ask for the bone out if you order the chicken to save yourself the trouble of fishing them out of your mouth. ⊠ *Main St., Road Town* ☎ *284/494–4196* ▭ *No credit cards* ☉ *Closed Sun.*

CONTEMPORARY ✕ **Palm Terrace Restaurant.** Relax over dinner in this open-air restaurant
$$–$$$$ at Long Bay Beach Resort. Tables are well spaced, offering enough privacy for intimate conversation. The menu changes daily, but several dishes show up regularly. Good appetizers are garlicky escargots in a pastry shell, Caribbean-style fish chowder, and shrimp fritters. Entrées include tuna glazed with tamarind and honey, pan-roasted duck with a rosemary glaze, or a filet mignon served with mushrooms. There are always at least five desserts to choose from, which might include Belgian chocolate mousse, strawberry cheesecake, or a fluffy lemon and coconut cake. ⊠ *Long Bay Beach Resort, Long Bay* ☎ *284/495–4252* ▭ *AE, D, MC, V* ☉ *No lunch.*

$$–$$$$ ✕ **Sebastian's Beach Bar & Restaurant.** The waves practically lap at your feet at this beachfront restaurant on Tortola's northern shore. The menu runs to seafood—especially lobster, conch, and local fish—

but you can also find dishes like ginger chicken and filet mignon. It's a perfect spot to stop for lunch on your around-the-island tour. Try the grilled dolphinfish sandwich, served on a soft roll with an oniony tartar sauce. Finish off with a cup of Sebastian's coffee spiked with home-brewed rum. ⊠ *North Coast Rd., Apple Bay* ☎ *284/494–4212* ⊟ *AE, D, MC.*

★ $$$ ✗ **Eclipse.** This popular waterfront spot isn't much more than a terrace filled with tables, but you can be caressed by the soft ocean breezes while you are impressed with the cuisine. With dishes from all over the globe, the menu is certainly well traveled. Sample several small dishes—maybe the cracked calamari, chèvre salad, and tuna carpaccio—as you peruse the two-page grazing menu. Or if you prefer, dig into the spicy curries, shrimp with chestnuts, grilled swordfish, and vegetarian dishes on the regular menu. ⊠ *Fat Hog's Bay, East End* ☎ *284/495–1646* ⊟ *MC, V* ☉ *No lunch.*

☾ $$$ ✗ **Skyworld.** The top of a mountain is the location for this casually elegant dining room. The menu changes constantly, but look for imaginative dishes such as pork tenderloin medallions on a bed of red onion marmalade and rabbit with roasted vegetables. Other specialties include grilled local fish, roast duck, rack of lamb with a sauce du jour, and key lime pie. The lunch menu runs to hamburgers and sandwiches with some interesting additions such as a goat cheese tartlet. The restaurant can be crowded for lunch when cruise ships dock. ⊠ *Ridge Rd., Joe's Hill* ☎ *284/494–3567* ⊟ *AE, D, DC, MC, V.*

$$$ ✗ **Turtles.** If you're touring the island, Turtles is a good place to stop for lunch or dinner. Sitting just back from the beach at Lambert Beach Resort, this casual place provides a relaxing respite from the rigors of navigating mountain roads. At dinner you might find tiger shrimp in a curry sauce or rack of lamb with a raspberry glaze. Lunch favorites include fried shrimp, fresh tuna on a bun, and pasta dishes. ⊠ *Lambert Beach Resort, Lambert Bay, East End* ☎ *284/495–2877* ⊟ *AE, D, MC, V.*

$$–$$$ ✗ **CalaMaya.** Casual fare is what you'll find at this waterfront restaurant. You can always order a burger or lobster salad; the grilled Kaiser sandwich—shrimp, cheese, and pineapple on a crisp roll—is a tasty alternative. For dinner, try the snapper with onions, peppers, and thyme. ⊠ *Hodge's Creek Marina, Blackburn Hwy.* ☎ *284/495–2126* ⊟ *AE, MC, V.*

$$–$$$ ✗ **Mountain View.** It's worth the drive up Sage Mountain for lunch or Fodor'sChoice dinner at this casual restaurant. The view is spectacular—one of the best ★ on Tortola. The small menu includes dishes like veal with a ginger sauce and grilled mahimahi in a lime-onion sauce. The lobster salad sandwich is the house lunch specialty. If it's on the menu, don't pass up the chicken roti. ⊠ *Sage Mountain* ☎ *284/495–9536* ⊟ *AE, MC, V.*

$$–$$$ ✗ **Sugar Mill Restaurant.** Candles gleam, and the background music is Fodor'sChoice peaceful in this romantic restaurant inside a 17th-century sugar mill. Well- ★ prepared selections on the à la carte menu, which changes nightly, include some pasta and vegetarian entrées. Lobster bisque with basil croutons and a curried lobster patty are good starters. Favorite entrées include grilled swordfish with a lime-and-chive butter, beef curry with *poppadoms* (Indian popovers), pan-seared roast duck, and fresh fish with

a spicy creole sauce. ⊠ *Sugar Mill Hotel, Apple Bay* ☎ *284/495–4355* ▤ *AE, MC, V* ☉ *No lunch.*

ECLECTIC
$–$$$

✕ **The Jolly Roger Restaurant.** This casual, open-air restaurant near the ferry terminal is as popular with locals as it is with visitors. The menu ranges from burgers to rib-eye steak to the island favorite, local lobster. Try the savory conch fritters filled with tender local conch and herbs for a good start to your dinner. End it with a slice of sweet key lime pie. ⊠ *West End* ☎ *284/495–4559* ▤ *D, MC, V.*

ITALIAN
$$$

Fodor'sChoice
★

✕ **Brandywine Bay.** Candlelit outdoor tables have sweeping views of neighboring islands, and owner Davide Pugliese prepares foods the Tuscan way: grilled with lots of fresh herbs. The remarkable menu always includes duck with a berry sauce and often has homemade mozzarella, beef carpaccio, grilled swordfish, and veal chop with ricotta and sundried tomatoes. The wine list is excellent, and the lemon tart and the tiramisu are irresistible. ⊠ *Sir Francis Drake Hwy., east of Road Town, Brandywine Bay* ☎ *284/495–2301* ⌂ *Reservations essential* ▤ *AE, MC, V* ☉ *Closed Sun. No lunch.*

## Beaches

Beaches in the BVI are less developed than those on St. Thomas or St. Croix, but they are simply not as inviting. The best BVI beaches are on deserted islands reachable only by boats, so take a snorkeling or sailing trip at least once. Tortola's north side has several perfect palm-fringed, white-sand beaches that curl around turquoise bays and coves, though none really achieve greatness. Nearly all are accessible by car (preferably one with four-wheel-drive), albeit down bumpy roads that corkscrew precipitously. Some of these beaches are lined with bars and restaurants as well as water-sports equipment stalls; others have absolutely nothing.

**Apple Bay.** If you want to surf, the area including Little Apple Bay and Capoon's Bay is the spot—although the white, sandy beach itself is narrow. Sebastian's, a very casual hotel, caters to those in search of the perfect wave. The legendary Bomba's Surfside Shack—a landmark festooned with all manner of flotsam and jetsam—serves drinks and casual food. Otherwise, there's nothing else in the way of amenities. Good surf is never a sure thing, but you're more apt to find it in January and February. If you're swimming and the waves are up, take care not to get dashed on the rocks. ⊠ *North Shore Rd. at Zion Hill Rd.*

**Brewers Bay.** The water here is good for snorkeling, and you can find a campground with showers and bathrooms and beach bar tucked in the foliage right behind the beach. An old sugar mill and ruins of a rum distillery are just north of the beach along the road. The beach is easy to find, but the paved roads leading down the hill to it can be a bit daunting. You can get there from either Brewers Bay Road East or Brewers Bay Road West. ⊠ *Brewers Bay Rd. E off Cane Garden Bay Rd., or Brewers Bay Rd. W off Ridge Rd.*

**Cane Garden Bay.** This enticing beach has exceptionally calm, crystalline waters and a silky stretch of sand except when storms at sea turn the water murky. Snorkeling is good along the edges. Casual guesthouses, restaurants, bars, and even shops are just steps off the beach in the growing village of the same name. It's a laid-back, even somewhat funky place to put down your beach towel. Water-sports shops rent equipment. It's the closest beach to Road Town—one steep uphill and downhill drive—and one of the BVI's best-known anchorages (unfortunately, it can be very crowded when cruise ships are in town). ⊠ *Cane Garden Bay Rd. off Ridge Rd.*

**Elizabeth Beach.** Home to Lambert Beach Resort, the palm-lined, wide, and sandy beach has parking for nonguests on its steep downhill access road. The undertow can be severe here in winter, but it's a nice place to spend a few hours. Other than at the hotel, which welcomes nonguests at its restaurant, there are no amenities aside from peace and quiet. Turn at the sign for Lambert Beach Resort. If you miss it, you wind up at Her Majesty's Prison. ⊠ *Lambert Rd. off Ridge Rd., on the eastern end of island.*

**Long Bay, Beef Island.** The scenery here is superlative: the beach stretches seemingly forever, and you can catch a glimpse of Little Camanoe and Great Camanoe islands. If you walk around the bend to the right, you can see little Marina Cay and Scrub Island. Long Bay is also a good place to find seashells. Swim out to wherever you see a dark patch for some nice snorkeling. There are no amenities, so come prepared with your own drinks and snacks. Turn left shortly after crossing the bridge to Beef Island. ⊠ *Beef Island Rd., Beef Island.*

**Long Bay West.** Have your camera ready to snap the breathtaking approach to this stunning, mile-long stretch of white sand. Although Long Bay Resort sprawls along part of it, the entire beach is open to the public. The water isn't as calm here as at Cane Garden or Brewers Bay, but it's still swimmable. Rent water-sports equipment and enjoy the beachfront restaurant at the resort. Turn left at Zion Hill Road; then travel about half a mile. ⊠ *Long Bay Rd.*

**Smuggler's Cove.** After bouncing your way down a pothole-filled dirt road to this beautiful, palm-fringed beach, you'll feel as if you've found a hidden piece of the island, although you probably won't be alone on weekends. There's a fine view of Jost Van Dyke, and the snorkeling is good as well. It's popular with Long Bay Resort guests who want a change of scenery, but there are no amenities. Follow Long Bay Road past Long Bay Resort, keeping to the roads nearest the water until you reach the beach. It's about a mile past the resort. ⊠ *Long Bay Rd.*

## Sports & the Outdoors

CRICKET Fans of this sport are fiercely loyal and exuberant. Matches are held at the New Recreation Grounds, next to the J. R. O'Neal Botanic Gardens, weekends from February to April. Check local newspapers or ask at your hotel front desk for information on times and teams.

DIVING & SNORKELING Clear waters and numerous reefs afford some wonderful opportunities for underwater exploration. In some spots, visibility reaches 100 feet, but in many locations colorful reefs teeming with fish are just a few feet below the sea surface. The BVI's system of marine parks means the underwater life visible through your mask will stay protected.

There are several popular dive spots around the islands. **Alice in Wonderland** is a deep dive south of Ginger Island with a wall that slopes gently from 15 feet to 100 feet. It's an area overrun with huge mushroom-shape coral, hence its name. Crabs, lobsters, and shimmering fan corals make their homes in the tunnels, ledges, and overhangs of **Blonde Rock,** a pinnacle that goes from just 15 feet below the surface to 60 feet deep. It's between Dead Chest and Salt Island. When the currents aren't too strong, **Brewers Bay Pinnacle** (20 to 90 feet down) teems with sea life. At the **Indians,** near Pelican Island, colorful corals decorate canyons and grottos created by four large, jagged pinnacles that rise 50 feet from the ocean floor. The **Painted Walls** is a shallow dive site where corals and sponges create a kaleidoscope of colors on the walls of four long gullies. It's northeast of Dead Chest.

The **Chikuzen,** sunk northwest of Brewers Bay in 1981, is a 246-foot vessel in 75 feet of water; it's home to thousands of fish, colorful corals, and big rays. In 1867 the **RMS Rhone,** a 310-foot royal mail steamer, split in two when it sank in a devastating hurricane. It's so well preserved that it was used as an underwater prop in the movie *The Deep.* You can see the crow's nest and bowsprit, the cargo hold in the bow, and the engine and enormous propeller shaft in the stern. Its four parts are at various depths from 30 to 80 feet (nearby Rhone Reef is only 20 to 50 feet down). Get yourself some snorkeling gear and hop a dive boat to this wreck, off Salt Island (across the channel from Road Town) and part of the BVI National Parks Trust. Every dive outfit in the BVI runs scuba and snorkel tours here, and if you go on only one trip, make it this one. Rates start at around $60 for a one-tank dive and $85 for a two-tank dive.

Your hotel probably has a dive company located right on the premises. If not, the staff can recommend one nearby. Using your hotel's dive company makes a trip to the offshore dive and snorkel sites a breeze. Just stroll down to the dock and hop aboard. All dive companies are certified by PADI, the Professional Association of Diving Instructors, which ensures your instructors are qualified to safely take vacationers diving. The boats are also inspected to make sure they're seaworthy. If you've never dived, try a short introductory dive, often called a resort course, which teaches you enough to get you under water. In the unlikely event you get a case of the bends, a condition that can happen when you rise to the surface too fast, your dive team will whisk you to the decompression chamber at Roy L. Schneider Regional Medical Center Hospital in nearby St. Thomas.

**Blue Waters Divers** (⊠ Nanny Cay ☎ 284/495–1200 ⊠ Soper's Hole, West End ☎ 284/294–1200 ⊕ www.bluewaterdiversbvi.com) teaches resort, open-water, rescue, and advanced diving courses and also makes daily trips. If you're chartering a sailboat, the company's boat will meet your boat at Peter, Salt, or CooperIsland for a rendezvous dive. Rates include all equipment as well as instruction. Make arrangements two days in advance. **Dive Tortola** (⊠ Prospect Reef ☎ 284/494–9200 ⊕ www.divetortola.com) offers beginner and advanced diving courses and daily trips. Trainers teach open-water, rescue, advanced diving, and resort courses. Dive Tortola also offers a rendezvous diving option for folks on charter sailboats.

FISHING  Most of the boats that take you deep-sea fishing for bluefish, wahoo, swordfish, and shark leave from nearby St. Thomas, but local anglers like to fish the shallower water for bonefish. A half-day of bone fishing runs about $480, a full day around $850. Call **Caribbean Fly Fishing** (⊠ Nanny Cay ☎ 284/499–4797 ⊕ www.caribfllyfishing.com).

HIKING  Sage Mountain National Park attacts hikers who enjoy the quiet trails that crisscross the island's loftiest peak. There are some lovely views and the chance to see rare species that grow only at higher elevations.

HORSEBACK  If you've ever wanted to ride a horse along a deserted beach, through
RIDING  a rain forest, or if you want to head up to mountain ridges for spectacular views, **Shadow Stables** (⊠ Ridge Rd., Todman Peak ☎ 284/494–2262) offers small group rides for $100 per person per hour.

SAILING  The BVI are among the world's most popular sailing destinations.
★ ☾  They're close together and surrounded by calm waters, so it's fairly easy to sail from one anchorage to the next. Most of the Caribbean's biggest sailboat charter companies have operations in Tortola. If you know how to sail, you can charter a bareboat (perhaps for your entire vacation); if you're unschooled, you can hire a boat with a captain. Prices vary depending on the type and size of the boat you wish to charter. In season, a weekly charter runs from $1,500 to $35,000. Book early to make sure you get the boat that fits you best. Most of Tortola's marinas have hotels, which give you a convenient place to spend the nights before and after your charter.

If a day sail to some secluded anchorage is more your spot of tea, the BVI has numerous boats of various sizes and styles that leave from many points around Tortola. Prices start at around $80 per person for a full-day sail, including lunch and snorkeling equipment.

**BVI Yacht Charters** (⊠ Inner Harbour Marina, Road Town ☎ 284/494–4289 or 888/615–4006 ⊕ www.bviyachtcharters.com) offers 31-foot to 56-foot sailboats for charter—with or without a captain and crew, whichever you prefer. **Catamaran Charters** (⊠ Nanny Cay Marina, Nanny Cay ☎ 284/494–6661 or 800/262–0308 ⊕ www.catamarans.com) charters catamarans with or without a captain. The **Moorings** (⊠ Wickham's Cay II, Road Town ☎ 284/494–2331 or 800/535–7289 ⊕ www.moorings.com), considered one of the best bareboat operations in the world, has a large fleet of well-maintained, mostly Beneteau sailing yachts. Hire a captain or sail the boat yourself. If you prefer a powerboat, call **Regency Yacht Vacations** (⊠ Wickham's Cay I, Road Town ☎ 284/495–1970 or 800/524–7676 ⊕ www.regencyvacations.com) for both bareboat and captained sail and powerboat charters. **Sunsail** (⊠ Hodge's Creek Marina, East End ☎ 284/495–4740 or 800/327–2276 ⊕ www.sunsail.com) offers a full fleet of boats to charter with or without a captain. **Voyages** (⊠ Soper's Hole Marina, West End ☎ 284/494–0740 or 888/869–2436 ⊕ www.voyagecharters.com) offers a variety of sailboats for charter with or without a captain and crew.

**Aristocat Charters** (✉ West End ☎ 284/499–1249 ⊕ www. aristocatcharters.com) sets sail daily to the Indians and Peter Island aboard a 48-foot catamaran. **White Squall II** (✉ Village Cay Marina, Road Town ☎ 284/495–2564 ⊕ www.whitesquall2.com) takes you on regularly scheduled day sails to the Baths at Virgin Gorda, Jost Van Dyke, or the Caves at Norman Island on an 80-foot schooner.

SURFING   Surfing is big on Tortola's north shore, particularly when the winter swells come in to Josiah's and Apple bays. Rent surfboards starting at $25 for a full day.

**HIHO** (✉ Waterfront Dr., Road Town ☎ 284/494–7694 ⊕ www.go-hiho. com) has a good surfboard selection for sale or rent. The staff will give you advice on the best spots to put in your board.

TENNIS   Tortola's tennis options range from simple, untended, concrete courts to professionally maintained facilities that host organized tournaments. Most hotels have a least one or two courts for guests. The courts listed below are all open to the public; some have restrictions for nonguests.

**Frenchman's Cay Hotel** (✉ West End ☎ 284/495–4844) has an unlit artificial-grass court with a pretty view of Sir Francis Drake Channel. Patrons of the hotel or restaurant can use the court for free; for others there's an hourly fee of $5. **Long Bay Beach Resort** (✉ Long Bay ☎ 284/495–4252) has two lighted soft courts. Private lessons are $60 per hour. Nonguests may rent a court for $8 an hour plus a weekly membership fee of $60 per couple. Tennis rackets can be rented for $7 an hour.

WINDSURFING   Steady trade winds make windsurfing a breeze. Three of the best spots for sailboarding are Nanny Cay, Slaney Point, and Trellis Bay on Beef Island. Rates for sailboards start at about $25 an hour or $75 for a full day.

**Boardsailing BVI** (✉ Trellis Bay, Beef Island ☎ 284/495–2447 ⊕ www. windsurfing.vi) rents equipment and offers private and group lessons.

# Shopping

The BVI aren't really a shopper's delight, but there are many shops showcasing original wares—from jams and spices to resort wear to excellent artwork.

## Shopping Areas

Many shops and boutiques are clustered along and just off Road Town's **Main Street.** You can shop in Road Town's **Wickham's Cay I** adjacent to the marina. **Crafts Alive Market** on the Road Town waterfront is a collection of colorful West Indian–style buildings with shops that carry items made in the BVI. You might find pretty baskets or interesting pottery or perhaps a bottle of home-brew hot sauce. There's an ever-growing number of art and clothing stores at **Soper's Hole** in West End.

## Specialty Stores

ART   The **Gallery** (✉ 102 Main St., Road Town ☎ 284/494–6680) carries photographs by local photographer Amanda Baker and paintings by other Tortola artists. **Sunny Caribbee** (✉ Main St., Road Town ☎ 284/494–

2178) has many paintings, prints, and watercolors by artists from throughout the Caribbean.

**CLOTHES & TEXTILES** **Arawak** (⊠ On the dock, Nanny Cay ☎ 284/494–5240 🖂 Hodge's Creek Marina, Hodge's Creek ☎ 284/495–1106) carries batik sundresses, sportswear, and resort wear for men and women. There's also a selection of children's clothing. **Latitude 18°** (⊠ Main St., Road Town 🖂 Soper's Hole Marina, West End ☎ 284/494–7807 for both stores) sells Maui Jim, Smith, Oakley, and Revo sunglasses; Freestyle, Quiksilver, and Roxy watches; and a fine collection of beach towels, sandals, sundresses, and sarongs. **Pusser's Company Store** (⊠ Main St. at Waterfront Rd., Road Town ☎ 284/494–2467 🖂 Soper's Hole Marina, West End ☎ 284/495–4599) sells nautical memorabilia, ship models, marine paintings, an entire line of clothes for both men and women, and gift items bearing the Pusser's logo, handsome decorator bottles of Pusser's rum, Caribbean books, Cuban cigars, and luggage. **Sea Urchin** (⊠ Mill Mall, Road Town ☎ 284/494–4108 🖂 Soper's Hole Marina, West End ☎ 284/495–4850) is the source for local books, jewelry, sunglasses, and resort wear—print shirts and shorts, colorful swimsuits, sandals, T-shirts—for the whole family. **Zenaida's of West End** (⊠ Soper's Hole Marina, West End ☎ 284/495–4867) displays the fabric finds of Argentine Vivian Jenik Helm, who travels through South America, Africa, and India in search of batiks, hand-painted and hand-blocked fabrics, and interesting weaves that can be made into pareus (women's wraps) or wall hangings. The shop also sells unusual bags, belts, sarongs, scarves, and ethnic jewelry.

**FOODSTUFFS** **Ample Hamper** (⊠ Inner Harbour Marina, Road Town ☎ 284/494–2494 🖂 Frenchman's Cay Marina, West End ☎ 284/495–4684 ⊕ www.amplehamper.com) has an outstanding collection of cheeses, wines, fresh fruits, and canned goods from the United Kingdom and the United States. You can have the management here provision your yacht or rental villa. **Best of British** (⊠ Wickham's Cay I, Road Town ☎ 284/494–3462) has lots of nifty British food sitting cheek and jowl with more American fare. Shop here for Marmite, Vegemite, shortbread, frozen meat pies, and delightful Christmas crackers filled with surprises. **K-Marks** (⊠ Waterfront Dr., at Port Purcell, Road Town ☎ 284/494–4649) carries the usual supermarket stuff—albeit a much smaller selection than you might find in your hometown supermarket.

**GIFTS** **Bamboushay** (⊠ Nanny Cay Marina, Nanny Cay ☎ 284/494–0393) sells handcrafted Tortola-made pottery in shades that reflect the sea. In a brightly painted West Indian house, **Sunny Caribbee** (⊠ Main St., Road Town ☎ 284/494–2178) packages its own herbs, teas, coffees, vinegars, hot sauces, soaps, skin and suntan lotions, and exotic concoctions—Arawak Love Potion and Island Hangover Cure, for example. There are also Caribbean books and art and hand-painted decorative accessories.

**JEWELRY** **Columbian Emeralds International** (⊠ Wickham's Cay I, Road Town ☎ 284/494–7477), a Caribbean chain catering to the cruise-ship crowd, is the source for duty-free emeralds plus other gems, gold jewelry, crystal, and china. **D'Zandra's** (⊠ Wickham's Cay I, Road Town

☎ 284/494–8330) carries mostly black coral items set in gold and silver. Many pieces reflect Caribbean and sea themes. **Samarkand** (⌧ Main St., Road Town ☎ 284/494–6415) crafts charming gold-and-silver pendants, earrings, bracelets, and pins, many with an island theme: seashells, lizards, pelicans, palm trees. There are also reproduction Spanish pieces of eight (old Spanish coins worth eight reals) that were found on sunken galleons.

PERFUMES & COSMETICS **Flamboyance** (⌧Palm Grove Shopping Center, Waterfront Dr., Road Town ☎ 284/494–4099) carries designer fragrances and upscale cosmetics.

STAMPS The **BVI Post Office** (⌧ Main St., Road Town ☎ 284/494–3701) is a philatelist's dream. It has a worldwide reputation for exquisite stamps in all sorts of designs. Although the stamps carry U.S. monetary designations, they can be used for postage only in the BVI.

# Nightlife & the Arts

## Nightlife

Like any other good sailing destination, Tortola has watering holes that are popular with salty and not-so-salty dogs. Many offer entertainment; check the weekly *Limin' Times* for schedules and up-to-date information. Bands change like the weather, and what's hot today can be old news tomorrow. The local beverage is the Painkiller, an innocent-tasting mixture of fruit juices and rums. It goes down smoothly but packs quite a punch, so give yourself time to recover before you order another.

By day **Bomba's Surfside Shack** (⌧ Apple Bay ☎ 284/495–4148), which is covered with everything from crepe-paper leis to ancient license plates to colorful graffiti, looks like a pile of junk; by night it's one of Tortola's liveliest spots and one of the Caribbean's most famous beach bars. There's a fish fry and a live band every Wednesday and Sunday. People flock here from all over on the full moon, when bands play all night long. At the **Jolly Roger** (⌧ West End ☎ 284/495–4559) an ever-changing roster of local and down-island bands plays everything from rhythm and blues to reggae and rock every Friday and Saturday—and sometimes Sunday—starting at 8. Local bands play at **Myett's** (⌧ Cane Garden Bay ☎ 284/495–9649) every night, and there's usually a lively dance crowd. Courage is what people are seeking at **Pusser's Road Town Pub** (⌧ Waterfront St., Road Town ☎ 284/494–3897)—John Courage by the pint. Other nights try Pusser's famous mixed drinks—Painkillers—and snack on the excellent pizza. At the **Pub** (⌧ Waterfront St., Road Town ☎ 284/494–2608) there's a happy hour from 5 to 7 every day and live blues on Thursday. BVI recording star Quito Rhymer sings island ballads and love songs at **Quito's Gazebo** (⌧Cane Garden Bay ☎284/ 495–4837), his rustic beachside bar-restaurant. Solo shows are on Tuesday and Thursday at 8:30; on Friday and Saturday nights at 9:30 Quito performs with his band. There's often live music at **Sebastian's** (⌧ Apple Bay ☎ 284/495–4212) on Sunday evenings, and you can dance under the stars.

### The Arts

Musicians from around the world perform in the series **Classics in the Atrium** (✉ H. Lavity Stoutt Community College, Paraquita Bay ☎ 284/494–4994 ⊕ www.hlscc.edu) from October to March each year. Past artists have included Britain's premier a cappella group, Black Voices; the Leipzig String Quartet; and Keith Lockhart and the Serenac Quartet (from the Boston Pops Symphony).

Every May, hordes of people head to Tortola for the three-day **BVI Music Festival** (✉ Cane Garden Bay ☎ 284/495–3378 ⊕ www.bvimusicfest. com) to listen to reggae, gospel, blues, and salsa music by musicians from around the Caribbean and the U.S. mainland.

## Exploring Tortola

Tortola doesn't have many historic sights, but it does have lots of beautiful natural scenery. Although you could explore the island's 10 square mi (26 square km) in a few hours, opting for such a whirlwind tour would be a mistake. There's no need to live in the fast lane when you're surrounded by some of the Caribbean's most breathtaking panoramas and beaches. Also, the roads are extraordinarily steep and twisting, making driving demanding. The best strategy is to explore a bit of the island at a time. For example, you might try Road Town (the island's main town) one morning and a drive to Cane Garden Bay and West End (a little town on, of course, the island's west end) the next afternoon. Or consider a visit to East End, a *very* tiny town located exactly where its name suggests. The north shore is where all the best beaches are found.

*Numbers in the margin correspond to points of interest on the Tortola map.*

### What to See in Road Town

The bustling capital of the BVI looks out over Road Harbour. It takes only an hour or so to stroll down Main Street and along the waterfront, checking out the traditional West Indian buildings painted in pastel colors and with high-pitched, corrugated-tin roofs, bright shutters, and delicate fretwork trim. For hotel and sightseeing brochures and the latest information on everything from taxi rates to ferry-boat schedules, stop in the BVI Tourist Board office. Or just choose a seat on one of the benches in Sir Olva Georges Square, on Waterfront Drive, and watch the people come and go from the ferry dock and customs office across the street.

**❸ Fort Burt.** The most intact historic ruin on Tortola was built by the Dutch in the early 17th century to safeguard Road Harbour. It sits on a hill at the western edge of Road Town and is now the site of a small hotel and restaurant. The foundations and magazine remain, and the structure offers a commanding view of the harbor. ✉ *Waterfront Dr., Road Town* ☎ *No phone* ☒ *Free* ☉ *Daily dawn–dusk.*

**★ ❷ Old Government House Museum.** The seat of government until 1987, this gracious building now displays a nice collection of items from Tortola's past. The rooms are filled with period furniture, hand-painted china, books signed by Queen Elizabeth II on her 1966 and 1977 visits, and

numerous items reflecting Tortola's seafaring legacy. ☒ *Waterfront Dr.,*
*Road Town* ☎ *284/494–3701* ☒ *$3* ☯ *Weekdays 9–2.*

★ ❶ **J. R. O'Neal Botanic Gardens.** Take a walk through this 4-acre showcase
of lush plant life. There are sections devoted to prickly cacti and succu-
lents, hothouses for ferns and orchids, gardens of medicinal herbs, and
plants and trees indigenous to the seashore. From the Tourist Board office in Road Town, cross Waterfront Drive and walk one block over to
Main Street and turn right. Keep walking until you see the high school.
The gardens are on your left. ☒ *Botanic Station, Road Town* ☎ *284/*
*494–3904* ☒ *$3* ☯ *Mon.–Sat. 9–4:30.*

## What to See Elsewhere on the Island

❽ **Cane Garden Bay.** Once a sleepy village, Cane Garden Bay is growing
into one of Tortola's important destinations. Stay here at a small hotel
or guesthouse or stop by for lunch, dinner, or drinks at a seaside restaurant. You can find a few small stores selling beachware and basics like
suntan lotion, and, of course, one of Tortola's most popular beaches is
at your feet. The roads in and out of this area are dauntingly steep, so
use caution when driving.

★ ☺ ❹ **Dolphin Discovery.** Get up close and personal with dolphins as they swim
in a spacious seaside pen. There are two different programs that provide a varying range of experiences. In the Royal Swim, dolphins tow
participants around the pen. The less expensive Encounter allows you
to touch the dolphins. ☒ *Prospect Reef Resort, Road Town* ☎ *284/494–*
*7675* ⊕ *www.dolphindiscovery.com* ☒ *Royal Swim $129, Encounter*
*$79* ☯ *Daily, by appointment only.*

❺ **Fort Recovery.** The unrestored ruins of a 17th-century Dutch fort, 30 feet
in diameter, sit amid a profusion of tropical greenery on the Villas of
Fort Recovery Estates grounds. There's not much to see here, and there
are no guided tours, but you're welcome to stop by and poke around.
☒ *Waterfront Dr., Road Town* ☎ *284/485–4467* ☒ *Free.*

❿ **Mount Healthy National Park.** The remains of an 18th-century sugar
plantation are here. The windmill structure has been restored, and you
can see the ruins of a mill, a factory with boiling houses, storage areas,
stables, a hospital, and many dwellings. It's also a nice place to picnic.
☒ *Ridge Rd., Todman Peak* ☎ *No phone* ⊕ *www.bvinationalparkstrust.*
*org* ☒ *Free* ☯ *Daily dawn–dusk.*

★ ❼ **Sage Mountain National Park.** At 1,716 feet, Sage Mountain is the highest peak in the BVI. From the parking area, a trail leads you in a loop
not only to the peak itself (and extraordinary views) but also to a small
rain forest, sometimes shrouded in mist. Most of the forest was cut down
over the centuries to clear land for sugarcane, cotton, and other crops;
to create pastureland; or simply to utilize the stands of timber. In 1964
this park was established to preserve what remained. Up here you can
see mahogany trees, white cedars, mountain guavas, elephant-ear vines,
mamey trees, and giant bullet woods, to say nothing of such birds as
mountain doves and thrushes. Take a taxi from Road Town or drive up
Joe's Hill Road and make a left onto Ridge Road toward Chalwell and

Doty villages. The road dead-ends at the park. ⊠ *Ridge Rd., Sage Mountain* ☎ *284/494–3904* ⊕ *www.bvinationalparktrust.org* ⊠ *$3* ☉ *Daily dawn–dusk.*

★ ❾ **Skyworld.** Drive up here and climb the observation tower for a stunning 360-degree view of numerous islands and cays. On a clear day you can even see St. Croix (40 mi [64½ km] away) and Anegada (20 mi [32 km] away). ⊠ *Ridge Rd., Joe's Hill* ☎ *No phone* ⊠ *Free.*

❻ **Soper's Hole.** On this little island connected by a causeway to Tortola's western end, you can find a marina and a captivating complex of pastel West Indian–style buildings with shady balconies, shuttered windows, and gingerbread trim that house art galleries, boutiques, and restaurants. Pusser's Landing is a lively place to stop for a cold drink (many are made with Pusser's famous rum) and a sandwich and to watch the boats in harbor.

# VIRGIN GORDA

Updated by Lynda Lohr

Virgin Gorda, or "Fat Virgin," received its name from Christopher Columbus. The explorer envisioned the island as a pregnant woman in a languid recline with Gorda Peak being her big belly and the boulders of the Baths her toes. Different in topography from Tortola, with its arid landscape covered with scrub brush and cactus, Virgin Gorda has a slower pace of life, too. Goats and cattle own the right of way, and the unpretentious friendliness of the people is winning.

## Where to Stay

Virgin Gorda's charming hostelries appeal to a select, appreciative clientele; repeat business is extremely high. Those who prefer Sheratons, Marriotts, and the like may feel they get more for their money on other islands, but the peace and pampering offered on Virgin Gorda are priceless to the discriminating traveler.

For approximate costs, *see* the lodging price chart on p. 133.

### Hotels & Inns

**$$$$** ▥ **Biras Creek Resort.** Although Biras Creek is tucked out of the way on the island's North Sound, the get-away-from-it-all feel is actually the major draw. Anyway, you're just a five-minute ferry ride from the dock at Gun Creek. There are a handful of other hotels in the area, but this resort's gourmet meal plan means you won't want to leave. A member of the exclusive Relais &Châteaux family of hotels, Biras Creek offers suites with separate bedroom and living areas, though only bedrooms have air-conditioning. Guests get around on complimentary bicycles. Rates are per couple, per night, and include everything but beverages. ⌂ *Box 54, North Sound* ☎ *284/494–3555 or 800/223–1108* 🖶 *284/494–3557* ⊕ *www.biras.com* ⇨ *31 suites* △ *2 restaurants, in-room safes, refrigerators, in-room data ports, 2 tennis courts, pool, spa, beach, snorkeling, windsurfing, boating, bicycles, hiking, bar, shop, Internet room; no room TVs* ▤ *AE, MC, V* ¶◎¶ *FAP.*

# Virgin Gorda

Mountain Pt.

Cockroach
Island

George
Dog

**Coastal Islands**
**6**

Nail Bay Point **15**

Great Dog

West Dog

Mango Bay

**5**

*Sir Francis Drake Channel*

**Virgin Gorda Peak
National Park**

Mahoe
Bay **14**

**13**

*Little Dix
Bay*

Colison Pt.

**11**

Pond Bay

**Savannah
Bay**

**12**

*Handsome
Bay*

St. Thomas
Bay

← TO TORTOLA

**8**

**Spanish Town**
Fort Pt. **2** **1**

**9**

**Virgin Gorda
Airport**

**10**

**Little Fort
National Park** **6**

**7**

The
Valley

*Copper Mine
Bay*

**1**

**Spring Bay Beach**
*Devil's Bay*

**4**

**3**

**3**

**4** **Copper Mine Point**

**3**

**The Baths**

**2**

*Crook's
Bay*

**5**

*Stoney Bay*

Fallen
Jerusalem

**6** **Coastal Islands**

0 ——————— 1 mi
0 ——————— 1 km

TO NECKER
ISLAND

TO
ANEGADA

Mosquito
Island

Blunder
Bay

Prickly Pear
Island

Eustatia
Island

Leverick
Bay

[16] [17]

North
Sound

[18]

[19]

Deep
Bay

Parjaros
Pt.

Gun Creek

[20]
[21]

South
Sound

Joe
Bay

Bercher's
Bluff

Valley
Hill

Sound
Bluff

South
Sound
Bluff

Caribbean Sea

☾ **$$$$**    🏨 **Bitter End Yacht Club.** Sailing's the thing at this busy hotel and marina
**Fodor'sChoice**    in the nautically inclined North Sound, and since the use of everything
★    from small sailboats to Windsurfers to kayaks is included in the price,
you have no reason not to get out on the water. If you're serious about
learning to sail, sign up for lessons with the acclaimed Nick Trotter Sailing School. Of course, if you just want to lounge about on the beachfront chaises or on your balcony, that's okay, too. There's a busy social
scene, with guests gathering to swap sailing tales at the hotel's bars. Rooms
are bright and cheery, with the decor leaning toward the blues and
whites. You reach the Bitter End only by a free private ferry. ⌂ *Box
46, North Sound* ☎ *284/494–2746 or 800/872–2392* ⎙ *284/494–
4756* ⊕ *www.beyc.com* ⇨ *87 rooms* ⌃ *3 restaurants, pool, beach, dive
shop, snorkeling, windsurfing, boating, waterskiing, bar, children's programs (ages 6–18), Internet room; no a/c in some rooms, no room TVs*
⊟ *AE, MC, V* ⦿ *AI.*

★ ☾ **$$$$**    🏨 **Little Dix Bay.** This laid-back luxury resort offers something for everyone, which is why we like it. You can swim, sun, and snorkel on a gor-
geous sandy crescent, play tennis or windsurf, or just relax with a good
book. The hotel's restaurants serve stellar food, but you're only a five-
minute drive from Spanish Town's less expensive restaurants and shopping. Rooms have rattan and wood furniture and a casual feel. The
grounds are gorgeous, with lots of lush plantings kept snipped to perfection. Depending on when you visit, your fellow guests will be honeymooners or folks who've spent a week or two in the winter season
for years. ⌂ *Box 70, Little Dix Bay* ☎ *284/495–5555* ⎙ *284/495–5661*
⊕ *www.littledixbay.com* ⇨ *98 rooms, 8 suites, 2 villas* ⌃ *3 restaurants,
in-room safes, refrigerators, in-room data ports, Wi-Fi, 7 tennis courts,
pool, gym, spa, beach, snorkeling, windsurfing, 2 bars, library, shops,
children's programs (ages 3–16), Internet room, business services, car
rental; no room TVs* ⊟ *AE, MC, V* ⦿ *EP.*

★ **$$–$$$$**    🏨 **Nail Bay Resort.** Rambling up the hill above the coast, this resort
offers a wide selection of rooms and suites to fit every need. The
beach is just a short walk away from the units at lower elevations, but
if you're staying higher up the hill, you might want to drive to avoid
the uphill trek back to your room. You get cooking facilities (at least
microwave, fridge, toaster oven, and coffee maker) no matter how small
your room. It's a bit of a drive down a miserable dirt road to reach
the resort, but it offers lots of activities and a restaurant, so you won't
need to leave unless you want to. The rooms and apartments have mod-
ern rattan furniture, tile floors, and nice views. There's some construc-
tion in the area, so check before you go if noise bothers you. ⌂ *Box
69, Nail Bay* ☎ *284/494–8000 or 800/871–3551* ⎙ *284/495–5875*
⊕ *www.nailbay.com* ⇨ *9 rooms, 4 suites, 1 studio apartment, 7 vil-
las* ⌃ *Restaurant, fans, some kitchens, some kitchenettes, in-room VCRs,
tennis court, beach, snorkeling, boccie, croquet, bar, Internet room*
⊟ *AE, MC, V* ⦿ *EP.*

**$$–$$$$**    🏨 **Saba Rock Resort.** Reachable only by a free ferry or by your own yacht,
this resort on its own tiny cay isn't for everyone. However, it's good for
folks who want to mix and mingle with the sailors who drop anchor
for the night. The bar and restaurant are busy with yachters gathering

for sundowners, lunch, and dinner. The rooms are spacious, each with a different decor. All have tile floors, rattan or wood furniture, and colorful spreads and drapes. A resort boat will drop you off at nearby North Sound resorts if you need a change of pace. ☐ *Box 67, North Sound* ☎ *284/495–7711 or 284/495–9966* ☐ *284/495–7373* ⊕ *www.sabarock. com* ⇋ *7 1-bedroom suites, 2 2-bedroom suites* ☐ *Restaurant, fans, some kitchens, refrigerators, cable TV, in-room data ports, Wi-Fi, beach, snorkeling, bar, recreation room, shop; no phones in some rooms* ▭ *MC, V* ℀ *CP.*

**$$$** ▣ **Olde Yard Village.** All the condos in this upscale complex have at least partial ocean views, and the location—a few minutes' drive outside Spanish Town—is ideal, close enough so that you can easily pop out to dinner but far enough out of town to make you feel as if you're more isolated than you are. You will need a car, though, to make those trips a breeze. The Olde Yard Village will be building new units over next five years, but construction is a bit removed from the existing accommodations. ☐ *Box 26, The Valley* ☎ *284/495–5544 or 800/653–9273* ☐ *284/495–5986* ⊕ *www.oldeyardvillage.com* ⇋ *26 condos* ☐ *Kitchens, microwaves, refrigerators, cable TV, in-room data ports, pool, bar* ▭ *AE, D, MC, V* ℀ *EP.*

**☺ $–$$** ▣ **Fischer's Cove Beach Hotel.** The rooms are modest, the walls thin, and the owners in the midst of upgrading the chipped furniture and tired bedspreads, but you can't beat the location. Budget travelers should consider this hotel if they want a good beach just steps away. If you plan to stay put, you won't even need to rent a car. Spanish Town's handful of restaurants and shopping at Virgin Gorda Yacht Harbor are an easy 15-minute walk away. For better views, opt for the beachfront rooms. ☐ *Box 60, The Valley* ☎ *284/495–5252* ☐ *284/495–5820* ⊕ *www. fischerscove.com* ⇋ *12 rooms, 8 cottages* ☐ *Restaurant, fans, some kitchenettes, refrigerators, beach, playground; no a/c in some rooms, no TV in some rooms* ▭ *AE, MC, V* ℀ *EP.*

**$** ▣ **Leverick Bay Resort & Marina.** With its colorful buildings and bustling marina, Leverick Bay is a good choice, but the resort does not have a great beach. With easy access to various water-sports activities, a tasty on-site restaurant, and comfortable and spacious rooms, it's still a good deal. If you prefer an apartment, opt for one of the units stretching up the hillside above the marina. There's a one-week minimum stay in the apartments. All the accommodations have tile floors and pastel accents with a tropical feel. ☐ *Box 63, Leverick Bay* ☎ *284/495–7421 or 800/848–7081* ☐ *284/495–7367* ⊕ *www.leverickbay.com* ⇋ *14 rooms, 4 condos* ☐ *2 restaurants, grocery, fans, in-room safes, some kitchens, refrigerators, cable TV, tennis court, pool, hair salon, spa, beach, dive shop, dock, boating, marina, bar, shops, laundry facilities, Internet room* ▭ *AE, D, MC, V* ℀ *EP.*

## Villas

Those craving seclusion would do well at a villa. Most have full kitchens and maid service. Prices per week in winter run from around $2,000 for a one- or two-bedroom villa up to $10,000 for a five-room beachfront villa. Rates in summer are substantially less.

On Virgin Gorda, a villa in the North Sound area means you'll pretty much stay put at night unless you want to make the drive on narrow roads to the Valley's restaurants. If you opt for a spot near the Baths, it's an easy drive to town.

The St. Thomas–based **McLaughlin-Anderson Luxury Villas** (⊠ 1000 Blackbeard's Hill, Suite 3, Charlotte Amalie, VI 00802-6739 ☎ 340/776–0635 or 800/537–6246 ⊕ www.mclaughlinanderson.com) handles nearly two dozen properties all over Virgin Gorda. Villas range in size from two bedrooms to six bedrooms and come with many amenities, including full kitchens, pools, and stellar views. The company can hire a chef and stock your kitchen with groceries. A seven-night minimum is required during the winter season.

**Virgin Gorda Villa Rentals** (⌂ Box 63, Leverick Bay ☎ 284/495–7421 or 800/848–7081 ⊕ www.virgingordabvi.com) manages more than 40 properties near Leverick Bay Resort and Mahoe Bay, so it's perfect for those who want to be close to activities. Many villas—from studios to houses with six or more bedrooms—have private swimming pools and air-conditioning, at least in the bedrooms; all have full kitchens, are well maintained, and have spectacular views.

★ $$–$$$  🏠 **Guavaberry Spring Bay Vacation Homes.** Rambling back from the beach, these hexagonal one- and two-bedroom villas give you all the comforts of home with the striking boulder-fringed beach just minutes away. The same company also manages 18 villas in the vicinity. The villas are best for independent travelers who want to be able to cook or simply head 10 minutes to Spanish Town for a night out. The popular Baths are a short walk away, and snorkeling is excellent. The rooms have dark-wood or white walls, tile floors, and tropical bright spreads and curtains. Not all have sea views. ⌂ *Box 20, The Valley* ☎ *284/495–5227* 🖷 *284/495–5283* ⊕ *www.guavaberryspringbay.com* ⤂ *12 1-bedroom units, 6 2-bedroom units, 18 villas* ⚷ *Grocery, fans, kitchens, beach, Internet room; no a/c, no room phones, no room TVs* ▭ *No credit cards* ❘O❘ *EP.*

$–$$$  🏠 **Mango Bay Resort.** Sitting seaside on Virgin Gorda's north coast, this collection of contemporary duplex apartments will make you feel at home in the tropics. Each apartment is individually owned, so each has a different decor, but you can count on tile floors and tropical accents. The homes come with floats, kayaks, and snorkeling equipment, so you can find plenty to do when you're tired of lounging in the chaise. The popular Giorgio's Table restaurant is a short walk away. ⌂ *Box 1062, Mahoe Bay* ☎ *284/495–5672* 🖷 *284/495–5674* ⊕ *www.mangobayresort.com* ⤂ *18 condos, 2 villas* ⚷ *Fans, kitchens, cable TV, beach* ▭ *MC, V* ❘O❘ *EP.*

## Where to Eat

Restaurants range from simple to elegant. Hotels that are accessible only by boat will arrange transport in advance upon request from nonguests who wish to dine at their restaurants. It's wise to make dinner reservations almost everywhere except really casual spots.

For approximate costs, *see* the dining price chart on p. 133.

AMERICAN-CASUAL

$$$–$$$$

✕ **The Restaurant at Leverick Bay.** This bi-level restaurant looks out over North Sound. The fancier upstairs dining room is slightly more expensive, with a menu that includes steaks, pork chops, chicken, and fresh fish. There's a prime rib special on Saturday nights. Below, the bar offers light fare all day—starting with breakfast and moving on to hamburgers, salads, and pizzas until well into the evening. There's a children's menu downstairs. ⊠ *Leverick Bay Resort & Marina, Leverick Bay* ☎ *284/495–7154* ▤ *MC, V.*

◔ $$–$$$$

✕ **The Flying Iguana Restaurant & Bar.** Local artwork is displayed in this charming restaurant's comfortable lounge. The open-air dining room looks past the island's tiny airport to the sea. Enjoy classic eggs and bacon for breakfast; for lunch there are sandwiches and juicy hamburgers. The dinner menu includes fresh seafood, grilled chicken, steaks, and a pasta special. ⊠ *Virgin Gorda Airport, The Valley* ☎ *284/495–5277* ▤ *MC, V.*

$$$

✕ **The Mine Shaft Café.** Perched on a hilltop that offers a 360-degree view of spectacular sunsets, this restaurant near Copper Mine Point serves simple yet well-prepared food, including grilled fish, chicken, steaks, and baby back ribs. Tuesday nights feature an all-you-can-eat Caribbean-style barbecue. The bar, as well as the monthly full-moon parties, draws a big local crowd. ⊠ *Copper Mine Point, The Valley* ☎ *284/495–5260* ▤ *AE, MC, V.*

$$–$$$

✕ **The Bath & Turtle.** You can sit back and relax at this informal tavern with a friendly staff—although the noise from the television can be a bit much. Well-stuffed sandwiches, homemade pizzas, pasta dishes, and daily specials like conch gumbo round out the casual menu. Live musicians perform Saturday nights. ⊠ *Virgin Gorda Yacht Harbour, Spanish Town* ☎ *284/495–5239* ▤ *AE, MC, V.*

$$–$$$

✕ **LSL Restaurant.** An unpretentious place along the road to the Baths, this small restaurant with pedestrian decor is a local favorite. You'll always find fresh fish on the menu, but folks with a taste for other dishes won't be disappointed. Try the veal with mushrooms and herbs in a white wine sauce or the breast of chicken with rum cream and nuts. ⊠ *Tower Rd., The Valley* ☎ *284/495–5151* ▤ *MC, V.*

◔ $$–$$$

✕ **Top of the Baths.** At the entrance to the Baths, this popular restaurant starts serving at 8 AM. Tables are on an outdoor terrace or in an open-air pavilion; all have stunning views of the Sir Francis Drake Channel. Hamburgers, sandwiches, and fish-and-chips are offered at lunch. Conch fritters and pumpkin soup are among the dinner appetizers. Entrées include fillet of yellowtail snapper, shrimp creole, and jerk chicken. For dessert, the mango raspberry cheesecake is excellent. The Sunday barbecue, with live music, is served from noon until 3 PM and is an island event. ⊠ *The Valley* ☎ *284/495–5497* ▤ *AE, MC, V.*

◔ $–$$

✕ **The Fat Virgins Café.** This casual beachfront eatery offers a straightforward menu of flying-fish sandwiches, baby back ribs, chicken roti, vegetable pasta, and fresh fish specials for lunch and dinner. Friday nights feature a special Chinese menu. There's a good selection of Caribbean beer. ⊠ *Biras Creek Resort, North Sound* ☎ *284/495–7052* ▤ *MC, V.*

🐚 ¢–$ ✗ **Mad Dog's.** Piña coladas are *the* thing at this breezy bar just outside the entrance to the Baths. The menu includes great triple-decker sandwiches and hot dogs. ⊠ *The Valley* ☎ 284/495–5830 ▭ *No credit cards* ⊘ *No dinner.*

CAJUN/CREOLE ✗ **Chez Bamboo.** This pleasant little hideaway isn't difficult to find;
$$–$$$$ look for the building with the purple and green latticework. Candles in the dining room and on the patio help make this a mellow place where you can enjoy a bowl of conch gumbo or one of the specialties like lobster curry. For dessert, try the chocolate bourbon mint cake or crème brûlée. Stop by Friday night for live music. ⊠ *Across from and a little north of Virgin Gorda Yacht Harbour, Spanish Town* ☎ 284/495–5752 ▭ *AE, MC, V* ⊘ *No lunch.*

CONTEMPORARY ✗ **Biras Creek Restaurant.** This hilltop restaurant at the Biras Creek
$$$$ Hotel has stunning views of North Sound. The four-course prix-fixe menu changes daily and includes several choices per course. For starters, there may be a five-spice duck salad drizzled with an orange-onion marmalade and beetroot dressing, or creamy leek and potato soup ribboned with thin strips of smoked salmon. Entrées may include pan-seared salmon wrapped in Parma ham, and the desserts, including a chocolate tart covered with caramelized bananas and warm chocolate sauce, are to die for. Dinner ends with Biras Creek's signature offering of cheese and port. ⊠ *Biras Creek Hotel, North Sound* ☎ 284/494–3555 *or* 800/223–1108 🖷 284/494–3557 ⟁ *Reservations essential* ▭ *AE, D, MC, V* ⊘ *No lunch.*

$$$–$$$$ ✗ **Little Dix Bay Pavilion.** For an elegant evening, you can't do better than this—the candlelight in the open-air pavilion is enchanting, the daily-changing menu sophisticated, the service attentive. The dinner menu always includes a fine selection of superbly prepared seafood, meat, and vegetarian entrées—sugarcane-skewered tuna with a smoked shrimp-ginger salsa, rack of lamb with a fresh mint sauce, and red snapper fillet baked in a banana leaf. The Monday breakfast, lunch, and evening buffets shine. ⊠ *Little Dix Bay Resort, Spanish Town* ☎ 284/495–5555 *Ext. 174* ⟁ *Reservations essential* ▭ *AE, D, MC, V.*

ITALIAN ✗ **Giorgio's Table.** Gaze out at the stars and listen to the water lap against
$$$–$$$$ the shore while dining on homemade ravioli, beef fillet in a brunello wine sauce, or truffle duck ragout over pappardelle pasta. House specialties include fresh lobster that you choose from a 5,000-gallon seawater pool. There's also a selection of 120 different wines kept in a temperature-controlled cellar. Lunch is more casual and includes pizzas and sandwiches. ⊠ *Mahoe Bay* ☎ 284/495–5684 ▭ *AE, D, MC, V.*

$$–$$$ ✗ **The Rock Café.** Surprisingly good Italian cuisine is served open-air among the waterfalls and giant boulders that form the famous Baths. For dinner, feast on spinach-and-ricotta gnocchi, spaghetti with lobster sauce, or fresh red snapper in a butter and caper sauces. For dessert, try the pear and chocolate pie with vanilla sauce. For lunch there's casual fare: pizza, burgers, and sandwiches. ⊠ *The Valley* ☎ 284/495–5482 ▭ *AE, D, MC, V.*

SEAFOOD ✕ **The Clubhouse.** The Bitter End Yacht Club's open-air waterfront
★ $$$$ restaurant is a favorite rendezvous for the sailing set—busy day and night.
You can find lavish buffets for breakfast, lunch, and dinner as well as
an à la carte menu. Dinner selections include grilled swordfish or tuna,
chopped sirloin, scallops, shrimp, and local lobster. ⊠ *Bitter End Yacht
Club, North Sound* ☎ *284/494–2745* ⌖ *Reservations essential* 🖃 *AE,
MC, V.*

## Beaches

Although some of the best beaches are reachable only by boat, don't
worry if you're a landlubber, because you can find plenty of places to
sun and swim. Anybody going to Virgin Gorda must experience swimming or snorkeling among its unique boulder formations, which can be
visited at several beaches along Lee Road. The most popular of these
spots is the Baths, but there are several other similar places nearby that
are easily reached.

**The Baths.** Featuring a stunning maze of huge granite boulders that ex-
tend into the sea, this national park beach is usually crowded midday
with day-trippers. The snorkeling is good, and you're likely to see a wide
variety of fish, but watch out for dinghies coming ashore from the numerous sailboats anchored just off the beach. Public bathrooms and a
handful of bars and shops are close to the water and at the start of the
path that leads to the beach. Beach lockers are available to keep belongings safe. ⊠ *About 1 mi (1½ km) west of Spanish Town ferry dock on
Tower Rd., Spring Bay* ☎ *284/494–3904* 🖾 *$3* ☉ *Daily dawn–dusk.*

**Nail Bay.** Head to the island's north tip and you'll be rewarded with a
trio of beaches within the Nail Bay Resort complex that are ideal for
snorkeling. Mountain Trunk Bay is perfect for beginners, and Nail Bay
and Long Bay beaches have coral caverns just offshore. The resort has
a restaurant, which is an uphill walk but perfect for beach breaks.
⊠ *Nail Bay Resort, off Plum Tree Bay Rd., Nail Bay* ☎ *No phone* 🖾 *Free*
☉ *Daily dawn–dusk.*

**Savannah Bay.** For a wonderfully private beach close to Spanish Town,
try Savannah Bay. It may not always be completely deserted, but it's a
long stretch of soft, white sand. Bring your own mask, fins, and snorkel,
as there are no facilities. The view from above is a photographer's delight. ⊠ *Off North Sound Rd., ¾ mi (1¼ km) east of Spanish Town ferry
dock, Savannah Bay* ☎ *No phone* 🖾 *Free* ☉ *Daily dawn–dusk.*

**Spring Bay Beach.** Just off Tower Road, this national-park beach gets much
less traffic than the nearby Baths, and has the similarly large, imposing
boulders that create interesting grottos for swimming. The snorkeling
is excellent, and the grounds include swings and picnic tables. ⊠ *Off
Tower Rd., 1 mi (1½ km) west of Spanish Town ferry dock, Spring Bay*
☎ *284/494–3904* 🖾 *Free* ☉ *Daily dawn–dusk.*

## Sports & the Outdoors

CRICKET You can catch a match at the Recreation Grounds in Spanish Town February to April. The BVI Tourist Board at Virgin Gorda Yacht Harbor
can give you information on game dates and times.

DIVING & SNORKELING

Where you go snorkeling and what company you pick depend on where you're staying. Many hotels have on-site dive outfitters, but if they don't, one won't be far away. If your hotel does have a dive operation, just stroll down to the dock and hop aboard—no need to drive anywhere. The dive companies are all certified by PADI. Costs vary, but count on paying about $75 for a one-tank dive and $95 for a two-tank dive. All dive operators offer introductory courses as well as certification and advanced courses. Should you get an attack of the bends, which can happen when you ascend too rapidly, the nearest decompression chamber is at Roy L. Schneider Regional Medical Center in St. Thomas.

There are some terrific snorkel and dive sites off Virgin Gorda, including areas around the Baths, the North Sound, and the Dogs. The Chimney at Great Dog Island sports a coral archway and canyon covered with a wide variety of sponges. At Joe's Cave, an underwater cavern on West Dog Island, huge groupers, eagle rays, and other colorful fish accompany divers as they swim. At some sites you can see 100 feet down, but divers who don't want to go that deep and snorkelers will find plenty to look at just below the surface.

The **Bitter End Yacht Club** (✉ North Sound ☎ 284/494–2746 ⊕ www. beyc.com) offers a number of snorkeling trips day and night. **Dive BVI** (✉ Virgin Gorda Yacht Harbour, Spanish Town ☎ 284/495–5513 or 800/848–7078 ⊕ www.divebvi.com) offers expert instruction, certification, and day trips. **Sunchaser Scuba** (✉ Bitter End Yacht Harbor, North Sound ☎ 284/495–9638 or 800/932–4286 ⊕ www. sunchaserscuba.com) offers resort, advanced, and rescue courses.

FISHING

The sportfishing here is so good that anglers come from all over the world. **Charter Virgin Gorda** (✉ Leverick Bay, North Sound ☎ 284/495–7421 ⊕ www.chartervirgingorda.com) offers a choice of trips aboard its 46-foot Hatteras, the *Mahoe Bay,* for full-day marlin hunting. Plan to spend $800 to $1,200.

GOLF

The 9-hole minigolf course, **Golf Virgin Gorda** (✉ Copper Mine Point, The Valley ☎ 284/495–5260), is next to the Mine Shaft Café, delightfully nestled between huge granite boulders. There's no charge to play.

SAILING & BOATING

The BVI waters are calm, and terrific places to learn to sail. You can also rent sea kayaks, waterskiing equipment, dinghies, and power boats, or take a parasailing trip. The **Bitter End Sailing & Windsurfing School** (✉ Bitter End Yacht Club, North Sound ☎ 284/494–2746 ⊕ www.beyc.com) offers classroom, dockside, and on-the-water lessons for sailors of all levels. Private lessons are $60 per hour. If you just want to sit back, relax, and let the captain take the helm, choose a sailing or power yacht from **Double "D" Charters** (✉ Virgin Gorda Yacht Harbour, Spanish Town ☎ 284/495–6150 ⊕ www.doubledbvi.com). Rates are $55 for a half-day trip and $90 for a full-day island-hopping excursion. Private full-day cruises or sails for up to eight people run $850. If you'd rather rent a Sunfish or Hobie Wave, check out **Leverick Bay Watersports** (✉ Leverick Bay, North Sound ☎ 284/495–7376 ⊕ www.watersportsbvi.com).

WINDSURFING  The North Sound is a good place to learn to windsurf: it's protected, so you can't be easily blown out to sea. The **Bitter End Yacht Club** (⊠ North Sound ☎ 284/494–2746 ⊕ www.beyc.com) gives lessons and rents equipment for $60 per hour for nonguests. A half-day Windsurfer rental runs $60 to $100.

**2**

## Shopping

Most boutiques are within hotel complexes or at Virgin Gorda Yacht Harbour. Two of the best are at Biras Creek and Little Dix Bay. Other properties—the Bitter End and Leverick Bay—have small but equally select boutiques.

CLOTHING  **Blue Banana** (⊠ Virgin Gorda Yacht Harbour, Spanish Town ☎ 284/495–5957) carries a large selection of name-brand swimsuits plus cover-ups, T-shirts, and accessories. At **Dive BVI** (⊠ Virgin Gorda Yacht Harbour, Spanish Town ☎ 284/495–5513), you can find books about the islands as well as snorkeling equipment, sportswear, sunglasses, and beach bags. **Fat Virgin's Treasure** (⊠ Biras Creek Hotel, North Sound ☎ 284/495–7054) sells cool island-style clothing in tropical prints, a large selection of straw sun hats, and unusual gift items like island-made hot sauces, artistic cards, and locally fired pottery. **Margo's Boutique** (⊠ Virgin Gorda Yacht Harbour, Spanish Town ☎ 284/495–5237) is the place to buy breezy, boldly printed sarongs and handmade accessories like shell and pearl jewelry. **Next Wave** (⊠ Virgin Gorda Yacht Harbour, Spanish Town ☎ 284/495–5623) sells T-shirts, canvas tote bags, and locally made jewelry. The **Pavilion Gift Shop** (⊠ Little Dix Bay Hotel, Little Dix Bay ☎ 284/495–5555) has the latest in resort wear for men and women, as well as jewelry, books, housewares, and expensive T-shirts. **Pusser's Company Store** (⊠ Leverick Bay ☎ 284/495–7369) has a trademark line of sportswear, rum products, and gift items.

FOODSTUFFS  The **Bitter End Emporium** (⊠ Bitter End Yacht Harbor, North Sound ☎ 284/494–2745) is the place for such edible treats as local fruits, cheeses, baked goods, and gourmet prepared food to take out. **Buck's Food Market** (⊠ Virgin Gorda Yacht Harbour, Spanish Town ☎ 284/495–5423 ⊠ Gun Creek, North Sound ☎ 284/495–7368) is the closest the island offers to a full-service supermarket and has everything from an in-store bakery and deli to fresh fish and produce departments. The **Chef's Pantry** (⊠ Leverick Bay ☎ 284/495–7677) has the fixings for an impromptu party in your villa or boat—fresh seafood, specialty meats, imported cheeses, daily baked breads and pastries, and an impressive wine and spirit selection. The **Wine Cellar & Bakery** (⊠ Virgin Gorda Yacht Harbour, Spanish Town ☎ 284/495–5250) sells bread, rolls, muffins, cookies, sandwiches, and sodas to go.

GIFTS  **Flamboyance** (⊠ Virgin Gorda Yacht Harbour, Spanish Town ☎ 284/495–5946) has a large line of fragrances, including those inspired by the scent of tropical flowers. The **Palm Tree Gallery** (⊠ Leverick Bay ☎ 284/495–7479) sells attractive handcrafted jewelry, paintings, and one-of-a-kind gift items, as well as games and books about the Caribbean. The **Reeftique** (⊠ Bitter End Yacht Harbor, North Sound ☎ 284/494–2745) carries island crafts and jewelry, clothing, and nautical odds and ends with the Bitter End logo. **Thee Artistic Gallery** (⊠ Virgin Gorda Yacht Harbour, Spanish Town ☎ 284/495–5104) has Caribbean-made jewelry, 14-karat-gold nautical charms, maps, collectible coins, crystal, and Christmas tree ornaments with tropical themes.

## Nightlife

Pick up a free copy of the *Limin' Times*—available at most resorts and restaurants—for the most current local entertainment schedule.

**The Bath & Turtle** (⊠ Virgin Gorda Yacht Harbour, Spanish Town ☎ 284/495–5239), one of the liveliest spots on Virgin Gorda, hosts island bands regularly in season from 8 PM until midnight. Local bands play at **Bitter End Yacht Club** (⊠ North Sound ☎ 284/494–2746) nightly during the winter season. **Chez Bamboo** (⊠ Across from Virgin Gorda Yacht Harbour, Spanish Town ☎ 284/495–5752) is the place on the island for live jazz on Friday nights. The bar at **Little Dix Bay** (⊠ Little Dix Bay ☎ 284/495–5555) presents elegant live entertainment several nights a week in season. The **Mine Shaft Café** (⊠ Copper Mine Point, The Valley ☎ 284/495–5260) has live bands on Tuesday and for Ladies Night on Friday from 7 PM to 9 PM. The **Restaurant at Leverick Bay** (⊠ Leverick Bay Resort & Marina, Leverick Bay ☎ 284/495–7154) hosts live music on Saturday through Wednesday nights in season. The **Rock Café** (⊠ The Valley ☎ 284/495–5177) has live bands Friday, Saturday, and Sunday nights.

## Exploring Virgin Gorda

One of the most efficient ways to see Virgin Gorda is by sailboat. There are few roads, and most byways don't follow the scalloped shoreline. The main route sticks resolutely to the center of the island, linking the Baths at the tip of the southern extremity with Gun Creek and Leverick Bay at North Sound and providing exhilarating views. The craggy coast, scissored with grottoes and fringed by palms and boulders, has a primitive beauty. If you drive, you can hit all the sights in one day. The best plan is to explore the area near your hotel (either the Valley or North Sound) first, then take a day to drive to the other end. Stop to climb Gorda Peak, which is in the island's center.

*Numbers in the margin correspond to points of interest on the Virgin Gorda map.*

### What to See

**③ The Baths.** At Virgin Gorda's most celebrated sight, giant boulders are

FodorsChoice scattered about the beach and in the water. Some are almost as large as

★ houses and form remarkable grottos. Climb between these rocks to swim in the many placid pools. Early morning and late afternoon are the best times to visit if you want to avoid crowds. If it's privacy you crave, follow the shore northward to quieter bays—Spring Bay, the Crawl, Little Trunk, and Valley Trunk—or head south to Devil's Bay. ⊠ *Off Tower Rd., The Baths* ☎ *284/494–3904* ⊕ *www.bvinationalparktrust. org* ⌂ *$3* ⊙ *Daily dawn–dusk.*

2

**6 Coastal Islands.** You can easily reach the quaintly named Fallen Jerusalem Island and the Dog Islands by boat. They're all part of the BVI National Parks Trust, and their seductive beaches and unparalleled snorkeling display the BVI at their beachcombing, hedonistic best. ☎ *No phone* 💷 *Free.*

**4 Copper Mine Point.** Here stand a tall stone shaft silhouetted against the sky and a small stone structure that overlooks the sea. These are the ruins of a copper mine established 400 years ago and worked first by the Spanish, then by the English, until the early 20th century. In April 2003 this historic site became the 20th park under the BVI National Parks Trust jurisdiction. ✉ *Copper Mine Rd.* ☎ *No phone* ⊕ *www.bvinationalparkstrust.org* 💷 *Free.*

**1 Spanish Town.** Virgin Gorda's peaceful main settlement, on the island's southern wing, is so tiny that it barely qualifies as a town at all. Also known as the Valley, Spanish Town has a marina, some shops, and a couple of car-rental agencies. Just north of town is the ferry slip. At the Virgin Gorda Yacht Harbour you can stroll along the dock and do a little shopping.

★ **5 Virgin Gorda Peak National Park.** There are two trails at this 265-acre park, which contains the island's highest point, at 1,359 feet. Small signs on North Sound Road mark both entrances; sometimes, however, the signs are missing, so keep your eyes open for a set of stairs that disappears into the trees. It's about a 15-minute hike from either entrance up to a small clearing, where you can climb a ladder to the platform of a wooden observation tower and a spectacular 360-degree view. ✉ *North Sound Rd., Gorda Peak* ☎ *No phone* ⊕ *www.bvinationalparkstrust.org* 💷 *Free.*

# JOST VAN DYKE

Updated by
Carol M.
Bareuther

Named after an early Dutch settler, Jost Van Dyke is a small island northwest of Tortola and is *truly* a place to get away from it all. Mountainous and lush, the 4-mi-long (6½-km-long) island—with fewer than 200 full-time residents—has one tiny resort, some rental houses and villas, a campground, a handful of cars and taxis, and a single road. Water conservation is encouraged, as the source of supply is rainwater collected in basement-like cisterns. Most lodgings will ask you to follow the Caribbean golden rule: "In the land of sun and fun, we never flush for number one." Jost is one of the Caribbean's most popular anchorages, and there's a disproportionately large number of informal bars and restaurants, which have helped earn Jost its reputation as the "party island" of the BVI.

## Where to Stay

For approximate costs, *see* the lodging price chart on p. 133.

**$$$** 🏠 **Sandy Ground Estates.** Each of these privately owned one- and two-bedroom villas is distinct in architecture, and interiors range from spar-

# The Laid-Back Lifestyle at its Best

**IT'S THE LAID-BACK ATTITUDE** of Jost Van Dyke, which boasts a beach as its main street and has had electricity only since the 1990s, that makes the famous feel comfortable and everyday folk feel glorious. At no locale is this more so than at Foxy's Tamarind. Foxy Callwood, a seventh-generation Jost Van Dyker and calypsonian extraordinaire, is the star here, strumming and singing rib-tickling ditties full of lewd and laughable lyrics that attract a bevy of boaters and even celebrities like Tom Cruise, Kelsey Grammer, and Steven Spielberg.

What began in the 1970s as a lemonade-stand-size bar, albeit with "modern" fixtures like a galvanized roof and plywood walls, has evolved into a bona fide beach bar with sand floor, wattle walls, and thatched roof that defines the eastern end of the beach at Great Harbour. Without the glitz of St. Thomas, glamour of St. John, or grace of Tortola, islanders like Foxy knew they needed to carve out their own unique niche—and have done so by appearing to have done nothing at all. Unhurried friendliness and a slice of quintessential Caribbean culture flow freely here.

Foxy, who fished for a living before he started singing for his supper, has traveled the world and had the world come to him for endless parties for Halloween, for Labor Day weekend, and for the New Year. The *New York Times* named Foxy's one of its three top picks to ring in the millennium. What's the appeal? Foxy sums it up himself: "It's the quantity of people and the quality of the party. You can dance on the tables and sleep on the beach. No one is going to bother you."

tan to stylish. The settings are unique, too. The House on the Hill, 80 feet above sea level, is assured of a cool breeze, complete privacy, and spectacular views of Sandy Cay. The Little House has a private path to the beach, three minutes away. Sunfish and kayaks are available for rent. Foliage, ranging from native greenery to cacti, abounds on this eastern end of the island. The closest civilization is Foxy's Taboo, about a half-mile away. Your kitchen can be prestocked, or you can bring or buy your own groceries. To get here, you need to take a water taxi from St. Thomas or West End, Tortola, to the resort's private dock. ⊠ *Sandy Ground Estates* 🕮 *Box 594, West End* ☎ *284/494–3391* 🖷 *284/495–9379* ⊕ *www.sandyground.com* ⮌ *7 houses* ⚲ *Fans, kitchens, beach; no a/c, no room phones, no room TVs* ▭ *MC, V* ⦿ *EP.*

★ **$$–$$$** 🏠 **Sandcastle.** This six-cottage hideaway sits on a half-mile stretch of white-sand beach shared by a half dozen beach bars and restaurants. The peach-color cottages are simply furnished. Two-bedroom cottages have outdoor showers and no air-conditioning, but the one-bedroom cottages do have these conveniences. Either way, the Caribbean is no more than 20 feet from your doorstep. There's nothing to do here except relax in a hammock, read, walk the beach, swim, and snorkel. Unfortunately, you may find your serenity shattered between 11 AM

2

and 3 PM by the bustle of charter-boat day-trippers who arrive on large catamarans for lunch and drinks at the Soggy Dollar Bar. At night, tuck into a casually elegant, four-course candlelight dinner at the Sandcastle Restaurant. For weeklong stays you have the option of a package that includes all breakfasts and most dinners. Long-time owners Debby Pearce and Bruce Donath sold the resort in 2005, but new owners Jerry and Tish O'Connell have maintained the same level of service. ☒ *White Bay* ☎ *284/495–9888* ☐ *284/495–9999* ⊕ *www. sandcastle-bvi.com* 🔊 *4 1-bedroom cottages, 2 2-bedroom cottages* ⚏ *Restaurant, beach, bar, shops; no a/c in some rooms, no room TVs* ▭ *D, MC, V* ⊺◯⦚ *EP, MAP.*

☺ **$–$$$** 🏨 **White Bay Villas & Seaside Cottages.** There's no missing the beautiful sea views from the verandas of these hilltop one- to three-bedroom villas and cottages. Accommodations are open-air, with screenless doors and shuttered windows, although there's mosquito netting over the beds. Almost everything is provided, from linens and beach towels to an occasional bunch of fresh bananas or a ripe papaya from the trees outside. Although there are some small markets on the island, it's a good idea to buy groceries on St. Thomas or Tortola before arriving. White Bay and five beach bars are less than a five-minute walk downhill. A mile farther down the beach there's a small supermarket, half a dozen beach bars and restaurants, a souvenir shop, and watersports rental. ☒ *White Bay* 🖃 *Box 3368, Annapolis, MD 21403* ☎ *410/571–6692 or 800/778–8066* ⊕ *www.jostvandyke.com* 🔊 *3 villas, 3 cottages* ⚏ *Fans, kitchens, cable TV, in-room VCRs, beach; no a/c* ⊺◯⦚ *EP.*

**$** 🏨 **Sea Crest Inn.** Perched on the hillside at the far east end of Great Harbour, this two-story white building with red trim has four one-bedroom apartments. Each has wicker furnishings, tropical-print bedspreads and curtains, and cool tile floors. From the balconies you get a sweeping view of the beach, where a half dozen bars and restaurants are within walking distance. Great Harbour does rock, especially on weekend nights, and the thumping bass from live bands at the beach bars may keep you awake, or it may entice you to join the party below. If you need tips on where to party, eat, or sightsee, just ask charming proprietor and Jost native Ivy Chinnery Moses. ☒ *Great Harbour* ☎ *284/ 495–9024* ☐ *284/495–9034* ⊕ *www.bviwelcome.com/seacrestinn/ seacrestinn.html* 🔊 *4 1-bedroom apartments* ⚏ *Kitchens, cable TV, beach* ▭ *MC, V* ⊺◯⦚ *EP.*

WHERE TO CAMP ★ ☺ **Ivan's Stress-Free Bar & White Bay Campground.** If you don't mind roughing it a bit, Ivan's will give you a quintessential Caribbean experience. You can pitch your tent 6 feet from the sea or farther back under the sea-grape trees where there's an electric hookup and lamp. Or opt for a primitive cabin, where you can find just a bed, fan, and bucket of water to wash the sand off your feet. There's an outhouse, sun showers (basically a plastic sack hung from a tree branch), and a communal kitchen stocked with pots and pans. Thursday-night barbecues attract campers and noncampers alike. Ivan will happily conduct nature walks and arrange island tours, sailing, and diving trips, but he's a musician at heart. Impromptu jam sessions are always a highlight, and if you pack a musical instrument, you can join in, too. ☼ *Flush toilets, drinking water, showers, picnic tables, food service, electricity, public telephone, swimming (ocean)* ⤴ *8 cabins, 5 tents, 15 campsites* ⊠ *White Bay* ☎ *284/ 495-9312* ⊕ *www.caribbeancruisingclub.com/ivan* ⤳ *Reservations essential* ▤ *No credit cards.*

## Where to Eat

Restaurants on Jost Van Dyke are informal (some serve meals family-style at long tables) but charming. The island is a favorite charter-boat stop, and you're bound to hear people exchanging stories about the previous night's anchoring adventures. Most restaurants don't take reservations, and in all cases dress is casual.

For approximate costs, *see* the dining price chart on p. 133.

**$$$$** ✕ **Sandcastle.** Candles illuminate this tiny beachfront dining room during the four-course, prix-fixe affairs. The menu changes frequently but can include a West Indian pumpkin or curried-apple soup; curried shrimp or three-mustard chicken; and, for dessert, rum bananas or key lime pie. Reservations are required by 4 PM for the single dinner seating at 7 PM. For lunch, you can get flying-fish sandwiches, hamburgers, and conch fritters at the Soggy Dollar Bar, famous as the purported birthplace of the lethal drink called the Painkiller. ⊠ *Sandcastle, White Bay* ☎ *284/495-9888* ⤳ *Reservations essential* ▤ *D, MC, V.*

☙ **$$–$$$$** ✕ **Foxy's Tamarind.** One of the true hot spots in the BVI—and a must-stop for yachties from the world over—Foxy's hosts the madcap Wooden Boat Race every May and throws big parties on New Year's Eve, April Fools' Day, and Halloween. This lively place serves local food, has terrific barbecue dinners on Friday and Saturday nights, mixes its own rum punch, and now offers its own Foxy's brand beer. Famed calypso performer and owner Foxy Callwood plays the guitar and creates calypso ditties about diners. Reservations for dinner are required by 5 PM. ⊠ *Great Harbour* ☎ *284/495-9258* ⤳ *Reservations essential* ▤ *AE, MC, V* ☽ *No lunch weekends.*

☙ **$$–$$$$** ✕ **Foxy's Taboo.** An oasis in the middle of uninhabited marshland at Diamond Cay, this simple, open-air eatery has plastic chairs and tiled wooden tables overlooking a "marina" (really a small dock). But the menu is definitely more upscale here than at Foxy's place in Great Harbour. The Taboo burger at lunch is a hand-formed mound of 100% beef, served with mango chutney and pepperjack cheese on ciabata bread. House-made pizzas have toppings ranging from jalapeño peppers to proscuitto and kalamata olives. Dinner selections include mango-tamarind chicken. There are a dozen or more wines available by the bottle or glass. Don't miss the tiramisu for dessert. Dinner reservations are required by 5 PM. ⊠ *Diamond Cay* ☎ *284/495-0218* ⤳ *Reservations essential* ▤ *AE, MC, V* ☽ *Closed Mon. No dinner Sun.*

**$$–$$$$** ✕ **Sydney's Peace & Love.** Here you can find great lobster, caught aboard owner Sydney Hendrick's own fishing boat, as well as barbecue chicken and ribs. All is served on an open-air terrace or an air-conditioned dining room at the water's edge. The find here is a sensational (by BVI standards) jukebox. The cognoscenti sail here for dinner, since there's no beach—meaning no irksome sand fleas. ✉ *Little Harbour* ☎ *284/495–9271* 🍽 *D, MC, V.*

**\$\$–\$\$\$**   ✗ **Abe's by the Sea.** Specialties at this popular, informal seaside spot include fresh lobster, conch, and spareribs. During the winter season there's a pig roast every Wednesday evening. ✉ *Little Harbour* ☎ *284/495–9329* 🍽 *D, MC, V.*

★
**\$\$–\$\$\$**   ✗ **Ali Baba's.** This sandy-floor eatery offers beach-bar dining at its best. Lobster and grilled local fish, including swordfish, kingfish, and wahoo, are a specialty. There's a pig roast on Monday night. Beware: Ali Baba's special rum punch is delicious but potent. Dinner reservations are required by 6 PM. ✉ *Great Harbour* ☎ *284/495–9280* ⚑ *Reservations essential* 🍽 *AE, MC, V.*

**\$\$–\$\$\$**   ✗ **Corsairs Beach Bar & Restaurant.** This beach bar is easily recognized by the restored U.S. Army Jeep that adjoins the dining area. Tex-Mex and Caribbean cuisine star at lunch, with selections ranging from lobster quesadillas to jerk chicken wings. Northern Italian takes over at night, when you can find seafood pomodoro, which is chock-full of shrimp, fish, squid, and lobster. Live music and a great drink menu keep things moving at night. ✉ *Great Harbour* ☎ *284/495–9294* 🍽 *MC, V.*

★
**\$\$–\$\$\$**   ✗ **Harris' Place.** Cynthia Harris is famous for her hospitality, along with her family's famous pig-roast buffets and Monday-night lobster specials. This is the hot spot to rub elbows with locals and the charter-boat crowd for breakfast, lunch, or dinner. ✉ *Little Harbour* ☎ *284/495–9302* 🍽 *AE, D, MC, V.*

**\$\$–\$\$\$**   ✗ **Rudy's Mariner's Rendezvous.** Hamburgers, cheeseburgers, and barbecue ribs are the specialties at this beachfront spot at the extreme western end of Great Harbour. There's a lobster buffet every Thursday night in season. You can also find a superette here where you can buy basic groceries. ✉ *Great Harbour* ☎ *284/495–9282* 🍽 *D, MC, V.*

**\$**   ✗ **Christine's Bakery.** The small porch of this two-story building, which is set back from the beach on Bun Road next to the icehouse, is a great spot to eat breakfast and watch the island come to life. The cinnamon buns are lush, especially if they've just come out of the oven. Coconut cake, banana bread, and white and whole wheat loaves are excellent, too. Order eggs and bacon for breakfast. Or for lunch have a hearty sandwich on home-baked bread. ✉ *Great Harbour* ☎ *284/495–9281* 🍽 *No credit cards* ⊗ *No dinner.*

**¢–\$**   ✗ **Jewel's Snack Shack.** This little wooden shack sells the best hot dogs on the island. You can find burgers, fries, and ice cream novelties too. ✉ *White Bay* ☎ *284/495–9286* 🍽 *No credit cards* ⊗ *No dinner.*

## Beaches & Activities

**Jost Van Dyke Safari Services.** Native Jost Van Dyker Dorsey Chinnery is expert at navigating the steep roads here in his big, red open-air safari cab. He knows all the best spots to visit on a sightseeing tour and can help you with everything from beach-hopping to barhopping. His tours cost \$20 per person. ☎ *284/495–9267 or 284/443–3832* ⊕ *www.bviwelcome.com/jvdsafari.*

**JVD Scuba.** See the undersea world around the island with divemaster Colin Aldridge. One of the most impressive dives in the area is off the north of Little Jost Van Dyke island. Here you'll find the Twin Towers: a pair of rock formations rising an impressive 90-feet. A one-tank dive costs $60, two-tank dive $95, and four-hour beginner course $120. ⊠ *Great Harbour* ☎ *284/495–0271* ⊕ *www.jvdwatersports.com.*

**Sandy Cay.** Just offshore, the little islet known as Sandy Cay is a gleaming scimitar of white sand, with marvelous snorkeling.

★ ☾ **White Bay.** On the south shore, west of Great Harbour, this long stretch of white sand is especially popular with boaters who come ashore for a libation at one of the beach bars.

## Nightlife

★ Jost Van Dyke is the most happening place to go bar-hopping in the BVI. In fact, yachties will sail over just to have a few drinks. All the spots are easy to find, congregated in two general locations: Great Harbour and White Bay (⇨ *see* Where to Eat, *above*). On the Great Harbour side you can find Foxy's, Rudy's, and Ali Baba's; on the White Bay side is the One Love Bar & Grill, where Seddy Callwood will entertain you with his sleight of hand, and the Soggy Dollar bar at the Sandcastle restaurant, where legend has it the famous Painkiller was first concocted. If you can't make it to Jost Van Dyke, you can have a Painkiller at almost any bar in the BVI.

# ANEGADA

Updated by
Lynda Lohr

Fodor'sChoice
★

Anegada lies low on the horizon about 14 mi (22½ km) north of Virgin Gorda. Unlike the hilly volcanic islands in the chain, this is a flat coral-and-limestone atoll. Nine miles (14 km) long and 2 mi (3 km) wide, the island rises no more than 28 feet above sea level. In fact, by the time you're able to see it, you may have run your boat onto a reef. (More than 300 captains unfamiliar with the waters have done so since exploration days; note that bareboat charters don't allow their vessels to head here without a trained skipper.) Although the reefs are a sailor's nightmare, they (and the shipwrecks they've caused) are a scuba diver's dream. Snorkeling, especially in the waters around Loblolly Bay on the north shore, is also a transcendent experience. You can float in shallow, calm, reef-protected water just a few feet from shore and see one coral formation after another, each shimmering with a rainbow of colorful fish. Such watery pleasures are complemented by ever-so-fine, ever-so-white sand (the northern and western shores have long stretches of the stuff) and the occasional beach bar (stop in for burgers, Anegada lobster, or a frosty beer). The island's population of about 150 lives primarily in a small south-side village called the Settlement, which has two grocery stores, a bakery, and a general store. Many local fisherfolk are happy to take visitors out bonefishing.

## Where to Stay

For approximate costs, *see* the lodging price chart on p. 133.

☾ **$$** 🏠 **Anegada Seaside Villas.** This tiny resort is a good place if you really want to get away from it all. There isn't much to do except sun, swim, snorkel, stroll miles of gorgeous white-sand beaches, and catch up on all that reading you've always wanted to do. The modern villas have those tropical touches like wicker furniture and tile floors that you've come to expect. When you tire of cooking in your well-equipped kitchen, head out to one of the island's very casual restaurants for lunch or dinner. Pomato Point Restaurant is five minutes away by foot. ☒ *Pomato Point* 🖧 *284/495–9466* ⊕ *www.anegadavillas.com* 📞 *7 villas* ⚄ *Fans, kitchens, beach, car rental; no a/c, no room phones, no room TVs* 🖃 *MC, V* �🍽 *EP.*

**$$** 🏨 **Anegada Reef Hotel.** This may be the busiest place on sleepy Anegada. Although boaters drop anchor in sheltered waters inside the reef and guests from other hotels stop by for lobster salad lunches, the resort itself remains a serene spot. Head here if you want to relax in the shade on a beach that stretches forever, enjoy the company of like-minded folks, and do nothing more strenuous than heading out once or twice to fish the nearby waters. Rooms are simple but fresh with pastel fabrics. ☒ *Setting Point* 🕾 *284/495–8002* 🖨 *284/495–9362* ⊕ *www.anegadareef. com* 📞 *16 rooms* ⚄ *Restaurant, beach, bar; no room phones, no room TVs* 🖃 *MC, V* �🍽 *AI.*

⚲ **$** 🏨 **Neptune's Treasure.** Basic beachside rooms with simple but squeaky-clean furnishings are the hallmark of this family-owned guesthouse. If you're happy with a simple place to rest your head (there aren't even TVs in the rooms) while you swim in crystal-clear waters, sun at the round-the-island beach, enjoy fresh-from-the-sea dinners at the hotel's restaurant, and watch the sun go down, this is the place. If you must move out of the hammock, the hotel will organize an island tour or a fishing expedition. ☒ *Between Pomato and Saltheap points* 🕾 *284/495–9439* 🖨 *284/495–8060* ⊕ *www.neptunestreasure.com* 📞 *9 rooms* ⚄ *Restaurant, beach; no room TVs* 🖃 *MC, V* �🍽 *EP.*

## Where to Eat

There are between 6 and 10 restaurants open at any one time, depending on the season and on whim. Check when you're on the island.

For approximate costs, *see* the dining price chart on p. 133.

AMERICAN- ✕ **Big Bamboo.** Ice-cold beer, fruity drinks, burgers, fresh fish, crab
CASUAL cakes, and grilled lobsters entice a steady stream of barefoot diners to
**$$–$$$$** this beach bar for lunch. Dinner is by request only. ☒ *Loblolly Bay West* 🕾 *284/495–2019* 🖃 *MC, V.*

SEAFOOD ✕ **Pomato Point Restaurant.** This relaxed restaurant-bar is on a narrow
**$$$–$$$$** beach a short walk from the Anegada Reef Hotel. Entrées include steak, lobster, stewed conch, and freshly caught seafood. Owner Wilfred Creque displays various island artifacts, including shards of Arawak pottery and 17th-century coins, cannonballs, and bottles. ☒ *Pomato Point* 🕾 *284/495–9466* ⚖ *Reservations essential* 🖃 *D, MC, V* ☾ *Closed Sept.*

**$$–$$$$** ✕ **Anegada Reef Hotel Restaurant.** Seasoned yachters gather here nightly to share tales of the high seas. Dinner is by candlelight and always includes famous Anegada lobster, steaks, and chicken—all prepared on the large grill by the little open-air bar. ⊠ *Anegada Reef Hotel, Setting Point* ☎ 284/495–8002 ⊛ *Reservations essential* ▤ *MC, V.*

**$$–$$$$** ✕ **Cow Wreck Bar & Grill.** Named for the cow bones that once washed up on shore, this open-air beachside eatery is a fun place to watch the antics of surfers and kite boarders skidding across the bay. Tuck into conch fritters or a lobster salad sandwich for lunch or freshly grilled lobster for dinner. ⊠ *Loblolly Bay East* ☎ 284/495–8057 ▤ *MC, V.*

☾ **$$–$$$$** ✕ **Neptune's Treasure.** The owners catch, cook, and serve the seafood (lobster is a specialty, as is garlic-studded shark, in season) at this casual bar and restaurant in the Neptune's Treasure guesthouse. ⊠ *Between Pomato and Saltheap points* ☎ 284/495–9439 ▤ *MC, V.*

## Shopping

**Anegada Reef Hotel Boutique** (⊠ Setting Point ☎ 284/495–8062) has a bit of everything: resort wear, hand-painted T-shirts, locally made jewelry, books, and one-of-a-kind gifts. At **Dotsy's Bakery** (⊠ The Settlement ☎ 284/495–9667) you can find a tempting array of fresh-baked breads, cookies, and desserts. Dotsy sells pizza and hamburgers too. **Pat's Pottery** (⊠ Nutmeg Point ☎ 284/495–8031) sells bowls, plates, cups, candlestick holders, and original watercolors.

# OTHER BRITISH VIRGIN ISLANDS

For approximate costs, *see* the dining and lodging price chart on p. 133.

## Cooper Island

This small, hilly island on the south side of the Sir Francis Drake Channel, about 8 mi (13 km) from Road Town, Tortola, is popular with the charter-boat crowd. There are no roads (which doesn't really matter, as there aren't any cars), but you can find a beach restaurant, a casual hotel, a few houses (some are available for rent), and great snorkeling at the south end of Manchioneel Bay.

**$$** ✕▨ **Cooper Island Beach Club.** Cooper Island is one of those Caribbean
Fodor'sChoice spots that hark back to an earlier era when frills were few but the
★ peaceful atmosphere was sublime. You usually either love the quiet or hate the isolation. Once you arrive via a complimentary ferry ride from Prospect Reef, Tortola, there's nothing to do but relax, enjoy the sun and the sea, and visit with old and new friends. Rooms are really small suites with basic cooking facilities, but the hotel's restaurant is nearby if you don't want to lug groceries on the ferry. Don't pack your hairdryer or electric shaver, because the hotel's primitive electrical system can't handle it. Meals run to basics like fish, chicken, and steak. Reservations are essential for the restaurant if you're not a resort guest. ⊠ *Manchioneel Bay* ⌖ *Box 859, Road Town, Tortola* ☎ 413/863–3162 or 800/542–4624 ⎙ 413/863–3662 ⊕ *www.cooper-island.com* ⇆ *12 rooms* ⌂ *Restaurant, fans, kitchens, beach, dive shop, bar; no a/c, no room phones, no room TVs* ▤ *MC, V* ⊠ *EP.*

## Guana Island

Guana Island sits off Tortola's northeast coast. Sailors often drop anchor at one of the island's bays for a day of snorkeling and sunning. The island is a designated wildlife sanctuary, and scientists often come here to study its flora and fauna. It's home to a back-to-nature resort that offers few activities other than relaxation. Unless you're a hotel guest or a sailor, there's no easy way to get here.

**$$$$** ☷ **Guana Island Resort.** Guana Island is a nature lover's paradise, and it's a good resort if you want to stroll the hillsides, snorkel around the reefs, and swim at its six beaches, and still enjoy some degree of comfort. Rooms are simple but charming, with rattan furniture and tile floors, and open to the tropical breezes. Once you're here, you're here. You can spend your time dining and socializing with the other guests or immersed in that book you never got around to reading. You can rent the entire 15-room resort if you'd like to vacation with a group of your friends or family. The hotel's launch picks you up at Terrence B. Lettsome Airport on Beef Island (Tortola's airport) for the short hop across the water to the resort. ✉ *Guana Island* ✆ *Box 32, Road Town, Tortola* ☎ *284/494–2354 or 800/544–8262* ☏ *284/495–2900* ⊕ *www.guana.com* ⇒ *15 rooms* ⚭ *Restaurant, fans, Wi-Fi, beach, dock, snorkeling, windsurfing, boating; no a/c, no room phones, no room TVs* ▤ *AE, MC, V* †◎† *FAP.*

## Necker Island

Necker Island sits off Virgin Gorda's northeast coast, reachable only by private ferry or helicopter. A mere speck in the British Virgin Islands, it's home to Sir Richard Branson's private estate. When he's not in residence, you and your friends are welcome to enjoy its gorgeous beaches and myriad amenities.

**$$$$** ✕☷ **Necker Island.** You probably won't run into British magnate Sir Richard Branson, but you can live in his luxurious style when you rent his estate on Necker Island. If you're rich, famous, or well heeled enough to spend thousands a day to get away from it all, this would be the place to do it. Actually, it's not such a bad deal if you and 25 of your family and friends want to enjoy a vacation together. The island comes fully staffed, and all meals and activities are included. Rooms are spread out over the main house and a handful of cottages located around the island. Arrival is by helicopter or private launch from Terrence B. Lettsome Airport on Tortola. For two weeks every year (usually in the fall), couples can book individual rooms for a one-week stay. ✉ *Necker Island* ✆ *Box 1091, The Valley, Virgin Gorda* ☎ *284/494–2757 or 800/557–4255* ⊕ *www.virgin.com/necker* ⇒ *10 rooms, 3 houses* ⚭ *Fans, Wi-Fi, tennis court, 2 pools, exercise equipment, beach, dock, snorkeling, windsurfing, boating; no room TVs* ▤ *AE, MC, V* †◎† *FAP.*

## Marina Cay

⏾ Beautiful little Marina Cay is in Trellis Bay, not far from Beef Island. Sometimes you can see it and its large J-shape coral reefs—a most dramatic sight—from the air soon after takeoff from the airport on Beef Island. With only 8 acres, this islet is considered small even by BVI standards. On it there's a restaurant, Pusser's Store, and a six-unit hotel. Ferry service is free from the dock on Beef Island.

### Where to Stay & Eat

$$–$$$$  ▦ **Pusser's Marina Cay Hotel & Restaurant.** If getting away from it all is your priority, this may be the place for you, because there's nothing more to do on this beach-rimmed island but swim, snorkel, and soak up the sun—there's not even a TV to distract you. Rooms, decorated in simple wicker and wood with floral-print fabrics, are on a hilltop facing the trade winds; two villas look right out to the morning sunrise. The laid-back tempo picks up at 4 PM for happy hour when charter boaters come ashore to hear local musicians entertain in the bar. The restaurant, open for lunch and dinner, offers a menu that ranges from fish and lobster to steak, chicken, and barbecued ribs. Pusser's Painkiller Punch is the house specialty. There's free ferry service from the Beef Island dock for anyone visiting the island, though ferry times and frequency vary with the seasons. ⊠ *West side of Marina Cay* ✉ *Box 76, Road Town, Tortola* ☎ *284/494–2174* 🖷 *284/494–4775* ⊕ *www.pussers.com/outposts* 🛏 *4 rooms, 2 2-bedroom villas* ⌂ *Restaurant, fans, beach, bar, shop; no a/c, no room phones, no room TVs* ▤ *AE, MC, V* ⦿ *CP.*

## Norman Island

This uninhabited island is the supposed setting for Robert Louis Stevenson's *Treasure Island*. The famed caves at Treasure Point are popular with day sailors and power boaters. If you land ashore at the island's main anchorage in the Bight, you can find a small beach bar and behind it a trail that winds up the hillside and reaches a peak with a fantastic view of the Sir Francis Drake Channel to the north.

$$–$$$  ✕ *Willy T.* The ship, a former Baltic trader and today a floating bar and restaurant anchored to the north of the Bight, serves lunch and dinner in a party-hearty atmosphere. Try the jalapeño poppers for starters. For lunch and dinner, British-style fish-and-chips, West Indian roti sandwiches, and the barbecued chicken are winners. If you don't have your own boat, you can take the free launch from Todman's, across from Nanny Cay Marina; it leaves at 5 PM and returns at 10 or 11 PM. ⊠ *The Bight* ☎ *284/496–8603* ⌕ *Reservations essential* ▤ *MC, V.*

## Peter Island

Although Peter Island is home to the resort of the same name, it's also a popular anchorage for charter boaters and a destination for Tortola vacationers. The scheduled ferry trip from Peter Island's shoreside base outside Road Town runs $15 round-trip for nonguests. The island is lush,

**2**

with forested hillsides sloping seaward to meet white sandy beaches. There are no roads other than those at the resort, and there's nothing to do but relax at the lovely beach set aside for day-trippers. You're welcome to dine at the resort's restaurants.

**$$$$** ✕▦ **Peter Island Resort.** Total pampering and the prices to match are the ticket at this luxury resort. If you want to while away your days at the beach, enjoy a morning at the spa, stroll the lushly planted grounds, and relax over dinner with other like-minded guests—and have the money to afford the steep rates—this is a good place to do it. For more active types, there are tennis and water sports galore. Peter Island is a half-hour ferry ride from Tortola, but once you arrive, you're in another world. The rooms are gorgeous, with thoughtful touches like showers with a view. A couple of villas sit above the hotel rooms. ⊠ *Peter Island* ☟ *Box 211, Road Town, Tortola* ☎ *284/495–2000 or 800/346–4451* 🖷 *284/495–2500* ⊕ *www.peterisland.com* ⬥ *52 rooms, 2 villas* ♨ *2 restaurants, fans, in-room safes, pool, gym, massage, spa, beach, dive shop, dock, snorkeling, windsurfing, boating, bar, shop, Internet room; no room TVs* ▭ *AE, MC, V* ℔ *FAP.*

**$$–$$$** ✕ **Deadman's Beach Restaurant.** Sitting just off the beach, this casual restaurant is popular with charter boaters, day-trippers, and hotel guests. The food is imaginative and served with style. The menu runs from a delicious shrimp pizza cooked in a wood-fired oven to more hearty fare like a crispy nori-wrapped tuna fillet served with glass noodles, shiitake mushrooms, and a saffron-tomato broth. ⊠ *Peter Island Resort* ☎ *284/ 495–2000* ▭ *AE, MC, V.*

# BRITISH VIRGIN ISLANDS ESSENTIALS

*To research prices, get advice from other travelers, and book travel arrangements, visit www.fodors.com.*

## Transportation

### BY AIR

There's no nonstop service from the continental United States to the BVI; connections are usually made through San Juan, Puerto Rico, or St. Thomas. You can also fly to Anegada and Virgin Gorda; these flights may originate in San Juan, St. Thomas, or Tortola.

All three of the BVI's airports—on Tortola (TOV), Virgin Gorda (VIJ), and Anegada (no code)—are classic Caribbean and almost always sleepy. However, the Terrence B. Lettsome Airport terminal at Beef Island can get crowded when several departures are scheduled close together.

☎ Airline Contacts **Air Sunshine** ☎ 284/495-8900 ⊕ www.airsunshine.com. **American Eagle** ☎ 284/495-2559 ⊕ www.aa.com. **Cape Air** ☎ 284/495-2100 ⊕ www. flycapeair.com. **Fly BVI** ☎ 284/495-1747 ⊕ www.fly-bvi.com. **LIAT** ☎ 284/495-2577 ⊕ www.liatairline.com.

☎ Airport Contacts **BVI Taxi Association** ☎ 284/494-3942. **Mahogany Rentals & Taxi Service** ⊠ Virgin Gorda ☎ 284/495-5469.

### BY BOAT & FERRY

Ferries connect the airport gateway of St. Thomas, USVI, with Tortola and Virgin Gorda. They leave from both Charlotte Amalie and Red Hook. Ferries also link St. John, USVI, with Tortola, Jost Van Dyke, and Virgin Gorda, as well as Tortola with Jost Van Dyke, Peter Island, and Virgin Gorda. Tortola has two ferry terminals—one at West End and one in Road Town—so make sure you hop a ferry that disembarks closest to where you want to go.

There's huge competition among the Tortola-based ferry companies on the St. Thomas–Tortola runs, with boats leaving close together. As you enter the ferry terminal to buy your ticket, crews may try to convince you to take their ferry. Ferries to Virgin Gorda land in the Valley. All ferries from the BVI to Red Hook, St. Thomas, stop in St. John to clear U.S. customs. Ferry schedules vary by day, and not all companies make daily trips. The BVI Tourist Board Web site ( ⇨ *see* Visitor Information, *below*) has links to all the ferry companies, which are the best up-to-date sources of information for specific routes and schedules.

🚢 **Inter-Island Boat Services** ☎ 284/495-4166. **Native Son** ☎ 284/495-4617 ⊕ www.nativesonbvi.com. **New Horizon Ferry Service** ☎ 284/495-9477. **North Sound Express** ☎ 284/495-2138. *Nubian Princess* ☎ 284/495-4999. **Peter Island Ferry** ☎ 284/495-2000 ⊕ www.peterisland.com. **Smith's Ferry** ☎ 284/495-4495 ⊕ www.smithsferry.com. **Speedy's Ferries** ☎ 284/495-5240 ⊕ www.speedysbvi.com.

### BY CAR

Driving in the BVI is on the left side of the road, British style—but your car will have left-hand drive like those used in the United States. Speed limits (rarely enforced) are 20 mph in town and 35 mph outside town. Gas tends to be expensive. Tortola's main roads are well paved, for the most part, but there are exceptionally steep hills and sharp curves; driving demands your complete attention. A main road circles the island, and several roads cross it, almost always through mountainous terrain. Virgin Gorda has a smaller road system, and a single, very steep road links the north and south ends of the island. Anegada's few roads are little more than sandy lanes.

You need a temporary BVI license, available at the rental-car company for $10 with a valid license from another country. The minimum age to rent a car is 25. Most agencies offer both four-wheel-drive vehicles and cars (often compacts).

🚗 **Avis** ✉ Opposite Police Station, Road Town, Tortola ☎ 284/494-3322. **D&D** ✉ Waterfront Dr., close to West End, Tortola ☎ 284/495-7676. **D. W. Jeep Rentals** ✉ The Settlement, Anegada ☎ 284/495-9677. **Hertz** ✉ West End, Tortola ☎ 284/495-4405 ✉ Airport, Tortola ☎ 284/495-2763 ✉ Road Town, Tortola ☎ 284/494-6228. **Itgo Car Rental** ✉ Wickham's Cay I, Road Town, Tortola ☎ 284/494-2639. **L&S Jeep Rental** ✉ South Valley, Virgin Gorda ☎ 284/495-5297. **Mahogany Rentals & Taxi Service** ✉ Spanish Town, Virgin Gorda ☎ 284/495-5469. **Speedy's Car Rentals** ✉ The Valley, Virgin Gorda ☎ 284/495-5240.

### BY TAXI

Your hotel staff will be happy to summon a taxi for you. Rates aren't set, so you should negotiate the fare with your driver before you start

2

your trip. It's cheaper to travel in groups because there's a minimum fare to each destination, which is the same whether you have one, two, or three passengers. The taxi number is also the license plate number. On Tortola, the BVI Taxi Association has stands in Road Town near the ferry dock. The Beef Island Taxi Association operates at the Beef Island–Tortola airport. You can also usually find a West End Taxi Association ferry at the West End ferry dock.

Andy's Taxi & Jeep Rental offers service from one end of Virgin Gorda to the other. Mahogany Rentals & Taxi Service provides taxi service all over Virgin Gorda.

🚖 **Andy's Taxi & Jeep Rental** ⊠ The Valley, Virgin Gorda ☎ 284/495-5511. **Beef Island Taxi Association** ⊠ Beef Island Airport, Tortola ☎ 284/495-1982. **BVI Taxi Association** ⊠ Near the ferry dock, Road Town, Tortola ☎ 284/494-2322. **Mahogany Rentals & Taxi Service** ⊠ The Valley, Virgin Gorda ☎ 284/495-5469. **West End Taxi Association** ⊠ West End ferry terminal, Tortola ☎ 284/495-4934.

## Contacts & Resources

### BANKS & EXCHANGE SERVICES

The currency is the U.S. dollar. Any other currency must be exchanged at a bank. Most hotels and restaurants in the BVI accept MasterCard and Visa, and some also accept American Express, Diners Club, and Discover. Some may have a minimum on credit-card purchases. Beware that a few accept only cash or traveler's checks. On Tortola, banks are near the Waterfront at Wickham's Cay I. All have ATM machines. Look for First Caribbean International Bank, First Bank, and Scotia Bank, among others. On Virgin Gorda, First Caribbean International isn't far from the ferry dock in Spanish Town.

### BUSINESS HOURS

Banking hours are usually Monday through Thursday from 9 to 2:30 and Friday from 9 to 2:30 and 4:30 to 6. Post offices are open weekdays from 9 to 5 and Saturday from 9 to noon. Stores are generally open Monday through Saturday from 9 to 5. Some may be open on Sunday.

### ELECTRICITY

Electricity is 110 volts, the same as in North America, so European appliances will require adapters. The electricity is quite reliable.

### EMERGENCIES

🚑 Ambulance, Fire & Police **General emergencies** ☎ 999.
🏥 Hospitals & Clinics **Anegada Government Health Clinic** ☎ 284/495-8049. **Jost Van Dyke Government Health Clinic** ☎ 284/495-9239. **Peebles Hospital** ⊠ Road Town, Tortola ☎ 284/494-3497. **Virgin Gorda Government Health Clinic** ⊠ The Valley ☎ 284/495-5337.
🚤 Marine Emergencies **VISAR** ☎ 767 from phone or Marine Radio Channel 16.
💊 Pharmacies **Island Drug Centre** ⊠ Spanish Town, Virgin Gorda ☎ 284/495-5449. **J. R. O'Neal Drug Store** ⊠ Road Town, Tortola ☎ 284/494-2292. **Medicure Pharmacy** ⊠ Road Town, Tortola ☎ 284/494-6189 ⊠ Spanish Town, Virgin Gorda ☎ 284/495-5479.

### HOLIDAYS

The following public holidays are celebrated in the BVI: New Year's Day, Commonwealth Day (Mar. 14), Good Friday (Fri. before Easter), Easter Sunday (usually Mar. or Apr.), Easter Monday (day after Easter), Whit Monday (1st Mon. in May), Sovereign's Birthday (June 16), Territory Day (July 1), BVI August Festival Days (usually 1st 2 wks in Aug.), St. Ursula's Day (Oct. 21), Christmas, and Boxing Day (day after Christmas).

### INTERNET, MAIL & SHIPPING

There are post offices in Road Town on Tortola and in Spanish Town on Virgin Gorda. Postage for a first-class letter to the United States and Canada is 50¢. The postage to Australia, New Zealand, or the United Kingdom is 60¢. Postcards to the United States and Canada are 35¢. To Australia, New Zealand, or the United Kingdom, they're 40¢. For a small fee, Rush It, in Road Town and in Spanish Town, offers most U.S. mail and UPS services (via St. Thomas the next day). If you wish to write to an establishment in the BVI, be sure to include the specific island in the address; there are no postal codes. Some businesses have a USVI postal address.

🛈 **Shipping Contacts Rush It** ✉ Road Town, Tortola ☎ 284/494-4421 ✉ Spanish Town, Virgin Gorda ☎ 284/495-5821.

### PASSPORTS REQUIREMENTS

U.S. and Canadian citizens, as well as citizens of all other countries, need a valid passport.

### SAFETY

Although crime is rare, use common sense: don't leave your camera on the beach while you take a dip or your wallet on a hotel dresser when you go for a walk.

### TAXES

The departure tax is $5 per person by boat and $20 per person by plane. There's a separate booth at the airport and ferry terminals to collect this tax, which must be paid in cash in U.S. currency. Most hotels add a service charge ranging from 5% to 18% to the bill. A few restaurants and some shops tack on an additional 10% charge if you use a credit card. There's no sales tax in the BVI. However, there's a 7% government tax on hotel rooms.

### TELEPHONES

Your mobile phone may or may not work in the BVI. If you are on the south side of Tortola, you may be able to connect to Cingular and Sprint, but other islands are problematic. The BVI has local companies only. Even if your U.S. mainland company assures you that your phone will work, don't count on it.

The area code for the BVI is 284; when you make calls from North America, you need only dial the area code and the number. From the United Kingdom you must dial 001 and then the area code and the number. From Australia and New Zealand you must dial 0011 followed by 1, the area code, and the number.

2

To call anywhere in the BVI once you've arrived, dial all seven digits. A local call from a pay phone costs 25¢, but such phones are sometimes on the blink. An alternative is a Caribbean phone card, available in $5, $10, and $20 denominations. They're sold at most major hotels and many stores and can be used to call within the BVI, as well as all over the Caribbean, and to access USADirect from special phone-card phones. For credit-card or collect long-distance calls to the United States, use a phone-card telephone or look for special USADirect phones, which are linked directly to an AT&T operator. USADirect and pay phones can be found at most hotels and in towns.

🛈 **USA Direct** ☎ 800/872-2881, 111 from a pay phone.

### TIPPING

Tip porters and bellhops $1 per bag. Sometimes a service charge (10%) is included on restaurant bills; it's customary to leave another 5% if you liked the service. If no charge is added, 15% is the norm. Cabbies normally aren't tipped because most own their cabs; add 10% to 15% if they exceed their duties.

### TOUR OPTIONS

Romney Associates/Travel Plan Tours can arrange island tours, boat tours, snorkeling and scuba-diving trips, dolphin swims, and yacht charters from its Tortola and Virgin Gorda bases.

🛈 **Romney Associates/Travel Plan Tours** ☎ 284/494-4000

### VISITOR INFORMATION

🛈 **BVI Tourist Board** ✉ Ferry Terminal, Road Town, Tortola ☎ 284/494-3134 ⊕ www. bvitourism.com. **Virgin Gorda BVI Tourist Board** ✉ Virgin Gorda Yacht Harbour, Spanish Town, Virgin Gorda ☎ 284/495-5181.

### WEDDINGS

Getting married in the BVI is a breeze, but you must make advance plans. To make things go smoother, hire a wedding planner to guide you through the ins and outs of the BVI system. Many hotels also have wedding planners on staff to help organize your event. Hotels often offer packages that include the ceremony; accommodations for you, your wedding party and your guests; and extras like massages, sailboat trips, and champagne dinners.

You must apply in person for your license ($110) weekdays at the attorney general's office in Road Town, Tortola. You must wait three days to pick it up at the registrar's office in Road Town. If you plan to be married in a church, announcements (called *banns* locally) must be published for three consecutive Sundays in the church bulletin. Only the registrar or clergy can perform ceremonies. The registrar charges $35 at the office and $100 at another location. No blood test is required.

🛈 **BVI Wedding Planners & Consultants** ☎ 284/494-5306 ⊕ www.bviweddings.com.

# UNDERSTANDING THE VIRGIN ISLANDS

# U.S. VIRGIN ISLANDS AT A GLANCE

## Fast Facts

**Capital:** Charlotte Amalie, St. Thomas
**National anthem:** *The Virgin Islands March*
**Type of government:** Unincorporated territory of the U.S., with governor and lieutenant governor, unicameral senate, and one non-voting representative in the U.S. House of Representatives
**Constitution:** July 22, 1954
**Legal system:** U.S. District Court of the Virgin Islands under Third Circuit jurisdiction; Territorial Court (judges appointed by the governor for 10-year terms)
**Suffrage:** 18 years of age; universal; indigenous inhabitants are U.S. citizens but do not vote in U.S. presidential elections as long as they reside in the U.S. Virgin Islands
**Legislature:** Unicameral Senate (15 seats; members are elected by popular vote to serve two-year terms); one non-voting representative elected to the U.S. House of Representatives
**Population:** 124,778
**Population density:** 938 people per square mi
**Median age:** female 33.7, male 28.6
**Life expectancy:** female 82.7, male 74.7
**Infant mortality rate:** 9 deaths per 1,000 live births
**Language:** English (official), Spanish, Creole
**Ethnic groups:** West Indian 81% (49% born in the Virgin Islands and 32% born elsewhere in the West Indies); U.S. mainland 13%; Puerto Rican 4%; other 2%
**Religion:** Baptist 42%; Roman Catholic 34%; Episcopalian 17%; other 7%

## Geography & Environment

**Land area:** 133 square mi, approximately twice the size of Washington, D.C.
**Coastline:** 116 mi
**Terrain:** Mostly hilly to rugged and mountainous with little level land (highest point: Crown Mountain 1,555 feet)
**Islands:** St. Croix, St. John, St. Thomas
**Natural hazards:** Hurricanes, frequent and severe droughts and floods, occasional earthquakes
**Environmental issues:** Lack of natural freshwater resources

## Economy

**Currency:** U.S. Dollar
**GDP:** $2.4 billion
**Per capita income:** $13,139
**Inflation:** 2%
**Unemployment:** 4.9%
**Work force:** 49,000; services/tourism 79%; industry 20%; agriculture 1%
**Major industries:** Construction, electronics, petroleum refining, pharmaceuticals, rum distilling, textiles, tourism, watch assembly
**Agricultural products:** Fruit, Senepol cattle, sorghum, vegetables
**Major export products:** Refined petroleum products
**Export partners:** U.S., Puerto Rico
**Major import products:** Building materials, consumer goods, crude oil, foodstuffs
**Import partners:** U.S., Puerto Rico

## Did You Know?

• On September 13, 2003, the world's largest underwater wedding took place off of Rainbow Beach in St. Croix. The bride, groom, minister, and more than 100 other guests in scuba equipment marked the matrimony in about 10 feet of water.

• The Hess Oil refinery on the south coast of St. Croix is one of the largest petroleum facilities in the world.

• If you're dying to drive on the wrong side of the road in America, this is your spot: The Virgin Islands are the only place in the U.S. where driving on the left side of the road is practiced.

• The marriage rate in the U.S. Virgin Islands is 35.1 per 1,000 people, the highest in the world.

• Point Udall on St. Croix is the farthest point east that U.S. territory stretches.

• The large, red cattle on St. Croix are Senepol, a breed handpicked to thrive on the island. Originally from Senegal, they've been bred to have a high tolerance for heat, no horns, and a strong immune system. After their success on the Virgin Islands, the cattle are now raised in the southern U.S.

• A leatherback turtle fitted with a depth recording device by scientists reached a depth of 3,973 feet off the Virgin Islands, a world record.

# BRITISH VIRGIN ISLANDS AT A GLANCE

## Fast Facts

**Capital:** Road Town, Tortola
**National anthem:** *God Save the Queen* (anthem of the United Kingdom)
**Type of government:** Overseas territory of the UK
**Constitution:** June 1, 1977
**Legal system:** English law
**Suffrage:** 18 years of age; universal
**Legislature:** Unicameral Legislative Council (13 seats; members are elected by direct popular vote, one member from each of 9 electoral districts, four at-large members; members serve four-year terms); next elections to be held in 2007
**Population:** 21,730

**Population density:** 229 people per square mi
**Median age:** female 30.4, male 31
**Life expectancy:** female 77.1, male 75.1
**Infant mortality rate:** 18.8 deaths per 1,000 live births
**Literacy:** 97.8%
**Language:** English (official)
**Ethnic groups:** Black 83%; white, Indian, Asian and mixed
**Religion:** Methodist 33%; Anglican 17%; other Protestant 15%; Roman Catholic 10%; Church of God 9%; Seventh-Day Adventist 6%; Baptist 4%; Jehovah's Witnesses 2%; other 2%; unaffiliated 2%

## Geography & Environment

**Land area:** The four major land masses are Tortola, Anegada, Virgin Gorda, and Jost Van Dyke, totaling 153-square-km (59-square-mi), about the size of Washington, D.C.
**Coastline:** 80 km (50 mi)
**Terrain:** Coral islands relatively flat; volcanic islands steep, hilly (highest point: Mount Sage 521 m [1,716 feet])

**Islands:** 60 islands and cays, including Tortola, Anegada, Virgin Gorda, and Jost Van Dyke
**Natural hazards:** Hurricanes and tropical storms (July to October)
**Environmental issues:** Limited natural fresh water resources (except for a few seasonal streams and springs on Tortola, most of the islands' water supply comes from wells and rainwater catchments)

## Economy

**Currency:** U.S. Dollar
**GDP:** $320 million
**Per capita income:** $11,000
**Inflation:** 2.5%
**Unemployment:** 3%
**Work force:** 4,911
**Debt:** $36.1 million
**Major industries:** Concrete block, construction, finance, light industry, offshore, rum, tourism
**Agricultural products:** Fish, fruits, livestock, poultry, vegetables

**Exports:** $25.3 million
**Major export products:** Animals, fresh fish, fruits, gravel, rum, sand
**Export partners:** U.S. Virgin Islands, Puerto Rico, U.S.
**Imports:** $187 million
**Major import products:** Automobiles, building materials, foodstuffs, machinery
**Import partners:** U.S. Virgin Islands, Puerto Rico, U.S.

## Did You Know?

• Almost half of BVI's economy is driven by tourism. An estimated 350,000 visit the islands each year, most from the United States.

• The world's smallest lizards live in this collection of islands. The sphaerodactylus parthenopion and sphaerodactylus ariasiae are about six-tenths of an inch long.

• This tiny nation has come up with big innovations for making money. An estimated 400,000 companies have taken advantage of a BVI offer allowing them to incorporate here to avoid paying taxes.

• There are five radio stations in the British Virgin Islands (one AM and four FM) and one TV station. The country does have a cable company.

• Pate here isn't the product of overfed ducks, it's a West Indian dish of pita bread filled with spiced meat, seafood, or vegetables.

• Watch for the misnamed "Century Plant," which blooms every eight years in the spring. Its yellow flowers can be seen in pods among its spiky leaves on a stalk that can reach 40 feet.

# VIRGIN ISLANDS CUISINE

The bunch of bananas sitting on the road-side stand's plywood counter was bigger than my father had ever seen in New Jersey. Each fruit was nearly a foot-long and thick as a summer sausage. Ripe black speckles burst over a sunny yellow peel. Money paid. Bunch in hand. He impatiently peeled the plumpest one and brought it to his mouth. A soft chuckle stopped him mid-bite. "Got to cook it first," said the market woman, grinning broadly. He set the plantain down, suddenly smarter. Foods in the Virgin Islands, he related to me later, weren't always as they seemed.

Take a mix of indigenous and imported ingredients, everything from papaya to salt cod. Blend this with the cooking styles of people like the ancient Amerindians, Africans, Europeans, East Indians and Asians and you have the melting pot that is traditional Virgin Islands cuisine. The best places to sample these foods are at local restaurants and bakeries, mobile food vans and the many food fairs and political fish fries that take place throughout the year.

Start the day with dumb bread and bush tea. Dumb bread takes its name from a style of cooking native to India, where hot coals set around a kettle filled with dough cooks loaves to crusty perfection. You can nibble four-inch-thick pie-shaped wedges plain or filled with Cheddar cheese.

In the local lingo, "bush" means herb. Parts of 420 different plants have been used to make tea in the Virgin Islands. Historically, these herbal blends have been touted as much for their medicinal value as for their taste. For example, there are bush teas like wormgrass, inflammation bush, and belly ache bush. When ordering bush tea in a restaurant, you'll most likely get lemongrass or mint.

You'll find bush for tea or seasoning at any of the roadside produce stands that dot the islands' roadways. While you're there, make sure to sample a mango, papaya, or finger-long fig banana. There are usually vegetables like small purple eggplants, green plantains, and gnarly root vegetables like tannia, cassava, and boniato. Elsewhere on the island you'll often find machete-wielding young men whacking the tops off of coconuts. They'll slip a straw into the nut's sturdy natural cup and hand it to you to drink the refreshing "coconut water" inside.

Pates are a popular snack, but don't envision goose or duck liver. Instead, these triangular-shaped fried pastries have an outer wrapping of bread and a spicy filling made from ground beef, conch, or salted fish. Do order a cup of mangoade, papaya punch, or soursop juice along with a pate. These tropical fruit drinks make the perfect partner to the pates, as these pastries often boast a touch of fiery scotch bonnet peppers among their ingredients.

Fish and fungi ranks as the unofficial national dish for the Virgin Islands. It's a combination as common as a hamburger and french fries on the U.S. mainland. The fish is pot fish, so called for it being caught offshore by fishermen using pots or traps. Favorites include oldwife, snapper, grouper and grunt, served whole; the meat from the head and eyes are considered a delicacy. Don't expect the fish to be served with mushrooms, however. Fungi is a polenta-like dish of African origin that is made up of cornmeal studded with chunks of chopped fresh okra. The fungi sops up the buttery tomato, onion, garlic and thyme flecked gravy from the fish to perfection.

Fungi is often served with kallaloo, a soupy stew made with spinach and okra, seasoned with fresh herbs, and made hearty with the addition of crab, fish, ham or a pig part like ear, tail or snout. Kallalo is traditionally eaten on the last evening of the year, known in these parts as Old Year's Night. The late Virgin Islands food writer and historian, Arona Petersen, once described how this tradition got its start: "By Old Year's Day, all that would be left of the ham served on Christmas day would be the bone. To make the kallaloo, someone would contribute the bone, another neighbor the fish or crab, and yet another person the greens." If you served kallaloo to your loved one on Old Year's Night, Petersen said, there would be a wedding by June.

Virgin Islanders love their kallaloo, as well as many other soups. Men especially enjoy spooning into a bowl of bullfoot soup or goat water, hearty dishes that are sworn to have aphrodisiac properties. Whether based of bull's feet, cow's heels, or some other type of meat, island soups are anything but anemic affairs. You'll find a full meal, for floating beside the namesake ingredient are a vast amount of vegetables and rib-stickers called dumplings.

Side dishes can be just as ambiguous in their names. For example, a plate of peas and rice is more likely to be made with red beans, kidney beans, black beans, or garbanzo beans than any type of pea. Potato stuffing, a mix of mashed white potatoes, tomato sauce, and seasonings, isn't used to stuff anything but it does accompany turkey at Thanksgiving. Boiled sweet potatoes, yams, and tannia are sliced and served with fish and poultry. On a menu, you'll find them referred to as "provisions", as these hearty root vegetables once sustained African slaves. Boiled green bananas and fried plantains are popular, too. Don't be surprised to find that a "plate of food," as a meal is called, includes an entrée, a green salad, and a choice of three starchy side dishes.

Dessert after a meal is more of an American than a West Indian convention, but Virgin Islanders do have their sweets. Tarts, filled with stewed sweetened coconut, guava, pineapple, or mango, are favorites—especially at Christmas. So is sweetbread, a dense fruitcake spiked with dried fruits that have been soaked for weeks in guavaberry rum. Coconut sugar cakes, a combination of shredded coconut and sugar boiled down into hard palm-sized rounds, more closely resemble candy than cake. Dundersloe, the Virgin Islands version of peanut brittle, is sold by ladies who have their "trays" set outside most of the island's shopping centers.

For all its American flag status, with its abundant fast-food and Continental-style restaurants, Virgin Islands cuisine does hold its share of delicious surprises. It's no wonder that a favorite saying is: "Better belly bus' than good food waste."

# BELOW THE WAVES

**COLORFUL REEFS AND WRECKS** rife with corals and tropical fish make the islands as interesting underwater as above. Bright blue tangs vie for your attention with darting blue-headed wrasses. Corals in wondrous shapes—some look like brains, others like elk antlers—live near colorful sponges. You might see a pink conch making its way along the ocean bottom in areas with seagrass beds. If you're really lucky, a turtle may swim into view, or a lobster may poke its antenna out of a hole in the reef or rocks. Scuba diving gets you up close and personal with the reefs and fish; snorkeling gives you a bird's eye view of the underwater world as you meander along the sea's surface. Whether scuba diving or snorkeling, take along an underwater camera to capture memories of your exciting adventure. You can buy disposable ones at most dive shops, though usually not as cheaply as at the drugstore back home.

## Scuba Diving

If you've never been diving, start with an introductory lesson—often called a "resort course"—run by any one of the Virgin Islands' dive shops. All meet stringent safety standards. If they didn't, they'd soon be out of business. If you're staying at a hotel, you'll often find the dive shop onsite; otherwise, your hotel probably has an arrangement with one nearby. If you're on a cruise, cruise-ship companies offer shore excursions that include transportation to and from the ship as well as the resort course.

The introductory course lasts a couple of hours and usually runs under $100. It starts with a video on the ins and outs of scuba diving. At the water's edge, you'll practice clearing your mask if it floods, breathing through the regulator, and learning to work your buoyancy compensator, which is called a "BC" in dive lingo. A shallow reef dive with the instructor practically holding your hand concludes the experience. This is the best way to learn if you'd like to take the plunge in to certification.

Certification, which requires much more study and practice, is required to rent air tanks, get air refills, and join others on guided dives virtually anywhere in the world. You can accomplish the entire 32- to 40-hour open-water certification course in as few as three days of vacation, but it's hard work. Assuming that you are fairly fit and able to swim, professionals suggest that you take a two-part approach: do the classroom study and pool exercises (basic swimming and equipment skills) through a dive school or a YMCA program at home, then, with a transfer form from your home instructor, certified Virgin Islands dive instructors will lead you through four open-water dives and check your qualifications for a certification card—called a "C card"—by the Professional Association of Diving Instructors (PADI) or the National Association of Underwater Instructors (NAUI). Most shops in the Virgin Islands offer certification from PADI, but you will find an occasional one that uses NAUI certification.

If you're really hooked, you can study further for advanced certification in fields such as night diving, wreck diving, search and recovery, underwater photography, and more. Who knows, you might like scuba diving so much, you'll go on to be a dive master or instructor so you can guide trips and teach others.

All certification courses stress diver safety. The basic rules for safe diving are simple, and fools ignore them at their own peril. Serious diving accidents are becoming increasingly rare these days, thanks to the high level of diver training. However, they *do* still occur occasionally. Surfacing too rapidly without exhaling—or going too deep for too long—can result in an air embolism or a case of the bends. Roy L. Schneider Hospital in St. Thomas has a decompression chamber that serves all the Virgin Islands. If you get the bends, you'll be whisked to the hospital for this necessary treatment.

Fauna is another concern. Though sharks, barracuda, and moray eels are on the most-feared list, more often it's sea urchins and fire coral that cause pain when you accidentally bump them. Part of any scuba-training program is a review of sea life and the importance of respecting the new world you're exploring. Dive professionals recognize the value of protecting fragile reefs and ecosystems in tropical waters, and instructors emphasize look-don't-touch diving (the unofficial motto is: take only pictures, leave only bubbles). Government control and protection of dive sites is increasing, especially in such heavily used areas as the Virgin Islands.

While you can scuba dive off a beach—and you'll find shops renting scuba equipment and providing airfills at the most popular beaches—a trip aboard a dive boat provides a more extensive glimpse into this wonderful undersea world. Since the dive shops can provide all equipment, there's no need to lug heavy weights and a bulky BC in your luggage. For the most comfort, you might want to bring your own regulator if you have one. The dive boat captains and guides know the best dive locations, can find alternatives when the seas are rough, and will help you deal with heavy tanks and cumbersome equipment. Trips are easy to organize. Dive shops on all islands make frequent excursions to a wide variety of diving spots, and your hotel, vacation villa, or cruise-ship staff will help you make arrangements.

If you fly too soon after diving, you're at risk for decompression sickness, which occurs when nitrogen trapped in your bloodstream doesn't escape. This creates a painful and sometimes fatal condition called the bends, not a sickness you want to develop while you're winging your way home after a fun-filled beach vacation. Opinions vary, but as a rule of thumb, wait at least 12 hours after a single dive to fly. However, if you've made multiple dives or dived several days in a row, you should wait at least 18 hours. If you've made dives that required decompression stops, you should also wait at least 18 hours before flying. To be safe, consult with your physician.

## Popular Dive Sites

The Virgin Islands offer a plethora of dive sites, and you'll be taken to some of the best if you sign on to a dive trip run by one of the many dive operations scattered around the islands.

The wreck of the **Rhone** tops the list for those who are willing to spend up to a few hours in a boat to reach the famous wreck. The mail ship **Rhone** went down off Salt Island in the British Virgin Islands in 1867 during a hurricane. It sits in two parts, one 15 feet down and the other 75 feet below the surface. The movie *The Deep* was filmed here in 1976.

St. Croix's Wall runs along that island's north shore. A boat trip with an operator makes reaching the dive site easy, but you can also swim out from Cane Bay Beach. Divers swim past coral, sponges, and numerous colorful fish. The wall drops off from about 30 feet to thousands of feet.

Grass and Mingo cays sit just a short boat ride off St. John. The water is usually calm, which makes for easier diving when winter swells come in from the north. Divers swim past colorful reefs that are studded with coral and home to many varieties of fish. You might even see a turtle or two.

Cow and Calf barely breaks water off the coast of St. Thomas. Divers swim through tunnels, overhangs, and archways only 40 feet below the surface. Colorful fish swim along with you, and you might even spot a harmless nurse shark.

## Snorkeling

Scuba diving always requires advance planning. Snorkeling, on the other hand, can be a far more casual affair. There's no heavy, expensive, complicated equipment involved. There's usually no need for a boat, since many of the finest snorkel sites are adjacent to a beach. Because lots of tropical marine life lives fairly near the water's surface, there's no link between the depth of a dive and your enjoyment. Many avid water-sports enthusiasts progress from swimming to snorkeling to scuba—and then gradually drift back to snorkeling. The silent world is even quieter without the hiss of a two-stage regulator. Just wade in, plop down on your stomach, and snorkel away. If you're a bit adventurous, hold your breath to dive down a few feet. You'll get a closer look at the entrancing marine life on the reefs and the ocean floor.

Few places on this planet are as convenient to snorkel as the Virgin Islands, and many dive shops rent snorkeling gear, provide instructions on how to use it, and give directions to nearby snorkeling sites. Hotels and vacation villas may provide you with complimentary gear or charge a small fee. And water-sports outfitters at the busiest beaches can outfit you with masks, fins, and snorkels. If you plan to do a lot of snorkeling, it may pay to buy your own gear either at a dive shop in your home area or in the Virgin Islands. Discount stores often sell snorkel equipment, but make sure you can try it on before you buy. To see if a mask fits, hold it up to your face and breath gently through your nose. It should stick there for a moment. If not, try another. Fins should fit well: if they're too loose, they'll fall off, and if they're too tight, they'll give you blisters. Usually, any snorkel with a mouthpiece that doesn't leak is fine.

To prevent your mask from fogging, spit in it and rub the saliva on the inside of the lens. (If you're on the squeamish side, a drop of ordinary dishwashing liquid or a commercial "mask defogger" also works.) Warning: it's difficult to walk in fins. Some people walk into the water backwards with them; a better idea is to put them on while sitting in shallow water. Practice clearing your snorkel (with a sharp blow of air) in very shallow water, bracing yourself with your hands on clear sand. This will help you develop confidence before venturing into deeper waters.

The dangers of snorkeling are few and easily avoided. As when scuba diving, don't touch mustard-colored coral. It's fire coral, as its name implies, and can give you a burn. Avoid spiny sea urchins, which have long black spines; if you step on one, you'll feel it for days. But you shouldn't touch *any* coral, both because it's better to be safe than sorry and also because it's very fragile and takes years to grow back. Don't put your hands into dark holes—unless you want to play "patty cake" with a defensive moray eel. Ignore sharks and barracudas unless they act particularly aggressive. If so, retreat calmly without excessive splashing. Don't wear shiny jewelry; it attracts sharks and barracudas. Never snorkel alone, and unless you're on a guided trip, don't snorkel at night. Avoid areas with heavy surf or strong currents.

Most busy beaches have swim areas marked with white buoys. For safety's sake, confine your snorkeling to those areas. Avoid busy harbors, dock areas, or navigational channels. While boats aren't usually a problem in marked swimming areas, if you hear a motorized vessel approaching, resurface immediately and clasp both hands together over your head. This makes you clearly visible and means "Diver Okay." (Waving your hands rapidly back and forth over your head means "Diver in trouble. Need Help!") In addition, make sure you don't get hit by one boat while watching another. Sound direction can be confusing underwater. Finally, towing a floating dive flag is your best protection against being run down.

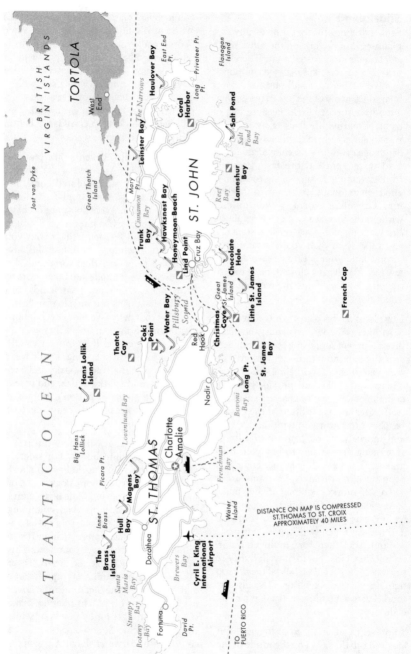

ATLANTIC OCEAN

*British Virgin Islands*

TORTOLA

*Jost van Dyke*

West End

*Great Thatch Island*

**Leinster Bay** *The Narrows*

**Haulover Bay**

*East End Pt.*

*Privateer Pt.*

*Long Pt.*

*Flanagan Island*

**Coral Harbor**

*Mary Pt.*

*Cinnamon Bay*

**Trunk Bay**

**Hawksnest Bay**

**Honeymoon Beach**

**Lind Point**

*Cruz Bay*

**ST. JOHN**

*Reef Bay*

**Salt Pond**

*Salt Pond Bay*

**Lameshur Bay**

**Chocolate Hole**

*Great St. James Island*

**Christmas Cove**

**Little St. James Island**

**Long Pt.**

**St. James Bay**

**French Cap**

**Hans Lollik Island**

*Big Hans Lollik*

*Inner Brass*

**The Brass Islands**

*Santa Maria Bay*

**Thatch Cay**

**Coki Point**

**Water Bay**

*Pillsbury Sound*

*Red Hook*

*Nadir*

*Boroni Bay*

*Picara Pt.*

*Loretiland Bay*

**Magens Bay**

**Hull Bay**

*Dorothea*

**ST. THOMAS**

**Charlotte Amalie**

*Frenchman Bay*

*Water Island*

*Brewers Bay*

**Cyril E. King International Airport**

*Stumpy Bay*

*Botany Bay*

*Fortuna*

*David Pt.*

**TO PUERTO RICO**

DISTANCE ON MAP IS COMPRESSED
ST. THOMAS TO ST. CROIX
APPROXIMATELY 40 MILES

*Caribbean Sea*

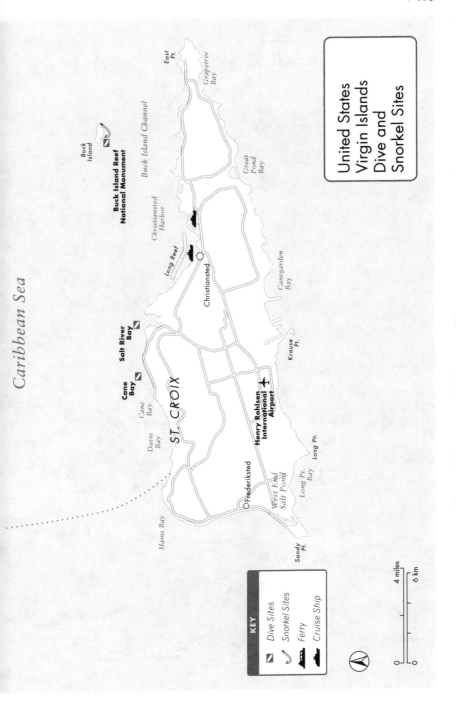

Caribbean Sea

**United States
Virgin Islands
Dive and
Snorkel Sites**

Buck Island

Buck Island Channel

*East Pt.*

*Grapetree Bay*

**Buck Island Reef
National Monument**

*Christiansted
Harbor*

*Long Reef*

Christiansted

*Great Pond Bay*

*Canegarden Bay*

**Salt River
Bay**

**Cane
Bay**

*Cane Bay*

*Davis Bay*

**ST. CROIX**

*Krause Pt.*

**Henry Rohlsen
International
Airport**

Frederiksted

*Hams Bay*

*West End
Salt Pond*

*Long Pt.*

*Long Pt.
Bay*

*Long Pt.*

*Sandy
Pt.*

**KEY**

Dive Sites

Snorkel Sites

Ferry

Cruise Ship

0     4 miles

0     6 km

British Virgin Islands
Dive and
Snorkel Sites

ATLANTIC O

Great
Tobago

Man
O?War
Bay

JOST VAN DYKE

West End
Pt.

Great
Harbour

**Green Cay**

Green
Cay

Little
Harbour

**Brewer's Bay**

Brewers
Bay

Long
Pt.
Guana Island

Trunk
Bay

Josiah's
Bay

E

**Great
Harbour**

**White
Bay**

Black
Pt.

Little Tobago

Pull &
Be Damn
Pt.

Cane Garden
Bay

Carrot Bay

Long Bay

West End

Todman
Pt.

Mt.
Sage

Road
Town

Fort
Shirley

Road Town
Harbour

Great Thatch
Island

West Pt.

**Frenchman's
Cay**

Frenchman's
Cay

TORTOLA

D
C

Great
Harbour

Rock
Hole

White
Bay

Pelican Island

Privateer
Bay

Norman
Island

TO ST. THOMAS

ST. JOHN
UNITED STATES VIRGIN ISLANDS

**The Caves
at Norman Island**

Money
Bay

West End
Pt.

Bones
Bight

Flamingo
Pond

Red
Pond

Loblolly
Bay

Table Bay

The
Settlement

**ANEGADA**
(15 miles north of Necker Is.)

Lower
Bay

Budrock
Pond

Horse
Shoe
Reef

**Wreck
of the
Rokus**

White
Bay

O C E A N

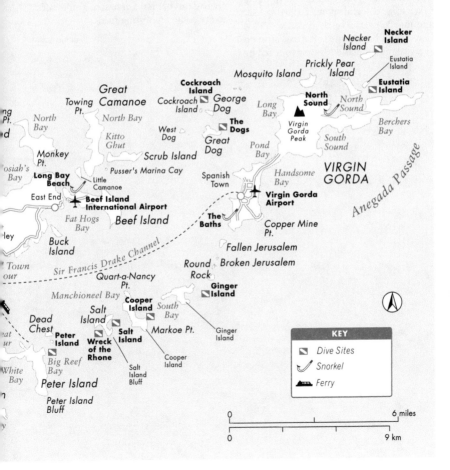

Necker
Island

**Necker
Island**

Eustatia
Island

Prickly Pear
Island

Mosquito Island

**Eustatia
Island**

Cockroach
**Island**

George
Dog

Long
Bay

**North
Sound**

North
Sound

Great
Camanoe

Cockroach
Island

Berchers
Bay

Towing
Pt.

North Bay

**The
Dogs**

Virgin
Gorda
Peak

South
Sound

North
Bay

Kitto
Ghut

West
Dog

Great
Dog

Pond
Bay

Handsome
Bay

**VIRGIN
GORDA**

ng
Pt.

d

Monkey
Pt.

Scrub Island

Spanish
Town

osiah's
Bay

**Long Bay
Beach**

Pusser's Marina Cay

Little
Camanoe

**Virgin Gorda
Airport**

Anegada Passage

East End

**Beef Island
International Airport**

**The
Baths**

Copper Mine
Pt.

ley

Fat Hogs
Bay

**Beef Island**

Fallen Jerusalem

Buck
Island

Sir Francis Drake Channel

Round
Rock

Broken Jerusalem

Town

our

Quart-a-Nancy
Pt.

**Ginger
Island**

Manchioneel Bay

**Cooper
Island**

South
Bay

Dead
Chest

Salt
Island

Markoe Pt.

Ginger
Island

eat
ur

**Peter
Island**

**Wreck
of the
Rhone**

**Salt
Island**

Cooper
Island

White
Bay

Big Reef
Bay

Salt
Island
Bluff

**Peter Island**

n

Peter Island
Bluff

y

| KEY | |
|---|---|
| ◹ | Dive Sites |
| ⌇ | Snorkel |
| ⛴ | Ferry |

0 ——————————————— 6 miles

0 ——————————————— 9 km

## Popular Snorkeling Sites

Snorkel spots abound in the Virgin Islands. Indeed, just about every beach has a lovely spot to tempt you into the salty sea. However, Trunk Bay in St. John gets the most attention. The national park service has created an underwater trail that lets you know what you're seeing in terms of coral and other underwater features. And the beach is easy to reach; taxis leave on demand from the Cruz Bay ferry dock, and Trunk Bay is on every St. John tour.

Magens Bay, the most popular beach on St. Thomas, provides lovely snorkeling if you head along the edges. You're likely to see some colorful sponges, darting fish, and maybe even a turtle if you're lucky. Like Trunk Bay, Magens Bay is a stop on every island tour, and it's easy to reach by rental car or taxi from wherever you're staying.

Snorkeling at Buck Island Reef National Monument in St. Croix provides a variety of experiences. The only way to reach this offshore cay is by boat. Once there, just jump into the water for a float over colorful reefs teaming with coral and fish. There's also a marked snorkeling trail here.

The BVI is a snorkeler's paradise, but if you happen to be in Virgin Gorda, you're in luck. The Baths attracts numerous snorkelers who enjoy floating around the huge pools created by the huge rocks that created this natural attraction. You're sure to see some interesting fish.

–Lynda Lohr

# TRY A YACHT CHARTER

**SAVORING A FRESHLY BREWED MUG OF COF-FEE,** I sat on the front deck of our chartered 43-foot catamaran and watched the morning show. Laser-like rays of sunlight streamed through a cottony cloudbank, bringing life to the emerald islands and turquoise seas surrounding our anchorage. My mind drifted back several centuries. What would it have been like to sail with Columbus and chart these waters for the first time? How would it feel to cast about the deserted beaches for the perfect place to bury plundered treasure? The aroma of freshly made banana pancakes roused me from my reverie. Our chef, Marcella, clad in khaki shorts and polo shirt with her blond hair tied back in a ponytail, playfully poured syrup over short stacks set on the cockpit table. The kids squealed in delight. My husband, who considered himself a confirmed landlubber, smiled and winked. As I scooted back to join him at the table, he whispered in my ear: "Let's tell everyone this trip was my idea."

## Bareboat or Crewed?

Once considered an outward-bound adventure or exclusive domain of the rich and famous, chartering a boat is an affordable and attractive vacation alternative. It's ideal for everyone from young honeymoon couples to families with kids and active seniors. If you're already a sailor, perhaps you've always wanted to explore beyond your own lake, river, or bay, but didn't feel confident to take your own boat on a long-haul transit to your dream destination. Or maybe your idea of boat travel has always been a cruise ship, but now you're ready for a more intimate voyage. Or perhaps you've never sailed before, but you are now curious to cast off and explore a whole new world.

The first question to answer in planning a charter is whether you'd like to go bareboat or crewed. Bareboat means without any crew. You are the captain. You sail the boat, chart the course, and cook the meals. On a crewed charter, you sit back and relax while the crew provides for your every want and need. Captains are U.S. Coast Guard licensed or the equivalent in the British maritime system. Cooks—preferring to be called chefs—have skills that go far beyond peanut butter and jelly sandwiches. There's four meals a day and many chefs boast certificates from culinary school ranging from the Culinary Institute of America in New York to the Cordon Bleu in Paris.

If you'd like to bareboat, don't be intimidated. It's a myth that you must be a graduate of a sailing school in order to pilot your own charter boat. A bareboat company will ask you to fill out a resume. The company checks for prior boat handling experience, the type of craft you've sailed (whether power boat or sailboat), and in what type of waters. Real life experience, meaning all those day and weekend trips close to home, count as valuable know-how. If you've done a bit of boating, you may be more qualified than you think to take out a bareboat.

The advantage of a crewed yacht charter, with captain and cook, is that it takes every bit of stress out of the vacation. With a captain who knows the local waters, you get to see some of the coves and anchorages that are not necessarily in the guidebooks. Your meals are prepared, cabins cleaned, beds made up everyday—and turned down at night, too. Plus, you can sail and take the helm as often as you like. But at the end of the day, the captain is the one who will take responsibility for anchoring safely for the night while the chef goes below and whips up a gourmet meal.

Costs can be very similar between a bareboat and crewed charter. For example,

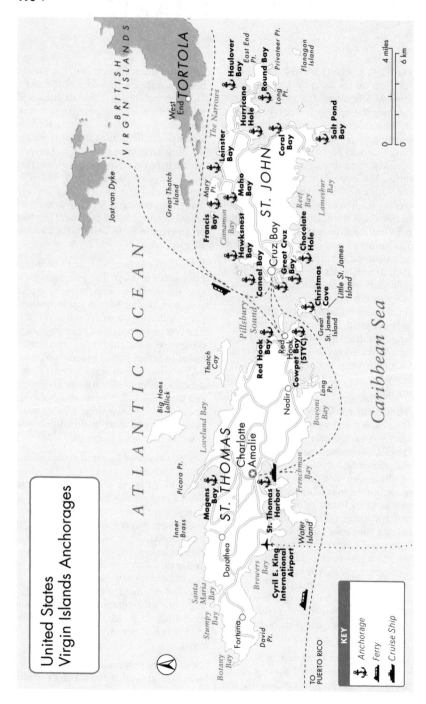

bareboats in the 50- to 55-foot range that carry six people start at $7,000 per week, excluding food, beverages, fuel, and other supplies. For the same size boat, prices for a weeklong charter with skipper and chef start at $3,000 for a couple and $9,000 for six people. The cost is all-inclusive, except for a 10% to 15% gratuity. The summer season, from May through mid-December, is generally less expensive than winter in the Caribbean. Christmas and New Year's are the most expensive times to travel. Between the U.S. and BVI, there are over 200 crewed yachts to choose from and well over 800 bareboats.

## Choosing a Charter

A decade ago, choosing a charter would mean calling a bareboat company or crewed yacht broker, describing the size of your group and where you'd like to sail, and then waiting to receive a set of brochures in the mail. You can still take this route, if you like. However, surfing the Internet has become a popular way to research and book bareboat and crewed yacht charters.

Bareboat company Web sites are like on-line brochures. They're a research tool that has made gathering information much more convenient. You can browse these sites to see different types of boats, photos of interiors and exteriors, layout schematics, a list of equipment and amenities, and sample itineraries. Many sites will allow you to book a charter directly, while others give you the option of calling a toll-free number to speak with an agent for further questions and final booking.

There are two types of Web sites for crewed charter yachts. The first is the type of informational site maintained by the Virgin Islands Charteryacht League (www.vicl.org) and the Charter Yacht Society of the British Virgin Islands (www.bvicrewedyachts.com). These sites let you know what to look for in a crewed charter, from the size of the boat to the amenities that are offered. You can't reserve on these sites, but they link to broker sites.

Brokers are the sales force for the charter yacht industry. Most brokers, whether they are based in the Caribbean, the United States, or Europe, attend annual charter yacht shows in St. Thomas, Tortola, and Antigua. At these shows, brokers visit the boats and meet the crews. This is what gives brokers their depth of knowledge for "match-making," or linking you with a boat that will meet your personality and preferences.

The second form of Web site is for individual boat companies. About 30 percent of the crewed charter yachts based out of the U.S. and British Virgin Islands book directly. This saves the commission an owner has to pay to the broker. But while "going direct" might seem advantageous, the final price tends to be the same whether you book through a broker or an owner. However, brokers put the down payment for the charter into an escrow account. If a boat owner has to cancel a trip for any reason, a broker can usually locate a similar boat so that you end up standing alone at the dock.

The Internet often has real deals on yacht charters. Companies may offer last-minute specials that are available only online. These special rates—usually for specific dates, destinations, and boats—are updated weekly or even daily. You can often score a discount off the cost of the charter or tack on a few free days to your trip.

## What to Consider

Whether bareboat or a crewed yacht, there are a few points to ponder when selecting your boat.

First, consider how many people are in your group and what kind of sleeping accommodations you want. As a general rule, count on one cabin for every two people. If there are three cabins, six people will usually fit comfortably. Don't try to squeeze in eight. Also the number of heads is important. Most people like one head per cabin. Choose a multihull, also called a catamaran, rather than a single-hulled

## British Virgin Islands Anchorages

ATLANTIC

Long Pt.

Guana Island

Great Tobago

Man O'War Bay

JOST VAN DYKE

West End Pt.

**Great Harbour**

Great Harbour

Little Harbour

**White Bay**

Pull & Be Damn Pt.

White Bay

Black Pt.

**Little Harbour**

Little Tobago

Brewers Bay

Trunk Bay

Josiah's Bay

Cane Garden Bay

**Cane Garden Bay**

Carrot Bay

Todman Pk.

Fort Shirley

**Baughers Bay**

Road Town

Great Thatch Island

Long Bay

West End

Mt. Sage

Road Harbour

**Sopers Hole**

West Pt.

Frenchman's Cay

**TORTOLA**

TO ST. THOMAS

Great Harbour

Rock Hole

**Peter Island**

White Bay

Pelican Island

Privateer Bay

**Norman Island**

Pe Bl

Money Bay

Norman Island

**ST. JOHN**

UNITED STATES VIRGIN ISLANDS

West End
Pt.

Bones
Bight

Loblolly
Bay

Table Bay

Flamingo
Pond

Red
Pond

**Anegada
Reef Hotel** ⚓

The
Settlement

**ANEGADA**
*(15 miles north of Necker Is.)*

Lower
Bay

Budrock
Pond

Horse
Shoe
Reef

White
Bay

O C E A N

**Necker
Island** ⚓

Necker
Island

Prickly Pear
Island ⚓

**Eustatia Island**

Mosquito Island

Eustatia Island

**Gorda
Sound** ⚓

**Saba
Rock** ⚓

**Deep Bay** ⚓

Long
Bay

*North
Sound*

Berchers
Bay

Great
Camanoe

Towing
Pt.

North Bay

Cockroach
Island

George
Dog

*Virgin
Gorda
Peak* ▲

*South
Sound*

**North
Bay**

Kitto
Ghut

West
Dog

Great
Dog

Pond
Bay

**VIRGIN
GORDA**

Monkey
Pt.

Scrub Island

**Marina
Cay** ⚓

Handsome
Bay

*Anegada Passage*

Little
Camanoe

**Trellis Bay** ⚓

**Virgin Gorda
Yacht Harbor** ⚓

**East End**

✈ **Beef Island
International Airport**

**Virgin Gorda
Airport** ✈

**Maya
Cove** ⚓

Fat Hogs
Bay

Beef Island

Spanish
Town

Copper Mine
Pt.

Buck
Island

*Sir Francis Drake Channel*

Fallen Jerusalem

**Ginger
Island** ⚓

Broken Jerusalem

Manchioneel
Bay

Quart-a-
Nancy Pt.

Round Rock

Dead
Chest

**Salt
Island** ⚓

**Cooper
Island** ⚓

South
Bay

Ginger Island

Salt
Island

Salt
Island
Bluff

Markoe Pt.

Cooper
Island

*Big Reef
Bay*

**Peter Island**

Peter Island
Bluff

| KEY | |
| --- | --- |
| ⚓ | *Anchorage* |
| 🚢 | *Ferry* |

0 _____ 6 miles

0 _____ 9 km

monohull yacht if you want to be more assured everyone has cabins of equal size and space.

Second, consider the type of boat. If you want to do some good old traditional sailing, where you're heeling over with the seas at your rails, monohulls are a good option. On the other hand, multihulls are more stable, easier to board, and have a big salon for families. They're also ideal if some people in the group tend to get seasick or aren't as gung-ho for the more traditional style of sailing. If you'd like to cover more ground, choose a power boat.

Third, be aware that some crewed charter boats specialize in certain types of charters. Among these are learn-to-sail excursions, honeymoon cruises, scuba-diving adventures, and family-friendly trips. Your broker can steer you to the boats that fit your specific needs.

Fourth and finally, bear in mind standard and optional equipment. Most charter boats have satellite navigation systems and autopilots, as well as regulation safety gear, dinghies with motors, and even stereos and entertainment systems. Generators will keep foods colder than battery-driven refrigeration systems. Air-conditioning really isn't needed during the winter, but can be a nice addition in the summer months. Crewed charter yachts can provide sea-to-shore communication, although phoning home is an extra charge and can be an expensive proposition at $4 or more per minute. For an added charge, you can request water toys like kayaks, boogie boards, and windsurfers. Many bareboat companies monitor the VHF round-to-clock to aid in case of breakdowns.

Now that you've decided on bareboat versus crewed charter and selected your craft, all you need to do is confirm the availability of the date with the company or broker and pay a nonrefundable deposit equal to 50 percent of the charter price.

## Preparing for Your Charter

Buying provisions is one key point you'll need to plan for in advance of a bareboat charter. You have three choices: choose a provisioning option from the charter company, shop from a local grocery via a faxed or e-mailed grocery list in advance of your trip, or buy groceries once you arrive on island and before you get on board the boat.

If you choose the company option, provisioning packages can cost from $25 to $35 per person per day. This may or may not include all three meals. Some companies have packages that include food for only three or four dinners, making it necessary for you to eat out some nights.

Some British Virgin Island grocery stores, like **Bobby's Market Place** (⊠ Wickham's Cay I, Road Town ☎ 284/494–2189 ⊕ www.bobbysmarketplace.com) and **Ample Hamper** (⊠ Inner Harbour Marina, Road Town ☎ 284/494–2494 ⊠ Frenchmans Cay Marina, West End ☎ 284/495–4684 ⊕ www.amplehamper. com) offer the option of provisioning via the Internet. For example, Bobby's Market Place offers three different packages that include all breakfasts and lunches: one with no dinners included, a second with four dinners included, and a third with all seven dinners included. Prices for these packages range from $15 to $23 per person per day. An 18-page list found on the company's Web site lets you to designate the number in your party and preferences for breakfast, lunch, dinner, and snacks. On the Ample Hamper's Web site there are more than 1,200 items divided into 33 categories ranging from prepared foods to vegetarian items. You can treat this just like a shopping list to check off a customized order around menus you've planned. It's a good idea to arrange this type of provisioning at least a week in advance. Many groceries will arrange free delivery to your boat.

If you want to provision before boarding your boat, be sure to arrive at your destination by midday. This will give you time to shop, unpack your groceries, and become familiar with the boat's kitchen while it is still daylight. There are several grocery stores, ranging from large mainland-style supermarkets to upscale gourmet groceries, on St. Thomas and Tortola, the two most common embarkation points. Beware of sticker shock, however. Food is about 30 percent more expensive than on the U.S. mainland. For example, a half-gallon of milk can range from $2.89 to $3.89, a loaf of wholewheat sandwich bread costs $2.29, and a dozen large eggs is $2.29. The U.S. dollar is the legal tender in both the U.S. and British Virgin Islands, and traveler's checks and major credit cards are widely accepted. Remember that most of the larger grocery stores are located inland and require a taxi ride to and from major marinas. Still, if you stick with the basics from big supermarkets, this could be the most economical route.

On a crewed charter the chef does all the cooking, so it's important to let the crew know just what you'd like to eat. In advance of your trip, your broker will send a preference sheet. On this sheet you can list your favorite foods. Are you a meat eater or vegetarian? Have allergies? Special requests for birthdays or anniversaries? Do you want a big breakfast or just a Continental-style meal and coffee? There is an added charge for fine wines and premium liquors.

This sheet is also where you can describe your wish for the trip. Perhaps you'd like lazy days of sleeping late, sunning, and swimming. Or you might prefer active days scooting across the seas with sails billowing and stops for snorkeling and exploring ashore. If there's a special spot you'd like to visit—Charlotte Amalie for shopping, Jost Van Dyke to hear calypsonian Foxy Callwood sing, or the giant boulder filled grottos of The Baths at Virgin Gorda—list it so your captain can plan the itinerary accordingly.

Pack light for any type of charter. Bring soft sided luggage, rather than hard suitcases, since space is limited and storage spots are usually odd shaped. Shorts, T-shirts and swimsuits are all you need for the bulk of your trip. Shoes are seldom required except ashore, but you might want beach shoes for exploring or snorkeling in areas that might be inhabited by sea urchins. If you'd like to dine out in a more formal restaurant, bring more formal clothing. This means a dress or skirt for women and long pants and collared shirts for men. There are a few upscale resort dining rooms that enforce this type of dress code. Most boats provide snorkel equipment, but double check before you go. Bring sunscreen, but a type that will not stain cockpit cushions and decks.

## What You'll See in the USBVI

The U.S. and British Virgin Islands boast over 100 stepping-stone islands and cays within a 50-nautical-mile radius. This means easy line-of-sight navigation and island-hopping in protected waters, and it's rare that you'll spend more than a few hours moving from one anchorage to another.

Tortola, in the British Virgin Islands, is the crewed charter and bareboat mecca of the Caribbean. This fact is plainly apparent from the forest of masts rising out of locales like Soper's Hole, Nanny Cay, and the capital of Road Town. The neighboring U.S. Virgin Islands fleet is based in St. Thomas' historic Charlotte Amalie and at the eastern end of the island in Red Hook. Direct flights from the mainland, luxurious accommodations, and duty-free shopping are drawing cards for departures from the U.S. Virgin Islands, whereas the British Virgins are closer to the prime cruising grounds.

On a typical weeklong charter, you could set sail from Red Hook, St. Thomas, then cross Pillsbury Sound to St. John's northshore anchorages in Honeymoon, Trunk or Francis bays. After clearing customs in West End, Tortola, many yachts hop along a series of smaller islands that run along the south side of the Sir Francis Drake Channel. Norman Island is the rumored site of Robert Lewis Stevenson's Treasure Island. Further east, off Salt Island, is the wreck of the Rhone—considered the most magnificent dive site in the eastern Caribbean. Giant boulders form caves and grottos called The Baths at Virgin Gorda's southern end, while the North Sound is home to several quiet anchorages as well as the Bitter End Yacht Club. A downwind run along Tortola's northshore ends at Jost Van Dyke, where that famous guitar-strumming calypsonian, Foxy Callwood, sings personalized ditties that make for a memorable finale.

If you're not sure whether a charter yacht vacation is right for you, consider this: Would you enjoy a floating hotel room where the scenery outside your window changed according to your desires? A "yes" enticed my husband to try chartering. After a single one-week trip, I had him hooked.

# FURTHER READING

If you have the time before your trip, read James Michener's *Caribbean;* it will enhance your visit. *Don't Stop the Carnival* by Herman Wouk is a classic Caribbean book, though some of its 1950s perspectives seem rather dated.

Once you get to the Virgin Islands, take time to book-shop; there are some prolific Virgin Islands writers and artists publishing on every subject from pirates to architecture. Look for books, art prints, and cards by Mapes de Monde, published by Virgin Islands native son Michael Paiewonsky, who splits his time between Rome and the USVI. Mapes de Monde also publishes *The Three Quarters of the Town of Charlotte Amalie* by local historian Edith Woods. It's richly printed and illustrated with Woods's fine pen-and-ink drawings. Photography buffs will want to look for the book of internationally known St. Croix photographer Fritz Henle. For BVI history buffs, Vernon Pickering's *Concise History of the British Virgin Islands* is a wordy but worthy guide to the events and personalities that shaped the region. Pickering also produces the *Official Tourist Handbook* for the BVI. Pick up a copy of *A Place Like This: Hugh Benjamin's Peter Island,* the charming and eloquent personal account of the Kittitian's past two decades in the British Virgin Islands. The book was written in collaboration with Richard Myers, a New York writer.

For children there's *Up Mountain One Time* by Willie Wilson, and a *St. John Historical Coloring Book.*

For linguists, *What a Pistarckle!* by Lito Valls gives the origins of the many expressions you'll be hearing, and historians will enjoy *St. John Backtime* by Ruth Hull Low and Rafael Valls, and *Eyewitness Accounts of Slavery in the Danish West Indies* by Isidor Paiewonsky. For sailors, Simon Scott has written a *Cruising Guide to the Virgin Islands.*

# SMART TRAVEL TIPS

*There are planners and there are those who, excuse the pun, fly by the seat of their pants. We happily place ourselves among the planners. Our writers and editors try to anticipate all the issues you may face before and during any journey, and then they do their research. This section is the product of their efforts. Use it to get excited about your trip to the U.S. & British Virgin Islands, to inform your travel planning, or to guide you on the road should the seat of your pants start to feel threadbare.*

## ADDRESSES

"Whimsical" might best describe USBVI addresses. Street names change for no apparent reason, and most buildings have no numbers. Streets in the main towns generally have names, though they may not have signs. Once you get out into the country on all islands, street names are rare. Areas are often known by their old plantation or estate names; for example, Estate Emmaus in St. John is found in what's now the heart of Coral Bay. Sometimes the estate names appear on maps, and sometimes they don't. The smaller the island, the less chance there is of a location having a specific street address. Addresses throughout this guide may include cross streets, landmarks, and other directionals. But to find your destination, you might have to ask a local—and be prepared for such directions as, "Go past the gas station, then take a right at the fish market. Stay on that road past the church and take a left after the palm tree."

## AIR TRAVEL

There are nonstop and connecting flights, usually through San Juan, from the United States mainland to both St. Thomas and St. Croix, with connecting ferry service from St. Thomas to St. John. There are no nonstop flights to the BVI from the United States or from Europe; you must connect in San Juan or St. Thomas for the short hop over to Tortola or Virgin Gorda. To reach Anegada, take a flight from Tortola. Several European airlines fly to other Caribbean destinations, such as Antigua or Barbados, where there are connections to the USVI and BVI. Canadians and Europeans must connect to flights in the U.S. or in San Juan. There are nonstop flights from London to Miami.

## CARRIERS

Some airlines have codeshare partnerships with airlines that fly to the Caribbean. The codeshare agreement allows an airline to sell a certain number of seats on a flight operated by its partner. Bear in mind, however, that if the flight is canceled because of weather or for any reason not the fault of the operating airline, you'll be rebooked on the next flight that has available seats specifically designated to the codeshare partner that issued your tickets. This may not be the next flight out.

Some islands in the British Virgin Islands are accessible only by small planes operated by local or regional carriers. International carriers will sometimes book those flights for you as part of your overall travel arrangements, or you can confidently book directly with the local carrier, using a major credit card, either online or by phone.

**U.S. Carriers: American Airlines** 800/433-7300 www.aa.com. **Continental Airlines** 800/523-3273 for U.S. and Mexico reservations, 800/231-0856 for international reservations www.continental.com. **Delta Airlines** 800/221-1212 for U.S. reservations, 800/241-4141 for international reservations www.delta.com. **Spirit Airlines** 800/772-7117 or 586/791-7300 www.spiritair.com. **United Airlines** 800/864-8331 for U.S. reservations, 800/538-2929 for international reservations www.united.com. **USAirways** 800/428-4322 for U.S. and Canada reservations, 800/622-1015 for international reservations www.usairways.com.

**Interisland carriers: Air Sunshine** 800/327-8900, 800/435-8900 in Florida www.airsunshine.com. **American Eagle** 800/433-7300 www.aa.com. **Cape Air** 800/352-0714 www.flycapeair.com. **Caribbean Sun** 866/864-6272 www.flycsa.com. **LIAT** 888/844-5428 www.liatairline.com. **Seaborne** 340/773-6442 www.flyseaborne.com.

## FLYING TIMES

The nonstop flight from New York to St. Thomas or San Juan takes about 4 hours; from Miami to St. Thomas or San Juan it's about three hours. Nonstop flights from London to Miami are about 7 to 8 hours, then it's another three hours to the USBVI. Once you've arrived in the USBVI, hops between the islands take 10 to 20 minutes.

## CHECK-IN & BOARDING

**Double-check your flight times,** especially if you made your reservations far in advance. Airlines change their schedules, and alerts may not reach you. Always **bring a government-issued photo ID to the airport** (even when it's not required, a passport is best), and **arrive when you need to and not before.** Check-in usually at least an hour before domestic flights and two to three hours for international flights. But many airlines have more stringent advance check-in requirements at some busy airports. The TSA estimates the waiting time for security at most major airports and publishes the information on its Web site. Note that if you aren't at the gate at least 10 minutes before your flight is scheduled to take off (sometimes earlier), you won't be allowed to board.

**Don't stand in a line if you don't have to.** Buy an e-ticket, check in at an electronic kiosk, or—even better—check in on your airline's Web site before you leave home. If you don't need to check luggage, you could bypass all but the security lines. These days, most domestic airline tickets are electronic; international tickets may be either electronic or paper.

You usually pay a surcharge (usually at least $25) to get a paper ticket, and its sole advantage is that it may be easier to endorse over to another airline if your flight is cancelled and the airline with which you booked can't accommodate you on another flight. With an e-ticket, the only thing you receive is an e-mailed receipt citing your itinerary and reservation and ticket numbers. Be sure to carry this with you as you'll need it to get past security. If you lose you receipt, though, you can simply print out another copy or ask the airline to do it for you at check-in.

Particularly during busy travel seasons and around holiday periods, if a flight is oversold, the gate agent will usually ask for volunteers and will offer some sort of compensation if you are willing to take a different flight. **Know your rights.** If you are bumped from a flight *involuntarily*, the airline must give you some kind of compensation if an alternate flight can't be found within one hour. If your flight is delayed because of something within the airline's control (so bad weather doesn't count), then the airline has a responsibility to get you to your destination on the same day, even if they have to book you on another airline and in an upgraded class if necessary. Read your airline's Contract of Carriage; it's usually buried somewhere on the airline's Web site.

**Be prepared** to quickly adjust your plans by programming a few numbers into your cell: your airline, an airport hotel or two, your destination hotel, your car service, and/or your travel agent. Bring snacks, water, and sufficient diversions, and you'll be covered if you get stuck in the airport, on the Tarmac, or even in the air during turbulence.

## CUTTING COSTS

It's always good to **comparison shop.** Web sites (aka consolidators) and travel agents can have different arrangements with the airlines and offer different prices for exactly the same flight and day. Certain Web sites have tracking features that will e-mail you immediately when good deals are posted. Other people prefer to stick with one or two frequent-flier programs, racking up free trips and accumulating perks that can make trips easier. On some airlines, perks include a special reservations number, early boarding, access to upgrades, and more roomy economy-class seating.

**Check early and often.** Start looking for cheap fares up to a year in advance, and keep looking until you see something you can live with; you never know when a good deal may pop up. That said, **Jump on the good deals.** Waiting even a few minutes might mean paying more. For most people, saving money is more important than flexibility, so the more affordable nonrefundable tickets work. Just remember that you'll pay dearly (often as much

as $100) if you must change your travel plans. Check on prices for departures at different times of the day and to and from alternate airports, and look for departures on Tuesday, Wednesday, and Thursday, typically the cheapest days to travel. Remember to **weigh your options,** though. A cheaper flight might have a long layover rather than being nonstop, or landing at a secondary airport might substantially increase your ground transportation costs.

Note that many airline Web sites—and most ads—show prices *without* taxes and surcharges. Don't buy until you know the full price. Government taxes add up quickly. Also **watch those ticketing fees.** Surcharges are usually added when you buy your ticket anywhere but on an airline's own Web site. (By the way, that includes on the phone–even if you call the airline directly—and for paper tickets regardless of how you book).

🔁 **Online Consolidators** AirlineConsolidator.com ⊕ www.airlineconsolidator.com; for international tickets. **Best Fares** ⊕ www.bestfares.com; $59.90 annual membership. **Cheap Tickets** ⊕ www.cheaptickets.com. **Expedia** ⊕ www.expedia.com. **Hotwire** ⊕ www.hotwire.com. **lastminute.com** ⊕ www.lastminute.com specializes in last-minute travel; the main site is for the UK, but it has a link to a U.S. site. **Luxury Link** ⊕ www.luxurylink.com has auctions (surprisingly good deals) as well as offers at the high-end side of travel. **Orbitz** ⊕ www.orbitz.com. **Onetravel.com** ⊕ www.onetravel.com. **Priceline.com** ⊕ www.priceline.com. **Travelocity** ⊕ www.travelocity.com.

## ENJOYING THE FLIGHT

**Get the seat you want.** Avoid those on the aisle directly across from the lavatories. Most frequent fliers say those are even worse than the the seats that don't recline (e.g., those in the back row and those in front of a bulkhead). For more legroom, you can request emergency-aisle seats, but only do so if you're capable of moving the 35- to 60-pound airplane exit door—a Federal Aviation Administration requirement of passengers in these seats. Seats behind a bulkhead also offer more legroom, but they don't have under-seat storage. Often, you can pick a seat when you buy your ticket on an airline's Web site. But it's not always a guarantee, particularly if the airline changes the plane after you book your ticket; check back before you leave. SeatGuru.com has more information about specific seat configurations, which vary by aircraft.

Fewer airlines are providing free food for passengers in economy class. **Don't go hungry.** If you're scheduled to fly during meal times, verify if your airline offers anything to eat; even when it does, be prepared to pay. If you have dietary concerns, request special meals. These can be vegetarian, low-cholesterol, or kosher, for example. It's a good idea to pack some healthful snacks and a small (plastic) bottle of water in your carry-on bag.

**Ask the airline about its children's menus, activities, and fares.** On some lines infants and toddlers fly for free if they sit on a parent's lap, and older children fly for half price in their own seats. Also inquire about policies involving car seats; having one may limit where you can sit. While you're at it, ask about seat-belt extenders for carseats. And note that you can't count on a flight attendant to automatically produce an extender; you may have to inquire about it again when you board.

### HOW TO COMPLAIN

If your baggage goes astray or your flight goes awry, complain right away. Most carriers require that you **file a claim immediately.** The Aviation Consumer Protection Division of the Department of Transportation publishes *Fly-Rights,* which discusses airlines and consumer issues and is available online. You can also find articles and information on mytravelrights.com, the Web site of the nonprofit Consumer Travel Rights Center.

▶ Airline Complaints **Office of Aviation Enforcement and Proceedings** (Aviation Consumer Protection Division) ☎ 202/366-2220 ⊕ airconsumer.ost. dot.gov. **Federal Aviation Administration Consumer Hotline** ☎ 866/835-5322 ⊕ www.faa.gov.

### RECONFIRMING

Reconfirming your flights on interisland carriers is not obsolete yet, as it is in major airlines, particularly when you're traveling to the smallest islands, like Anegada. You may be subjected to a carrier's whims: If no other passengers are booked on your flight, you may be asked (or told) to take another flight later in the day, or your plane may make unscheduled stops to pick up more passengers or cargo. It's all part of the excitement—and unpredictability—of travel in the Caribbean. In addition, regional carriers use small aircraft with limited baggage space, and they often impose weight restrictions; travel light, or you could be subject to outrageous surcharges or delays in getting very large or heavy luggage, which may have to follow on another flight.

### AIRPORTS

The major airports are Terrence B. Lettsome International Airport on Beef Island, Tortola, Cyril E. King Airport on St. Thomas, and Henry Rohlsen Airport on St. Croix. There are smaller airports (so small that they don't have phone numbers; call the individual airlines if you need information) on Anegada and Virgin Gorda.

▶ Airline and Airport Links.com ⊕ www. airlineandairportlinks.com has links to many of the world's airlines and airports. **Terrence B. Lettsome International Airport** ☎ 284/495-2525. **Cyril E. King Airport** ☎ 340/774-5100. **Henry Rohlsen Airport** ☎ 340/778-1012.

▶ Airline Security Issues **Transportation Security Agency** ⊕ www.tsa.gov/public has answers for almost every question that might come up.

### BOAT & FERRY TRAVEL

Ferries travel between St. Thomas and St. John. You can also travel by ferry from both St. Thomas and St. John to the British Virgin Islands, and between the British Virgin Islands themselves. For more information, *see* Boat Ferry Travel *in* the Essentials section at the end of each chapter.

### BUSINESS HOURS

Bank hours are generally Monday through Thursday 9 to 3 and Friday 9 to 5; a handful open Saturday (9 to noon). Walk-up windows open at 8:30 on weekdays. Hours may vary slightly from branch to branch and island to island, but they are generally weekdays 7:30 or 8 to 4 or 5:30 and Saturday 7:30 or 8 to noon or 2:30.

Shops, especially those in the heavily touristed areas, are open Monday to Saturday 9 to 5. Those near the cruise ships may also be open on Sunday.

## CAR RENTAL

Request car seats and extras such as GPS when you book, and make sure that a confirmed reservation guarantees you a car. Agencies sometimes overbook, particularly for busy weekends and holiday periods. Rates are sometimes—but not always—better if you book in advance or reserve through a rental agency's Web site. There are other reasons to book ahead, though: for popular destinations, during busy times of the year, or to ensure that you get a certain type of car (vans, SUVs, exotic sports cars).

Rates range from $50 a day/$300 a week for an economy car with air-conditioning, automatic transmission, and unlimited mileage to $80 a day/$400 a week for a four-wheel-drive vehicle. Both the USVI and the BVI have major companies (with airport locations) as well as numerous local companies (near the airports, in hotels, and in the main towns), which are sometimes cheaper. Most provide pick-up service; some ask that you take a taxi to their headquarters.

### CUTTING COSTS

**Really weigh your options.** Find out if a credit card you carry or organization or frequent-renter program to which you belong has a discount program. And check that such discounts really are the best deal. You can often do better with special weekend or weekly rates offered by a rental agency. (And even if you only want to rent for five or six days, ask if you can get the weekly rate; it may very well be cheaper than the daily rate for that period of time.)

Price local car-rental companies as well as the majors. Also investigate wholesalers, which don't own fleets but rent in bulk from those that do and often offer better rates (note you must usually pay for such rentals before leaving home). Consider adding a car rental onto your air/hotel vacation package; the cost will often be cheaper than if you had rented the car separately on your own.

When traveling abroad, **look for guaranteed exchange rates,** which protect you against a falling dollar. With your rate locked in, you won't pay more, even if the price goes up in the local currency. (Note to self: Not the best thing if the dollar is surging rather than plunging.)

**Beware of hidden charges.** Those great rental rates may not be so great when you add in taxes, surcharges, cancellation penalties, taxes, drop-off charges (if you're planning to pick up the car in one city and leave it in another), and surchages (for being under or over a certain age, for additional drivers, or for driving over state or country borders or out of a specific radius from your point of rental).

Note that airport rental offices often add supplementary surcharges that you may avoid by renting from an agency whose office is just off airport property. Don't buy the tank of gas that's in the car when you rent it unless you plan to do a lot of driving. Avoid hefty refueling fees by filling the tank at a station well away from the rental agency (those nearby are often more expensive) just before you turn in the car.

🚗 **Major Agencies Alamo** ☎ 800/522-9696 ⊕ www.alamo.com. **Avis** ☎ 800/331-1084 ⊕ www.avis.com. **Budget** ☎ 800/472-3325 ⊕ www.budget.com. **Hertz** ☎ 800/654-3001 ⊕ www.hertz.com. **National Car Rental** ☎ 800/227-7368 ⊕ www.nationalcar.com.

## INSURANCE

Everyone who rents a car wonders about whether the insurance that the rental companies offer is worth the expense. No one—not even us—has a simple answer. This is particularly true abroad, where laws are different than at home.

If you own a car, your personal auto insurance may cover a rental to some degree, though not all policies protect you abroad; always read your policy's fine print. If you don't have auto insurance, then seriously consider buying the collision- or loss-damage waiver (CDW or LDW) from the car-rental company, which eliminates your liability for damage to the car. Some credit cards offer CDW coverage, but it's usually supplemental to your own insurance and rarely covers SUVs, minivans, luxury models, and the like. If your coverage is secondary, you may still be liable for loss-of-use costs from the car-rental company. But no credit-card insurance is valid unless you use that card for *all* transations, from reserving to paying the final bill. All companies exclude car rental in some countries, so be sure to find out about the destination to which you are traveling.

Some countries require you to purchase CDW coverage or require car-rental companies to include it in quoted rates. Ask your rental company about issues like these in your destination. In most cases, it's cheaper to add a supplemental CDW plan to your comprehensive travel insurance policy ( ⇨ Insurance *below*) than to purchase it from a rental company. That said, you don't want to pay for a supplement if you're required to buy insurance from the rental company.

Note that you can decline the insurance from the rental company and purchase it through a third-party provider such as Travel Guard (www.travelguard.com)—$9 per day for $35,000 of coverage. That's sometimes just under half the price of the CDW offered by some car-rental companies. Also, Diner's Club offers primary CDW coverage on all rentals reserved and paid for with the card. This means that Diner's Club's company—not your own car insurance—pays in case of an accident. It *doesn't* mean your car-insurance company won't raise your rates once it discovers you had an accident.

## CAR TRAVEL IN THE US&BVI

A car gives you mobility. You'll be able to spend an hour browsing at that cozy out-of-the-way shop instead of the 10 minutes allotted by your tour guide. You can beach-hop without searching for a ride, and you can sample that restaurant you've heard so much about that's a half-hour (and an expensive taxi ride) away. On parts of some of the islands, you may need to rent a four-wheel-drive vehicle to really get out and about.

## EMERGENCY SERVICES

To reach police, fire, or ambulance, dial 911 in the USVI and 999 in the BVI. There are no emergency-service companies such as AAA in the USBVI. Before driving off into the countryside, check your rental car for tire-changing equipment, including an inflated spare.

## GASOLINE

Except in St. Croix, where it may be cheaper than in many parts of the U.S., gas is expensive throughout the Virgin Islands. Prices rise to well over $3 a gallon on most islands. The USVI stations sell gas by the gallon; in the BVI, you'll buy it by the liter or the gallon, depending on the station. Most stations take major credit cards. Gas stations are found at key points on St. Croix and St. Thomas; on Tortola, Virgin Gorda, and St. John, and other islands, be sure to fill up before you leave the main towns. Most stations are open from early morning until early evening. On smaller islands, they may be closed on Sunday.

## ROAD CONDITIONS

Island roads, particularly in mountainous regions that experience heavy tropical rains, are often potholed and bumpy—as well as narrow, winding, and hilly. Drive with extreme caution, especially if you venture out at night. You won't see guardrails on every hill and curve, although the drops can be frighteningly steep. And pedestrians (including children and the elderly) and livestock often share the roadway with vehicles.

## RULES OF THE ROAD

Driving in the Virgin Islands can be tricky. Traffic moves on the left in *both* the USVI and BVI. (The BVI obviously followed the British tradition; no one knows why the USVI followed suit.) Except for the odd right-hand drive car in the BVI, cars on both the BVI and USVI have left-hand drive, the same as cars on the U.S. mainland. This means the driver sits on the side of the car next to the road's edge, a position that makes some people nervous. Note that you may turn left from the left-hand lane when the light is red.

Buckle up before you turn the key. Police in the USVI are notorious for giving $25 tickets to unbelted drivers and front-seat passengers. The police are a bit lax about drunk driver enforcement, but why risk it? Take a taxi or appoint a designated driver when you're out on the town.

Drivers throughout the island often stop in the middle of the road to chat with people or pick up passengers. Watch out for such situations. Traffic moves at about 10 mph in town; on major highways—in St. Croix, for example—you can fly along at 50 mph. On other roads, the speed limit may be less. Traffic jams in major towns such as Christiansted on St. Croix, Charlotte Amalie on St. Thomas, and Road Town on Tortola aren't unheard of. Try to avoid the 7:30 AM–9 AM and 4 PM–6 PM rush hours.

Main roads in the USVI carry route numbers, but locals may not know them, nor are they always marked. (Be prepared for such directions as "turn left at the big tree.") Few USVI secondary roads have signs; throughout the BVI, roads aren't very well marked either. Parking laws are enforced in all major towns. Your best bet is to park in public lots found on all the islands. There are no meters, but there are still fees on some islands, with some lots charging a mere 50¢ an hour. And never, ever park in a space for disabled drivers or block its access in the USVI unless you have a handicap sticker for your windshield. Police give out $1,000 tickets for this offense.

## CRUISE TRAVEL

Cruising is a relaxing and convenient way to tour this beautiful part of the world. You get all of the amenities of a resort hotel and enough activities to guarantee fun, even on the occasional rainy day. All your important decisions are made long before you board. Your itinerary is set, and you know the basic cost of your vacation beforehand. Ships usually call at several ports on a single voyage but are at each port for only one day. Thus, while you don't get much of a feel for any specific island, you get a taste of what several islands are like and can then choose to vacation on your favorite one for a longer

time on a future trip. While cruises are never restricted solely to the USBVI, St. Thomas is one of the Caribbean's most popular cruise destinations, and ships also call at St. John, Tortola, and Virgin Gorda.

If you are planning a Caribbean cruise, consider Fodor's *The Complete Guide to Caribbean Cruises* (available in bookstores everywhere).

🚢 Cruise Lines **Carnival Cruise Line** ☎ 305/599-2600 or 800/227-6482 ⊕ www.carnival.com. **Celebrity Cruises** ☎ 305/539-6000 or 800/647-2251 ⊕ www.celebrity.com. **Clipper Cruise Line** ☎ 314/655-6700 or 800/325-0010 ⊕ www.clippercruise.com. **Costa Cruises** ☎ 954/266-5600 or 800/462-6782 ⊕ www.costacruise.com. **Crystal Cruises** ☎ 800/446-6625 or 310/785-9300 ⊕ www.crystalcruises.com. **Cunard Line** ☎ 661/753-1000 or 800/728-6273 ⊕ www.cunard.com. **Disney Cruise Line** ☎ 407/566-3500 or 800/325-2500 ⊕ www.disneycruise.com. **Holland America Line** ☎ 206/281-3535 or 877/932-4259 ⊕ www.hollandamerica.com. **MSC Cruises** ☎ 954/662-6262 or 800/666-9333 ⊕ www.msccruises.com. **Norwegian Cruise Line** ☎ 800/327-7030 ⊕ www.ncl.com. **Oceania Cruises** ☎ 305/514-2300 or 800/531-5658 ⊕ www.oceaniacruises.com. **Princess Cruises** ☎ 661/753-0000 or 800/774-6237 ⊕ www.princess.com. **Regent Seven Seas Cruises** ☎ 954/776-6123 or 800/477-7500 ⊕ www.rssc.com. **Royal Caribbean International** ☎ 305/539-6000 or 800/327-6700 ⊕ www.royalcaribbean.com. **Seabourn Cruise Line** ☎ 305/463-3000 or 800/929-9391 ⊕ www.seabourn.com. **SeaDream Yacht Club** ☎ 305/856-5622 or 800/707-4911 ⊕ www.seadreamyachtclub.com. **Silversea Cruises** ☎ 954/522-4477 or 800/722-9955 ⊕ www.silversea.com. **Star Clippers** ☎ 305/442-0550 or 800/442-0551 ⊕ www.starclippers.com. **Windjammer Barefoot Cruises** ☎ 305/672-6453 or 800/327-2601 ⊕ www.windjammer.com. **Windstar Cruises** ☎ 206/281-3535 or 800/258-7245 ⊕ www.windstarcruises.com.

## CUSTOMS & DUTIES

You're always allowed to bring goods of a certain value back home without having to pay any duty or import tax. There's also a limit on the amount of tobacco and liquor you can bring back duty-free, and some countries have separate limits for perfumes; for exact figures, check with your customs department. The values of so-called "duty-free" goods are included in these amounts. When you shop abroad, save all your receipts as customs inspectors may ask to see them as well as the items you purchased. If the total value of your goods is more than the duty-free limit, then you'll have to pay a tax (most often a flat percentage) on the value of everything beyond that limit.

🔚 U.S. Information **U.S. Customs and Border Protection** ⊕ www.cbp.gov.

## EATING OUT

Everything from fast food to fine cuisine in elegant settings are available in the USBVI, and prices run about the same as what you'd pay in New York or any other major city. Most chefs at top-of-the-line restaurants and even some small spots went to a major culinary school, which means innovative and interesting cuisine. Don't be afraid to sample local dishes at the roadside restaurants located on all the islands. Throughout the book, the restaurants we list are the cream of the crop in each price category. For information on food-related health issues see Health *below.*

### MEALS & MEALTIMES

Your hotel is your best bet for breakfast in the USBVI, where you'll easily find American-style food. Local restaurants serve fish and other heavy dishes for breakfast. Other meals are similar to those in the U.S.

For fast food, island-style, try a pate from a roadside stand. It's a fried pastry filled with conch, salted fish, or hamburger, which islanders call meat. Maubi, made from tree bark, is a unique drink popular in the USBVI.

Most restaurants open for lunch from around 11:30 AM to about 3 PM; they serve dinner from around 6:30 PM to about 10 PM. Unless otherwise noted, the restaurants listed in this guide are open daily for lunch and dinner.

### PAYING

Major restaurants take at least two major credit cards, most often MasterCard and Visa, but that off-the-beaten path spot you've heard so much about may accept only cash. For guidelines on tipping see Tipping *below.*

## RESERVATIONS & DRESS

Regardless of where you are, it's a good idea to make a reservation if you can. In many places in the Caribbean, it's expected, particularly at nicer restaurants. We only mention specifically when reservations are essential (there's no other way you'll ever get a table) or when they are not accepted. For popular restaurants, book as far ahead as you can (often 30 days), and reconfirm as soon as you arrive. (Large parties should always call ahead to check the reservations policy.) We mention dress only when men are required to wear a jacket or a jacket and tie. Beach attire is universally frowned upon in restaurants throughout the Caribbean.

## WINE, BEER & SPIRITS

Top-notch restaurants offer good selections of fine wines. Beer and spirits are available on all islands at all kinds of restaurants and roadside stands, but you may not find the brand you prefer.

Was the service stellar or not up to snuff? Did the food give you shivers of delight or leave you cold? Did the prices and portions make you happy or sad? Rate restaurants and write your own reviews in Travel Ratings or start a discussion about your favorite places in Travel Talk on www.fodors.com. Your comments might even appear in our books. Yes, you, too, can be a correspondent!

## ELECTRICITY

The USBVI use the same current as the U.S. mainland—110 volts. European appliances will require adaptors. Since power fluctuations occasionally occur, bring a heavy-duty surge protector (available at hardware stores) if you plan to use your computer.

## ETIQUETTE & BEHAVIOR

Cover up when you're not at the beach; Virgin Islanders are modest folks. Say good morning, good afternoon, or good night when you enter a store or business; that's the best way to ensure that you start your conversation off right. It's considered rude if you don't begin your interactions with some kind of pleasantry. In the US & BVI, too much assertiveness is considered rude in any interaction, even when you are making a valid complaint. When passing people on hiking trails or when walking on narrow country roads, be sure to greet fellow hikers or walkers. Casual clothes are generally fine, but men should wear a tie and jacket and women summer business attire when dealing with government offices, insurance companies, and the like. Only wear shorts to the most casual of marine-related businesses.

## GAY & LESBIAN TRAVELERS

Gay and lesbian travelers are welcome in the USBVI, but some unfriendly attitudes still exist. Ask at your hotel for advice on places to go. St. Thomas has a thriving gay community, and you'll be made very welcome. St. Croix has several gay-friendly resorts perfect for couples as well as singles.

🚩 Gay- & Lesbian-Friendly Travel Agencies **Different Roads Travel** ⊠ 8383 Wilshire Blvd., Suite 520, Beverly Hills, CA 90211 ☎ 323/651-5557 or 800/429-8747 (Ext. 14 for both) 🖷 323/651-5454 ⤴ lgernert@tzell.com. **Kennedy Travel** ⊠ 130 W. 42nd St., Suite 401, New York, NY 10036 ☎ 212/840-8659, 800/237-7433 🖷 212/730-2269 ⊕ www.kennedytravel.com. **Now, Voyager** ⊠ 4406 18th St., San Francisco, CA 94114 ☎ 415/626-1169 or 800/255-6951 🖷 415/626-8626 ⊕ www.nowvoyager.com. **Skylink Travel and Tour/Flying Dutchmen Travel** ⊠ 1455 N. Dutton Ave., Suite A, Santa Rosa, CA 95401 ☎ 707/546-9888 or 800/225-5759 🖷 707/636-0951; serving lesbian travelers.

## HEALTH

The most common types of illnesses are caused by contaminated food and water. Especially in developing countries, drink only bottled, boiled, or purified water and drinks; don't drink from public fountains or use ice. You should even consider using bottled water to brush your teeth. Make sure food has been thoroughly cooked and is served to you fresh and hot; avoid vegetables and fruits that you haven't washed (in bottled or purified water) or peeled yourself. If you have problems, mild cases of traveler's diarrhea may respond to Imodium (known generically as loperamide) or Pepto-Bismol. Be sure to drink plenty of fluids; if you can't keep fluids down, seek medical help immediately.

Infectious diseases can be airborne or passed via mosquitoes and ticks and through direct or indirect physical contact with animals or people. Some, including Norwalk-like viruses that affect your digestive tract, can be passed along through contaminated food. If you are traveling in an area where malaria is prevalent, use a repellant containing DEET and take malaria-prevention medication before, during, and after your trip as directed by your physician. Condoms can help prevent most sexually transmitted diseases, but aren't absolute and the quality of them varies from country to country. Speak with your physition and/or check the CDC or World Health Organization Web sites for health alerts, particularly if you're pregnant, traveling with children, or have a chronic illness.

Water in the USBVI is generally safe to drink. Mosquitoes can be a problem here, particularly after a spate of showers. Off! insect repellent is readily available, but you may want to bring something stronger. Also a nuisance are the little pests from the sand-flea family known as no-see-ums. You don't realize you're being had for dinner until it's too late, and these bites stay, and itch, and itch, and itch. No-see-ums start getting hungry around 3 PM and are out in force by sunset. They're always more numerous in shady and wooded areas (such as the campgrounds on St. John). Take a towel along for sitting on the beach, and keep reapplying insect repellent.

Beware of the manchineel tree, which grows near the beach and has green apple-like fruit that is poisonous and bark and leaves that burn the skin.

Even if you've never been sunburned in your life, believe the warnings and use sunscreen in the USBVI. If you're dark-skinned, start with at least an SPF of 15 and keep it on. If you're fair-skinned, use a sunscreen with a higher SPF and stay out of the sun during the midday. Rays are most intense between 11 and 2, so move under a sea grape tree (although you can still burn here) or, better yet, take a shady lunch break. You can also burn in this part of the world when it's cloudy, so putting sunscreen on every day no matter what the weather is the best strategy.

## DIVERS' ALERT
**Do not fly within 24 hours of scuba diving.**
🔒 Health Warnings **National Centers for Disease Control & Prevention** (CDC) ☎ 877/394-8747 international travelers' health line ⊕ www.cdc.gov/travel. **World Health Organization** (WHO) ⊕ www.who.int.

## HOLIDAYS
In addition to the U.S. federal holidays, locals in the USVI celebrate Three Kings Day (Jan. 6); Transfer Day (commemorates Denmark's 1917 sale of the territory to the United States, Mar. 31); Holy Thursday and Good Friday; Emancipation Day (when slavery was abolished in the Danish West Indies in 1848, July 3); Columbus Day and USVI–Puerto Rico Friendship Day (always on Columbus Day weekend); and Liberty Day (honoring David Hamilton Jackson, who secured freedom of the press and assembly from King Christian X of Denmark, Nov. 1).

Although the government closes down for 23 days a year, most of these holidays have no effect on shopping hours. Unless there's a cruise-ship arrival, expect most stores to close for Christmas and a few other holidays in the slower summer months.

The following public holidays are celebrated in the BVI: New Year's Day, Commonwealth Day (Mar. 14), Good Friday (Fri. before Easter), Easter Sunday (usually Mar. or Apr.), Easter Monday (day after Easter), Whit Monday (1st Mon. in May), Sovereign's Birthday (June 16), Territory Day (July 1), BVI August Festival Days (usually 1st 2 wks in Aug.), St. Ursula's Day (Oct. 21), Christmas, and Boxing Day (day after Christmas).

## INSURANCE
What kind of coverage do you honestly need? Do you even need trip insurance at all? Take a deep breath and read on.

We believe that comprehensive trip insurance is especially valuable if you're booking a very expensive or complicated trip (particularly to an isolated region) or if you're booking far in advance. Who knows what could happen six months down the road? But whether or not you get insurance has more to do with how comfortable you are assuming all that risk yourself.

Comprehensive travel policies typically cover trip-cancellation and interruption, letting you cancel or cut your trip short because of a personal emergency, illness, or, in some cases, acts of terrorism in your destination. Such policies also cover evacuation and medical care. Some also cover you for trip delays because of bad weather or mechanical problems as well as for lost or delayed baggage. Another type of coverage to look for is financial default—that is, when your trip is disrupted because a tour operator, airline, or cruise line goes out of business. Generally you must buy this when you book your trip or shortly thereafter, and it's only available to you if your operator isn't on a list of excluded companies.

If you're going abroad, consider buying medical-only coverage at the very least. Neither Medicare nor some private insurers cover medical expenses anywhere outside of the United States besides Mexico and Canada (including time aboard a cruise ship, even if it leaves from a U.S. port). Medical-only policies typically reimburse you for medical care (excluding that related to pre-existing conditions) and hospitalization abroad and provide for evacuation. You still have to pay the bills and await reimbursement from the insurer, though.

Expect comprehensive travel insurance policies to cost about 4% to 7% of the total price of your trip (it's more like 12% if you're over age 70). A medical-only policy may or may not be cheaper than a comprehensive policy. Always read the fine print of your policy to make sure that you are covered for the risks that are of the most concern to you. Compare several policies to make sure you're getting the best price and range of coverage available.

Just as an aside: You know you can save a bundle on trips to warm-weather destinations by traveling in rainy season. But there's also a chance that a severe storm will disrupt your plans. The solution? Look for hotels and resorts that offer storm/hurricane guarantees. Although they rarely allow refunds, most guarantees do let you rebook later if a storm strikes.

**⊡ Insurance Comparison Sites Insure My Trip. com** ⊕ www.insuremytrip.com. **Square Mouth.com** ⊕ www.quotetravelinsurance.com.

**⊡ Comprehensive Travel Insurers Access America** ☎ 866/807-3982 ⊕ www.accessamerica.com. **CSA Travel Protection** ☎ 800/729-6021 ⊕ www. csatravelprotection.com. **HTH Worldwide** ☎ 610/ 254-8700 or 888/243-2358 ⊕ www.hthworldwide. com. **Travelex Insurance** ☎ 888/457-4602 ⊕ www.travelex-insurance.com. **Travel Guard International** ☎ 715/345-0505 or 800/826-4919 ⊕ www.travelguard.com. **Travel Insured International** ☎ 800/243-3174 ⊕ www.travelinsured.com.

**⊡ Medical-Only Insurers Wallach & Company** ☎ 800/237-6615 or 504/687-3166 ⊕ www.wallach. com. **International Medical Group** ☎ 800/628-4664 ⊕ www.imglobal.com. **International SOS** ☎ 215/942-8000 or 713/521-7611 ⊕ www. internationalsos.com.

## LODGING

Decide whether you want to pay the extra price for a room overlooking the ocean or pool. At less expensive properties, location may mean a difference in price of only $10 to $20 per room; at luxury resorts, however, it could amount to as much as $100 per room. Also find out how close the property is to a beach. At some hotels you can walk barefoot from your room onto the sand; others are across a road or a 10-minute drive away.

Nighttime entertainment is often alfresco in the USBVI, so if you go to sleep early or are a light sleeper, ask for a room away from the dance floor. Air-conditioning isn't a necessity on all islands, many of which are cooled by trade winds, but it can be a plus if you enjoy an afternoon snooze or are bothered by humidity. Breezes are best on upper floors, particularly corner rooms. If you like to sleep without air-conditioning, make sure that windows can be opened, have screens, and won't cause security problems if opened. If you're staying away from the water, make sure the room has a ceiling fan and that it works.

In even the most luxurious resorts, there are times when things simply *don't* work; it's a fact of Caribbean life. No matter how diligent the upkeep, humidity and salt air take their toll, and cracked tiles and chipped paint are common everywhere.

The lodgings we list are the cream of the crop in each price category. We always list the facilities that are available, but we don't specify whether they cost extra; when pricing accommodations, always ask what's included and what costs extra. Properties are assigned price categories based on the range between their least and most expensive standard double rooms at high season (excluding holidays).

Did the resort look as good in real life as it did in the photos? Did you sleep like a baby, or were the walls paper thin? Did you get your money's worth? Rate hotels and write your own reviews in Travel Ratings or start a discussion about your favorite places in Travel Talk on www. fodors.com. Your comments might even appear in our books. Yes, you, too, can be a correspondent!

Most hotels and other lodgings require you to give your credit card details before they will confirm your reservation. If you don't feel comfortable e-mailing this information, ask if you can fax it (some places even prefer faxes). However you book, get confirmation in writing and have a copy of it handy when you check in.

Be sure you understand the hotel's cancellation policy. Some places allow you to cancel without any kind of penalty—even if you prepaid to secure a discounted rate—if you cancel at least 24 hours in advance. Others require you to cancel a week in advance or penalize you for the cost of one night. Small inns and B&Bs are most likely to require you to cancel far in advance. Most hotels allow children under a certain age to stay in their parents' room at no extra charge, but others charge for them as extra adults; find out the cutoff age for discounts.

Assume that hotels operate on the European Plan (**EP**, no meals) unless we specify that they use the Breakfast Plan (**BP**, with full breakfast), Continental Plan (**CP**, Continental breakfast), Full American Plan (**FAP**, all meals), Modified American Plan (**MAP**, breakfast and dinner) or are **all-inclusive** (all meals and most activities).

### APARTMENT & VILLA RENTALS
Renting a villa lets you settle in. You'll have room to spread out, you can cook any or all of your meals, and you will have all the privacy you desire. Since most villas are located in residential neighborhoods, your neighbors probably won't appreciate late-night parties. And you may be disturbed by your neighbor's weekend yard maintenance. That said, there's no better way to experience life in the USBVI.

Many villas are set up specifically for the rental market with bedrooms at opposite ends of the house. This makes them perfect for two couples who want to share an accommodation but still prefer some privacy. Others with more bedrooms are sized right for families. Ask about the villa layout to make sure young children won't have to sleep too far away from their parents. Villas with separate bedroom buildings, called pods, are probably not a good idea unless your children are in their teens.

You can book your villa through the numerous agencies that show up on the Internet, but they are usually not based on the island you want to visit. Booking through an island-based manager means that you can talk to a person who knows the villa and can let you know whether it meets your specifications. You villa manager can arrange for a maid, a chef, and other staffers to take care myriad other details that make your vacation go smoothly. They're only a phone call away when something goes wrong or you have a question.

🏠 **At Home Abroad** ☎ 212/421-9165 ⊕ www.athomeabroadinc.com. **Barclay International Group** ☎ 516/364-0064 or 800/845-6636 ⊕ www.barclayweb.com. **Vacation Home Rentals Worldwide** ☎ 201/767-9393 or 800/633-3284 ⊕ www.vhrww.com. **Villanet** ☎ 206/417-3444 or 800/964-1891 ⊕ www.rentavilla.com. **Villas & Apartments Abroad** ☎ 212/213-6435 ⊕ www.vaanyc.com. **Villas of Distinction** ☎ 707/778-1800 or 800/289-0900 ⊕ www.villasofdistinction.com. **Villas International** ☎ 415/499-9490 or 800/221-2260 ⊕ www.villasintl.com. **Wimco** ☎ 800/449-1553 ⊕ www.wimco.com.

### CAMPING
Camping in the USBVI is limited to established campgrounds. Except for the National Park Service's Cinnamon Bay Campground on St. John, all are privately operated. Camping is a big draw on St. John, so be sure to make reservations as early as possible. Most campgrounds do not have hot showers, game rooms, or swimming pools; instead, your entertainment comes on the beach and along hiking trails.

🏕 **Campgrounds Brewers Bay Campground** ✉ Tortola ☎ 284/494-3463. **Cinnamon Bay Campground** ✉ St. John ☎ 340/776-6330 or 800/539-9998 ⊕ www.cinnamonbay.com. **Maho Bay Camps** ✉ St. John ☎ 340/776-6240 or 800/392-9004 ⊕ www.maho.org. **Mount Victory Camp** ✉ St. Croix ☎ 340/772-1651 or 866/772-1651 ⊕ www.mtvictorycamp.com. **White Bay Campground** ✉ Jost Van Dyke ☎ 284/495-9358 ⊕ www.caribbeancruisingclub.com/ivan.

### HOME EXCHANGES
With a direct home exchange, you stay in someone else's home while they stay in yours. Some outfits also deal with vacation homes, so you're not actually staying in someone's full-time residence, just their vacant weekend place.

🏠 **Exchange Clubs HomeLink International** ☎ 813/975-9825 or 800/638-3841 ⊕ www.homelink.org; $80 yearly for Web-only membership; $125 with Web access and two directories. **Home Exchange.com** ☎ 800/877-8723 ⊕ www.homeexchange.com charges; $49.95 yearly for a 1-year online listing; this is a Web-based company with no catalog. **Intervac U.S.** ☎ 800/756-4663 ⊕ www.intervacus.com; $128.88 yearly for a listing, online access, and a catalog; $78.88 without catalog.

### HOTELS
**Weigh all your options (we can't say this enough).** Join "frequent guest" programs. You may get preferential treatment in room choice and/or upgrades in your favorite chains. Check general travel sites and hotel Web sites as not all chains are represented on all travel sites. Always research or inquire about special packages and corporate rates. If you prefer to book by phone, note you can sometimes get a better price if you call the hotel's local toll-free

number (if one is available) rather than the central reservations number.

If your destination's high season is December through April and you're trying to book, say, in late April, you might save considerably by changing your dates by a week or two. Note, though, that many properties charge peak-season rates for your entire stay even if your travel dates straddle peak and nonpeak seasons. High-end chains catering to businesspeople are often busy only on weekdays and often drop rates dramatically on weekends to fill up rooms.**Ask when rates go down.**

**Watch out for hidden costs,** including resort fees, energy surcharges, and "convenience" fees for such things as unlimited local phone service you won't use and a free newspaper—possibly written in a language you can't read. Always verify whether local hotel taxes are or are not included in the rates you are quoted, so that you'll know the real price of your stay. In some places, taxes can add 20% or more to your bill. If you're traveling overseas **look for price guarantees,** which protect you against a falling dollar. With your rate locked in, you won't pay more, even if the price goes up in the local currency.

All hotels listed have private bath unless otherwise noted.

🔢 Discount Hotel Rooms **Accommodations Express** ☎ 800/444-7666 or 800/277-1064. **Hotels.com** ☎ 800/219-4606 or 800/364-0291 ⊕ www.hotels.com. **Quikbook** ☎ 800/789-9887 ⊕ www.quikbook.com. **Turbotrip.com** ☎ 800/473-7829 ⊕ w3.turbotrip.com.

## MAIL & SHIPPING
Airmail between the USBVI and cities in the United States or Canada takes 7 to 14 days; surface mail can take 4 to 6 weeks. Airmail to the United Kingdom takes 2 to 3 weeks; to Australia and New Zealand, 3 to 4 weeks. For island-specific information on post office locations, postal rates, and opening hours, *see* Mail & Shipping *in* the Essentials sections of individual island chapters.

### SHIPPING PACKAGES
Courier services (such as Airborne, DHL, Federal Express, UPS, and others) operate in the USBVI, although not every company serves each island. "Overnight" service is more likely to take two or more days, because of the limited number of flights on which packages can be shipped. Service to St. John and the smaller of the British Virgin Islands can take even longer.

## MONEY MATTERS
The U.S. dollar is the currency on both the USVI and BVI. Prices throughout this guide are given for adults. Substantially reduced fees are almost always available for children and students. For information on taxes, *see* Taxes.

### ATMS
You'll find ATMs at most banks in the USBVI. The ATMs at FirstBank and Scotia Banks, the only two in St. John, sometimes run out of cash on long holiday weekends. Your own bank will probably charge a fee for using ATMs abroad; the foreign bank you use may also charge a fee. Nevertheless, you'll usually get a better rate of exchange via an ATM than you will at a currency-exchange office or even when changing money in a bank. And extracting funds as you need them is a safer option than carrying around a large amount of cash. Note that PIN numbers with more than four digits are not recognized at ATMs in many countries.

### CREDIT CARDS
Major credit cards are widely accepted at hotels, restaurants, shops, car-rental agencies, other service providers, and ATM machines throughout the Caribbean. The only places that might not accept them are open-air markets or tiny shops in out-of-the way villages. Villa renters should be forewarned that some managers may not accept credit cards.

Throughout this guide, the following abbreviations are used: **AE,** American Express; **D,** Discover; **DC,** Diners Club; **MC,** MasterCard; and **V,** Visa.

It's a good idea to inform your credit card company before you travel, especially if you're going abroad and don't travel internationally very often. Otherwise, the credit-card company might put a hold on your card owing to unusual activity—not a good thing halfway through your trip. Record all your credit card numbers—as well as the phone numbers to call in the if your cards are lost or stolen—in a safe place so you're prepared should something go wrong. Both Mastercard and Visa have general numbers you can call (collect if you're abroad) if your card is lost, but you're better off calling the number of your issuing bank since Mastercard and Visa usually just transfer you to your bank; your bank's number is usually printed on your card.

**Reporting Lost Cards American Express** 800/992-3404 in the U.S. or 336/393-1111 collect from abroad ⊕ www.americanexpress.com. **Diners Club** 800/234-6377 in the U.S. or 303/799-1504 collect from abroad ⊕ www.dinersclub.com. **Discover** 800/347-2683 in the U.S. or 801/902-3100 collect from abroad ⊕ www.discovercard.com. **MasterCard** 800/622-7747 in the U.S. or 636/722-7111 collect from abroad ⊕ www.mastercard.com. **Visa** 800/847-2911 in the U.S. or 410/581-9994 collect from abroad ⊕ www.visa.com.

## TRAVELER'S CHECKS

Some consider this the currency of the cave man, and it's true that fewer establishments accept traveler's checks these days. Nevertheless, they're a cheap and secure way to carry extra money, particularly on trips to urban areas. Both Citibank (under the Visa brand) and American Express issue traveler's checks in the United States, but Amex is better known and more widely accepted; you can also avoid hefty surcharges by cashing Amex checks at at Amex offices. Whatever you do, keep track of all the serial numbers in case the checks are lost or stolen.

American Express now offers a stored-value card called a Travelers Cheque Card, which you can use wherever American Express credit cards are accepted, including ATMs. The card can carry a minimum of $300 and a maximum of $2,700, and it's a very safe way to carry your funds. Although you can get replacement funds in 24 hours if your card is lost or stolen, it doesn't really strike us as a very good deal. In addition to a high initial cost ($14.95 to set up the card, plus $5 each time you "reload"), you still have to pay a 2% fee

for each purchase in a foreign currency (similar to that of any credit card). Further, each time you use the card in an ATM you pay a transaction fee of $2.50 on top of the 2% transaction fee for the conversion—add it all up and it can be considerably more than you would pay for simply using your own ATM card. Regular traveler's checks are just as secure and cost less.

**American Express** 888/412-6945 in the U.S., 801/945-9450 collect outside of the U.S. to add value or speak to customer service ⊕ www.americanexpress.com.

## PACKING

Why do some people travel with a convoy of suitcases the size of large-screen TVs and yet never have a thing to wear? How do others pack a toaster-oven-size duffle with a week's worth of outfits *and* supplies for every possible contingency? We realize that packing is a matter of style—a very personal thing—but there's a lot to be said for traveling light. The tips in this section will help you win the battle of the bulging bag.

**Make a list.** In a recent Fodor's survey, 29% of respondents said they make lists (and often pack) at least a week before a trip. Lists can be used at least twice—once to pack and once to repack at the end of your trip. You'll also have a record of the contents of your suitcase, just in case it disappears in transit.

**Think it through.** What's the weather like? Is this a business trip or a cruise or resort vacation? Going abroad? In some places and/or sights, traditions of dress may be more or less conservative than you're used to. As your itinerary comes together, jot activities down and note possible outfits next to each (don't forget those shoes and accessories).

**Edit your wardrobe.** Plan to wear everything twice (better yet, thrice) and to do laundry along the way. Stick to one basic look—urban chic, sporty casual, etc. Build around one or two neutrals and an accent (e.g., black, white, and olive green). Women can freshen looks by changing scarves or jewelry. For a week's trip, you can look smashing with three bottoms, four or five tops, a sweater, and a jacket you can wear alone or over the sweater.

**Be practical.** Put comfortable shoes at the top of your list. (Did we need to tell you this?) Pack items that are lightweight, wrinkle resistant, compact, and washable. (Or this?) Try a simple wrinkling test: Intentionally fold a piece of fabric between your fingers for a couple minutes. If it refuses to crease, it will probably come out of your suitcase looking fresh. That said if you stack and then roll your clothes when packing, they'll wrinkle less

**Check weight and size limitations.** In the United States you may be charged extra for checked bags weighing more than 50 pounds. Abroad some airlines don't allow you to check bags weighing more than 60 to 70 pounds, or they charge outrageous fees for every pound your luggage is over. Carry-on size limitations can be stringent, too.

**Be prepared to lug it yourself.** If there's one thing that can turn a pack rat into a minimalist, it's a vacation spent lugging heavy bags over long distances. Unless you're on a guided tour or a cruise, select luggage that you can readily carry. Porters, like good butlers, are hard to find these days.

**Lock it up.** Several companies sell locks (about $10) approved by the Transportation Safety Administration that can be unlocked by all U.S. security personnel should they decide to search your bags. Alternatively, you can use simple plastic cable ties, which are sold at hardware stores in bundles.

**Tag it.** Always put tags on your luggage with some kind of contact information; use your business address if you don't want people to know your home address. Put the same information (and a copy of your itinerary) inside your luggage, too.

**Don't check valuables.** On U.S. flights, airlines are only liable for about $2,800 per person for bags. On international flights, the liability limit is around $635 per bag. But just try collecting from the airline for items like computers, cameras, and jewelry. It isn't going to happen; they aren't

covered. And though comprehensive travel policies may cover luggage, the liability limit is often a pittance. Your homeowners' policy may cover you sufficiently when you travel—or not. You're really better off stashing baubles and gizmos in your carryon—right near those prescription meds.

**Report problems immediately.** If your bags—or things in them—are damaged or go astray, file a written claim with your airline *before you leave the airport*. If the airline is at fault, it may give you money for essentials until your luggage arrives. Most lost bags are found within 48 hours, so alert the airline to your whereabouts for two or three days. If your bag was opened for security reasons in the United States and something is missing, file a claim with the TSA.

**WHAT YOU'LL NEED IN THE USBVI**

Unless you just have to have a certain cut of meat, think breakfast isn't breakfast without one particular brand of cereal, or must have a specific type of coffee, there's really no need to bring food on your USBVI vacation. After all, the folks who live there year-round find plenty to fill their refrigerators. You'll find stateside brands in both the USBVI as well as other unfamiliar labels. There are occasional shortages of some goods, but do like the islanders do and substitute. No bananas at the supermarket? Eat papayas instead.

There are no prohibitions about bringing any food items to the USVI, but you can't bring meat into the BVI without a $25 agricultural permit. You need to apply in advance at the Agriculture Department, but it's hardly worth the effort when you can buy what you'll need at the island's grocery stores. You can't take most meat and agricultural products back to the U.S. mainland, so don't plan on packing an apple in your carry-on luggage for your trip home.

Frugal folks who don't want to buy an entire jar of spices or plan to make something that needs just a cup of flour should pack what they need so they don't have to throw out the leftovers or lug them home. Film cans make perfect spice containers and anything else can go in plastic bags. Double bag bottled liquids to make sure you don't have leaks. To bring your favorite cut of meat, freeze it thoroughly, pack in a cooler with ice packs, and tape the cooler shut with duct tape. Unless the cooler is small enough to fit in the overhead compartment of the airplane, you'll have to check it as luggage. This means you're using up your luggage allowance and you run the risk of it getting lost.

Remember to **pack light.** There are no luggage carts at USBVI airports, and porters can be scarce. Small interisland planes have very limited carry-on space. Suitcases that fit under seats on major carriers just won't fit in these tiny places, so check your luggage and pack some toiletries, a change of clothes, and perhaps a bathing suit in your carry-on bag—just in case your checked luggage arrives on a later flight (which may be the next day).

Dress is generally casual. On all islands, bathing suits and immodest attire are frowned upon off the beach. A sun hat is advisable. Night-time dress can range from really informal to casually elegant, depending on the establishment. A tie is practically never required, but a jacket may be appropriate in the fanciest restaurants and casinos. You may need a light sweater or long-sleeve T-shirt for breezy nights (or overly air-conditioned restaurants) or for the ferry ride home after a day in the sun.

## PASSPORTS & VISAS

Upon entering the USVI from the U.S., there are no immigration procedures to face. If you're arriving from an international destination—even from the BVI—you'll have to clear customs as well as immigration. When you depart for the U.S. or if you're connecting in San Juan, you'll clear customs and immigration at the USVI airport. If you arrive in the USVI by ferry from the BVI, you must also go through customs and immigration procedures. If you're arriving by air or ferry in the BVI from the USVI or San Juan, you must go through customs and immigration. There are no special procedures for departure from the BVI.

Even though one is not required for travel to or from the USVI, a passport works best; officials will still accept a birth or citizenship certificate. In the BVI, U.S. citizens must have a valid passport, but Canadians may be able to use a certified birth certificate and government-issued photo I.D.

## PASSPORTS

We're always surprised at how few Americans have passports—only 25% at this writing, though the number is expected to grow in coming years, when it becomes impossible to re-enter the United States from trips to neighboring Canada or Mexico without one. Remember this: A passport verifies both your identity and nationality—a great reason to have one.

U.S. passports are valid for 10 years. Applications are available online and at post offices as well as passport offices. The cost to apply is $97 for adults, $82 for children under 16; renewals are $67. Allow six weeks to process the paperwork for either a new or renewed passport. For an expediting fee of $60, you can reduce the time to about two weeks. If your trip is less than two weeks away, you can get a passport even more rapidly by going to a passport office with the necessary documentation. Private expediters can get things done in as little as 48 hours but charge hefty fees for their services. Children under 14 must appear in person to apply for or renew a passport; both parents must accompany the child (or send a notarized statement with their permission) and provide proof of their relationship to the child.

Before your trip, make two copies of your passport's data page (one for someone at home and another for you to carry separately). Or scan the page and e-mail it to someone at home and/or yourself.

## VISAS

Visas are essentially formal permissions to travel to a country. They allow countries to keep track of you and other visitors and to generate revenue (from visa fees). You *always* need a visa to enter a foreign country; however, many countries routinely issue tourist visas on arrival, particularly to U.S. citizens. When your passport is stamped or scanned in the immigration line, you're actually being issued a visa. Sometimes you have to stand in a separate line and pay a small fee to get your stamp before going through immigration, but you can still do this at the airport on arrival. Getting a visa isn't always that easy. Some countries require you to arrange for one in advance of your trip. There's usually—but not always—a fee involved, and said fee may be nominal ($10 or less) or substantial ($100 or more).

If you must apply for a visa in advance, you can usually do it in person or by mail. When you apply by mail, you send your passport to a designated consulate, where your passport will be examined and the visa issued. Expediters—usually the same ones who handle expedited passport applications—can do all the work to obtain your visa for you; however, there's always an additional cost (often more than $50 per visa).

Most visas limit you to a single trip—basically during the actual dates of your planned vacation. Other visas allow you to visit as many times as you wish for a specific period of time. Remember that requirements change, sometimes at the drop of a hat, and the burden is on you to make sure that you have the appropriate visas. Otherwise, you'll be turned away at the airport or, worse, deported after you arrive in the country. No company or travel insurer gives refunds if your travel plans are disrupted because you didn't have the correct visa.

🔢 **U.S. Passport & Visa Expediters A. Briggs Passport & Visa Expeditors** ☎ 800/806-0581 or 202/464-3000 ⊕ www.abriggs.com. **American Passport Express** ☎ 800/455-5166 or 603/559-9888 ⊕ www.americanpassport.com. **Passport Express** ☎ 800/362-8196 or 401/272-4612 ⊕ www.passportexpress.com. **Travel Document Systems** ☎ 800/874-5100 or 202/638-3800 ⊕ www.traveldocs.com. **Travel the World Visas** ☎ 866/886-8472 or 301/495-7700 ⊕ www.world-visa.com.

## PHONES

The good news is that you can now make a direct-dial telephone call from virtually any point on earth. The bad news? You can't always do so cheaply. Calling from a hotel is almost always the most expensive option; hotels usually add huge surcharges to all calls, particularly international ones. In some countries, you can phone from call centers or even the post office. Calling cards usually keep costs to a minimum, but only if you purchase them locally. And then there are mobile phones ⇨ *below*, which are sometimes more prevalent—particularly in the developing world—than land lines; as expensive as mobile phone calls can be, they are still usually a much cheaper option than calling from your hotel.

Phone service to and from the Virgin Islands is up-to-date and efficient. Phone cards are used throughout the islands; you can buy them (in several denominations) at many retail shops and convenience stores. They must be used in special card phones, which are also widely available.

### CALLING WITHIN THE USBVI

Local calls from USBVI pay phones run 25¢, although some privately owned phones are now charging 35¢. Calls from the USVI to the BVI and vice versa are charged as international toll calls. In the USVI and BVI, you dial just as if you were anywhere else in the U.S.

The area code for the USVI is 340; for the BVI, 284.

In the USVI, dial 913 to reach the operator. In the BVI, dial 119. In both locations, dial 0 for advice on how to place your call.

### CALLING OUTSIDE THE USBVI

Calling the United States and Canada from the USBVI is just like making a long distance call within those countries: dial 1, plus the area code. To reach Europe, Australia, and New Zealand, dial 011 followed by the country code.

The country code is 1 for the United States and Canada, 61 for Australia, 64 for New Zealand, and 44 for the United Kingdom.

If you are using a U.S.-based calling card, the U.S. access number should be on the back of the card. If you are using a local calling card, the access number will be on the back of your calling card.

## MOBILE PHONES

If you have a multiband phone (some countries use different frequencies than what's used in the United States) and your service provider uses the world-standard GSM network (as do T-Mobile, Cingular, and Verizon), you can probably use your phone abroad. Roaming fees can steep, though: 99¢ a minute is considered reasonable. And overseas, you normally pay the toll charges for incoming calls. It's almost always cheaper to send a text message than to make a call since text messages have a very low set fee (often less than 5¢). Some companies count the USVI as part of their domestic network; for others, the USVI are considered international. The BVI are always considered international.

Cell phones from most U.S. companies, including Sprint, work in most locations in the USVI if you have a roaming feature; if you are on St. John's north coast, you may have some difficulties with service, where you may find yourself connected to Boat-Phone, a Tortola service. If you are on the south side of Tortola, you may be able to connect to Cingular and Sprint, but other islands in the BVI are problematic. Phones from other companies may work, but only Cingular and Sprint have offices in the USVI. The BVI has local companies only. Even if your U.S. mainland company assures you that your phone will work in the USBVI, don't count on it. Both companies use GSM and TDMA networks with single- and dual-band phones.
🔲 **Cingular** ☎ 340/777-7777. **Sprint** ☎ 340/715-5400.

## SAFETY

In the USVI, ask hotel staff members about the wisdom of venturing off the beaten path. Although it may seem like a nice night for a stroll back to your hotel from that downtown restaurant, it's better to take a taxi than face an incident. Although local police go to great lengths to stop it, crime does happen. The BVI has seen less crime than its neighbors to the west, but again, better safe than sorry.

Follow the same precautions that you would anywhere. Look around before using the ATM. Keep tabs on your pocketbook; put it on your lap—not the back of your chair—in restaurants. Stow valuable jewelry or other items in the hotel safe when you leave your room; hotel and villa burglaries do occur infrequently. Deserted beaches on St. John and the BVI are usually safe, but think twice about stopping at that luscious strand of lonely sand on St. Croix and St. Thomas. Hotel or public beaches are your best bets. Never leave your belongings unattended at the beach or on the seats of your rental car.

Distribute your cash, credit cards, IDs, and other valuables between a deep front pocket, an inside jacket or vest pocket, and a hidden money pouch. Don't reach for the money pouch once you're in public.

## TAXES & SERVICE CHARGES

There's no sales tax in the USVI, but there's an 8% hotel-room tax; most hotels add a 10% service charge to the bill. The St. John Accommodations Council members ask that hotel and villa guests voluntarily pay a $1 a day surcharge to help fund school and community projects and other good works. Many hotels add additional energy surcharges and the like, so please ask about any additional charges, but these are not government-imposed taxes.

In the BVI, the departure tax is $5 per person by boat and $20 per person by plane. There's a separate booth at the airport and ferry terminals to collect this tax, which must be paid in cash in U.S. currency. Most hotels in the BVI add a service charge ranging from 5% to 18% to the bill. A few restaurants and some shops tack on an additional 10% charge if you use a credit card. There's no sales tax in the BVI. However, there's a 7% government tax on hotel rooms.

## TIME

The USBVI are in the Atlantic Standard Time zone, which is one hour later than Eastern Standard or four hours earlier than GMT. During Daylight Savings Time, between April and October, Atlantic Standard is the same time as Eastern Daylight Time.

## TIPPING

Many hotels in the USVI add a 10% to 15% service charge to cover the room maid and other staff. However, some hotels may use part of that money to fund their operations, passing on only a portion of it to the staff. Check with your maid or bellhop to determine the hotel's policy. If you discover you need to tip, give bellhops and porters 50¢ to $1 per bag and maids $1 or $2 per day. Special errands or requests of hotel staff always require an additional tip. At restaurants bartenders and waiters expect a 10%–15% tip, but always check your tab to see whether service is included. Taxi drivers in the USVI get a 15% tip.

In the BVI, tip porters and bellhops $1 per bag. Sometimes a service charge of 10% is included on restaurant bills; it's customary to leave another 5% if you liked the service. If no charge is added, 15% is the norm. Cabbies normally aren't tipped because most own their cabs; add 10% to 15% if they exceed their duties.

## TOURS & PACKAGES

Of the major U.S. airline packagers, only American Airlines Vacations offers packages in both the U.S. and British Virgin Islands. US Airways Vacations and Delta Vacations offer trips on all three U.S. Virgin Islands; Continental Vacations offers only St. Thomas.

You'll usually find the best deals on packages in the slower summer season, when hoteliers have lots of vacant rooms. Check with your travel agent, online, airlines, or in the pages of your local major newspaper for the best deals. The best packages for the USVI can often be found through Liberty/GoGo, Travel Impressions, and Apple Vacations. For the BVI, Liberty/GoGo Travel, Apple Vacations, and Classic Custom Vacations offer packages. They often tout last-minute specials, so late planning may save you money.

Online travel agencies such as Orbitz, Expedia, and Travelocity, also offer packages to the Virgin Islands.

## VACATION PACKAGES

Packages *are not* guided tours. Packages combine airfare, accommodations, and perhaps a rental car or other extras (theater tickets, guided excursions, boat trips, reserved entry to popular museums, transit passes), but they let you do your own thing. During busy periods, packages may be your only option because flights and rooms may be otherwise sold out. Packages will definitely save you time. They can also save you money, particularly in peak seasons, but—and this is a really big "but"—you should price each part of the package separately to be sure. And be aware that prices advertised on Web sites and in newspapers rarely include service charges or taxes, which can up your costs by hundreds of dollars.

Note that local tourism boards can provide information about lesser-known and small-niche operators that sell packages to just a few destinations. And don't always assume that you can get the best deal by booking everything yourself. Some packages and cruises are sold only through travel agents.

Each year consumers are stranded or lose their money when packagers—even large ones with excellent reputations—go out of business. How can you protect yourself? First, always pay with a credit card; if you have a problem, your credit-card company may help you resolve it. Second, buy trip insurance that covers default. Third, choose a company that belongs to the United States Tour Operators Association, whose members must set aside funds ($1 million) to cover defaults. Finally choose a company that also participates in the Tour Operator Program of the American Society of Travel Agents (ASTA), which will act as mediator in any disputes. You can also check on the tour operator's reputation among travelers by posting an inquiry on one of the Fodors.com forums.

🛫 **Airline Vacation Packagers American Airlines Vacations** ☎ 800/321-2121 ⊕ www.aavacations. com. **Continental Airlines Vacations** ☎ 800/301-3800 ⊕ www.covacations.com. **Delta Vacations** ☎ 800/654-6559 ⊕ www.deltavacations.com. **US Airways Vacations** ☎ 800/422-3861 ⊕ www. usairwaysvacations.com.

🛫 **Large Agency Packagers Apple Vacations** ⊕ www.applevacations.com. **Classic Custom Vaca-**

tions ☎ 800/635-1333 ⊕ www.classicvacations. com. **Liberty Travel** ☎ 888/271-1584 ⊕ www. libertytravel.com. **Travel Impressions** ⊕ www. travelimpressions.com.

📶 Online Agency Packagers **Cheap Tickets** ⊕ www.cheaptickets.com. **Expedia** ⊕ www. expedia.com. **Orbitz** ⊕ www.orbitz.com. **Priceline** ⊕ www.priceline.com. **Travelocity** ⊕ www. travelocity.com.

📶 Organizations **American Society of Travel Agents** (ASTA) ☎ 703/739-2782 or 800/965-2782 24-hr hotline ⊕ www.astanet.com. **United States Tour Operators Association** (USTOA) ☎ 212/599-6599 ⊕ www.ustoa.com.

## TRAVEL AGENTS

If you use an agent—brick-and-mortar or virtual—you'll pay a fee for the service. And know that the service you get from some online agents isn't comprehensive. For example Expedia or Travelocity don't search for prices on budget airlines like JetBlue, Southwest, or small foreign carriers. That said, some agents (online or not) *do* have access to fares that are difficult to find otherwise, and the savings can more than make up for any surcharge.

A knowledgeable brick-and-mortar travel agent can be a godsend if you're booking a cruise, a package trip that's not available to you directly, an air pass, or a complicated itinerary including several overseas flights. What's more travel agents that specialize in a destination may have exclusive access to certain deals and insider information on things such as charter flights. Agents who specialize in types of travelers (senior citizens, gays and lesbians, naturists) or types of trips (cruises, luxury travel, safaris) can also be invaluable.

A top-notch agent planning your trip to Russia will make sure you get the correct visa application and complete it on time; the one booking your cruise may get you a cabin upgrade or arrange to have bottle of champagne chilling in your cabin when you embark. And complain about the surcharges all you like, but when things don't work out the way you'd hoped, it's nice to have an agent to put things right.

📶 Agent Resources **American Society of Travel Agents** ☎ 703/739-2782 ⊕ www.travelsense.org.

📶 Online Agents **Expedia** ⊕ www.expedia.com. **Onetravel.com** ⊕ www.onetravel.com. **Orbitz** ⊕ www.orbitz.com. **Priceline.com** ⊕ www. priceline.com. **Travelocity** ⊕ www.travelocity.com.

## VISITOR INFORMATION

For general information on the islands, contact these tourist offices before you go.

Learn more about foreign destinations by checking government-issued travel advisories and country information. For a broader picture, consider information from more than one country.

📶 USVI: United States Virgin Islands Department of Tourism **USVI Government Tourist Office** ✉ 245 Peachtree St., Center Ave. Marquis One Tower MB-05, Atlanta, GA 30303 ☎ 404/688-0906 ✉ 500 N. Michigan Ave., Suite 2030, Chicago, IL 60611 ☎ 312/670-8784 ✉ 3460 Wilshire Blvd., Suite 412, Los Angeles, CA 90010 ☎ 213/739-0138 ✉ 2655 Le Jeune Rd., Suite 907, Coral Gables, FL 33134 ☎ 305/442-7200 ✉ 1270 Ave. of the Americas, Room 2108, New York, NY 10020 ☎ 212/332-2222 ✉ Hall of Streets, #298, 444 N. Capital St. NW, Washington, DC 20006 ☎ 202/624-3590 ✉ 703 Evans Ave., Suite 106, Toronto, Ontario, Canada M9C5E4 ☎ 416/622-7600 ✉ 114 Power Rd., Chiswick, London W4 5PY, U.K. ☎ 207/978-5222 ⊕ www.usvitourism.vi.

📶 BVI: British Virgin Islands Tourist Board **BVI Tourist Board (U.K.)** ✉ 15 Upper Grosvenor St., London W1K 7PS, U.K. ☎ 207/355-9585. **BVI Tourist Board (U.S.)** ✉ 1270 Broadway, Suite 705, New York, NY 10001 ☎ 212/696-0400 or 800/835-8530 ✉ 1275 Shiloh Rd., Suite 2930, Kennesaw, GA 30144 ☎ 770/874-5951 ✉ 3450 Wilshire Blvd., Suite 1202, Los Angeles, CA 90010 ☎ 213/736-8931.

## WEB SITES

We're really proud of our Web site: Fodors.com is a great place to begin any journey. Scan Travel Wire for suggested itineraries, travel deals, restaurant and hotel openings, and other up-to-the-minute info. Check out Booking to research prices and book plane tickets, hotel rooms, rental cars, and vacation packages. Head to Talk for on-the-ground pointers from travelers who frequent our message boards. You can also link to loads of other travel-related resources.

After your trip, be sure to rate the places you visited and share your experiences and travel tips with us and other Fodorites in Travel Ratings and Talk on www.fodors.com.

On the USVI Department of Tourism's Web site (www.usvitourism.vi) information on St. Croix, St. Thomas, or St. John is just a click away. In addition to the usual lodging, dining, and shopping categories, the BVI Tourism Bureau's site (www.bvitouristboard.com) has a separate "At Sea" category, a nod to the popularity of water sports on these islands. And of course every Caribbean traveler should bookmark the Caribbean Tourism Organization's comprehensive site (www.doitcaribbean.com). A quick search on

an Internet search engine such as Google or Yahoo will turn up myriad Web sites providing various types of information about the USBVI.

🔃 Time Zones **Timeanddate.com** ⊕ www.timeanddate.com/worldclock can help you figure out the correct time anywhere in the world.

🔃 Weather **Accuweather.com** ⊕ www.accuweather.com is an independent weather-forecasting service with especially good coverage of hurricanes. **Weather.com** ⊕ www.weather.com is the Web site for the Weather Channel.

🔃 Other Resources **CIA World Factbook** ⊕ www.odci.gov/cia/publications/factbook/index.html has profiles of every country in the world. It's a good source if you need some quick facts and figures.

# INDEX

## PHOTO CREDITS

**Chapter 1: United States Virgin Islands:** 23, *U.S. Virgin Islands Department of Tourism.* 24 (top), *U.S. Virgin Islands Department of Tourism.* 24 (bottom), *Philip Coblentz/Medioimages.*

**Chapter 2: British Virgin Islands:** 129, *Philip Coblentz/Medioimages.* 130 (top), *Philip Coblentz/Digital Vision.* 130 (bottom), *Philip Coblentz/Digital Vision.* 133 (left), *Philip Coblentz/Digital Vision.* 133 (right), *Philip Coblentz/Digital Vision.*

# NOTES

# NOTES

# NOTES

# NOTES

# NOTES

# ABOUT OUR WRITERS

Writer and dietitian **Carol M. Bareuther,** who lives in St. Thomas, works part-time for the government of the U.S. Virgin Islands. In her other life as a writer, she writes for local, regional, and international publications on the topics of food, travel, and watersports. She's the author of two books, *Sports Fishing in the Virgin Islands* and *Virgin Islands Cooking.* She is the mother of 12-year-old Nikki and 15-year-old Rian, as well as the longtime partner of photographer Dean Barnes. She covered St. Thomas as well as all of the British Virgin Islands—except for Tortola—for this edition, and she also contributed the essays on island cuisine and chartering a yacht.

Longtime St. John resident **Lynda Lohr** lives above Coral Bay with her significant other and two chubby cats. She moved to St. John in 1984 for a bit of adventure; she's still there and still enjoying the adventure. The editor of *Island News,* a newsletter for people with a serious interest in the Virgin Islands, she also writes for numerous national, regional, and local publications as well as travel Web sites. On her rare days off, she swims at Great Maho Bay and hikes the island's numerous trails. For this edition, she covered St. John, St. Croix, Tortola, and many of the smaller islands. She also updated Smart Travel Tips and the Essentials sections for both the U.S. and British Virgin Islands.